THE

CREATIVE CURRICULUM®
FOR INFANTS, TODDLERS & TWOS

Second Edition

Diane Trister Dodge

Sherrie Rudick

· Kai-leé Berke

Donna Bloomer, Laura J. Colker, Amy Laura Dombro,
and Diane Woodard, Contributing Authors

Teaching
Strategies Inc.
Washington, DC

Editor: Toni Bickart and Laurie Taub
Cover and book design: Carla Uriona
Cover and interior illustrations: Jennifer Barrett O'Connell
Layout/production: Jennifer Love King, Elia Seba, and Kristina W. Lowe

The drawings of toys, equipment, and furniture on pages 91, 235, 258,
and 267 are based on products offered by Community Playthings.

The drawings of toys, equipment, and furniture on pages 29, 364, and
414 are based on products offered by Kaplan Early Learning Company.

The drawing of toys, equipment, and furniture on page 398 is based on
products offered by Lakeshore Learning Materials.

Teaching Strategies, Inc.
P.O. Box 42243
Washington, DC 20015
www.TeachingStrategies.com
ISBN: 978-1-879537-99-6

Teaching Strategies and *The Creative Curriculum* names and logos are
registered trademarks of Teaching Strategies, Inc., Washington, DC.

Library of Congress Cataloging-in-Publication Data

Dodge, Diane Trister.
   The creative curriculum for infants, toddlers & twos / Diane Trister
Dodge, Sherrie Rudick, Kai-leé Berke. -- 2nd ed.
      p. cm.
   2nd ed. of: The creative curriculum for infants & toddlers, Revised ed. /
Amy Laura Dombro, Laura J. Colker, Diane Trister Dodge, 1997, 1999.
   Includes bibliographical references and index.
   ISBN-13: 978-1-879537-99-6
   ISBN-10: 1-879537-99-0
   1. Education, Preschool--Curricula--United States. 2. Child care--United
States. 3. Curriculum planning--United States. 4. Child development--
United States. I. Rudick, Sherrie. II. Berke, Kai-leé. III. Title.
   LB1140.4.D66 2006
   372.19--dc22
                          2006018619

Printed and bound in the United States of America
2012   2011   2010   2009   2008   2007
10 9 8 7 6 5 4 3

Acknowledgments

Writing a curriculum—even a new edition—is a journey with many players and numerous steps. We have a number of people to thank for the role they played in helping us write and redesign this new edition of *The Creative Curriculum for Infants, Toddlers & Twos*.

The very first step in the journey was to develop and validate our tool for ongoing observation and assessment, *The Creative Curriculum Developmental Continuum for Infants, Toddlers & Twos*. We thank Amy Laura Dombro and Laura J. Colker, who helped conceptualize the continuum, identified many of the objectives, and worked with us to produce multiple drafts. In addition to the three authors of this book, Toni Bickart, Laurie Taub, and Jennifer Park-Jadotte actively participated in developing the final version of the *Developmental Continuum*. We also thank Jenna Bilmes and Rachel Zigler, who generously shared their expertise. Jennifer Park-Jadotte, Jeffrey Capizzano, and Maha Jafri oversaw an extensive field test of *The Creative Curriculum for Infants, Toddlers & Twos* Developmental Continuum Assessment System. It was piloted with over 550 children under age 3 in the following programs: University of Oklahoma, Center for Early Childhood Professional Development, Moore, Oklahoma; Community Partnership for Child Development, Colorado Springs, CO; Delaware Department of Education, Early Childhood Education/IDEA-Preschool, Dover, Delaware; Human Development Institute, University of Kentucky, Lexington, Kentucky; JCCEO Early Head Start, Birmingham, AL; and The Sunshine House Inc., Greenwood, SC. We are very grateful to the teachers and administrators in these programs who used the tool for over a year and gave us invaluable feedback, and to Donna Bloomer, who provided training for each site.

After drafting this new edition of *The Creative Curriculum for Infants, Toddlers & Twos*, we asked a group of experts to review our work. We would like to thank the following people for their very thoughtful and insightful comments, which greatly enhanced the final product: Tess Bennett, Laura Colker, Amy Dombro, Carol Gestwicki, Janice Im, Gail Kelso, Jean Monroe, Sherry Nolte, Jerry Parr, Miriam L. Perreira, Sarah Semlak, and Kim Thuerauf. Thanks also to Monica Vacca for reviewing the sections on children with disabilities, Betsy Shelby-Morris for her suggestions on sharing stories and books with children with disabilities, and Dawn Terrill for her comments on dual language learners.

This book benefited in many ways from the thoughtful and detailed editing it received from Toni Bickart and Laurie Taub. They challenged us to refine our writing continually, contributed their own excellent ideas, and ensured that every page is correct.

The beautiful illustrations of Jennifer Barrett O'Connell bring our children and teachers to life and provide a vision of what we hope to convey through our words. We thank our design and production team for the attractive and engaging design and layout of the book: Carla Uriona, Jennifer Love King, Elia Seba, and Kristina W. Lowe.

Table of Contents

Introduction

The care that infants, toddlers, and twos receive and their experiences during the first 3 years of life have a powerful influence on how they view the world, how they relate to others, and their ability to succeed as learners. As a teacher, you have a unique opportunity to make a difference in the lives of very young children and their families.

Infants, toddlers, and 2-year-olds are in the most vulnerable and important period of life. Initially, they are totally dependent on adults to meet their every need. If the care and experiences they have are nurturing, consistent, and loving, children flourish. Almost every day you can see exciting changes as children learn to trust you, joyfully explore the environment you have created, make discoveries, care about others, and begin to see themselves as competent learners. Infants, toddlers, and twos who receive high-quality care are more likely to become sociable, capable preschoolers who get along with others, demonstrate self-control, and love learning.

The opportunity to have a positive influence on children and families depends on the quality of the program you provide. Organizations like ZERO TO THREE and the National Association for the Education of Young Children have identified the factors that define a quality program for infants, toddlers, and twos. Caring for children under age 3 is too important to leave to chance. Teachers must be intentional about what they do each day in their work with children and families. That is why we offer this comprehensive, developmentally appropriate curriculum.

What a Comprehensive Curriculum Offers

A curriculum is like a roadmap; it helps you get where you want to go. A comprehensive, developmentally appropriate curriculum, like *The Creative Curriculum for Infants, Toddlers & Twos*, includes goals and objectives for children's learning in all areas of development: social/emotional, physical, cognitive, and language. Goals and objectives show where you want to go; the curriculum tells you how to get there. Curriculum is the what, why, how, and when of providing a high-quality program. It also guides the interactions you have with children and families. *The Creative Curriculum* explains all aspects of a developmentally appropriate program and leads you through the processes of planning and implementing every aspect of caring for and teaching infants, toddlers, and twos.

Just as a roadmap gives you choices about what routes to take, *The Creative Curriculum* offers choices and encourages flexibility. What makes caring for infants, toddlers, and twos so enjoyable and satisfying is your ability to appreciate the everyday discoveries that delight a child: the colors dancing on the wall from a prism, the bells that chime in a pull toy, the amazing accomplishment of a first step, finally fitting a puzzle piece into place. *The Creative Curriculum* helps you be intentional about the experiences you offer infants, toddlers, and twos while still having the flexibility to respond to the changing interests and abilities of young children.

The Creative Curriculum for Infants, Toddlers & Twos Developmental Continuum Assessment System, which is linked to *The Creative Curriculum,* helps you identify and respond to children's changing interests and abilities. It is a powerful tool for observing children, documenting their growing skills, and individualizing your approach. Using ongoing assessment to decide how to respond to each child and to plan appropriate experiences enables you to care for and teach children well. This system is based on the goals and objectives of *The Creative Curriculum* and shows the typical sequence of development for each objective.

Our Fundamental Beliefs

Certain fundamental beliefs underlie *The Creative Curriculum for Infants, Toddlers & Twos.* You will find them reflected throughout the book:

- Building a trusting relationship with each child
- Providing responsive, individualized care
- Creating environments that support and encourage exploration
- Ensuring children's safety and health
- Developing partnerships with families
- Observing and documenting children's development in order to plan for each child and the group
- Recognizing the importance of social/emotional development
- Appreciating cultural, family, and individual differences
- Taking advantage of every opportunity to build a foundation for lifelong learning
- Supporting dual language learners
- Including children with disabilities in all aspects of the program

What Is Different About the Second Edition

This new edition retains its focus on building relationships, responsive care, and routines and experiences, but it has been updated in many important ways:

- Uses the same organizational structure as *The Creative Curriculum® for Preschool* to create continuity for programs.

- Introduces *The Creative Curriculum® Developmental Continuum for Infants, Toddlers & Twos* to help teachers thoughtfully observe children and use what they learn to be responsive to children's interests and needs.

- Addresses language and literacy, math, and science, because very young children are already exploring ideas and developing important skills that become the building blocks for future learning.

- Offers specific guidance on how to meet the needs of 2-year-olds, dual language learners, and children with disabilities.

- Highlights the research and theory on which the curriculum is based and the implications for everyday practice.

How the Curriculum Is Organized

As you can see, *The Creative Curriculum* rests on a solid foundation of research. Its organizational structure has five components that help you make good decisions about the routines and experiences you provide for infants, toddlers, and twos.

Here is an overview of what you will find in the book.

The **Foundation** outlines the theory and research that underlie and explain the curriculum's focus on the importance of meeting basic needs, fostering social/emotional development, developing secure attachments, and supporting cognition and brain development.

Part 1: The Five Components (chapters 1–5) presents the organizational structure of *The Creative Curriculum for Infants, Toddler & Twos* and gives you the information you need to set up your program and work with children and their families.

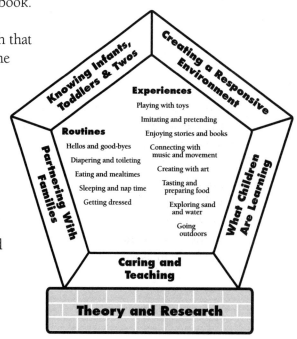

Knowing Infants, Toddlers & Twos

Creating a Responsive Environment

Experiences
Playing with toys
Imitating and pretending
Enjoying stories and books
Connecting with music and movement
Creating with art
Tasting and preparing food
Exploring sand and water
Going outdoors

Routines
Hellos and good-byes
Diapering and toileting
Eating and mealtimes
Sleeping and nap time
Getting dressed

Partnering With Families

What Children Are Learning

Caring and Teaching

Theory and Research

Knowing Infants, Toddlers, and Twos describes the social/emotional, physical, cognitive, and language development of children. It also discusses the characteristics and experiences that make each child unique, including temperament, life experiences, dual language learning, and disabilities. It presents our goals and objectives for children and the *Developmental Continuum*, a tool for observing children's development and following their progress in relation to the 21 objectives.

Creating a Responsive Environment offers a model for setting up the physical environment for routines and experiences in ways that address the developing abilities and interests of infants, toddlers, and twos. It shows how to create a daily schedule and make weekly plans in ways that give you direction but allow flexibility.

What Children Are Learning shows how the responsive relationship you form with each child, the interactions you have every day, and the materials and experiences you offer become the building blocks for successful learning. Language and literacy, discovering mathematical relationships, and scientific explorations are part of this discussion. Art and music and movement are addressed in later chapters.

Caring and Teaching describes the varied and interrelated roles of teachers who work with infants, toddlers, and twos. It offers strategies for building positive relationships, helping children develop self-regulation, and responding to challenging behaviors. It shows how to guide children's learning during daily routines and everyday experiences. Finally, it explains the role of ongoing assessment in learning about each child, following children's progress, and planning.

Building Partnerships With Families explores the benefits of working with families as partners in the care of their children. It explains how partnerships are built by exchanging information on a daily basis, involving families in all aspects of the program, communicating in respectful ways, and working through differences in ways that sustain the partnership and benefit the child.

Part 2: Routines (chapters 6–10) shows how daily routines are an important part of the curriculum and important times to put research and theory into practice. Routines are opportunities to build relationships with children that promote the development of trust. The one-on-one time you spend easing a child and family through hellos and good-byes, diapering and toileting, feeding, dressing, and soothing a child to sleep helps infants, toddlers, and twos learn to trust and feel secure with you. As they gain new skills and can participate more actively in daily routines, they develop a sense of their own competence. Routines are also times to nurture children's curiosity and guide them as they make increasing sense of their world.

Part 3: Experiences (chapters 11–18) offers guidance about providing appropriate materials and interactions. It discusses ways to engage children in playing with toys, imitating and pretending, enjoying stories and books, connecting with music and movement, creating with art, tasting and preparing food, exploring sand and water, and going outdoors. This section also explains that, while planning for these experiences is important, you are only *planning for possibilities* because you must be able to respond to whatever interests a child.

Getting Started

You may not have used a curriculum or assessment system in your work with infants, toddlers, and twos before now. Do not think that you have to read the entire book or learn the entire assessment process before beginning to use these resources. Find the topics that are of most importance to your work and start with those chapters. You will find a lot that immediately supports your daily work, especially your interactions with children and families.

We describe how you plan and how you provide responsive care for children in four age groups. The ages overlap a bit because children develop on individual timetables and programs define age groups in a number of ways. The four groups in *The Creative Curriculum* are

- Young infants (0–9 months)
- Mobile infants (8–18 months)
- Toddlers (16–25 months)
- Twos (24–36 months)

In every chapter, we provide examples of what children do at different ages and what responsive care is like. For each age group, we have created several children and their teachers. They are introduced here.

Julio, 4 months, with his teacher, Linda

Jasmine, 8 months, with her teacher, Janet

Willard, 11 months, with his teacher, Grace

Abby, 14 months, with her teacher, Brooks

Leo, 18 months, with his teacher, Barbara

Matthew, 22 months, with
his teacher, Mercedes

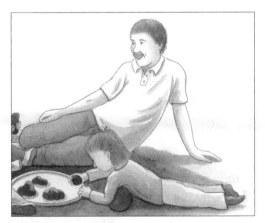

Gena, 30 months, with her teacher, Ivan

Valisha and Jonisha, 33-month-old twins,
with their teacher, LaToya

The Foundation: Theory and Research

Until the 20th century, scientific researchers gave little attention to children's development and learning. In the past 75 years, however, research has generated new information about childhood as a separate and distinct stage of life. Developmentally appropriate practice is the application of this knowledge to teaching. *The Creative Curriculum for Infants, Toddlers & Twos* shows you how to implement developmentally appropriate practice in your program for young children.

Developmentally appropriate practice means teaching in ways that match the way children develop and learn. According to the National Association for the Education of Young Children, quality care requires that early childhood professionals make decisions about the care and education of children based upon information in three areas:[1]

- knowledge of child development and how children learn

- knowledge of the individual needs, strengths, and interests of each child

- knowledge of the social and cultural context in which each child lives

This chapter summarizes some of the major theories behind developmentally appropriate practice and *The Creative Curriculum*. Each of the theories or research described has influenced the design of *The Creative Curriculum* and its view of how children develop and learn. The chapter also explains how *The Creative Curriculum* helps you put theory and research into practice in your program. It will help you decide what to do when, for example, an infant cries for the first several days in your care. It will help you understand such things as why a mobile infant pushes her toys one by one off the table, watching them fall. You will know what to do when a toddler shouts, "No!" when you ask him to do something. Understanding early childhood theory and research is essential to knowing what children think and feel and how you can help them become caring people and joyful learners.

Meeting Children's Basic Needs

All people have basic needs. Abraham Maslow, a 20th century psychologist, suggested that people's basic needs must be met before higher level learning can take place. Stanley Greenspan and T. Berry Brazelton, two of today's most respected child development experts, focus on the particular needs of children. They have taken a broader, more comprehensive approach to addressing children's needs.

Abraham Maslow

Abraham Maslow described a hierarchy of needs common to all human beings.[2] Needs that involve physiology, safety, belonging, and esteem are extremely important in the care of very young children. Physiological needs are hunger, thirst, and bodily comfort. Knowing that a hungry child has difficulty focusing on relationships and learning, many early childhood programs provide breakfast, snacks, and lunch, and they feed each infant according to his or her own schedule. Safety involves security and freedom from danger. When children feel protected and believe that no harm will come to them, they are better able to interact with others and to explore their environment. Belonging is the sense of being comfortable with and connected to others. Feeling connected depends upon being accepted, respected, and loved. Esteem involves self-respect and respect from others. Esteem emerges from daily experiences that give children the opportunity to discover that they are capable learners.

More recent reviewers of Maslow's theory have argued that meeting people's needs in a particular order is not always necessary, and basic needs are not as simplistic as Maslow's hierarchy suggests. However, his research did demonstrate that certain basic needs must be met in order for children to benefit from the experiences you offer.

T. Berry Brazelton and Stanley Greenspan

T. Berry Brazelton and Stanley Greenspan describe children's specific needs in their book, *The Irreducible Needs of Children*.[3] They explain that children need

- ongoing, nurturing relationships
- physical protection, safety, and regulation
- experiences tailored to their individual differences
- developmentally appropriate experiences
- limit setting, structure, and expectations
- stable, supportive communities and cultural continuity
- adults to protect their future

These seven needs expand upon Maslow's basic needs. They underlie the principles of developmentally appropriate practice, particularly the important role that families, teachers, and communities play in children's lives. When parents, teachers, and communities meet all seven of these needs, children are prepared socially, emotionally, and intellectually for future life success.

In *The Creative Curriculum*, your ability to meet children's needs is essential to providing responsive care and education. Children are able to learn and grow when they feel safe and cared for, are appropriately challenged and guided, and have strong relationships with nurturing adults.

Valisha *(33 months) is busy adding animals to her block building when LaToya announces that it is clean-up time. Jonisha (33 months) says, "You gotta clean up now, Valisha." Valisha looks at her angrily and says, "No!" as she reaches to push Jonisha away. LaToya immediately intervenes, knowing that she must make sure that the children in her care are safe. She says, "Valisha, be safe. I will not let you push your sister." By saying this, LaToya intentionally and clearly limits Valisha's behavior.*

To show Valisha that she respects her feelings, LaToya adds, "It sounds as though you are frustrated because you don't want to clean up your building." When Valisha says, "I'm making a house for my animals. I don't wanna go outside," LaToya considers what to say. She wants to honor Valisha's feelings and preference while clarifying expectations for group behavior. "Valisha, I have to go outside with the other children now. It isn't safe for you to be inside by yourself. Would you like to put a Please save sign on your building so that no one puts it away? Then you can come back and play with it when we come inside again." Valisha nods her head, "Yes."

Major Ideas	The Creative Curriculum
Abraham Maslow Needs that involve physiology, safety, belonging, and esteem must be met in order for children to be able to build relationships and learn.	• Create an environment in which children are safe, feel emotionally secure, and have a sense of belonging. • Provide responsive caregiving to meet the individual needs of children.
T. Berry Brazelton and Stanley Greenspan Seven needs must be met in order for children to develop and learn. They underlie the principles of developmentally appropriate practice, particularly the important role that families, teachers, and communities play in children's lives.	• Establish and maintain nurturing relationships with children. • Provide safe, developmentally appropriate learning experiences. • Individualize schedules, routines, and experiences to meet each child's needs. • Create partnerships with families to support children's development and learning. • Set limits and guide learning in ways that reflect realistic expectations for children's behavior.

Fostering Social/Emotional Development

The positive social/emotional development of infants, toddlers, and twos is nurtured when they develop trusting relationships with the important adults in their lives. As trust develops, they begin to see themselves as separate, capable human beings who can understand and control their emotions.

Erik Erikson

Erik Erikson's theory of the "Eight Stages of Man" identifies a sequence of main psychological tasks that need to be resolved for healthy development to occur.[4] According to Erikson, each stage builds on successfully resolving the conflict of earlier stages. During the first 3 years, children are challenged by the conflicts of trust versus mistrust (infancy) and autonomy versus shame and doubt (ages 1–3). For each stage, Erikson describes what adults need to provide in order to help children meet the challenges facing them.

According to Erikson, **trust** develops when your experiences show you that the world around you is safe, reliable, and responsive to your needs. Infants who receive consistent and loving care learn to trust themselves, others, and the world around them. They are then free to explore their environment and have the foundation for developing positive relationships with others. Infants develop mistrust when they cry but get no response, are not fed when they are hungry, or are not comforted when they are hurt. They learn that they cannot count on adults to meet their needs, and they mistrust their own ability to affect the world around them. Maintaining a reliable, safe, and comforting atmosphere reinforces the trust children learn at home and helps children who may mistrust because of difficult experiences.

Autonomy, or independence, requires a sense of one's own power. It is built on the foundation of trust described in Erikson's first stage of development. Children develop autonomy when adults give them opportunities to do things successfully on their own. When adults make too many demands or criticize children's efforts, children develop shame and doubt. You help children become autonomous by honoring their efforts and providing experiences that foster their sense of competence. You also set clear limits so toddlers feel safe to explore their newfound independence.

Your most important role is to establish trusting relationships with the children in your care. When children learn that they can trust you, they are open to exploring the world around them and they will be able to develop autonomy.

Stanley Greenspan

In a separate body of work, Stanley Greenspan charted six milestones in young children's emotional growth.[5] Like Erikson, Greenspan believes that children need supportive, trusting relationships with the important adults in their lives. He explains that, when children have such relationships as their foundation, they grow socially, emotionally, and cognitively. The milestones mark the emotional development of children from birth through age 4.

Milestone 1: Self-regulation and interest in the world—During this first stage, young infants have their own ways of dealing with sensations, taking in and acting on information, and finding ways to calm and soothe themselves. They need you and their parents to take note of these individual differences and respond to them accordingly. *The Creative Curriculum* guides you to learn and appreciate each child's unique ways of being and to respond to them appropriately.

Milestone 2: Falling in love (relating to others in a warm, trusting manner)—Mastery of this milestone means that a baby has learned that relationships can be joyful and that warmth and love are possible. That is why your major responsibility is to establish trusting, nurturing relationships with the children in your care. Important motor, cognitive, and language skills also develop that help the baby establish relationships with primary caregivers. By 5 months, some infants eagerly reach out for relationships. They return your smiles, watch your face with great interest, and relax when held. Others may be more hesitant to establish relationships. These infants need you and their parents to continue to reach out to them, even when they ignore or reject some of your attempts to engage them.

Milestone 3: Developing intentional, two-way communication—By this stage, infants need to know that their families and teachers will understand and respond appropriately to the signals they use to communicate. For example, they need adults to interpret the cues that signal their need for calm or their readiness to play. *The Creative Curriculum* places a high priority on responding appropriately to children's communication attempts. When you do this, you reinforce their intentional expression of needs and wants through gestures, facial expressions, and vocalizations.

Milestone 4: Emergence of an organized sense of self and problem-solving ability—Infants, toddlers, and twos need adults to recognize and appreciate their ability to assert themselves and their new abilities. *The Creative Curriculum* encourages you to follow a child's lead during play, extend her play, and help her shift from one experience to another. By doing this, you help her see herself as an individual. *The Creative Curriculum* also shows you how to enforce appropriate limits, offer her opportunities to explore, respond to her requests, and help her solve problems.

Milestone 5: **Creating emotional ideas**—During this stage, children use pretend play to explore their feelings and make sense of their world. When you help children express their feelings through words and gestures, you promote their emotional development. If children's emotions make you uncomfortable, you may find yourself stopping play that includes anger and aggression. Rather than limiting children's exploration of these emotions, *The Creative Curriculum* encourages you to acknowledge their feelings and model or suggest an appropriate way to express them.

Milestone 6: **Emotional thinking**—By this milestone, children link ideas and begin to deal with the world logically. For example, rather than simply hugging a doll, a child might explain that the doll is sad because she fell down and hurt her knee. They begin to connect ideas that pertain to "me" and "not me" and to distinguish reality from fantasy. *The Creative Curriculum* explains how to help toddlers and twos connect their ideas by asking them about their opinions and by extending their play. You also help them realize that actions have consequences and that the present has implications for the future.

Major Ideas	The Creative Curriculum
Erik Erikson Social and emotional learning is a lifelong process that begins at birth. When adults are responsive to children's needs, children resolve the tension between trust and mistrust, and between autonomy and shame.	• Develop and maintain a trusting relationship with each child. • Implement nurturing, trust-building routines. • Provide responsive caregiving to meet the individual needs of children. • Provide learning experiences that help children feel competent. • Offer children appropriate choices and challenges.
Stanley Greenspan Six emotional milestones mark the emotional development of very young children. Children develop an understanding of themselves and the world through relationships and emotions.	• Assign primary caregivers to infants and toddlers, to help build trusting, loving relationships. • Talk with children, even before they understand anything you are saying. • Respond to children's communication attempts. • Help children express their emotions appropriately. • Provide many opportunities for pretend play.

Developing Relationships

Research about attachment and resilience provides guidance about other aspects of social/emotional development of infants, toddlers, and twos. It confirms the importance of the development of trusting relationships with the important adults in their lives.

Attachment

Attachment theory describes the processes through which people form close relationships with others. **John Bowlby's** research recognized that infants become attached to the important people in their lives.[6] On the basis of their deep emotional bonds, young children learn about their self-worth, relationships with others, and which emotions should be expressed and how. Their first relationships create the foundation for future relationships with others.

When children's needs are consistently met in a nurturing, responsive way by a trusted adult and when they have many positive interactions with that adult, children learn that they are important and that they can count on others. However, not all attachments are based on trusting, loving relationships. **Mary Ainsworth's** research on attachment demonstrated that there are two primary types: secure and insecure. Each has a different effect on how infants and toddlers behave, develop, and learn.[7]

Secure attachments develop when infants are cared for by adults who meet their needs consistently, accurately, and lovingly. These infants know that they can rely on the important people in their lives to meet their basic needs, to provide comfort when they are upset, and to share the joy of their everyday interactions. Consistent, nurturing care teaches children that they are important and helps them develop a positive sense of self. Children who develop secure attachments to one or more adults are more likely to develop positive social skills. They gradually acquire an understanding of their emotions and the emotions of others because of their interactions with nurturing caregivers.

Insecure attachments develop when adults are unpredictable, insensitive, uninformed, unresponsive, or threatening. A mother who pays attention to her child only when she wants, rather than when the baby needs her to, is being insensitive and unpredictable. A teacher who sometimes responds lovingly when the baby cries but who generally does not respond at all is being unresponsive. Children also develop insecure attachments when their caregivers are threatening, such as when they respond angrily to a baby's crying or when they physically or emotionally abuse the baby or other members of the household. Insecure attachments can make children feel badly about themselves, lack self-control, and struggle to develop positive relationships with others.

These two types of attachment reflect the quality of the relationship between the adult and the child; they are not determined by the child, himself. *The Creative Curriculum* supports and encourages secure attachments between you and the children in your care.

Grace *and her co-teacher each have three babies for whom they are primarily responsible. Every day during Willard's (11 months) first week in Grace's care, he cried most of the time. Grace held Willard close to her body for periods of time, using a baby carrier that his family offered. This allowed her to have her hands free while still being responsive to Willard's need for physical closeness. Grace also used diaper changing, meals, and naps as key times during the day to talk with Willard, reassure him that she would meet his needs, and respond empathetically to his crying.*

During the beginning of the second week, as Willard began to understand that he could count on Grace to be a consistent, loving presence for him, he was able to relax. He cried less frequently and began to explore his exciting new environment.

Resilience

(The ability to recover from stress or to manage the effects of a difficult situation and function effectively is called *resilience*.) The research on resilience, which began in the 1970s, has focused on children who develop well despite hardships. Perhaps the most significant result of this work has been to challenge the assumption that children growing up under the threat of disadvantage and hardship are doomed to a life of problems. Research has shown that children can develop the strength and skills necessary to deal positively with adversity.[8]

This research has also begun to provide information about the kind of help that children threatened by harmful conditions need in order to thrive. Not surprisingly, the research consistently notes the importance of teachers.

The basic foundation of resilience is developed when very young children

- form close, trusting relationships with the important adults in their lives

- have adults who help them understand their feelings and the feelings of others

- receive the necessary adult support to develop self-control

- have opportunities to develop a sense of their own competence

These findings inform the core belief that underlies *The Creative Curriculum*: It is essential for teachers to develop a positive, nurturing, supportive relationship with each child. As young children develop language, responsive adults help them learn about themselves and others and the need to learn self-control. Their positive relationships with caring adults help children develop social/emotional skills and a positive self image. The strategies that *The Creative Curriculum* presents encourage these foundations of resiliency and enable teachers to help children develop and learn, even though they cannot change the difficult circumstances in which some families live.

Julio (4 months) wakes from his nap and begins to cry. Knowing that it is extremely important for him to trust her, Linda immediately lifts him out of his crib. She gently pats his back, trying to soothe him. Over time, as he learns that he can rely on her, this trusting relationship helps him develop resilience.

Holding him, she realizes that he has a wet diaper. Linda knows that talking with Julio about his discomfort will eventually help him understand his emotions. As they walk to the diaper changing table, she says, "Oh, sweet bebé. You are sad because your diaper is wet. Let's go put on a dry one."

Major Ideas	The Creative Curriculum
Attachment When children's needs are met consistently in a nurturing way by a trusted adult and when they have many positive interactions with that adult, children learn that they are important and that they can count on others. When they develop a secure attachment with one or more caregivers, children feel more confident about exploring the world around them and developing relationships with others.	• Assign a primary teacher to each child. • Provide responsive, loving care that meets the individual needs of children. • Use nurturing routines (diaper changing, eating and mealtime, hellos and good-byes, sleeping, and getting dressed) to develop and maintain a trusting relationship with each child. • Respond appropriately to children's communication attempts.
Resilience When young children develop close, trusting relationships with the important adults in their lives, the most basic foundation for the further development of resiliency is laid.	• Develop and maintain a trusting relationship with each child. • Teach language for the expression of feelings. • Offer appropriate levels of support to help children develop self-control. • Provide opportunities for children to practice their new skills.

Supporting Cognition and Brain Development

Infants, toddlers, and twos develop cognitively when they have many opportunities to explore the world around them, interact with others, and play. The work of Jean Piaget and Lev Vygotsky, as well as recent brain research, provide a deeper understanding of why these experiences are so important for young children. Research findings also help us determine what teachers and families can do to support cognitive development.

Jean Piaget

Jean Piaget was interested in the way logical thinking develops.[9] Like Erikson and Greenspan, Piaget described development as a progression through stages. He showed that infants think differently from young children, that young children think differently from older children, and that older children think differently from adults.

Piaget thought that children refine their logic and construct understandings about the world through play. By handling materials of different sizes, shapes, and colors, children eventually learn to sort, classify, compare, and sequence. Their knowledge grows as they experiment, make discoveries, and modify their earlier way of thinking to incorporate new insights. Piaget called the processes *accommodation* and *assimilation*.

Accommodation occurs when a child's experience does not fit his previous understanding. He must change his thinking about the subject in order for it to make sense again. For example, imagine a toddler who lives in a house with several small dogs and who believes all dogs are small. When she sees a big animal that barks and her father tells her that it is a dog, she has to change her thinking to accommodate this new knowledge: Some dogs are small, but some are big.

Assimilation occurs when a child takes in various experiences and fits them into a current mental model for thinking or acting. For example, imagine that the same child in a different situation sees a big animal that barks. Because she now knows now that some dogs are big and some are small, she is able to assimilate this new information: The barking animal is a dog.

Piaget's theory identifies four stages of cognitive development: sensorimotor, preoperational, concrete operational, and formal operational. The sensorimotor stage and the preoperational stage are relevant to *The Creative Curriculum*. Older children reach the concrete and formal operational stages.

The **sensorimotor stage** begins at birth and lasts until about age 2. In this stage, children learn by reacting to what they experience through their senses and physical activity, especially through manipulation of objects. For example, they put books in their mouths, kick play gyms with their feet, and pull at the strings of wheeled toys to discover what they can do with these objects. Through many interactions and opportunities to explore objects, they learn that a book has a cover and pages, that kicking a mobile will cause it to spin, and that pulling the string on a toy will bring it to them. Piaget believed that their motor development underlies their cognitive development.

When babies learn that the mother seen from the back and the mother seen from the front are the same mother and that a ball still exists when it rolls out of sight, they understand *object permanence*. This means that they understand that objects maintain their identities when they change location and usually continue to exist when they are out of sight.

At about age 2, children enter a stage that Piaget calls the **preoperational period.** During this stage, which lasts throughout the preschool years, children begin to notice the properties of the objects they explore. However, their observations are limited to only one attribute of an object at a time. They focus on how things look and do not use adult logic. For example, children at this stage may think that the tallest person in the room must also be the oldest. They are unable to understand that height and age do not always correspond directly.

Children who are at the preoperational stage also tend to see the world from their own point of view. Piaget calls this quality *egocentrism*. The following conversation is an example of egocentrism:

> "I'm going to read this book about trucks," the teacher explains. "I have a truck," says one child. Another comments, "My daddy drives a truck." "My daddy is tall," observes a third child. "I'm tall," responds a fourth.

Each child responds to what was said with information about himself, rather than staying with the other's idea.

Piaget believed that pretend play is essential to cognitive development during this stage. By taking on pretend roles and using objects in unconventional ways (for example, using a block as a telephone) children are thinking symbolically. Symbolic play experiences lay the foundation for more abstract symbolic thinking later, such as using letters, numbers and numerals, and words.

Recent research has also shown that child development is more fluid and more tied to specific content knowledge than Piaget's stages suggest. For instance, a child who thinks that the tallest person must be the oldest might often draw valid conclusions about other situations. She might conclude that not all men are daddies, because she has had many experiences with men who are daddies and men who are not. Nevertheless, the sequential development of logic that Piaget identified still holds. He also helped us understand the role of the child's actions in development. Piaget's descriptions of how children construct understanding inform the teaching techniques, selection of materials, and suggested experiences of *The Creative Curriculum*.

Lev Vygotsky

The social aspect of children's cognitive development was a primary interest of Lev Vygotsky. [10] While Piaget paid more attention to the relationship between physical and cognitive development, Vygotsky recognized that social interaction is crucial to children's cognitive learning. According to Vygotsky, children grow cognitively not only by acting on objects but also by interacting with adults and more knowledgeable peers. Teachers' verbal directions, physical assistance, and probing questioning help children improve skills and acquire knowledge. Peers who have advanced skills can also help other children grow and learn by modeling strategies or providing other assistance.

Vygotsky uses the term *zone of proximal development* (ZPD) to describe the range of a child's learning about a particular experience. The lower limit of the zone is what a child can do independently. The upper limit of the zone is what a child can learn by watching and talking to peers and teachers. With the support of others, the child organizes new information to fit what he already knows. As a result, he can function at a higher level than he could by working on his own. This process of helping a child build knowledge and understanding is called *scaffolding*, just as a scaffold holds you up so you can reach a higher place when you are building a house.

To be able to scaffold children's learning, Vygotsky, like Piaget, taught that teachers need to be expert observers of children. By interacting with children, asking questions, and thinking carefully about children's development, teachers can determine each child's developmental level and consider ways to extend children's learning.

The Creative Curriculum is grounded in Vygotsky's theory that social interaction is key to children's learning. Your primary role is to establish and maintain trusting relationships with children by being responsive to their individual needs. Learning takes place through positive relationships between and among children and adults. Planning and teaching is based on observing and documenting what children do and say. In Vygotsky's terms, you need to determine each child's ZPD. Then you can provide individualized experiences for children that are challenging enough to help them move to a higher level of learning but not so challenging as to frustrate them.

Brain Research

Brain research has improved our understanding of how and when children learn best. Experimental studies of animals and recent innovations in medical technology have led to many new insights. Here are some of the elements of brain research that inform *The Creative Curriculum.*

What We Know From Brain Research	Implications for Teachers
Learning is not a matter of nature versus nurture; it is both. We used to think that heredity (a person's inborn characteristics) is more important than environment (what he or she is exposed to) in determining how well a person learns. In fact, both play a major role.	The ability to learn is not as fixed as we once thought. All children benefit from rich experiences and interactions in early childhood. Teachers can have a profound influence on all children's learning and development.
The human brain is affected by experiences. Children's learning changes the physical structure of their brains.	Every appropriate sensorimotor experience that teachers provide helps children build brain connections.
Learning needs to be reinforced again and again. For a brain connection to become permanent, it must be used repeatedly. Connections that are not used eventually disappear.	Children need many different opportunities to practice new skills. Rather than constantly rotating materials and interrupting children's repetitive play (such as dropping a block off a table and picking it up again and again), teachers give children time to practice new skills.
In order to learn, children need to feel safe and confident. Stress, on the other hand, can trigger chemical changes that begin in the brain and affect many processes in the body. The changes probably affect attention, memory, planning, and behavioral control.	Secure relationships with family members, teachers, and other significant people in a child's life are essential to learning. *Creative Curriculum* teachers make it their first priority to develop trusting, nurturing relationships with the children in their care.

▶

What We Know From Brain Research	Implications for Teachers
Nutrition, health, and physical activity affect learning. Movement stimulates connections in the brain. A well-balanced diet, sufficient sleep, and plenty of exercise support healthy brain growth.	Daily exercise and time outdoors are essential for health and well-being, even for young infants. Many programs also provide health screening, as well as meals and snacks.
Evidence shows that visual impairments, auditory deficits, and perceptual-motor delays have serious negative effects on children's developing nervous systems. There might also be sensitive periods when the brain is more receptive to certain types of learning (including emotional control, social attachment, and language), but questions about the brain areas involved in such learning are still being explored. It appears that the brain remains open to experiences, so interventions are important.[11]	Teachers focus on the skills that provide a foundation for all future learning and offer corrective efforts when children have disabilities. The development of self-regulation, skills for forming relationships with others, strategies for solving problems, language, and music should be important aspects of the curriculum.
During the early years, the brain is more receptive to phonology, learning the individual sounds that make up languages.	Teachers support children's phonological development and language acquisition by talking, singing, reading, and playing with the sounds of words. Dual language learners are supported in learning their home languages as well as the primary language spoken in the program.

Brain research has found physical evidence to support what Maslow, Erikson, and other theorists have taught us. It shows that the wiring in children's brain development is positively affected when they are healthy and well fed; feel safe from threats; and have nurturing, stable relationships. Because of this research, *The Creative Curriculum* emphasizes the primary role that teachers play.

Major Ideas	The Creative Curriculum
Jean Piaget Children's logical thinking develops in stages. They need many opportunities to explore the world around them in order to refine their understandings about how things work. Infants learn by reacting to what they experience through their senses and physical activity. Toddlers and twos are egocentric (see things from their point of view) and overgeneralize their limited experiences.	• Provide safe opportunities for infants to explore their environment through play. • Create a system for collecting and sanitizing mouthed toys and materials, because infants use all of their senses to explore. • Provide opportunities for toddlers and twos to make choices. • Schedule uninterrupted periods of time for children to play and explore their environment. • Ask open-ended questions to encourage children's thinking.
Lev Vygotsky Interactions with teachers and peers are an important part of children's cognitive development. Teachers scaffold children's learning by offering assistance and giving supporting information. Teachers must observe children closely to understand how to support their learning.	• Observe children carefully. • Organize a system for recording observation notes and documenting children's development. • Use information from your observations to plan routines and experiences that encourage children's development and learning. • Encourage social interaction between children with varying skill levels so that they can learn from one another. • Offer assistance to children as needed.
Learning and the Brain Knowledge of young children's cognitive development has grown with the newer understanding of how the brain develops. Brain development is affected by learning and experiences, which need to be repeated. Emotions, physical health, nutrition, and movement affect learning. There are sensitive periods when the brain is at its peak for certain kinds of learning, but the brain remains open to experiences. Early and sustained stress affects brain development negatively.[12]	• Provide many and varied experiences for children. • Allow children time to practice new skills. • Develop positive relationships with each child. • Create a safe environment where children can explore confidently and learn. • Provide many rich language experiences throughout the day, by describing what is happening, asking questions, singing, and reading. • Offer continuity of care and primary caregiving.

The Five Components

The organizational structure of *The Creative Curriculum for Infants, Toddlers & Twos* includes five components. They give you the information you need to set up your program and to make decisions as you work with children and families. Each of the chapters in Part 1 discusses one of the components. The graphic below shows how the components fit together.

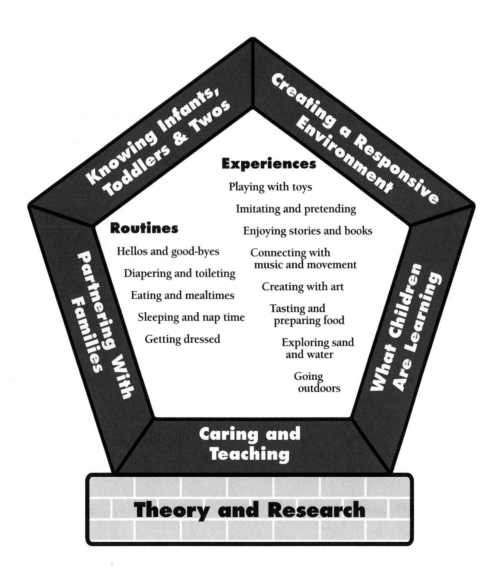

inside | this chapter

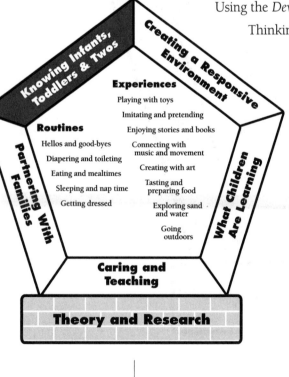

Knowing Infants, Toddlers, and Twos

The first 3 years of life are a time of tremendous development and learning. Think about a newborn baby. Every experience is new to her. Her reactions are limited to such things as turning her head toward what she likes (such as her mother's breast for feeding) or turning her head away from what she does not like (such as loud noises). She can relax her body and become quiet, or tense her body and cry. She depends completely on adults to take care of her and respond to her needs, to clean and feed her, move her, offer her the appropriate level of activity, and soothe her when she is upset.

Two and a half years later, the same child who once had only a few ways to communicate her needs has become a skilled communicator, pointing and using other gestures, and speaking in sentences. As she developed relationships with the important adults in her life, she began learning to relate to other people. In addition to observing actively, she can now manipulate, group, and sort objects. Her motor skills have progressed from the basic reflexive movements of a newborn to the complex skills of an energetic, running, climbing 2-year-old.

This chapter explains the first component of *The Creative Curriculum for Infants, Toddlers & Twos*. Curriculum begins with knowing children.

There are three sections in this chapter:

What Infants, Toddlers, and Twos Are Like presents an overview of the developmental characteristics of children from birth to 36 months. Four areas of child development are discussed: social/emotional, physical, cognitive, and language. The influence of culture upon various aspects of child development is also examined briefly.

Individual Differences discusses the ways in which temperament, life circumstances, dual language learning, and disabilities might affect the development of individual children.

Using the *Developmental Continuum* to Observe Children explains a tool that describes children's development and that guides teachers' observations, assessment of children's progress, and program planning.

What Infants, Toddlers, and Twos Are Like

Child development information may be divided into four areas: social/emotional, physical, cognitive, and language. While it is helpful to consider these areas for planning and discussion, development does not really divide into neat categories. Rather, the four categories are closely related and often overlap. Development in one area affects and is influenced by development in all other areas. This is why teachers have to pay attention to all four areas.

Leo (18 months) is developing expressive language. He approaches his teacher, Barbara, and says, "Up, p'ease." She promotes Leo's language development when she expands on his communication by saying, "You would like me to pick you up, please." She supports his social/emotional development when she returns Leo's smile and lifts him into her arms. Leo practices physical skills when he stands and raises his arms toward her. When she acts on this request, Barbara reinforces Leo's understanding of cause and effect, an important element of cognitive development.

The following sections provide an overview of the four areas of child development for children from birth to 36 months.

Social/Emotional Development

Young children's social/emotional development involves the way they feel about themselves, their understanding of feelings, their ability to regulate emotions and express them appropriately, and their capacity for building relationships with others. It flourishes when they have close, supportive, and trusting relationships with adults. When adults are responsive, when they share the pleasure of children's accomplishments and discoveries, and when they create an environment in which children can participate actively in daily routines and experiences, they show children that they are important, interesting, and competent. Through positive interactions, children learn about themselves and how to relate to others.

Young infants have little ability to regulate their emotions. Initially, they express themselves by such things as turning slightly toward or away from what they like or dislike and by crying and smiling. With attentive, responsive care, infants quickly learn which behaviors lead to having their needs met, to being fed, being changed when soiled or wet, being comforted to sleep, and being held and loved.

Sometimes adults worry that they will spoil infants if they always respond to their needs. However, infants whose needs are met consistently and lovingly are more easily comforted, are better able to pay attention to what is going on around them, and are more open to exploring their environment and to new experiences. They also learn more quickly to calm themselves and regulate their emotions in other ways. Adults who do not respond to an infant's cries until the infant becomes extremely distressed encourage the baby to rise to a frantic level of crying more quickly in the future. This kind of delayed response makes it harder for parents and teachers to settle the baby and harder for the baby to learn to regulate his emotions.

At around 2 months, something wonderful happens. Babies smile for the first time. By 3 or 4 months, babies begin to laugh in response to very active stimuli.

Julio (4 months) coos with laughter when Linda covers his toes with kisses and says, "Where are the baby's toes? Dónde están los dedos del pie del bebé? Oh, there are the little toes. I'm going to gobble up those toes!"

At about 5–6 months, young infants begin to develop an understanding that they are separate individuals. As they explore, they pull at their parents' hair, study their teachers' faces, and reach for the jewelry or glasses worn by familiar adults.

Young infants are fascinated by other people and soon learn to use facial expressions, other movements, and vocalizations to initiate, return, and end interactions with others. With teachers who respond to their emotional and social cues (crying, laughing, smiling), infants begin to learn that they can affect others through their actions. This understanding helps them to see themselves as competent individuals who can influence the world around them.

By about 8 months of age, when most infants have established secure attachments with the important adults in their lives, they become upset when their preferred adult leaves (separation anxiety) and anxious when a new adult is present (stranger anxiety). They show their secure attachment to their parents and teachers with more intensified clinging. Their anxiety is usually resolved as infants become more mobile, spend more time away from the people to whom they first became securely attached, and develop close relationships with other important adults in their lives, such as their teachers.

Mobile infants are active, enthusiastic explorers who are in love with the world. They are often so busy crawling, cruising, walking, and practicing their other new skills that, to get their attention, their families sometimes have to stand in front of them and wave.

Mobile infants enjoy watching other children and begin to imitate each other. They also engage in *social referencing*, looking at others' faces, recognizing emotional expressions, and using this information to react to new situations and people.

Willard (11 months) discovers a tray of water placed on a low table. He looks at Grace as if to ask, "May I play with this?" Grace smiles and nods encouragingly. Willard turns back to the tray and splashes it enthusiastically with his hand.

Mobile infants can also crawl or walk to their trusted teachers when they feel sad or frightened or just need some reassurance. Increased mobility gives them a new strategy for regulating their emotions (actively seeking protection and comfort from a teacher). Development of *emotional regulation* (in this case, increased awareness that a trusted teacher will help them if they become scared, sad, or unsure of themselves) also motivates them to master physical skills. This is another example of how all areas of development are related.

As their motor and cognitive abilities increase, mobile infants feel more capable. They want to control their actions and the effects those actions produce. When things do not go the way they would like—as when a favorite toy is out of reach, a pop-up toy does not pop up, or their hands are blocked from grabbing a fragile item—they react with frustration and sometimes anger. Their happiness is also powerful. When enjoying a toy, older mobile infants stop their play and smile with delight at a trusted adult to communicate their pleasure. A simple game of peek-a-boo may prompt lots of happy laughter.

Toddlers busily explore their independence as they learn about and respond increasingly appropriately to the feelings of others and as they gain better control over their emotions. The world is an exciting place for toddlers, but it sometimes overwhelms them. As a result, toddlers typically find themselves wanting the impossible: to be big and to stay little at the same time. The same toddler who screams, "No!" when his teacher says it is time to wash his hands may be crying five minutes later, wanting to be cuddled like a baby. Responsive and caring teachers understand that toddlers want to practice their new skills, make their own decisions, and do things themselves.

Matthew (22 months) pushes Mercedes' hands out of the way and says, "No, me," when she tries to help him put on his coat. She listens to what Matthew is telling her. She asks, "Do you want to put your coat on by yourself?" and Matthew nods his head.

Twos' increased language skills provide them with a greater ability to regulate their emotions and explore their sense of self. They develop a vocabulary for talking about feelings and about themselves. While toddlers fondly use the words *me* and *mine,* twos are soon able to use words like *sad, mad, scary, love, silly,* and *yucky* to describe their thoughts and feelings. Being able to express their emotions to a responsive teacher gives them new control over their emotions and behavior. As twos become more self-aware and as they understand the expectations that adults have for their behavior, self-conscious emotions, such as shame, pride, and guilt, also develop. They also use this new understanding of emotions to empathize with others. Twos not only begin to use words to express their emotions, they can also recognize and respond appropriately to the emotions of others.

How Culture Might Affect Social/Emotional Development

Young children learn by observing the important people in their lives. Their families' home cultures greatly influence their understanding of which emotions to express and how and when to express them. Some cultures value the group's well-being over the individual's (collectivism). In these cultures, it is often more important not to express strong emotions in order to maintain the harmony of the group. Cultures that value the individual's well-being over the group's (individualism) tend to appreciate the expression of an individual's feelings, such as by smiling broadly, laughing loudly, crying mightily, or scowling deeply.

Culture may also determine whether children are encouraged to express pride about individual accomplishments or whether to feel shame or embarrassment at being recognized individually in front of a group. Families who value individualism often encourage children to express pride and happiness about personal accomplishments, whereas families who value collectivism might feel shame or embarrassment if someone calls attention to an individual's success in front of a group.

Barbara, knowing that the majority of the families she serves have home cultures that value collectivism, is careful to share children's individual accomplishments with families when they are alone rather than with others.

Physical Development

Physical development refers to gradually gaining control over large and small muscles. Gross motor (or large muscle) skills allow a child to do such things as roll over, sit, crawl, walk, run, and throw a ball. Fine motor (or small muscle) skills, such as holding, pinching, and flexing fingers, eventually enable children to do such things as draw, write, eat with utensils, and cut with scissors. The development of new motor skills allows young children to make other new discoveries. As they explore, they begin to make sense of their environment.

Julio (4 months), having gained control of his head, can better use his eyes and ears to locate the source of a sound.

Willard (11 months) is able to use his fingers, hands, and wrists to touch, taste, and smell the slice of pear on the table.

Jonisha (33 months) can turn the pages of her book one at a time. She identifies pictures of common objects and animals and recalls a familiar story.

Although they develop at different rates, infants learn to control their bodies in the same progression. Control develops from head to toe, and from the center of their bodies out through their arms and legs to their fingers and toes. You can see this general pattern as you watch a child learn to lift his head and then sit, crawl, walk, and run.

Young infants move primarily by reflex when they are newborns. They move automatically in response to various stimuli. Some reflexes help ensure that infants will get what they need to survive. For example, when you touch the cheek of a newborn, she starts moving her mouth in search of a nipple. When you touch her mouth or when her mouth touches the nipple of a breast or bottle, she begins sucking. Young infants have other reflexes, too. For example, reciprocal kicking occurs when an infant kicks first one foot, then the other. This reflex suggests skills yet to be developed, such as crawling and walking. During the first eight months, however, infants change from having little control over their muscles to developing motor skills such as rolling over, reaching for and grasping objects, transferring items from hand to hand, sitting without help from an adult, and often beginning to crawl.

Mobile infants quickly become skilled at moving themselves from place to place. They pull themselves up to standing, using the support of furniture, toys, or a trusted adult. They begin to cruise from this upright position, holding onto the edges of furniture while walking. Next, they take their first steps and walk without support. When they are about a year old, they begin to stack blocks or other toys. Their *pincer grasp*—holding something with the thumb and index finger—becomes more coordinated, so they can pick up small pieces of cereal, turn knobs on toys, and open and close small boxes.

Toddlers have a wide range of gross and fine motor skills. They can walk and run, and they are developing new skills such as hopping and throwing a ball.

Mercedes notices that, now that Matthew (22 months) has begun to run, he usually runs from one activity to another, practicing this new skill.

Toddlers use their fingers and hands to put puzzle pieces in place; make marks with a crayon; roll, pound, and squeeze playdough; and paint.

Twos continue to refine their motor skills. They combine various gross motor skills during play and move more easily from running to jumping to climbing. They begin to coordinate their arms and legs to try complicated tasks such as pedaling and steering a tricycle. As their fine motor skills advance, their scribbling gets smaller and more controlled, and they enjoy stringing large beads to make necklaces.

Valisha (33 months) refines her fine motor skills as she begins to use scissors successfully to cut paper. LaToya notices this as she observes Valisha during art experiences.

Toddlers and twos need many opportunities and a safe environment to practice, refine, and master physical skills. You can promote motor development by encouraging children to try new skills and sometimes by helping them to slow down a little so they can gain more control.

How Culture Might Affect Physical Development

A family's cultural practices can influence the rate at which children develop motor skills. If a child's home culture believes strongly in independence, then a child may be encouraged to move in order to do things on her own at an earlier age. If a child's home culture values relationships with others more than personal independence, she may be discouraged from doing things independently at a young age.

Abby's mother explains to Brooks that she spoonfeeds Abby at home and will probably continue to do so for several years. Abby's mother believes that this culturally supported practice is one way that she can show Abby (14 months) how much she loves her and how important it is for people to depend on and help each other.

Cognitive Development

Cognitive development involves the way children think, develop understandings about the world, and use what they learn to reason and solve problems. Infants, toddlers, and twos interact with others and use all of their senses and motor skills actively to construct their own understandings about the people and objects in their environment. Children learn when they roll over, crawl around and over everything in their paths, run, jump, knock things over, and pick things up. They learn as they grasp a rattle, pound playdough, and smell the grilled cheese sandwiches you make for lunch. They learn as they play and as they live their everyday lives with you and their families. As they eat, get dressed, have their diapers changed, sit on a toilet, or move a chair across the room, they collect information about how things work.

Young infants are experiencing everything for the first time and are trying to make sense of their world. Their ability to focus on and explore objects increases as their vision and grasp develops.

As infants are able to sit up, reach for toys, and explore things with their hands and mouths, they experiment with such properties as soft and hard, smooth and rough, heavy and light, and big and little.

When they consistently experience predictable routines, young infants learn to anticipate events. For example, an infant who is crying because he is wet might stop crying when he sees you pick up a diaper. He has learned that, when you pick up a diaper, his discomfort will end soon. Infants also learn that they can control their environments when they intentionally try to repeat something interesting that they originally did unintentionally. A child who pushes a car accidentally and likes the way it rolls may pound on the car, touch it, and knock it over before he tries pushing it again. He is beginning to understand the connection between his pushing and the car's rolling.

Jasmine (8 months) opens and closes a cupboard door repeatedly, making it bang. She learns that her repeated behavior affects objects in consistent ways. This understanding helps her to make sense of her world.

Mobile infants begin to show their increasing ability to act intentionally, use tools, and understand cause and effect. They learn that particular actions have particular results. They continue to build understandings about cause and effect and use new problem-solving skills.

Willard (11 months) wants the pull toy that is on the other side of the table. He gets it by pulling the string. He has learned that pulling the string makes the toy attached to the string move.

Children this age often imitate the actions of others.

Abby (14 months) bangs a drum as she watches Leo doing so.

As children learn more and more about the world and the objects in it, they begin to categorize new information. Once mobile infants begin talking, they frequently ask, "Dat?" as they try to collect more information about the new things they encounter.

Toddlers' developing language and memory skills affect other aspects of their thinking. For example, they can separate from their families more easily because they have begun to understand that people leave and come back. As their ability to remember events and people increases, they engage in lots of pretend play, exploring daily and special events and social roles.

Children at this age tend to be egocentric. This means that they believe that they can control the world and that everyone thinks and feels as they do. For example, a toddler may believe he can make the traffic on a busy street come to a standstill, simply by yelling, "Stop!" Toddlers also believe that all moving things are alive.

Leo (18 months) is afraid of the sounds of a flushing toilet and a running vacuum cleaner, believing that these objects are alive because they make such loud sounds and have moving parts.

Twos are better able to collect new information and link it to what they already know. As they push a play vacuum cleaner around the room, they discover that they can control the toy, just as you control the real vacuum. With consistent, predictable routines, they begin to understand basic concepts about time and to recognize that there is an order to daily events.

Valisha (33 months) begins looking for her parents after story time, knowing that they usually arrive after that time of the day.

As their attention span increases, twos are able to persist with more complex problem solving and may investigate the cause when something unexpected happens.

Gena (30 months) is building a block tower. She places a large block on top of a stack of small blocks, and the tower falls to the ground. She looks at it with a frown and says, "Blocks fell down." After a few minutes of stacking and unstacking the blocks, Gena begins to rebuild the tower with the large block on the bottom.

How Culture Might Affect Cognitive Development

A child's home culture can influence the way he learns and processes new information. Cultures encourage children to explore their environments in different ways. In some cultures, experimenting with toys, manipulating objects, and solving problems by using materials are highly valued as the way children learn best. Other cultures value observation more than handling materials. In some communities, children learn by observing their environments, watching others interact, and focusing on people rather than materials.

Mercedes has a toddler in her class whose family values observation more than active manipulation of objects. She frequently sees him standing or sitting in one place, focusing intently on an interaction between adults or other children. She knows that, if she approaches and encourages him to interact with the others or tries to distract him with a toy or game, she would interrupt his way of learning. By talking with this child's family, Mercedes has come to understand how much he learns when he watches intently.

Language Development

Language development is one of children's major accomplishments during the first 3 years of life. They progress from communicating needs through facial expressions, gestures, body movements, and crying to communicating through verbal or sign language. They can acquire a vocabulary of thousands of words and learn the rules for using them by being around and interacting with adults who communicate with them, encourage their efforts to communicate, and guide their exploration and learning.

Learning to talk takes practice. By sharing your pleasure in children's communication rather than correcting their mistakes, and by talking with them even before they understand what you are saying or can respond verbally, you help children build on their desire to communicate.

Young infants are born with a unique ability to relate to other human beings. They come into the world ready to communicate. A newborn turns her head to the sound of her mother's voice. When their eyes meet, the baby's face brightens and quiets. Infants cry to communicate their needs, but crying is not their only means of communication. During the first few months, they begin making other sounds as well. They gurgle, coo, and squeal, using sounds to initiate, continue, and end interactions with others. By about 6–9 months, infants begin to babble language sounds, practicing rising and falling intonation, and experimenting with volume. By age 1, they focus on their own culture's language rather than the full range of sounds used in the world's languages.[13] In addition to making sounds, infants also listen and respond.

As they get older, infants respond by smiling, kicking, and turning their heads to look at someone who is talking. They also cry, turn away, or withdraw when they are unhappy with their environments.

Mobile infants are able to understand much more than they can say. Before they are able to talk, they look at objects you name and make gestures, such as waving good-bye when someone leaves or pointing at a book that is just out of reach. They can respond to requests and questions by using gestures, sounds, and sometimes words.

Brooks asks Abby (14 months) if she would rather have apples or pears with her lunch. Abby points to the apples and says, "Appa."

At about one year, some mobile infants say a few recognizable words, usually the names of people and things that are important to them. In English-speaking families, early words often include *mama, dada, ba* (for bottle), *bow-wow*, or *ball*. Children soon start to mix words and babble, speaking with great expression.

Mobile infants enjoy looking at pictures in books, particularly illustrations of familiar things: people's faces, babies, toys, trucks, and animals. You can help them build strong vocabularies by sharing books with them and naming the objects in pictures. Mobile infants like turning the pages of their favorite books and pointing to familiar pictures when you offer prompts.

Toddlers continue to understand much more than they can say, and they are able to listen to and enjoy more complex stories.

Matthew (22 months) giggles in response to a book that Mercedes reads about a dog who loves to dance.

Many toddlers have at least 50 words in their expressive vocabularies by the time they are 18 months old.[14] Estimates of children's expressive vocabularies (the words they say) vary widely at age 2, but researchers agree that young children's receptive vocabularies (the words they understand when they hear them) are much larger. Mobile infants learn that one of the functions of language is to help them get what they want or need. They begin putting two words together to express other thoughts as well, such as "Daddy go" or "Me do."

Twos continue to increase their language skills, both their ability to listen (receptive language) and their ability to speak (expressive language). Between the ages of 2 and 3 years, their vocabularies continue to increase dramatically, and their sentences become more complex. They engage in conversations, offering ideas and asking questions.

As their language skills develop, so does their interest in and ability to talk about books.

Gena (30 months) says, "Night Moon," as she brings the book Goodnight Moon *to Ivan every afternoon before she naps.* *Jonisha and* *Valisha* (33 months) enjoy choosing books from the shelf, turning the pages, and telling the story to each other from memory.

How Culture Might Affect Language Development

As in all other aspects of development, young children's use of speech varies. Some say their first words at 8 months, while others hardly speak at all until they are almost 2 years old. Many factors influence how and when language develops. Some are individual differences present from birth. Others depend on a child's experiences with language and whether a child is learning two languages at once. Dual language learning is discussed in the next section.

A child's home culture can influence when a child speaks and the way in which he uses verbal language, facial expressions, gestures, and silence to communicate. Some families rely heavily on verbal language and direct speech. Others rely more on the facial expressions of the speaker and on indirect communication strategies. Children reared by families who value direct communication and who use many words to explain a situation or to express thoughts and feelings will probably use speech in the same way.

A child whose family culture values indirect communication is generally physically closer to his parents (being carried, sitting on a lap, or touching a family member). That physical closeness allows the adult to read the child's body signals—a change in position, a tensing of the muscles, a subtle change in expression—and respond to them. This encourages the child to continue to communicate nonverbally rather than relying on words. Understanding these different styles will help you to recognize each child's communication attempts and better support the language development of the children in your care.

Individual Differences

Your understanding of individual differences helps you build a trusting relationship with each child and makes each child feel comfortable in your care. Children have different temperaments, prior experiences, and life circumstances. Some may be learning English at the same time as they are learning their home language (dual language learners). Some children have formally identified special needs.

Think about the children in your care. Perhaps you have an infant who loves to explore her environment and who opens every drawer, cabinet, and box she gets her hands on. She never seems to stop moving, even during nap time. Perhaps you have a toddler who hides behind his mother's legs and needs constant encouragement and support to interact with others and play with new toys.

Understanding children means appreciating their unique ways of interacting with the world and with people. It means taking time to learn about children's strengths, interests, challenges they like, challenges that frustrate them, and ways they are comforted. With this knowledge, you can respond in ways that address each child's needs. The planning forms discussed in the next chapter give you a way to use what you learn about each child and your group of children.

Temperament

Children are born with behavioral styles called *temperaments*. For example, some children approach new situations cautiously, without a fuss, and adapt slowly. Others have an immediate positive response to new situations, are generally cheerful, and have regular patterns of behavior. Still others withdraw or cry in new situations. When you are aware of a child's temperament, you can sometimes predict how that child will behave in certain types of situations. Thinking about temperament may help you to understand and interpret children's behaviors.

Research suggests that temperamental differences can be identified even in newborns. There are significant differences in the way babies respond to different stimuli, such as to loud noises or gentle rocking. Stella Chess and Alexander Thomas examined how the temperament of newborns influenced the further development of some personality traits.[15]

1. **Activity Level**—How active is the child? Does he kick vigorously or is he often still? Does he squirm while having his diaper changed? Does he prefer to explore the world by watching and listening or by crawling and climbing?

2. **Biological Rhythms**—How predictable are the child's sleeping and eating habits? Does he wake up, get hungry, and get sleepy at the same times each day?

3. **Tendency to approach or withdraw**—Does the child respond positively to (approach) something new or does she pull away (withdraw) from it? When something new happens, does she fuss, do nothing, or seem to like it? For example, does she reach for a new toy or push it away? Does she swallow a new food or spit it out? Does she smile at a new person or cry and move away?

4. **Adaptability**—How does the child react to change? Does he have a hard time with changes in routines or with new people? How long does it take him to get used to new foods, new people, and other new circumstances?

5. **Sensory threshold**—At what point does a child become bothered by noise or light, changes in temperature, different tastes, or the feel of clothing?

6. **Intensity or energy level of reactions**—How does the child respond emotionally? Does she react loudly and dramatically to even the most minor disappointment, or does she become quiet when she is upset?

7. **Mood**—Does the child have a positive or negative outlook? Is she generally in a light-hearted mood, or does she take things very seriously?

8. **Distractibility**—Is the child readily distracted from a task by what is going on around her? When being fed her bottle, does she turn her head to look in the direction of every new sound she hears or movement she sees?

9. **Persistence**—How long does the child stay with a task when it is challenging? How does he react to interruptions or requests to clean up when he is playing?

Children with different personality traits need to be treated differently.

Julio (4 months) has very predictable eating and sleeping patterns. Linda knows to have his bottle ready at 2:00 when he wakes up from his nap.

Gena (30 months) tends to be cautious in group situations. Knowing this, Ivan makes sure to invite her to play with him and another child every day.

While temperament may be inborn, providing appropriate support for children can help them function comfortably. An active child can calm down, and a child who tends to withdraw can learn strategies for feeling more comfortable in group situations.

Life Circumstances

In addition to other individual differences, varying life circumstances contribute to the uniqueness of each child. Consider how each of these factors affects the children you care for and teach.

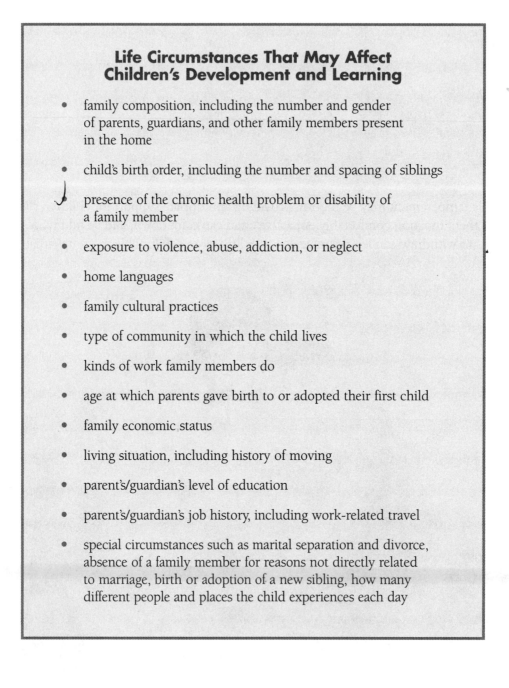

Life Circumstances That May Affect Children's Development and Learning

- family composition, including the number and gender of parents, guardians, and other family members present in the home

- child's birth order, including the number and spacing of siblings

- presence of the chronic health problem or disability of a family member

- exposure to violence, abuse, addiction, or neglect

- home languages

- family cultural practices

- type of community in which the child lives

- kinds of work family members do

- age at which parents gave birth to or adopted their first child

- family economic status

- living situation, including history of moving

- parent's/guardian's level of education

- parent's/guardian's job history, including work-related travel

- special circumstances such as marital separation and divorce, absence of a family member for reasons not directly related to marriage, birth or adoption of a new sibling, how many different people and places the child experiences each day

Try to be aware of each child's circumstances when he or she enters your program. Your program's enrollment forms may be helpful in learning more about individual families. Talking with family members and taking notes about what you learn is an important first step. Encourage families to communicate with you about anything new taking place in children's lives, and honor their styles of communication. This process will take time as you develop a trusting relationship with family members. Remember to honor the confidentiality of information that family members share with you. If a family shares information with you that you do not know how to handle, seek advice from your supervisor or an outside expert.

Dual Language Learners

Children whose home language is not English are very likely to be in your care, if not now, then in the future. The number of children who speak a first language that is not English (English Language Learners) or who are learning English at the same time they are learning another language (Dual Language Learners) has increased dramatically and continues to increase in the United States.

Young children in your program may be learning two languages simultaneously, English in your program and another language or languages at home. Children may arrive in your classroom without ever having heard English anywhere other than on television, which is not a very good teacher. You may have several children who share a common home language other than English, or you may have children whose first languages are rare in your community.

Just as all children have very different strengths and needs, children who are learning English while they are learning another language vary greatly. The extent of children's knowledge of their primary language can vary, just as it does for children who speak only English at home.

Some children have language-rich home environments and arrive with strong language skills in their primary language. Other children have a weaker foundation on which to build language skills. Immersing them in a language-rich environment while they are in your care can help them increase their skills.

A number of misconceptions about learning two languages can cause unnecessary anxiety for teachers and parents. The following chart dispels some of these common misunderstandings.[16]

Misunderstandings About Dual Language Learning

Misunderstandings	Reality
Children who are exposed to more than one language are at a clear disadvantage.	Bilingual children are often very creative and good at problem solving. Compared with children who speak one language, those who are bilingual can communicate with more people, read more, and benefit more from travel. Such children will have an additional skill when they enter the workforce.
Learning two languages at the same time confuses a child.	Children do not get confused, even when they combine languages in one sentence. Mixing languages is a normal and expected part of learning and speaking two languages. In fact, bilingual adults frequently do this as well. This is particularly true for dual language learners.
Learning two languages as a young child will slow down children's readiness to read.	Actually, the opposite is often true. Because they have been exposed to the sounds and letter combinations of two languages, their phonological awareness is often better developed than children who have only been exposed to one language.
When children are exposed to two languages, they never become as proficient in either language as children who have to master only one language.	As long as they consistently use both languages, children can become proficient in both languages.
Only the brightest children can learn two languages without encountering problems. Most children have difficulty because the process is so complex.	Nearly all children are capable of learning two languages during the early childhood years. While the process may be complex for adults, young children's brains are still developing the structures for language, so they are able to learn multiple languages. After the early childhood years, those structures are mostly formed. Rather than learning two languages at the same time, older children and adults must learn to translate from one language to another. That is a much more difficult and time-consuming task.

Specific strategies for supporting dual language learners are discussed in other chapters. Exposure to rich language experiences in two languages is a definite asset. All children can benefit from learning another language.

Disabilities

All children have needs. However, you may feel more comfortable meeting some needs than others. For example, you may have several ideas for helping a child who has difficulty saying good-bye to his parents in the morning or for helping another who has temper tantrums. At the same time, you may be hesitant about working with a child who has cerebral palsy or who is visually impaired. You may wonder, "How can I ever meet the needs of these children?" Considering how to meet the needs of all children in your program is challenging. However, with an understanding of their individual development and the support of other professionals, you can help all children develop and learn.

Children are identified for special services in many ways. A child may be identified as having a disability at birth; during a checkup at the pediatrician's office; by a specialist such as a physical therapist; or by someone providing care and education, such as you.

Under Part C of The Individuals with Disabilities Education Act (IDEA), state or community teams work with family members to create an Individualized Family Service Plan (IFSP). These teams may include speech and physical therapists, physicians, social workers, public health nurses, and educators. Federal law (Public Law 108-446, 2004) requires that IFSPs contain this information:

- current developmental information, including a detailed account of a child's abilities and emerging skills

- desired developmental outcomes for the child on which team members agree

- desired developmental outcomes for the family on which team members agree

- a listing of the resources and services necessary to meet the unique needs of the child and family and a description of the environment in which these services will be provided

- specific developmental objectives that allow team members to see what progress is being made

- for children 30–36 months, a transition plan to support the children as they move to preschool or other appropriate services

The emphasis in *The Creative Curriculum* on building trusting relationships is extremely important for young children with disabilities and their families. Some children may have been isolated because their families were anxious about bringing their child into the world beyond their home. Some of the children with disabilities in your group may receive special services, such as occupational, physical, or speech and language therapy. Invite specialists in these fields to your program to share ideas about common goals, strategies, and expectations.

Your involvement with a local early intervention program may come about in a variety of ways. You may be the person who suspects a developmental delay and initiates the intervention process by suggesting to the family that they call the state's Part C Coordinator, who will help them contact local service providers. You may know about a family's IFSP because you were contacted as the family's primary entry point into the system and have been involved from the beginning. Perhaps you were overlooked when the IFSP was written, or you might be meeting the family for the first time. If so, talk with the child's family about requesting a time to discuss their child's IFSP goals and adding your name to the team. You are an important member of the early intervention team because you work with the child each day to achieve developmental goals.

Federal legislation requires each state to have a lead agency with central responsibility for early intervention and a central directory of services. More information about Part C and how it can support the children and families in your program is available from The Council for Exceptional Children (www.cec.sped.org). The central office of your local public schools is another good resource.

The Americans with Disabilities Act requires child care providers to make reasonable accommodations to care for children with disabilities. This includes children who have chronic medical conditions, such as asthma, seizures, and sickle cell disease. Work with the child's family and health care providers to develop a detailed Individualized Health Plan (IHP) for the child. The IHP details all the accommodations needed for feeding, explains routine medication and other health procedures, outlines measures to prevent medical crises, and includes information about recognizing and responding to medical emergencies. You will also need to have the necessary medication and supplies, participate in training in the necessary health procedures, and have an emergency backup plan.

When working with children who have disabilities, first think about their strengths. Also learn about each child's interests before considering the child's special needs. Remember that there are individual differences in the way a disability affects each child.

Gena's parents were nervous about what to expect when she entered the program for the first time. Ivan put them at ease by asking Gena (30 months) about the stuffed lamb she was carrying before talking with them about Gena's impaired speech and dexterity. During that conversation, Ivan learned that, while Gena's cerebral palsy affects her motor development, her cognitive development is typical for a child her age.

All children need to feel included and successful. For this to happen, you must look beyond the specific diagnosis to see how the disability affects the particular child. Be careful not to make assumptions about the child because of the diagnosis, although it is important to learn about the usual effects of the child's specific disability. Consider how a specific disability may or may not affect the child's daily life in your program. Use this information to decide what adjustments you need to make, if any. For example, you may need another adult to help you during certain parts of the day, or you may need to move furniture so a child's special equipment will fit in every part of your room.

Using the *Developmental Continuum* to Observe Children

To provide quality care, you need to know how children develop and what you want them to learn. Each of the four goals of *The Creative Curriculum for Infants, Toddlers & Twos* corresponds to an area of child development:

> **Goal 1:** To learn about self and others—Social/emotional development
>
> **Goal 2:** To learn about moving—Physical development
>
> **Goal 3:** To learn about the world—Cognitive development
>
> **Goal 4:** To learn about communicating—Language development

As the chart shows, the 21 *Creative Curriculum* objectives for infants, toddlers, and twos are organized according to the goals to which they most closely relate. They address the important aspects of a child's development and learning that can be influenced by your care. A larger version of this *Goals and Objectives at a Glance* chart is included in the *Appendix*.

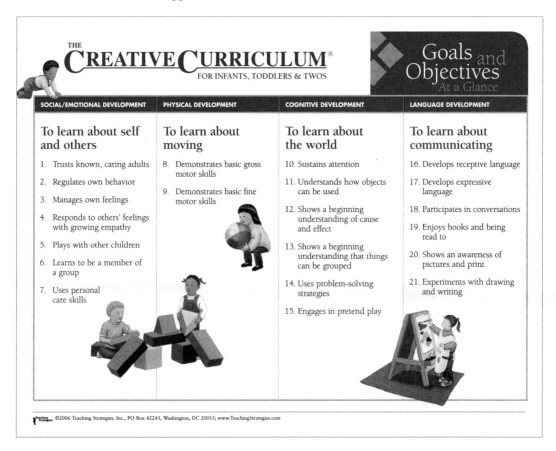

THE **CREATIVE CURRICULUM**®
FOR INFANTS, TODDLERS & TWOS

Goals and Objectives
At a Glance

SOCIAL/EMOTIONAL DEVELOPMENT	PHYSICAL DEVELOPMENT	COGNITIVE DEVELOPMENT	LANGUAGE DEVELOPMENT
To learn about self and others	**To learn about moving**	**To learn about the world**	**To learn about communicating**
1. Trusts known, caring adults	8. Demonstrates basic gross motor skills	10. Sustains attention	16. Develops receptive language
2. Regulates own behavior	9. Demonstrates basic fine motor skills	11. Understands how objects can be used	17. Develops expressive language
3. Manages own feelings		12. Shows a beginning understanding of cause and effect	18. Participates in conversations
4. Responds to others' feelings with growing empathy		13. Shows a beginning understanding that things can be grouped	19. Enjoys books and being read to
5. Plays with other children		14. Uses problem-solving strategies	20. Shows an awareness of pictures and print
6. Learns to be a member of a group		15. Engages in pretend play	21. Experiments with drawing and writing
7. Uses personal care skills			

©2006 Teaching Strategies, Inc., PO Box 42243, Washington, DC 20015; www.TeachingStrategies.com

You also want to know whether each child is developing and learning as expected, and you want to be aware of each child's strengths and needs. *The Creative Curriculum Developmental Continuum for Infants, Toddlers & Twos* shares the same goals and objectives as *The Creative Curriculum for Infants, Toddlers & Twos*. It is a tool to help teachers observe children and guide their development and learning.

How to Read the *Developmental Continuum*

Children do not master a skill or objective all at once. Instead, development typically follows sequential steps. The *Developmental Continuum* therefore shows five developmental steps for each of the 21 objectives and gives three increasingly mature examples to illustrate each step.

As an example, the figure below shows Objective 18, "Participates in conversations." It is one of the six objectives related to Goal 4, "To learn about communicating." The examples for each step give you an idea of what you may observe a child doing.

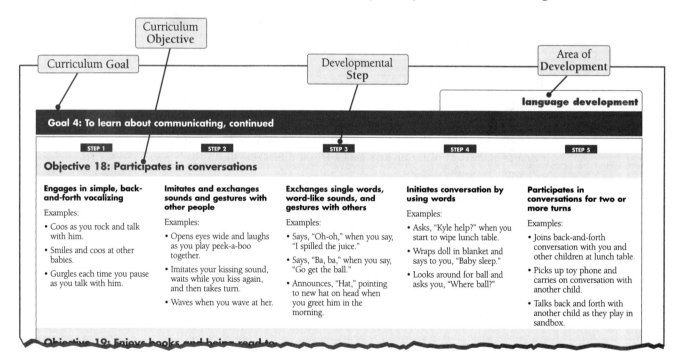

| Curriculum Goal | Curriculum Objective | | Developmental Step | | Area of Development |

language development

Goal 4: To learn about communicating, continued

STEP 1	STEP 2	STEP 3	STEP 4	STEP 5

Objective 18: Participates in conversations

Engages in simple, back-and-forth vocalizing	**Imitates and exchanges sounds and gestures with other people**	**Exchanges single words, word-like sounds, and gestures with others**	**Initiates conversation by using words**	**Participates in conversations for two or more turns**
Examples:	Examples:	Examples:	Examples:	Examples:
• Coos as you rock and talk with him.	• Opens eyes wide and laughs as you play peek-a-boo together.	• Says, "Oh-oh," when you say, "I spilled the juice."	• Asks, "Kyle help?" when you start to wipe lunch table.	• Joins back-and-forth conversation with you and other children at lunch table.
• Smiles and coos at other babies.	• Imitates your kissing sound, waits while you kiss again, and then takes turn.	• Says, "Ba, ba," when you say, "Go get the ball."	• Wraps doll in blanket and says to you, "Baby sleep."	• Picks up toy phone and carries on conversation with another child.
• Gurgles each time you pause as you talk with him.	• Waves when you wave at her.	• Announces, "Hat," pointing to new hat on head when you greet him in the morning.	• Looks around for ball and asks you, "Where ball?"	• Talks back and forth with another child as they play in sandbox.

Objective 19: Enjoys books and being read to

For each objective, you will need to decide whether a child is at Step 1, 2, 3, 4, or 5. Step 1 is a beginning stage of typical development, and Step 5 is the most advanced stage of typical development for children under age 3. Children demonstrate their mastery of skills in a variety of ways. Because the examples presented in the *Developmental Continuum* are sample behaviors, you may or may not see those particular behaviors when you observe the children in your care. Look for behaviors that are of a similar type and skill level. For example, consider a child who points at his cup, says "'up," and then nods his head in affirmation when you ask, "Would you like your cup?" He is functioning at Step 3 of Objective 18. While his behavior is not precisely one of the given examples, he is demonstrating his ability to "Exchange single words, word-like sounds, and gestures with others."

If a child does not seem to be making progress in a particular developmental area as a whole, consider whether the child needs to be observed further and screened for possible developmental delays. The *Developmental Continuum* is not a screening tool.

The Value of Looking at Goals and Objectives on a Continuum

Looking at goals and objectives on a continuum has a number of advantages. Specifically, *The Creative Curriculum Developmental Continuum for Infants, Toddlers & Twos*

- helps you understand typical child development by outlining a progression of behaviors that can be observed in group care settings

- presents a sequence of realistic expectations for each objective, to help you plan your program and respond to children's needs

- provides a way of determining children's progress over time and thereby helps you observe and plan for all children in your program

- fosters a positive approach to teaching by encouraging teachers and families to focus on what children can do and by suggesting what children will be able to do next, rather than focusing on what they cannot do

- gives you a wealth of information to share with families that will reassure them about their child's progress

- includes all children, those who are following a typical pattern of development and learning and those who are not following the typical pattern

The 21 objectives of the *Developmental Continuum* follow, with the steps of each objective and the examples of each step.

Goal 1: To learn about self and others

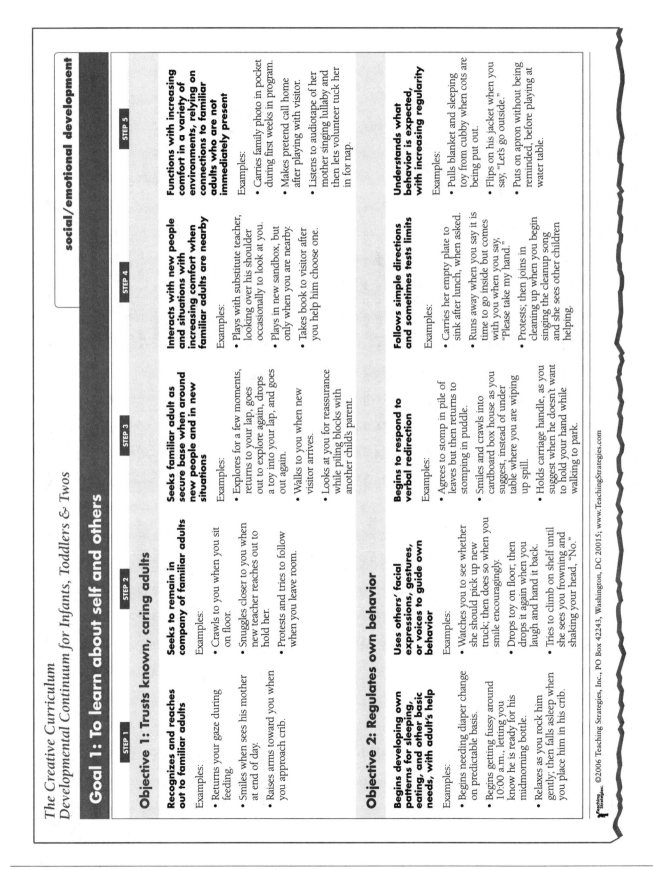

Objective 1: Trusts known, caring adults

STEP 1	STEP 2	STEP 3	STEP 4	STEP 5
Recognizes and reaches out to familiar adults	**Seeks to remain in company of familiar adults**	**Seeks familiar adult as secure base when around new people and in new situations**	**Interacts with new people and situations with increasing comfort when familiar adults are nearby**	**Functions with increasing comfort in a variety of environments, relying on connections to familiar adults who are not immediately present**
Examples:	Examples:	Examples:	Examples:	Examples:
• Returns your gaze during feeding.	• Crawls to you when you sit on floor.	• Explores for a few moments, returns to your lap, goes out to explore again, drops a toy into your lap, and goes out again.	• Plays with substitute teacher, looking over his shoulder occasionally to look at you.	• Carries family photo in pocket during first weeks in program.
• Smiles when sees his mother at end of day.	• Snuggles closer to you when new teacher reaches out to hold her.	• Walks to you when new visitor arrives.	• Plays in new sandbox, but only when you are nearby.	• Makes pretend call home after playing with visitor.
• Raises arms toward you when you approach crib.	• Protests and tries to follow when you leave room.	• Looks at you for reassurance while piling blocks with another child's parent.	• Takes book to visitor after you help him choose one.	• Listens to audiotape of her mother singing lullaby and then lets volunteer tuck her in for nap.

Objective 2: Regulates own behavior

STEP 1	STEP 2	STEP 3	STEP 4	STEP 5
Begins developing own patterns for sleeping, eating, and other basic needs, with adult's help	**Uses others' facial expressions, gestures, or voices to guide own behavior**	**Begins to respond to verbal redirection**	**Follows simple directions and sometimes tests limits**	**Understands what behavior is expected, with increasing regularity**
Examples:	Examples:	Examples:	Examples:	Examples:
• Begins needing diaper change on predictable basis.	• Watches you to see whether she should pick up new truck; then does so when you smile encouragingly.	• Agrees to stomp in pile of leaves but then returns to stomping in puddle.	• Carries her empty plate to sink after lunch, when asked.	• Pulls blanket and sleeping toy from cubby when cots are being put out.
• Begins getting fussy around 10:00 a.m., letting you know he is ready for his midmorning bottle.	• Drops toy on floor; then drops it again when you laugh and hand it back.	• Smiles and crawls into cardboard box house as you suggest, instead of under table where you are wiping up spill.	• Runs away when you say it is time to go inside but comes with you when you say, "Please take my hand."	• Flips on his jacket when you say, "Let's go outside."
• Relaxes as you rock him gently; then falls asleep when you place him in his crib.	• Tries to climb on shelf until she sees you frowning and shaking your head, "No."	• Holds carriage handle, as you suggest when he doesn't want to hold your hand while walking to park.	• Protests; then joins in cleaning up when you begin singing the cleanup song and she sees other children helping.	• Puts on apron without being reminded, before playing at water table.

The Creative Curriculum
Developmental Continuum for Infants, Toddlers & Twos

social/emotional development

Goal 1: To learn about self and others, continued

	STEP 1	STEP 2	STEP 3	STEP 4	STEP 5

Objective 3: Manages own feelings

Expresses a variety of emotions and needs, using facial expressions, body movements, and vocalizations

Examples:
- Puts fist in mouth and curls arms and legs when hungry; relaxes and extends arms and legs when full.
- Smiles and kicks when you talk to her.
- Breaks eye contact and arches back when tired of peek-a-boo game.

Uses others' facial expressions, gestures, or voices to guide own feelings

Examples:
- Tenses when new teacher approaches; then relaxes when you give big smile of recognition.
- Starts to cry when another child takes his toy; then stops when you offer duplicate.
- Startles when door slams; then relaxes when you rub his back and calmly say, "It's okay. It's just the door."

Begins applying strategies to manage feelings by self

Examples:
- Gets favorite stuffed animal when tired.
- Asks for bottle ("Ba-ba") after crying about father's departure.
- Stamps foot after dropping one of the boxes she wants to carry to the corner; then goes back to get box.

Begins to use strategies learned from adults

Examples:
- Looks at you to intervene when another child pushes him.
- Says, "No! Mine!" when another child takes his toy; then looks at you.
- Takes out family photo album, as you have often encouraged, after his mother leaves.

Begins to use feeling words

Examples:
- Says, "Uh-oh, a doggie! No!" on walk to park.
- Points to picture of smiling monster in book and says, "He's happy."
- Explains, "She's sad," when she sees crying child.

Objective 4: Responds to others' feelings with growing empathy

Mirrors others' expressions of feelings

Examples:
- Smiles back at smiling face.
- Quiets when sees that you have a concerned expression.
- Cries when hears another baby crying.

Becomes aware of others' expressions of emotion

Examples:
- Looks at group of laughing children; then returns to playing with ball.
- Stops playing and stares at you when you frown about applesauce you spilled.
- Looks up when two children struggle over a toy.

Responds to the emotions of others, sometimes with adult prompting

Examples:
- Approaches a crying child.
- Laughs excitedly when other children laugh.
- Pats other child's back while you hold other child and say, "She needs some love. She is sad."

Shows awareness that others' feelings are separate from own feelings

Examples:
- Points to an infant and says, "Baby crying."
- Asks, "Why crying?" when sees another child crying at water table.
- Points to picture of pig that is hiding from wolf, when you ask him to find something in the book illustration that is scared.

Responds to others' feelings with caring behavior, without adult prompting

Examples:
- Kisses your finger after you say it hurts.
- Smiles and claps excitedly when another child exclaims, "I did it!"
- Brings crying child's blanket to her.

The Creative Curriculum
Developmental Continuum for Infants, Toddlers & Twos

social/emotional development

Goal 1: To learn about self and others, continued

Objective 5: Plays with other children

STEP 1	STEP 2	STEP 3	STEP 4	STEP 5
Watches and responds to other children	**Reaches out to and engages momentarily with other children**	**Has brief play encounters with other children**	**Participates in longer play encounters with children who are engaged with identical or similar activities**	**Participates in coordinated play with other children**
Examples:	Examples:	Examples:	Examples:	Examples:
• Turns her head toward toddler who is singing.	• Pats arm of another infant sitting nearby.	• Goes to child who is holding doll and pats doll's head.	• Scoops sand in bucket, next to child who is scooping sand in own bucket.	• Runs with another child, shouting, "Go!" when they pass tree.
• Kicks legs while watching other babies.	• Squeals and holds out arms as another child crawls to him.	• Sits next to child to whom you are reading; listens briefly; then picks up puppet and moves away.	• Sits with children at art table and scribbles on paper with marker.	• Pushes another child in wagon; then exchanges places.
• Rolls over to look at another infant lying on nearby blanket.	• Pushes musical ball toward another child.	• Follows another child into rocking boat but climbs out after a few minutes.	• Notices children pouring at water table, goes over, and also pours.	• Joins another child who is pretending to cook breakfast and makes believe she is eating eggs.

Objective 6: Learns to be a member of a group

Shows interest in being with others	**Finds security in being with familiar people**	**Begins to participate in group routines**	**Begins to accept that others' needs are important, in addition to own**	**Participates actively in group experiences**
Examples:	Examples:	Examples:	Examples:	Examples:
• Kicks his legs with delight when two toddlers sit with you near his blanket.	• Reaches for you after bumping her head.	• Comes to table when he sees you putting out snacks.	• Gives another child piece of her playdough.	• Shakes tambourine and parades with other children.
• Smiles and babbles as you hold him on your lap at lunch table.	• Protests when her father leaves in the morning; then settles into play with your help.	• Pulls blanket off shelf after lunch, in preparation for nap.	• Stands next to you, waiting for turn with ride-on toy.	• Helps others at table put all the crayons in basket during cleanup.
• Looks around as you hold him, smiling at familiar adults and children.	• Reaches for her mother and snuggles, sucking her thumb, after tiring day.	• Starts looking toward door as you sing songs each afternoon before pick-up time.	• Moves over so another child can fit at sand table.	• Answers questions that you ask as you read to small group.

©2006 Teaching Strategies, Inc., PO Box 42243, Washington, DC 20015; www.TeachingStrategies.com

The Creative Curriculum
Developmental Continuum for Infants, Toddlers & Twos

social/emotional development

Goal 1: To learn about self and others, continued

Objective 7: Uses personal care skills

STEP 1	STEP 2	STEP 3	STEP 4	STEP 5
Begins to participate as adult attends to personal needs	**Attempts simple personal care tasks**	**Tries more complex personal care tasks, with limited success**	**Tries more complex personal care tasks, with increasing success**	**Does many complex personal care tasks successfully**
Examples:	Examples:	Examples:	Examples:	Examples:
• Sucks eagerly when offered bottle.	• Takes own socks off.	• Brings spoon to mouth, frequently turning spoon over as he does so.	• Puts on slip-on shoes, although not always on correct feet.	• Hangs coat on own hook when arriving in morning.
• Closes eyes and extends neck as you pull shirt over her head.	• Feeds self finger foods from tray.	• Holds hands under faucet after diaper change, waiting for you to turn on water.	• Begins to let you know of need to "go potty."	• Feeds self at lunch, using fingers, spoon, and sometimes fork.
• Raises knees to chest when placed on back on diaper-changing table.	• Tries to unfasten diaper tabs after you take her pants off.	• Places knit cap on top of his head but does not pull it down over his ears.	• Washes and then pats hands with paper towel when you say, "Wash your hands for lunch."	• Pulls pants down and up to help with toileting.

©2006 Teaching Strategies, Inc., PO Box 42243, Washington, DC 20015; www.TeachingStrategies.com

Goal 2: To learn about moving

Objective 8: Demonstrates basic gross motor skills

STEP 1	STEP 2	STEP 3	STEP 4	STEP 5
Begins moving purposefully	**Begins to gain balance and to move from place to place**	**Walks forward with increasing coordination**	**Attempts a variety of large-muscle activities**	**Balances while moving arms and legs in active play**
Examples:	Examples:	Examples:	Examples:	Examples:
• Holds head up when you hold her.	• Sits steadily without assistance.	• Toddles without support.	• Walks to ball and kicks it.	• Moves along obstacle course by crawling, walking, climbing, sliding, and jumping.
• Rolls over when placed on blanket on floor of protected area.	• Rocks back and forth on hands and knees; may crawl.	• Walks across room, starting and stopping.	• Throws ball overhand, using both arms, while standing.	• Attempts to pedal and steer riding toy.
• Holds head and chest up, with weight on forearms.	• Pulls self to standing position; cruises while holding onto furniture.	• Walks up and down stairs, with support.	• Runs with increasing speed; jumps in place.	• Catches ball with straight arms.

Objective 9: Demonstrates basic fine motor skills

STEP 1	STEP 2	STEP 3	STEP 4	STEP 5
Uses whole hand to grasp and drop objects	**Uses thumb and index finger to grasp and drop objects**	**Uses one hand to hold an object and the other hand to manipulate another object**	**Uses eye-hand coordination while doing simple tasks**	**Uses eye-hand coordination while doing increasingly complex tasks**
Examples:	Examples:	Examples:	Examples:	Examples:
• Bats at rattle that you hold near him.	• Pulls your nose, using thumb and index finger.	• Holds sippy cup in one hand and bangs spoon with other hand.	• Places large pegs into pegboard.	• Threads shoelace through large bead.
• Reaches for toy with whole hand.	• Picks up Cheerios® one by one.	• Dumps pail with one hand and retrieves shovel that fell out with other hand.	• Makes chain with large snap beads.	• Begins to button large buttons.
• Opens hand to release toy when new toy is offered.	• Picks up large bead and hands it to you.	• Holds paper in place with one hand while scribbling with other hand.	• Pours water from small pitcher into cup.	• Begins using scissors to snip edges of paper.

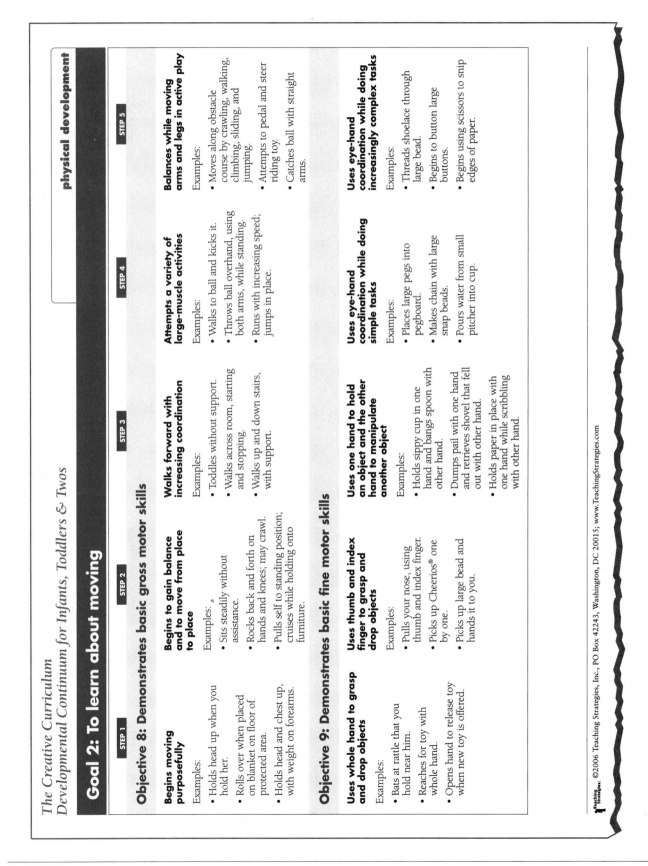

The Creative Curriculum
Developmental Continuum for Infants, Toddlers & Twos

cognitive development

Goal 3: To learn about the world

Objective 10: Sustains attention

STEP 1	STEP 2	STEP 3	STEP 4	STEP 5
Attends to sights and sounds	**Continues an activity when an adult interacts**	**Focuses on activity of choice but is easily distracted**	**Continues an activity, despite distractions**	**Continues an activity until own goal is reached, despite distractions**
Examples:	Examples:	Examples:	Examples:	Examples:
• Turns head toward sound of mother's voice.	• Takes small block from you and puts it in container.	• Stops working puzzle when sees you stirring cereal.	• Looks up from toy when others begin to clean up; then returns to playing with toy.	• Puts all of blocks in storage container.
• Watches you walk across room.	• Turns page and studies picture when you read together.	• Stops eating when others leave table to wash hands.	• Continues to dig in sand, after glancing at children who are struggling over another shovel.	• Completes simple puzzle.
• Watches leaves moving in wind.	• Resumes stacking rings when you come over and sit with her.	• Reads book to self but throws it down to join friend at water table.	• Tells friend, "Wait, wait," and continues to stack blocks.	• Announces, "I used every color!" when he stops painting.

Objective 11: Understands how objects can be used

STEP 1	STEP 2	STEP 3	STEP 4	STEP 5
Explores objects, using all senses	**Learns how objects work by handling them and watching others use them**	**Uses familiar objects in conventional ways**	**Plans ways to use objects to perform one-step tasks**	**Plans ways to use objects to perform multi-step tasks**
Examples:	Examples:	Examples:	Examples:	Examples:
• Reaches for teether; then brings it to mouth.	• Watches you make soft toy squeak; then squeezes it.	• Puts pieces in simple puzzle.	• Uses scarf to make dress for stuffed animal.	• Moves storage cube; then climbs on it to water plants on windowsill.
• Pats and then mouths soft toy.	• Takes large pegs out of pegboard after watching another child do so.	• Holds baby doll and feeds him bottle.	• Pulls cushion closer to her, to retrieve doll on top of it.	• Gets spoon and apron, then comes to table to help mix playdough.
• Looks at spoon; then bangs it on tray.	• Holds empty cup to mouth and imitates way you drink.	• Picks up shovel to dig in sandbox.	• Uses toy broom handle to free ball from corner.	• Arranges large blocks, puts on fire hat, and then pretends to drive to fire.

©2006 Teaching Strategies, Inc., PO Box 42243, Washington, DC 20015; www.TeachingStrategies.com

The Creative Curriculum
Developmental Continuum for Infants, Toddlers & Twos

cognitive development

Goal 3: To learn about the world, continued

Objective 12: Shows a beginning understanding of cause and effect

STEP 1	STEP 2	STEP 3	STEP 4	STEP 5
Explores objects and notices how they react	**Discovers that repeated actions yield similar effects**	**Explores ways to make something happen**	**Expects people and objects to respond to actions in particular ways**	**Begins to investigate causes when something unexpected happens**
Examples:	Examples:	Examples:	Examples:	Examples:
• Kicks at blanket when in crib.	• Slaps water in shallow pan repeatedly, making it splash.	• Bangs and then shakes windup toy, trying to get it to work.	• Darts away and laughs with delight when you swoop her up; then darts away again.	• Looks puzzled when block tower falls and asks, "Fell down?"
• Shakes arm when holding rattle.	• Raises bottle as level of milk drops.	• Requests, "Up, p'ease"; then tugs on your pants when you do not pick him up immediately.	• Says, "Again, again!" and looks at you for response when you reach end of book you are reading together.	• Reaches inside shoe when it will not go on and finds sock in toe.
• Bangs toy on floor.	• Beats pot with spoon, making clanging sound.	• Turns faucet handle to make water start and stop.	• Puts cassette in player and presses *Play* button.	• Smells odor from another room and asks, "Who made popcorn?"

Objective 13: Shows a beginning understanding that things can be grouped

STEP 1	STEP 2	STEP 3	STEP 4	STEP 5
Explores objects, using all senses	**Notices particular characteristics of objects**	**Begins to manipulate objects according to particular attributes**	**Begins to match objects by similarities**	**Groups objects with similar characteristics**
Examples:	Examples:	Examples:	Examples:	Examples:
• Reaches for toy, using whole hand.	• Rubs fingers over soft velvet cushion.	• Stacks wooden rings on post.	• Places blue block next to another blue block.	• Puts all of red Duplos® in your lap.
• Touches beads of your necklace as you hold him on your lap.	• Makes a face when she first tastes peas; then turns away from spoon.	• Eats all of mandarin orange slices first from fruit salad.	• Sees picture of donkey and says, "Horsie."	• Sorts round beads from pile of assorted beads.
• Grasps object and gums it.	• Squeals as she mashes piece of banana on plate with her palm.	• Nests two measuring cups.	• Plays simple game of matching pictures.	• Puts cars in one labeled box and airplanes in another labeled box during cleanup.

©2006 Teaching Strategies, Inc., PO Box 42243, Washington, DC 20015; www.TeachingStrategies.com

The Creative Curriculum
Developmental Continuum for Infants, Toddlers & Twos

cognitive development

Goal 3: To learn about the world, continued

Objective 14: Uses problem-solving strategies

STEP 1	STEP 2	STEP 3	STEP 4	STEP 5
Demonstrates awareness of a problem	**Imitates the way others solve problems, immediately after seeing them do so**	**Experiments with trial-and-error approaches to simple problems**	**Persists with trial-and-error approaches to solving a problem**	**Carries out own plan for solving simple problems**
Examples:	Examples:	Examples:	Examples:	Examples:
• Indicates hunger or pain with different cries.	• Holds tissue to own nose after seeing you sneeze and wipe your nose.	• Uses fingers to eat cooked noodles, after trying unsuccessfully to use spoon.	• Experiments with different objects to free ball that rolled under bush.	• Goes to pretend play area, gets large spoon, and takes it to sand table to use as scoop.
• Kicks foot when it becomes stuck in blanket.	• Blows on cereal after seeing you blow on your bowl.	• Tries unsuccessfully to pick up large box; then pushes it to new location.	• Looks in several places until he finds toy that dropped out of sight.	• Gets socks and shoes; then sits on floor to put them on.
• Grunts when toy rolls out of reach.	• Tries to pull cover off container after watching you do so.	• Uses spoon; then reaches for shovel when trying to fill large bucket with sand.	• Moves puzzle piece in various positions until it fits.	• Asks you for tape after accidentally tearing page in book she is reading.

Objective 15: Engages in pretend play

STEP 1	STEP 2	STEP 3	STEP 4	STEP 5
Watches the actions of others	**Imitates the actions of others**	**Uses objects in pretend play as they are used in real life**	**Substitutes one object for another in pretend play**	**Uses real and imaginary objects in pretend play**
Examples:	Examples:	Examples:	Examples:	Examples:
• Watches your face as you talk with him.	• Claps her hands after seeing toddlers clap to music.	• Pulls blanket over self and pretends to sleep; then giggles to let you know she is pretending.	• Pushes block across floor and says, "Vroom."	• Holds hands as if turning steering wheel and pretends to be driving car.
• Follows you with his eyes when you walk across room.	• Pats back of doll gently, just as you pat her back.	• Gives doll a bottle.	• Puts bowl upside down on head to wear as hat.	• Holds empty hand out to doll and says, "Here's a cookie for you."
• Stares at other children playing nearby.	• Moves spoon in bowl after watching you stir applesauce.	• Picks up toy phone and says, "Hello."	• Scoots on ride-on toy and says, "My car."	• Uses imaginary hose to put out imaginary fire.

The Creative Curriculum
Developmental Continuum for Infants, Toddlers & Twos

Goal 4: To learn about communicating

Objective 16: Develops receptive language

STEP 1	STEP 2	STEP 3	STEP 4	STEP 5
Shows interest in speech of others	**Responds to simple gestures and to the intonation, pitch, and volume of simple speech**	**Demonstrates understanding of simple multiword speech in familiar contexts**	**Demonstrates understanding of simple directions, questions, explanations, and stories**	**Demonstrates understanding of increasingly complex and abstract spoken language**
Examples:	Examples:	Examples:	Examples:	Examples:
• Watches face of person who is speaking to him.	• Stops whimpering when you talk in quiet, soothing manner.	• Hugs you when you ask, "May I have a hug?"	• Gets special blanket when you say, "It's nap time. Please get your blanket."	• Moves next to you when you tell her, "Sit beside me on the rug, please."
• Turns head toward speaker and smiles.	• Releases other child's shirt when you say firmly, "Gentle touches."	• Touches your nose when you ask, "Where's my nose?"	• Laughs when something silly happens in book you read aloud.	• Matches actions to story as you describe what characters are doing.
• Coos as you talk to him while dressing him.	• Crawls toward door when she hears her father's voice in hall.	• Points to picture of bananas in book when you say, "Show me the bananas."	• Says, "My doll," when you ask, "Whose doll is this?"	• Gets paper towel after you tell her, "Don't forget to use a paper towel to turn off the faucet."

Objective 17: Develops expressive language

STEP 1	STEP 2	STEP 3	STEP 4	STEP 5
Uses facial expressions, body positions and movements, and distinct cries or other vocalizations to communicate	**Gestures, babbles, and combines sounds to communicate, using the rising and falling patterns of adult speech, and produces first words**	**Uses gestures, word-like sounds, and single words to communicate**	**Speaks in two-word phrases**	**Uses simple sentences and questions with three or more words**
Examples:	Examples:	Examples:	Examples:	Examples:
• Croons, "M-m-m-m," while sucking.	• Babbles combined sounds, such as "Ba-da, ba-da."	• Says, "Uh," holding arms out to be picked up.	• Says, "My book," while holding book out to you.	• Says, "Go home now," when leaving.
• Smiles and squeals when you enter room.	• Calls, "Eh-eh-eh," to get your attention.	• Points at new toy and asks, "Dat?"	• Asks for "more juice" for a snack.	• Asks, "What we doing now?" when you open box of new puppets.
• Coos, "A-a-ah," and kicks while looking at toy.	• Points at sippy cup that is out of reach and looks at you.	• Picks up toy car and says, "Car."	• Says, "Mommy bye-bye," a few minutes after mother leaves.	• Tells about weekend experiences, saying, "Daddy pushed me on the swing."

©2006 Teaching Strategies, Inc, PO Box 42243, Washington, DC 20015; www.TeachingStrategies.com

The Creative Curriculum
Developmental Continuum for Infants, Toddlers & Twos

language development

Goal 4: To learn about communicating, continued

Objective 18: Participates in conversations

STEP 1	STEP 2	STEP 3	STEP 4	STEP 5
Engages in simple, back-and-forth vocalizing	**Imitates and exchanges sounds and gestures with other people**	**Exchanges single words, word-like sounds, and gestures with others**	**Initiates conversation by using words**	**Participates in conversations for two or more turns**
Examples:	Examples:	Examples:	Examples:	Examples:
• Coos as you rock and talk with him.	• Opens eyes wide and laughs as you play peek-a-boo together.	• Says, "Oh-oh," when you say, "I spilled the juice."	• Asks, "Kyle help?" when you start to wipe lunch table.	• Joins back-and-forth conversation with you and other children at lunch table.
• Smiles and coos at other babies.	• Imitates your kissing sound, waits while you kiss again, and then takes turn.	• Says, "Ba, ba," when you say, "Go get the ball."	• Wraps doll in blanket and says to you, "Baby sleep."	• Picks up toy phone and carries on conversation with another child.
• Gurgles each time you pause as you talk with him.	• Waves when you wave at her.	• Announces, "Hat," pointing to new hat on head when you greet him in the morning.	• Looks around for ball and asks you, "Where ball?"	• Talks back and forth with another child as they play in sandbox.

Objective 19: Enjoys books and being read to

STEP 1	STEP 2	STEP 3	STEP 4	STEP 5
Manipulates books as adult reads aloud	**Engages briefly with books as they are read aloud and finds pleasure in the experience**	**Becomes increasingly engaged with the content of books that are read aloud**	**Begins to make connections between own life and the stories in books**	**Pretends to read favorite books**
Examples:	Examples:	Examples:	Examples:	Examples:
• Sucks on pages of board book as you hold child and book.	• Turns pages of board book, pausing to study a page.	• Points to cow in book illustration when you moo.	• Gets toy tractor from shelf after hearing story about tractors.	• Brings book, turns pages, and retells familiar story by using pictures as prompts.
• Takes book from you; then bangs it on floor.	• Vocalizes and smiles when he recognizes picture of familiar object.	• Repeats word from refrain of repetitive story.	• Asks, "Park, p'ease?" when you read story about child who goes to park.	• Recites part of familiar story to another child.
• Attempts to crumple pages of cloth book while you read to her.	• Smiles when he sees cover of familiar book.	• Finds same picture in book about trains, repeatedly.	• Points to picture of airplane and says, "Daddy up, up."	• Completes some of the rhymes as you reread familiar book.

Teaching Strategies ©2006 Teaching Strategies, Inc., PO Box 42243, Washington, DC 20015; www.TeachingStrategies.com

The Creative Curriculum
Developmental Continuum for Infants, Toddlers & Twos

language development

Goal 4: To learn about communicating, continued

Objective 20: Shows an awareness of pictures and print

STEP 1	STEP 2	STEP 3	STEP 4	STEP 5
Notices pictures	**Recognizes and shows a beginning understanding of pictures**	**Recognizes that pictures have meaning and can tell a story**	**Demonstrates interest in print**	**Shows beginning understanding that print is useful**
Examples:	Examples:	Examples:	Examples:	Examples:
• Gazes at pictures of faces on mobile.	• Touches pictures in book with various textures.	• Points to picture and asks, "Dat?"	• Chooses book from shelf and says, "Read, p'ease."	• Recognizes some popular logos.
• Looks and coos at photo on wall.	• Vocalizes when pointing to a picture.	• Says, "Cat'pillar," when she sees cover of *The Very Hungry Caterpillar.*	• Watches teacher write name on painting and asks, "What dat?"	• Scribbles, folds paper, and announces, "Happy birthday!"
• Glances at picture in board book.	• Points to picture of baby when you ask, "Where is the baby?"	• Turns pages of book to find favorite pictures.	• Points to "Itsy-Bitsy Spider" fingerplay chart on wall and says, "Bitsy spider."	• Points to letter on book cover and says, "That's my letter."

Objective 21: Experiments with drawing and writing

Notices drawing and writing tools	**Begins to handle drawing and writing tools**	**Scribbles spontaneously**	**Experiments with scribbling**	**Scribbles with intention of communicating**
Examples:	Examples:	Examples:	Examples:	Examples:
• Bats at pen you are using to write observation notes.	• Picks up crayon and holds it in fist.	• Holds crayon, moving hand all around paper.	• Scribbles on paper, watching lines form as he moves his hands.	• Scribbles picture; then says, "My kitty cat."
• Reaches for marker on floor, until you offer substitute object.	• Bangs piece of stubby chalk on paper, occasionally making marks.	• Moves paintbrush across paper, making lines.	• Paints, first with paintbrush and then with sponge.	• Scribbles all over paper; then says, "This letter for grandma."
• Watches as you draw line with marker.	• Runs marker over palm and smiles, before you again encourage writing on paper.	• Fills paper with marks.	• Fills one patch of paper with one kind of mark; then fills another patch with different marks.	• Scribbles several small shapes and says, "That's my name."

Teaching Strategies   ©2006 Teaching Strategies, Inc., PO Box 42243, Washington, DC 20015; www.TeachingStrategies.com

Appreciating Individual Differences While Using the *Developmental Continuum*

The *Developmental Continuum* helps you understand how children typically develop and learn. Many factors influence a child's development. Understanding the individual differences discussed in this chapter, such as a child's home culture, life circumstances, disabilities, and temperament, can help you find additional indicators of a child's developmental level.

Brooks knows that Abby (14 months) does not feed herself at home because her parents do not encourage this behavior. Brooks knows that this will affect what she observes in relation to Abby's development of personal care and fine motor skills. She decides to look for other behaviors that show Abby's developing abilities, such as putting a shirt away in her cubby (an example of personal care skills) or picking up large beads (an example of fine motor development).

When you use the *Developmental Continuum* to assess the progress of children with disabilities, you may need to consider the objectives and steps especially carefully. For example, a child with a hearing impairment might use sign language rather than oral language to convey his message. The child's teacher would adapt the related objectives to include sign language. For Objective 17, his teacher would know that combining two signs is an indication that the child has reached Step 4, "Speaks in two-word phrases." Making adjustments are also necessary for children with disabilities that influence motor development.

Ivan assesses Gena's (30 months) ability to move with her assistive device, rather than without it. When considering the steps in Objective 8, "Demonstrates basic gross motor skills," Ivan documents his observations of how Gena uses her walker to move.

Individual differences also affect a child's rate of progress.

Mercedes knows that children's temperaments affect the way they relate to new situations and people. Matthew (22 months) is slow to adapt. Because of this, Mercedes is not concerned that he has only recently reached Step 3 of Objective 1, "Trusts known caring adults," although he is at Step 4 of many other objectives. Mercedes knows that, with continued support and close, nurturing relationships, Matthew will eventually feel more comfortable around new people.

Thinking About Development After 36 Months

How children develop and what they learn during their first 3 years of life lay the foundation for the preschool years and beyond. While the *Developmental Continuum for Infants, Toddlers & Twos* spans the ages from entry into your program to 36 months, some children might remain with you briefly beyond their third birthday. Sometimes even younger children show development that is more mature than the steps of the *Developmental Continuum for Infants, Toddlers & Twos* with regard to some objectives. Whatever the reason for their relative maturity, you will need a way to assess the children's continuing development and learning, and you will want to know what to expect in terms of next steps.

Each of the 21 objectives of the *Developmental Continuum for Infants, Toddlers & Twos* leads to one or more of the 50 objectives in the *Developmental Continuum for Ages 3–5*. Some of the objectives for infants, toddlers, and twos correlate directly with one objective for preschool-age children. For instance, Objective 12, "Shows a beginning understanding of cause and effect" corresponds with preschool Objective 25, "Explores cause and effect." However, most objectives of the continuum for infants, toddlers, and twos lead to several preschool objectives. The following chart shows how an objective for infants, toddlers, and twos provides the foundation for three preschool objectives.

Objective for Infants, Toddlers, and Twos	Objectives for Preschoolers
17. Develops expressive language	39. Expresses self using words and expanded sentences
	41. Answers questions
	42. Asks questions

As children in your group reach age 3, you may observe development that goes beyond the scope of continuum for infants, toddlers, and twos. You may want to refer to *The Creative Curriculum Developmental Continuum for Ages 3–5* in order to support the child's development. You can read more about the relationship between the two continuums in *The Creative Curriculum for Infants, Toddlers & Twos Developmental Continuum Assessment System Teacher's Guide.*

Jonisha and *Valisha* (33 months) reached Step 5 of Objective 8, "Demonstrates basic gross motor skills," in March. Their teacher, LaToya, wanted to be able to plan for their further development and keep track of their progress, so she referred to The Creative Curriculum Developmental Continuum for Ages 3–5. This helped her think about the next progression of steps in young children's gross motor development.

The *Developmental Continuum* helps you look for each child's progress in each area of development. Remember that children develop different skills at different rates, both in comparison with other children and in terms of particular objectives. Children who are advanced in one area of development may not necessarily be advanced in all areas or all objectives in a given area. For example, a child who is at Step 5 for Objective 8, which relates to gross motor skills, may only be at Step 4 for Objective 9, which relates to fine motor skills.

Conclusion

Knowing how infants, toddlers, and twos develop is the starting point for every *Creative Curriculum* teacher. When you also know the unique characteristics of every child, you can build trusting relationships that enable all children to thrive. Looking at children's development on a continuum gives you a full idea of each child's learning and a roadmap for tracking children's progress. The *Developmental Continuum* guides your observations and decisions as you plan, offer learning experiences, and provide responsive care. The next chapter describes how to set up a responsive environment that meets the needs of infants, toddlers, and twos and supports their development.

inside this chapter

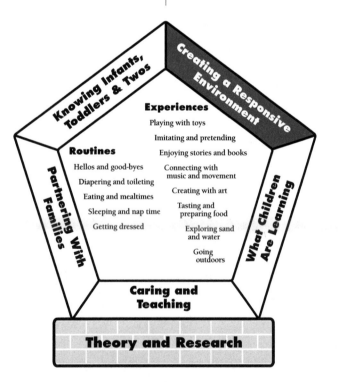

2 Creating a Responsive Environment

Your knowledge of the social/emotional, physical, cognitive, and language development of infants, toddlers, and twos and the many ways in which each child is unique enables you to create an environment that addresses the needs and growing abilities and interests of young children. Creating a responsive environment is the second component of *The Creative Curriculum for Infants, Toddlers & Twos.*

This chapter discusses the environment in which you care for children and welcome families. It includes two sections:

> **Setting Up the Physical Environment** explains how to arrange a welcoming place for children and families, and a pleasant, efficient place in which to work. It describes ways to create places for routines and experiences, discusses the design of spaces for each age group, and offers guidelines for selecting and displaying materials. Special environmental considerations and ways the environment conveys positive messages to children and families are also discussed.

> **Creating a Structure for Each Day** explains daily and weekly planning, individualizing the schedule for infants, and creating a schedule for toddlers and twos. Transitions and responsive planning are also included.

Setting Up the Physical Environment

A well-planned room for infants, toddlers, or twos is a welcoming place for children and families, and a pleasant, efficient place in which to work. Children spend many hours in your program. They are most comfortable when they are in a place that includes sights and sounds that are like those of their own homes. A child care environment that is similar to their homes encourages the feelings of safety and security that young children experience with their families.

A warm and friendly environment is also reassuring to families. Areas designed with family members in mind send the message that they are always welcome. Families can share ideas for making your environment more homelike, and they might be willing to contribute items and skills.

The next box outlines general space-planning guidelines that are discussed further in other sections of this chapter.

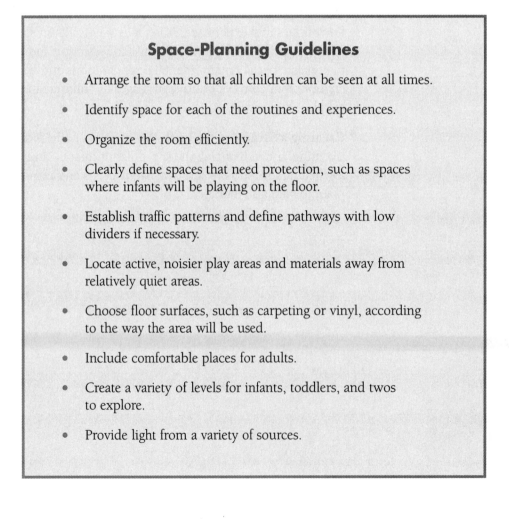

Space-Planning Guidelines

- Arrange the room so that all children can be seen at all times.

- Identify space for each of the routines and experiences.

- Organize the room efficiently.

- Clearly define spaces that need protection, such as spaces where infants will be playing on the floor.

- Establish traffic patterns and define pathways with low dividers if necessary.

- Locate active, noisier play areas and materials away from relatively quiet areas.

- Choose floor surfaces, such as carpeting or vinyl, according to the way the area will be used.

- Include comfortable places for adults.

- Create a variety of levels for infants, toddlers, and twos to explore.

- Provide light from a variety of sources.

Creating Places for Routines and Experiences

Areas that are conveniently located, organized, and well-equipped make routines easier to manage and allow you to focus on your interactions with children. Areas for experiences also need to be arranged according to the strengths and needs of the children.

Greeting Area

Locate the greeting area just inside the room. It serves as an entryway and a transition area between the outdoors or hallway and the room. Separate this area from the rest of the space to make it feel cozy and welcoming. It should be large enough to accommodate two or more parents with their children. Here are some items that will make your greeting area welcoming and functional:

- a bulletin- or message board for family notices

- cubbies or a coat rack and individual storage tubs

- photos of the children at play and with their families

- children's artwork

- a bench or counter at adult-height to make it easier to dress and undress children

- comfortable seating for two or more adults

Diapering and Toileting Areas

One of the challenges of organizing a diapering area is setting it up so you can see what the other children in the group are doing while you are changing a child's diaper. Ideally, the space should be designed so that you face the room—rather than a wall—while diapering. If this is not possible, place a mirror on the wall so that you can see behind you. Infant and toddler teachers spend a lot of time in the diapering area, so choose a convenient location. Handwashing is an integral part of diapering, so locate the diaper-changing table near a hand sink, and, to prevent the spread of disease, away from food-preparation areas. Storage is essential because you need to have many supplies nearby. In your diapering area, include

- storage for bleach solution, diapers, wipes, and extra clothing

- a safe changing table with a smooth, easily cleaned surface and a raised rim

- steps for older infants and toddlers to climb to the changing table

- a lined diaper can

Toddlers and twos often prefer to stand to be diapered. Check with your local licensing organization for ways to accommodate this preference while making sure that the diapering process is sanitary and safe.

Twos and their teachers spend a lot of time in the bathroom, so make it a pleasant place. Ideally, bathrooms are inside classrooms and have child-size toilets, sinks, and paper towel holders so children can learn to function in the area independently. If you do not have child-size fixtures, the American Academy of Pediatrics and the American Public Health Association recommend that you use modified toilet seats and step aids for toilet learning. The use of potty chairs is discouraged because they are difficult to clean and sanitize. If you use potty chairs, follow the guidance on cleaning and sanitizing them.[17]

Sleeping Area

Some programs have separate sleeping areas for infants in cribs, while others incorporate cribs into the general space. Your state licensing requirements and the design of your facility will determine your options. Ideally, your sleeping area will be separate from noisy, active play areas so it can accommodate each child's individual sleeping schedule and preferences. If infants sleep within the classroom, you can group a few cribs together, creating the atmosphere of a bedroom rather than of an institution. By the time they are toddlers, children sleep on cots or mats that are set in the play areas of the room. Reserve some space for one or two children who sleep on a different schedule from the other children in the group. In your sleeping area, include

- lighting that can be dimmed
- storage space for sheets, blankets, and children's comfort items
- a glider or other comfortable chair for cuddling children and for watching them as they nap or play quietly
- a compact disc player for soft music

Nursing Area

The nursing area can be part of your sleeping area, or it can be located in another quiet area of the room. The nursing area should have comfortable seating, a footstool, and a small pillow to support the nursing mother's arm. A small folding screen or room divider provides some privacy.

Eating Area

A separate eating area is not necessary for young infants. Create quiet comfortable places where you can hold young infants while you feed them their bottles without being interrupted or distracted by other children. Mobile infants, toddlers, and twos need a space for eating, although the space can also used for play experiences such as dabbling in art or tasting and preparing food. Make sure that the eating area is separated from the diapering area.

A well-equipped eating and food preparation area includes

- a washable floor

- a counter and cupboards for storing food, dishes, and utensils

- a sink (preferably a double sink, which is convenient during mealtimes and for washing and sanitizing toys)

- a small refrigerator

- assigned space for each child's food in the cupboard and refrigerator, if families provide food, formula, or breast milk

- tables and chairs where mobile infants, toddlers, and twos can eat together in small groups (Once infants can sit comfortably and no longer need to be held to be fed, they can sit in sturdy chairs at low tables, rather than in high chairs.)

- a counter or cart that is large enough to hold serving dishes

- a comfortable place for teachers to sit if bottle-feeding children

- safety latches on lower cabinets, unless the entire storage area is inaccessible to children

Areas for Experiences

Chapters 11–18 discuss a variety of play experiences that infants, toddlers, and twos enjoy. These include playing with toys, imitating and pretending, enjoying stories and books, connecting with music and movement, creating with art, tasting and preparing food, exploring sand and water, and going outdoors. While all of these experiences require particular supplies and materials, not all require separate space. The next section provides information about how to design appropriate spaces for each age group.

Designing Spaces for Each Age Group

One of the most important ways to put your knowledge of child development into practice is to design spaces that accommodate children's developmental needs, abilities, and interests. As infants, toddlers, and twos develop and learn, you will need to change the environment to keep children safe, provide new challenges, and inspire new interests.

Setting Up a Room for Young Infants

The infant room is a place where infants and adults can be comfortable and interact positively with each other. The youngest infants need soft, comfortable places throughout the room and a variety of views. Good, variable lighting is important. Take advantage of natural light whenever possible and consider using diffusers that minimize the glare from ceiling fixtures.

Arrange several protected areas where infants can watch the action from the floor. Provide soft toys for children to choose. As children develop, plan changes and additions to the environment. The next chart lists some characteristics of young infants and describes ways to arrange the environment to support their development and learning.

What Young Infants Can Do	Ways You Can Arrange the Environment	How This Supports Development
Notice and look at what is around them	Place pictures at children's eye level on the wall, ends of cribs, and shelves (including eye level when seated on an adult's lap and when held by a standing adult).	Encourages infants to focus and attend to objects
Distinguish familiar from unfamiliar sights and sounds	Provide familiar items, such as clothing, taped voices, and music.	Comforts infants with sights and sounds from home
Reach for, bat, and poke objects; grasp objects that can be held easily	Place toys within infants' reach.	Encourages infants to practice fine motor skills; encourages children to explore objects and notice how they react
Bring toys to their mouths to explore	Include a container for toys that need to be washed after play.	Supports exploration while keeping children healthy
Respond to being held and rocked	Have comfortable seating for when adults hold infants, such as soft chairs and gliders.	Builds trusting relationships
Develop the ability to roll, sit, and crawl	Provide soft surfaces, such as carpets, mats, and grass, so infants can move safely.	Promotes gross motor skills

Setting Up a Room for Mobile Infants

One of the most important things to remember in setting up an environment for mobile infants is that they move from place to place. They need protected spaces where they can crawl; low, carpeted risers that they can navigate; secure railings that they can pull on to stand and hold to cruise; and spaces where they can walk, fall safely, and walk again.

Many aspects of the environment for young infants are also appropriate for mobile infants. For example, soft areas and places to sit with adults continue to be important as children become more mobile. Even though mobile infants can move on their own, they still need adults to comfort and cuddle them.

Mobile infants are beginning to have preferences and like to choose what to play with and what to do. Organize the room to offer different play experiences, such as places to play with toys, roll balls, and look at books. You might also designate a few areas for experiences such as imitating and pretending.

The next chart lists some characteristics of mobile infants and suggests ways to arrange the environment to promote their development and learning.

What Mobile Infants Can Do	Ways You Can Arrange the Environment	How This Supports Development
Pull themselves to a standing position	Be sure furniture is sturdy, with rounded edges. Provide railings that children can use to pull themselves up.	Allows mobile infants to explore safely and to gain balance
Repeat a movement to learn it well	Provide space and time so children can play without being disturbed.	Encourages the development of attention and of motor skills
Push, pull, fill, and dump objects	Offer a variety of playthings and containers, including household objects.	Builds motor skills, eye-hand coordination, and a beginning understanding of cause and effect
Take comfort from familiar objects and reminders of home	Display pictures of family members and invite families to make audiotapes.	Strengthens secure attachments by helping children feel connected to their families throughout the day
Use familiar adults as a base for exploration	Use low dividers so children and adults can see each other while the children explore freely.	Helps children feel safe and secure

There are many ways to set up a room for both young and mobile infants. Here is a sample layout to help you to think about your own infant room. Make sure you have enough open space. Infants are little, but they need space to move around and explore.

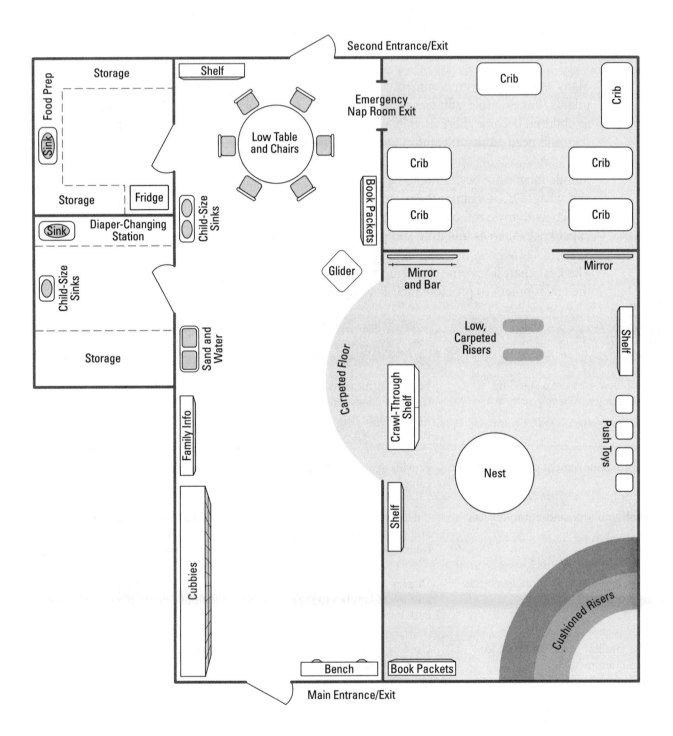

Setting Up Rooms for Toddlers and Twos

Toddlers are very active learners who change moment by moment. Sometimes they want help, but they often want to be independent. They are usually sociable, but sometimes they want to be alone. They love to move, but at times they want to be held like young infants. Their environments must be extremely rich in opportunities that support all aspects of development.

Many of the suggestions for young and mobile infant environments also apply to toddler spaces. However, some differences are necessary. Toddlers become comfortable in their use of low tables and chairs. They begin to nap on a more regular schedule, and they sleep on cots or mats rather than in cribs.

Designate a few experience areas for young toddlers and add more over the next few months. Separate noisier, more active spaces from quiet ones so that children may play freely. Remember that toddlers often gather spontaneously in larger groups when they are interested in what other children doing. Allow space for this to happen.

You can enhance toddlers' experiences by adding an increasing variety of materials and props. An indoor gross motor area, lofts or platforms, and carpeted risers help support their interest in moving and climbing. A low loft provides interesting spaces for toddlers to explore, underneath as well as on top.

Twos have additional needs. Two-year-olds usually eat together, so you need enough tables and chairs so that all of your twos can eat at the same time, although still in small groups. Define more areas for creating with art, imitating and pretending, sand and water, stories and books, playing with toys, and playing with blocks. Plan to use some of those places for music and movement and for tasting and preparing food. One of the areas should be large enough for all of the children to gather for a short time. Spaces for quiet activities, such as stories and books, should be located away from noisier activities. The increasingly complex room arrangement later helps twos make the transition to a preschool classroom.

Your decisions about the environment for toddlers and twos are based on your understanding of what they can do. The following chart lists some characteristics of toddlers and twos, and it describes ways to arrange the environment to support their development and learning.

What Toddlers and Twos Can Do	Ways You Can Arrange the Environment	How This Supports Development
Walk, run, climb, and jump	Allow space for movement and arrange equipment for safety.	Encourages toddlers to explore freely and independently
Make choices and have favorite toys	Organize toys on low shelves and label the containers and shelves with pictures and words.	Supports the development of autonomy
Eat as part of a small group	Use low tables and chairs for meals.	Helps children learn to be a member of a group and encourages conversation
Sleep at scheduled times	Provide cots or mats for napping.	Optimizes space for movement and play; allows them to get the rest they need to participate actively in the program
Sometimes want to do more than they can do	Offer materials and experiences that match children's levels of development.	Provides appropriate challenges but minimizes children's frustration
Play near and with others	Define areas where two or three children can play. Provide duplicates of toys.	Promotes children's ability to sustain social play

There are many ways to organize an environment for toddlers and twos. Use this sample layout to think about your own room.

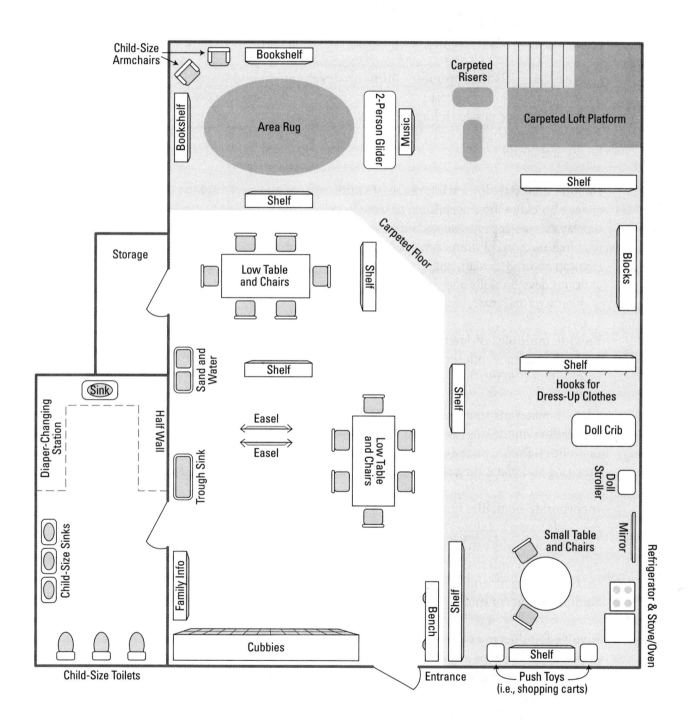

Selecting Materials

The materials you select make your environment interesting for young children to investigate. Choose materials that gently challenge children's developing abilities and skills and keep some of the familiar items that still interest them. Consider the following ideas when selecting materials.

Choose materials that promote children's development and learning. Young children learn about the world through the materials they explore during play. Include materials that encourage children to use their senses; explore shape, size, color, and balance; strengthen their muscles; experiment with cause and effect; and explore books and writing.

Include materials for a wide range of skills. Infants, toddlers, and twos grow and change quickly. Observe children to make sure that the materials you select and display are age-appropriate and challenging but not frustrating for them. Choose toys that react to children's actions. Include an assortment of open-ended materials that can be used in many different ways, such as Duplos®, blocks, and balls. As children develop skills and discover new interests, they find new ways to use familiar toys and materials.

Provide multiples of favorite toys. Young children often want to play with the same toy as their friends, but they are not developmentally ready to take turns or share. Duplicates of favorite items minimize disagreements and waiting time.

Choose materials that honor diversity. Materials should depict people similar to the children in the class as well as the diversity of society, including people with disabilities. Books, puzzles, photographs, dolls, music, art supplies, and props for imitating and pretending should portray people positively.

Incorporate homelike touches and noncommercial materials. Familiar, homelike materials remind children of their families and help them feel secure. Mobile infants, toddlers, and twos can play for long periods of time with measuring cups that nest or pots and pans with matching lids. You can make toys, too. An oatmeal box and large spools can be a fill-and-dump toy. Magazine pictures can be mounted on cardboard, laminated, and cut into three pieces to make simple puzzles for twos.

Involve families in collecting materials. Ask families to help collect materials, such as pretend play props and empty appliance boxes to crawl through. Families can bring pictures for homemade books and for you to display around the room. Ask families to bring items that they would otherwise throw away, such as empty juice cans, coffee cans and lids, large spools, fabric scraps, and so forth.

Good Toys and Materials

To promote fine motor skills

see-through rattles	clutch balls	containers to fill and dump
bean bags	busy boxes	cardboard boxes with lids
nesting cups	interlocking blocks	large beads and shoelaces
Duplos® and Bristle Blocks™	shape-sorting boxes	puzzles (3–8 pieces)

To promote gross motor skills

riding toys	large cardboard boxes	balls of various sizes
climber and slide wagons	push-and-pull toys	low steps covered with carpet
tractor tires	tumbling mats	foam furniture covered with vinyl
	cars and trucks	

To explore with their senses

playdough	large nontoxic crayons	paper for scribbling and tearing
finger paint	sand and water table with containers and scoops	ribbons, scarves, and fabrics

To explore shape, size, color, and balance

small wooden blocks	unit blocks	rubber animals
people props	large cardboard blocks	small cars and trucks
nesting toys	foam blocks	

To encourage quiet play

tape recorder or compact disc player	cardboard and cloth books	picture books for toddlers
	blankets	soft cushions
music and story tapes and CDs		

Displaying Materials

If materials are organized and displayed thoughtfully with children's strengths and needs in mind, the children are more likely to use and care for them. Here are some suggestions for organizing and displaying toys and materials.

Store toys and related materials in the area where they will be used most often. Arrange them neatly on low shelves so children can reach them safely. Out of children's reach, store toys that are not currently in use or that need to be used with supervision.

Display toys so children can see what is available and choose what they want. Display a few carefully selected toys. An uncluttered display of carefully chosen toys is more helpful to children than crowded shelves. Offer interesting and varied toys that serve a range of abilities. Natural wood and neutral paint and surfaces make it easier for children to see brightly colored toys. Store toys with many pieces in clear plastic containers.

Use picture and word labels on containers and shelves. Labels show that everything has a place, and they help children participate in cleanup. Make labels from photographs or pictures in catalogs, or draw them on cardboard. Write labels in conventional form as the words would appear in a book. Avoid using all uppercase letters.

Rotate materials regularly. Clean and exchange materials for stored items as children outgrow or lose interest in the toys that have been displayed. In your room and in long-term storage, keep them sorted by type of toy or by the area where they will be used. This organization makes it easier to rotate toys.

Hang pictures, unbreakable mirrors, and interesting toys where children can see and touch them. Remember that eye level changes according to whether children are being held or carried, lying on a blanket on the floor, crawling around the room, or beginning to walk. Attach to the walls things that children can feel or manipulate, such as a steering wheel, beads on a wire, or boards with various textures. Mount these items either permanently or temporarily.

Special Considerations in Setting Up the Physical Environment

Think about ways to arrange the environment to address children's special requirements. First consider the need to keep children safe and healthy. In addition, think about arrangements for mixed-age groups, for children with disabilities, and for the needs of adults.

Keeping Children Safe and Healthy

Every family's primary concern is their child's safety. Your program's task is to keep children safe while allowing them to explore freely. As children develop, safety concerns change. A fully childproofed environment, designed in accordance with your knowledge of child development, can prevent or at least minimize injuries. Conduct a safety check of your indoor environment each day, and check the outdoor environment every day before the first child goes outdoors. Hazards emerge overnight. Outlet covers disappear during vacuuming. Mushrooms sprout, and litter may blow or be thrown onto the playground. Pay special attention to what is on the floor and within reach of children who are playing on the floor.

Here are some suggestions for providing a safe environment.

A Safe Environment

- Maintain appropriate staff-child ratios, and supervise all children at all times.

- Have furniture and equipment that is sized for the ages and developmental levels of the children who use the space.

- Make sure that equipment is in good repair and will not tip over. Report any equipment that needs to be repaired, and follow up to make sure it gets fixed.

- Check every day to make sure that toys are in good condition. They must not have broken parts, chipping paint, or splinters.

- Check to see that furnishings, cloth toys, bedding, and carpeting are flame resistant.

- Cover electrical outlets and use child safety locks on cupboards when appropriate.

- Keep electrical cords and electrical devices out of children's reach. Make sure that cords from window coverings are also out of children's reach.

- Check all toys and other materials to make sure that they do not present choking hazards. Remove anything with small parts. If an object can go through a choke tube or fit entirely into a child's mouth, it is too small.

- Display heavy toys on bottom shelves.

- Be sure that the water from faucets will not scald children. (It should be under 120 degrees Fahrenheit.)

- Store hazardous equipment and materials, including adult purses and tote bags, plastic bags, and cleaning supplies, out of the reach of children.

- Keep a well-stocked first-aid kit easily available and take additional kits along on walks or trips.

- Keep emergency contact information up-to-date and make sure that emergency exits are free of clutter.

Keeping infants, toddlers, and twos healthy is another challenge. Communicable diseases cannot be eliminated, but you can minimize their spread. Keep the environment as hygienic as possible. Make sure that play spaces are clean, that [...] and soft toys are laundered, and that hard-surfaced toys are regularly cleaned [...]itized.

[...]nt handwashing is critical to everyone's health. Everyone entering your program [...]d wash his or her hands (or have them washed) before beginning work or play, [...]ll as periodically throughout the day. Handwashing is necessary before feeding an [...]t, before preparing or serving food, after diapering and toileting, after touching [...], and after blowing noses. It can dramatically reduce child and adult illnesses. Post a sign to remind visitors, staff members, and families to wash their hands. Invite families to wash their hands and their children's hands as part of their good-bye routine when they arrive. It will give them something to do together to ease separation.

Here are suggestions for providing a healthy environment for infants, toddlers, and twos.

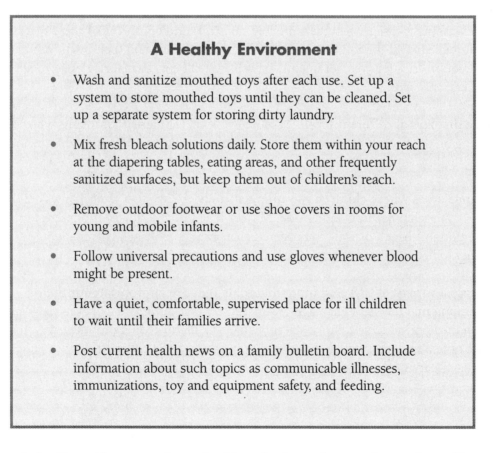

A Healthy Environment

- Wash and sanitize mouthed toys after each use. Set up a system to store mouthed toys until they can be cleaned. Set up a separate system for storing dirty laundry.

- Mix fresh bleach solutions daily. Store them within your reach at the diapering tables, eating areas, and other frequently sanitized surfaces, but keep them out of children's reach.

- Remove outdoor footwear or use shoe covers in rooms for young and mobile infants.

- Follow universal precautions and use gloves whenever blood might be present.

- Have a quiet, comfortable, supervised place for ill children to wait until their families arrive.

- Post current health news on a family bulletin board. Include information about such topics as communicable illnesses, immunizations, toy and equipment safety, and feeding.

Provide families with a copy of your health and safety policies and procedures. This shows that health and safety practices are priorities in your program.

Organizing the Environment for Mixed-Age Groups

One of the ways that programs promote continuity of care and primary caregiving is by grouping children of mixed ages. (See chapter 4, *Caring and Teaching,* for a discussion of continuity of care and primary caregiving.) Children in mixed-age groups usually remain in the same space with the same teachers over time. Here are some ideas for organizing the environment for mixed-age groups.

Keep quiet and active zones separated. Care for younger infants in protected areas, while offering mobile infants, toddlers, and twos opportunities for both quiet and very active play.

Vary the heights of tables and chairs. Review manufacturer's recommendations for children's ages and furniture heights before purchasing equipment. Look for equipment that can be adjusted to different heights.

As you choose equipment, plan for a wide range of developmental levels among the children. Both changing tables and child-size toilets are needed for mixed-age groups. Handwashing is easier when there are low sinks for toddlers and twos and sinks at a comfortable height for adults to wash young infants' hands and their own. Nap time may require cribs for younger infants, as well as small cots or mats for older infants, toddlers, and twos.

Place displays at different levels, because eye-level is different for infants who are playing on the floor, for toddlers and twos who are walking, and for children who are being held by adults.

Arrange areas where children can interact safely. A Plexiglas® panel allows children to peek at each other from either side. Mirrors that attract toddlers also interest infants. A comfortable bench or wide upholstered chair near a bookshelf will encourage a toddler to help you read a story to an infant.

Include a variety of toys and other materials that are appropriate for the developmental levels of each age group. Expect that most toys will eventually end up on the floor, and use a choke test tube to check all toys for appropriate size. Toys of a size or texture that is not good for infant play should be kept apart, for use only with teacher supervision.

Store materials for infants on lower shelves and materials for toddlers and twos on higher shelves. The lowest shelves are best for infant toys, so mobile infants can reach them from a crawling position. Children who stand can reach items on shelves at the levels of their waists and chests.

Adapting the Environment for Children With Disabilities

You may have a child with a special need or a diagnosed disability in your group. It may be a mild disability, such as a child born prematurely who uses a heart monitor when she sleeps and needs extra time to finish a bottle. Other disabilities require more complicated adaptations. For example, a child with cerebral palsy or spina bifida may need a special chair and require your help to change positions. With support from the child's family and specialists, you can adapt your environment and materials to enable the child with disabilities to participate and interact as fully as possible.

Physical Disabilities

Most of the furnishings and equipment typically found in programs for young children are appropriate for children with physical disabilities. For example, a pool of balls, soft mats to crawl on, and foam shapes to climb over are useful for children who do not have serious motor disabilities. In some instances, however, you will need to rearrange furniture and obtain adaptive equipment.

Wheel chairs or walkers—If you have a child who uses a wheelchair or walker, you may need to have some doorways widened and to install ramps and grab bars. Some simple environmental changes include rearranging tables or play areas to provide space to maneuver special equipment. Make sure your program's outdoor environment is also arranged for wheelchairs and walkers.

Support for sitting and standing—To participate fully in the program, some children with physical disabilities need physical support when they sit and stand. A large cushion can be shaped to provide support for sitting. Several types of specialized chairs are also available. *Educube®* chairs are hard chairs with a raised back and sides. *Tumbleform* chairs are firm foam chairs in various sizes, and *pummel* chairs have a knob between the spaces for children's legs. Other therapeutic chairs and prone standers, which provide support for the child's trunk and lower body, are designed and manufactured specifically for a child's size and special need.

Help in changing positions—Some children with physical disabilities need help to change their positions. They need assistance to stay comfortable and to be able to explore their environments. Family members and physical or occupational therapists working with the child can show you the best positions for different kinds of play. Positioning children with physical disabilities might require bolsters, wedges, or other positioning tools, along with chairs and prone standers. Positioning equipment should be kept near experience areas so that the child can change activities easily. In classroom displays, include photographs of children with motor impairments who are positioned comfortably for play. The photos will help visiting adults and substitute teachers as they interact with the children.

Sensory Impairments

Sensory problems include visual impairment and blindness, hearing impairment and deafness, and sensory integration disorders. Children with sensory impairments need clear cues the encourage them to use their strengths. Children with sensory integration disorders need environments in which sensory stimulation can be adjusted.

Children with **visual impairments** learn to pay attention to the information they receive by listening, touching, smelling, and tasting. The sounds of music and familiar voices are reassuring. Clear pathways and well-defined areas help them move from place to place. Textural cues, such as change of texture from carpet to tile, help children know that they have entered a different part of the room. A piece of material such as felt or fur can help children with visual impairments find their cubbies.

Children with **hearing impairments** use visual cues, touch, vibration, tastes, and smells to interpret what is happening around them. Good acoustics and minimal conflicting noise help children who have at least some hearing. Since these children rely heavily on visual information, make sure that the inside lighting is adequate and free of glare. Play areas that encourage face-to-face interactions help children with hearing impairments read the facial cues of their playmates.

Some children with physical and developmental disabilities have **tactile defensiveness**, which causes them to avoid directly touching some materials, such as paint, water, or playdough. Provide gloves, sticks, paint brushes, and other tools and props to encourage them to participate in sensory activities as they choose.

Meeting the Needs of Adults for Comfort

Caring for young children is a physically challenging job. Rather than forcing yourself to do physically difficult tasks, make them easier by using techniques such as these.

Minimize physical strain whenever possible. Place resilient cushioned mats in front of the diapering table and other places where adults stand a great deal. A small armrest pillow reduces strain when bottle-feeding infants. When working with mobile infants, low carpeted risers and cubes for adult seating help you observe, join floor play, and stand up easily. Steps for children to climb to the diapering table limit your need to lift them. Toddlers and twos can push low chairs to the table, assist with wiping tables with soapy water after meals, and pick up some toys. Keep a small dustpan and broom nearby so you can pick up toys from the floor without bending. Provide several kinds of comfortable adult seating as well.

Well-organized storage areas help you find things easily and enable you to remain attentive to the children. Adults also need places to store their personal belongings out of children's reach. Purses, bags, and coat pockets are filled with fascinating things that are sometimes dangerous for young children. You need spaces to store extra children's clothing, medications if they are stored in the room, and materials that are not currently in use.

Sending Positive Messages

Have you ever watched children and their family members when they first visit your room? They look around to decide what kind of place it is. They may be wondering:

- Do I belong here?
- Do these people know who I am? Do they like me?
- Is this a place I can trust?
- Will I be safe here?
- Will I be comfortable here?
- Can I move around and explore?
- Is this a calm and interesting place to be?
- Can I count on these people to take care of me?

Because you are the most important part of the learning environment, your daily interactions with infants, toddlers, and twos are the most important way to answer these concerns. Your arrangement of the physical environment also sends powerful messages to children and their families. Think about whether it conveys the messages you intend.

You belong here. We like you.

- At children's eye levels, display photos of the children at play and with their families. Change them occasionally. Laminate them or use a Plexiglas® cover so children can touch them without tearing them. Put photos in unbreakable cube frames that children may carry around.

- Provide places for each child to store belongings from home.

- Make sure that pictures and materials honor the ethnic and individual characteristics of the children and families.

- Change the environment on the basis of your observations of children. For example, when children begin to climb on the bookshelf, add large cushions or plastic boxes that children may climb on instead.

- Encourage family members to bring interesting materials for children to explore, such as colorful bandanas, stackable bottle caps, or a guitar.

This is a place you can trust. You will be safe here.

- Arrange the furniture with safety in mind. Cushion surfaces where children are learning to move on their own, making sure that the cushioning does not interfere with balance.

- Store items near the places where they will be used. Label containers, cupboards, and shelves so that substitute teachers, adult visitors, and family members can find things easily.

- Limit environmental changes to help cautious children know that they can depend on the room arrangement.

This is a comfortable place to be.

- Include homelike touches and familiar household objects in the environment, such as curtains, large floor cushions, nontoxic plants, and even plastic tumblers to stack.

- Make sure that children's comfort items are available to them.

- Provide soft furniture, such as stuffed chairs and couches.

- Have enough space for teachers and family members to join children in their play.

- Place reading materials in many places around the room so children and adults may sit and enjoy them.

- Use soft textures and furnishings to help moderate noisy sounds. Soft colors, lights, and sounds foster a peaceful atmosphere.

You can move freely and explore on your own.

- Set aside sufficient space so that children can turn over, crawl, creep, pull up, stand, cruise, and walk around as they grow and change. Borrow this space from other areas when necessary. For instance, you can push cribs closer together temporarily, to leave more floor space when children are not napping.

- Block off areas that are unsafe for children.

- Store a variety of materials on shelves that are low enough for children to reach.

- Make sure that all of the materials stored or set out on low shelves are intended for children's use.

- Label shelves and containers with pictures and words so children know where to find and return materials.

- Display toys, books, and other materials in consistent places so children know where to find them.

- Designate areas for experiences as children's strengths, needs, and interests change.

We will take care of you.

- Set up areas for routines.

- Designate a crib, cot, or mat for each child.

- Provide a comfortable, supervised place where sick children may rest until their parents come.

Scan your room regularly to look for ways the environment can be enhanced to convey these positive messages. Small, special touches make the environment warm and welcoming to everyone: children, families, and you.

Creating a Structure for Each Day

Structure is the second aspect of creating a responsive environment for infants, toddlers, and twos. A predictable sequence of events enables children, their families, and you to feel a sense of order. While your daily schedule and plans need to be flexible, they give you direction for your work with children.

Planning a Daily Schedule

Infants, toddlers, and twos need a schedule that is regular enough to be predictable but flexible enough to meet their individual needs and to take advantage of the learning opportunities that emerge continually every day. In general, the younger the children, the more flexible and individualized the schedule must be. Yet even babies feel more secure when the schedule is somewhat consistent. Responsive care respects children's biological rhythms and their interests.

When an infant falls asleep soon after arriving at child care, she needs a nap even though the other children are awake and playing. When the wind begins swirling leaves in the backyard, 2-year-olds might want to play outside even though the schedule suggests that it is time to come inside for lunch.

Parts of a Daily Schedule

When you create a daily schedule, remember to allow adequate time for these routines:

- hellos and good-byes
- diapering and toileting
- eating and mealtimes
- sleeping and nap time
- dressing

These routines are discussed in depth in chapters 6–10.

In addition to providing routine care, you plan experiences that promote children's development and learning. These include

- playing with toys

- imitating and pretending

- enjoying stories and books

- connecting with music and movement

- creating with art

- tasting and preparing food

- exploring sand and water

- exploring outdoors

These experiences are discussed in chapters 11–18. Your task is to create daily schedules that include routines and a variety of experiences when individual children and small groups are ready for them.

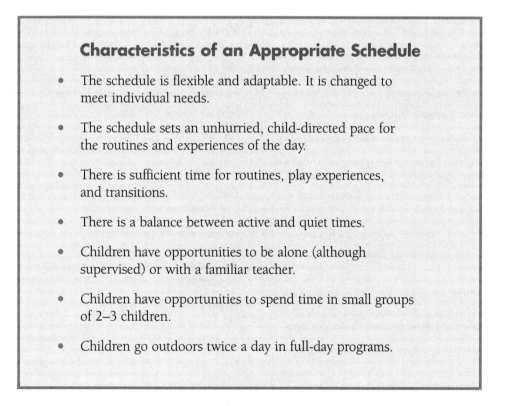

Characteristics of an Appropriate Schedule

- The schedule is flexible and adaptable. It is changed to meet individual needs.

- The schedule sets an unhurried, child-directed pace for the routines and experiences of the day.

- There is sufficient time for routines, play experiences, and transitions.

- There is a balance between active and quiet times.

- Children have opportunities to be alone (although supervised) or with a familiar teacher.

- Children have opportunities to spend time in small groups of 2–3 children.

- Children go outdoors twice a day in full-day programs.

The schedule you develop for your program may vary from those outlined. However, the sample schedules that are suggested here will give you ideas for planning a schedule that meets the needs of your children and your program.

Individualizing the Schedule for Infants

Each child in your care has his or her own schedule for eating, diapering and toileting, playing, and sleeping. In an infant room, each infant is fed when hungry, sleeps in a familiar place when tired, and has his or her diaper changed when it is wet or soiled. With adult help, infants begin to develop their own patterns for sleeping, eating, and other basic needs, but each has his own schedule. In an infant room, there are as many schedules as there are infants.

The next chart shows the sequence of events during one day in the lives of two infants, Julio (4 months) and Willard (11 months). Notice that, although they do many of the same activities, the timing and specific content of what they do differ.

Julio's Day	Willard's Day
Morning	**Morning**
Arrival: Julio arrives with his mother. She takes a while to say good-bye and gives Julio to Linda.	**Arrival:** Willard arrives at the center with his mother. Willard cries as his mother says good-bye. Grace comforts him by reading a book with him.
Mealtime: Julio sits in a glider with Linda. She cradles him in her arm as she gives him a bottle.	**Mealtime:** Grace helps Willard wash his hands to get ready for breakfast. He sits in a small sturdy chair at a low table. He feeds himself the apple slices on his plate and drinks milk from a training cup. After breakfast, he swipes his hands with a wet paper towel, and then Grace helps him wash them more thoroughly.
Diaper change: Julio gazes at Linda as she changes his diaper and talks to him. He begins rubbing his eyes.	
Nap time: Julio falls asleep in his crib after Linda pats him gently and softly sings a lullaby.	**Indoor play:** Willard squeezes, pounds, and pokes a soft squeaky toy. He looks at Grace and laughs with delight each time the toy squeaks.
Diaper change: Julio's diaper is dry when Linda checks it.	**Diaper change:** Grace changes Willard's diaper, naming body parts as she touches them.
Indoor play: Julio lies on a mat with two other babies near a low, shatterproof mirror. Linda sits at the edge of the mat and talks with the three children about what they are seeing and doing.	**Indoor play:** Grace sings with Willard and two other children. Willard notices his family picture album, picks it up, and turns the pages. He points to his mother's picture when Grace asks, "Where's Mommy?"
Mealtime: Julio drinks part of a bottle while he sits on Linda's lap. Then he burps as Linda gently pats his back.	**Diaper change:** Willard protests as Grace picks him up to change his diaper. Grace assures him that it will only take a minute. He lies still and helps open the diaper tabs.
Diaper change: Julio kicks his legs as Linda changes his diaper. "You're kicking your legs," she explains. "I'm going to put your pants back on those legs now."	**Dressing:** Willard takes his jacket off its hook. Grace helps him put it on.
Dressing: Linda puts on Julio's jacket. She sings to him as she dresses him.	**Outdoor play:** Grace spreads a big blanket near the fence and puts Willard on the blanket. He pulls to standing by holding onto the fence. He points to cars, dogs, and people as they pass by.
Outdoor play: Linda takes Julio outdoors, walking around the playground with him. He closes his eyes when a gust of wind blows across his face. Linda tells him that the moving air he feels on his face is wind.	

Julio's Day	Willard's Day

◀

Midday

Diaper change: Linda changes Julio, focusing on him but remaining attentive to the other children.

Mealtime: Linda puts Julio on her lap and offers him his bottle. He turns his head away, indicating that he is not ready to eat just now. She tries again in 10 minutes. He is hungry and drinks his bottle.

Nap time: Julio begins dozing off. Linda puts him on his back in his crib and gently pats his tummy a few times before letting him fall asleep on his own.

Diaper change: Linda talks quietly to Julio as she changes his diaper. They enjoy a game of peek-a-boo together.

Mealtime: Julio drinks part of a bottle while Linda cradles him on her lap.

Afternoon

Indoor play: Julio sits on Linda's lap as she sings with older infants.

Diaper change: Linda notices that Julio is wet and changes his diaper. He squirms, so she talks to him calmly and finishes quickly.

Indoor play: Linda places Julio under a play gym on a floor mat. Julio bats the objects on the gym with his fist.

Dressing: Linda puts Julio's jacket on again.

Outdoor play: Linda carries Julio outside. She sings "Ring Around a Rosie," and Julio laughs every time she stoops as she sings, "All fall down!"

Departure: Julio sits on a glider with his mother while she relaxes and talks with Linda. After about 10 minutes, she puts on Julio's jacket, says good-bye, and they leave for home.

Midday

Diaper change/handwashing: Willard's diaper is dry when Grace checks it. With Grace's help, Willard washes his hands

Mealtime: Willard sits at a low table with Grace and three other children. He takes the spoon from Grace and tries to feed himself applesauce. Grace laughs and asks, "Willard, are you feeding yourself or the table?" After lunch, Grace helps Willard wash his hands, and she brushes his teeth.

Diaper change: Willard yawns and lies quietly as Grace changes his diaper.

Nap time: Willard falls asleep almost instantly when Grace puts him in his crib. After sleeping for about an hour, Willard begins to make quiet sounds in his crib.

Diaper change: Grace checks Willard's diaper and changes it, singing one of his favorite songs.

Snack: Willard drinks formula from a training cup and eats some pear slices with his fingers.

Afternoon

Indoor play: Willard pushes a plastic crate around the room, stopping repeatedly to put things into it, dump them out, and fill the box again.

Cleanup: Grace encourages Willard to help put the balls back in the basket. She takes turns with him to make it into a game.

Diaper change: Willard's diaper is wet when Grace checks it. Before picking him up, she explains, "Okay, let's change this wet diaper."

Dressing: Willard squirms as Grace helps him put on his jacket. "Willard, here's your hat," Grace says. "Please put it on your head while I put on your jacket."

Outdoor play: Willard sits in the sandbox, filling and dumping a bucket of wet sand.

Departure: Willard exclaims, "Da-da!" when he hears his father's voice. He takes two steps toward his father and then crawls over, sits, holds his arms up, and smiles as his father picks him up.

The *Individual Care Plan* you develop with each family will enable you to create a personal schedule for each infant (see chapter 5, *Partnering With Families*). Janet completed the *Individual Care Plan* for Jasmine (8 months) after her conversation with the Jones family.

THE CREATIVE CURRICULUM® FOR INFANTS, TODDLERS & TWOS

Individual Care Plan

Child:	Jasmine
Child's Date of Birth:	Infants
Teacher:	Janet & Tamika
Family Member(s):	Donna & Lee Jones
Date:	March 25, 2006

Arrival	Eating
Jasmine arrives by 7:30. Dad usually brings her.	Jasmine eats jarred baby food that her family provides. She also eats some finger foods: Cheerios®, bread, bananas, peaches, and very tender potatoes and carrots. She has a bottle before she naps. She usually eats lunch after she wakes up from her nap at around 11:30 and has an afternoon snack around 3:30.
Diapering	**Dressing**
Jasmine usually needs her diaper changed about 30–45 minutes after eating. She likes to be actively involved and enjoys playing with her toes and fingers during diapering.	Jasmine has a couple of extra sets of clothes in her cubby. It is important that she be in a clean outfit when her grandma picks her up in the afternoon.
Sleeping	**Departure**
Jasmine takes two naps, one from 10:00–11:30 and another from 2:30–3:30. She likes to have her back rubbed before her morning nap, and she is used to hearing a song before her afternoon nap.	Jasmine's grandma usually picks her up by 4:30.

Once you have completed the *Individual Care Plan* for each of the infants in your primary care group, you can develop an overall schedule for your group that shows the approximate times of the daily routines for each child. The actual times will change from day to day, but a general routines schedule will help you and your co-teachers coordinate responsibilities. The routines schedule will also help you decide when to provide experiences for children who are awake but not eating or having their diapers changed. You will also have an idea about when to schedule morning and afternoon outdoor times.

Schedules for Toddlers and Twos

By the time children are toddlers, their days are more consistent and group-oriented. For example, toddlers and twos typically eat and sleep as a group and have designated times for playing. A consistent daily schedule helps them feel more in control and thus more competent and secure. It is still important to be flexible about responding to individual children's needs and to maintain an unhurried pace each day.

Here is a sample schedule for toddlers who are enrolled in a full-day program. Notice that several activities often take place at the same time. The actual times on your schedule may vary, depending upon your children's needs.

DAILY SCHEDULE

7:00–8:30 **Planning/preparation time:** Review the plans for the day. Conduct health and safety checks. Refill bathroom and diaper changing supplies. Make bleach solution. Set out materials for children to use as they arrive. Think about individual children and any special needs.

Hellos and good-byes: As children transition from home to school, greet each child and help them say good-bye to each other.

Dressing: Help children take off and store their outerwear.

Diapering and toileting: Check diapers and change as necessary. Take older children to the toilet as needed.

Eating and mealtimes: Help children wash hands and eat breakfast. Sit with children and enjoy breakfast together. Wash hands and brush teeth.

8:30–10:15 **Indoor Play:** Guide children in selecting what they want to play with and how. Observe and interact with children to extend play and learning. Find time to read to children individually or in a very small group.

Diapering and toileting: Check diapers and change as necessary. Take older children to the toilet as needed.

Sleeping and nap time: Allow tired children to sleep according to their needs, even if they usually sleep at the same time as the rest of the group.

Dressing: Change children's wet or soiled clothing as necessary.

Cleanup: Help children put materials away.

Eating and mealtimes: Help children wash hands and eat morning snack. Sit with children and enjoy a snack and conversation together.

10:15 – 11:30 **Dressing:** Help children put on outerwear before going outdoors.

Outdoor play: Supervise and interact with children as they explore the playground environment and equipment. Roll balls back and forth, blow bubbles, paint with water, make natural discoveries, and so on.

Dressing: Help children take off and store their outerwear.

DAILY SCHEDULE

11:30–12:30   **Diapering and toileting:** Check diapers and change as necessary. Take older children to the toilet as needed.

          Eating and mealtimes: Help children wash hands and eat lunch. Sit with children and encourage conversation about the day's events, the meal itself, and other things of interest to the children. Wash hands and faces; brush teeth.

12:30–2:30   **Sleeping and nap time:** Help children relax so they can fall asleep. Supervise napping children, sharing duties so each teacher gets a break. Provide quiet activities for children who do not sleep. Adjust length of nap time to suit the group pattern and the needs of individual children.

2:30–3:00   **Diapering and toileting:** Check diapers as children awaken and change as needed. Take older children to the toilet.

          Eating and mealtimes: Set up snack so children can eat as they wake up.

3:00–4:00   **Experiences:** Guide children in selecting what they want to play with and how. Observe and interact with children to extend play and learning. Read and sing with children individually or in a small group.

4:00–5:00   **Dressing:** Help children put on outerwear before going outdoors.

          Outdoor play: Use outdoor playground or take children on walks.

          Dressing: Help children take off and store their outerwear.

5:00–6:00   **Experiences:** Set out a limited number of choices for children so they are engaged until their parents arrive. Read stories to a child or a small group of children.

          Diapering and toileting: Check diapers and change as needed. Take older children to the toilet.

          Dressing: Send home wet or soiled clothing and bedding.

          Hellos and good-byes: Help children and families reconnect at the end of the day. Greet each parent and share something special about their child's day.

As time allows during the day   **Planning and reflection:** Discuss with colleagues how the day went and what you observed about individual children's needs, interests, and accomplishments. Make plans for the next day.

Adapting the Daily Schedule for 2-Year-Olds

Twos can engage in more extended play. They are also ready to sit with a small group of 2–4 children during a planned story time. Here are some things to keep in mind when planning a schedule for this age group:

- Include active and quiet times.

- Schedule time for outdoor play in the morning and in the afternoon.

- Be aware of children's individual needs for sleeping, eating, and toileting.

- Keep group times short. Allow children to decide how long they want to stay with the group. Be ready to stop when you see that most children are losing interest.

- Display your schedule at children's eye level, illustrated with drawings or photographs of scheduled activities.

- Plan for transitions.

Planning for Transitions

Every day is filled with transitions, the periods between one routine or experience and the next. Transitions are more apparent for toddlers and twos than for infants, because the older children have a more structured schedule. The most important transitions, and often most difficult, are at the beginning and end of the day. (This is discussed in detail in chapter 6, *Hellos and Good-Byes*.) However, any transition can be a problem if children do not know what to do or if they are required to wait too long. Young children cannot wait happily. When they have to do so while adults get organized, disruptive behavior such as pushing and hitting often occurs.

Here are some suggestions for preparing for transitions.

Plan ahead. Thinking and organizing supplies ahead of time allows you to give the children your full attention.

Be organized. Have the supplies for the next activity ready so you do not have to search for them while the children wait.

Give children a warning. Before a change takes place, tell them that it is coming. For example, before cleaning up toys and washing hands for lunch, you might say, "It's almost time to clean up. Finish what you are doing, and then we will help each other put the toys away. It is almost time for lunch."

Give clear directions. Make sure your instructions are appropriate for the developmental level of the child. For example, a child who can only follow one-step directions will be confused if you tell him to put the balls in the shed, go inside, hang up his coat, and wash his hands.

Avoid having children wait. Divide the group so children will not have to wait. For example, while some 2-year-olds are brushing their teeth, the others might be listening to a story or helping you put blankets on cots.

Guide children through transitions. Do this by describing what you are doing or by singing or chanting together. For example, you can have a special song for clean-up time or for getting ready for lunch.

Planned transitions help children build a sense of order. They feel competent when they know what is expected and when they are engaged. A well-organized day will help you remain calm and allow you to observe children and enjoy their development.

Responsive Planning

The importance of building responsive relationships is emphasized throughout *The Creative Curriculum*. Teachers must observe children purposefully, think about what they learn about each child, and respond in supportive ways. Even though you develop a plan for each day, you must always be open to following children's interests and addressing their needs.

As you care for and teach infants, toddlers, and twos, you balance planning—thinking ahead about what you might do during a week or a day—with following the child's lead at particular moments. You need to know when to watch, when to step in, and how to extend each child's learning. When you know individual children's interests and developmental levels, you can offer experiences that engage and delight children and build their competence.

Using Observations to Respond to and Plan for Each Child

As you work with infants, toddlers, and twos, you continually observe what they are doing and saying. Refer to the *Developmental Continuum* and keep the goals and objectives in mind as you observe children. Think about what you see and hear and determine how to respond at the moment. Later, you can use your observation notes to complete weekly planning forms. Ongoing observation will help you shape daily routines and experiences and continually enhance your relationship with each child. In chapters 11–18, you will see examples of how teachers observe children at different points during the day, what they think about, how they respond at the moment, and their ideas for incorporating the information into their weekly plans.

Using the Weekly Planning Forms

To help you prepare for each day and still respond to children's changing interests and abilities, *The Creative Curriculum* includes two weekly planning forms: the *Child Planning Form* and the *Group Planning Form*. (These are available in *The Creative Curriculum for Infants, Toddlers & Twos Developmental Continuum Assessment Toolkit.*)

The *Child Planning Form* is used on a weekly basis to record current information about each child. It helps you use what you know about each child to plan experiences that support his development and learning. This enables you individualize your program.

To offer a program that meets each child's needs, you need to know and appreciate what makes each child unique. When you understand what motivates a child, how the child approaches new tasks, and his preferred learning style, you can plan for him. The *Child Planning Form* helps you do this. Each week, take a few minutes to review your observation notes, examine portfolio samples, think about recent events and interactions, and analyze the information you have about each child in your primary care group. Record the most important facts in the section called "Current Information." Then note how you will use this information in the coming week. For example, describe changes you might make to routines and list materials you might introduce to the child.

This is how Brooks completed the *Child Planning Form* for the four children in her group.

Child Planning Form

CREATIVE CURRICULUM
FOR INFANTS, TODDLERS & TWOS

Teacher(s):	Brooks
Group:	Infants
Week of:	February 2–6

Child: Abby (14 months)

Current information:
Abby has been filling purses with small toys and carrying them around. She's also starting to nap earlier in the morning.

Plans:
Add some small baskets to the room for filling and carrying. Adjust the schedule to accommodate her new nap time.

Child: Max (16 months)

Current information:
Max played with two simple puzzles every day.

Plans:
Add two new knob puzzles and leave the old ones. Encourage him to discover and try the new ones.

Child: Devon (18 months)

Current information:
Devon enjoyed hearing *The Itsy-Bitsy Spider* board book. He's started to do the hand motions.

Plans:
Continue reading the book. Bring the spider puppet to use with the book.

Child: Shawntee (18 months)

Current information:
Shawntee needs to be by me when new adults are around.

Plans:
Make sure I'm available to her on Friday when Max's dad comes to volunteer.

The *Group Planning Form* helps you think about all of the children in your group and decide what changes to make to the environment, general schedule, and routines. It also helps you decide what experiences to offer during the week. It gives you an overall sense of direction for the week and a list of the materials you want to have available.

Think about weekly planning as *planning for possibilities.* You prepare for routines and meaningful experiences and then follow each child's lead. Infants, toddlers, and twos often respond in unexpected ways to new materials and to planned experiences. Observing and responding to what children do each day is one of the joys of working with young children. If your plans are flexible and you feel free to revise them as often as you think best, you are more likely to take advantage of learning opportunities that arise during the course of daily life in the program. To complete the *Group Planning Form,* think about the following questions:

- What experiences interest the children now?

- Which materials are the children using most?

- What skills are children developing?

- What is working well? What is not working well?

- How are we providing meaningful roles for family members who visit the program?

Your answers to these questions will help you make decisions about your program. The *Group Planning Form* includes five main sections.

Changes to the environment—Record the changes you will make to the environment next week. Your observations guide the changes. For example, if puzzle pieces were often scattered on the floor, you might decide that the puzzles are too difficult and should be put away for now. Perhaps you will decide that the puzzles are not stored so that children can use them independently, and you might decide to put them on a lower shelf. If a child shows a particular interest in playing with a ball, you might decide to include balls of different sizes in the play area. Perhaps it is time to add new labels to the shelves to help toddlers clean up after themselves. You might plan to rotate toys that children have not played with for a while, replacing them with different toys that capture children's interest.

Changes to routines and schedule—Record the ways you will change routines next week. For example, if a child has been having trouble going to sleep, organize his sleeping routine so you can rock him until he is drowsy. If a child is too hungry before lunch time, you might offer lunch earlier or find ways to eliminate waiting when it is time for the meal. If you and a toddler's parents agree that it is time to begin toilet learning, note that on the *Group Planning Form.*

Family involvement—Include your ideas about involving family members next week. These may include asking for their help in making materials and inviting them to participate in an experience or in daily routines.

Special experiences I plan to offer this week—Enter experiences you will offer to support children's exploration and discoveries. Think about the experiences you can provide indoors and outdoors. Remember to give children opportunities to choose what they want to do and the people with whom to play. Chapters 11–18 discuss experiences. You do not have to plan a different experience every day or offer every kind of experience every day. Infants, toddlers, and twos master skills through repetition, and they take delight in repeating the same thing again and again.

Thoughts for next week—Complete this section when you think about your current week. Include information about how engaged the children were. Did one child roll balls down a ramp for 20 minutes? Were other children involved? Think about what actually happened and about any changes you want to make for the following week. For example, do you want to add more balls or balls of different sizes? Perhaps you want to see what happens if you add a large inclined tube for the children to roll balls down, instead of a ramp.

Here is an example of the *Group Planning Form* that Brooks completed by using the information from the *Child Planning Form*.

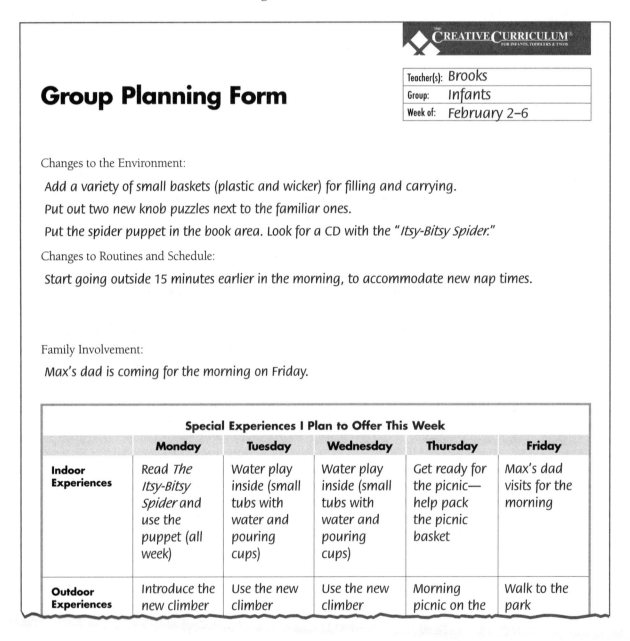

Teacher(s):	Brooks
Group:	Infants
Week of:	February 2–6

Group Planning Form

Changes to the Environment:

Add a variety of small baskets (plastic and wicker) for filling and carrying.

Put out two new knob puzzles next to the familiar ones.

Put the spider puppet in the book area. Look for a CD with the "*Itsy-Bitsy Spider.*"

Changes to Routines and Schedule:

Start going outside 15 minutes earlier in the morning, to accommodate new nap times.

Family Involvement:

Max's dad is coming for the morning on Friday.

Special Experiences I Plan to Offer This Week				
Monday	**Tuesday**	**Wednesday**	**Thursday**	**Friday**
Indoor Experiences Read *The Itsy-Bitsy Spider* and use the puppet (all week)	Water play inside (small tubs with water and pouring cups)	Water play inside (small tubs with water and pouring cups)	Get ready for the picnic— help pack the picnic basket	Max's dad visits for the morning
Outdoor Experiences Introduce the new climber	Use the new climber	Use the new climber	Morning picnic on the	Walk to the park

Planning for Twos

Sometimes you may notice that many 2-year-olds are interested in the same topic. You might want to expand on their interest by incorporating several different experiences related to the topic into your weekly plans. In order to do this, you need to consider their developmental skills as well as their interests.

LaToya and her assistant teacher looked at their observation notes from the week as they prepared to write next week's plans. They had several notes about children who discovered and collected leaves on the playground. Abraham, Jonisha, Marcus, Valisha, Donovan, Josie, and Annemarie were interested in the leaves. Jonisha, Marcus, and Abraham had asked why the leaves fell off the tree. Another note said that Donovan and Josie chased leaves as they fell from the trees, jumping to try to catch them. In considering what they might do to encourage the children's interest in leaves, they also thought about the children's skills. They knew that the children can

- *sit in a small group and listen to a short story*
- *group objects that have similar characteristics*
- *use writing and painting tools such as crayons and paint brushes*
- *use language to describe objects*

LaToya wondered, "How I can I extend the children's learning?" After discussing their ideas, LaToya and her assistant decided to include the exploration of leaves in their plans. They agreed to observe the children's level of interest this coming week to decide whether they should continue the exploration of leaves for the following week or two. Here are their ideas for experiences:

Books: *Red Leaf, Yellow Leaf,* by Lois Ehlert; *Look What I Did With a Leaf,* by Morteza Sohi; *A Tree is Nice,* by Marc Simon; *Leaf Man,* by Lois Ehlert; *A Simple Brown Leaf,* by L. J. Davis

Encourage the children to collect leaves on the playground to examine inside.

Take a walk around the neighborhood and look at and collect other leaves.

Bring magnifying glasses outside to examine leaves there.

Talk about the sizes, shapes, and colors of the leaves and ask questions:

- What do they feel like?

- What do they look like?

Put paint of the colors of the leaves at two art easels outside.

Creative movement inside (moving like leaves falling from the trees).

Provide crayons without wrappings and thin paper for leaf rubbings.

Sort the leaves into simple categories (same color, big/little).

Add leaves to the collage materials in the art area.

Bring child-size rakes outside.

Here is the *Child Planning Form* that LaToya completed for her group after observing the children.

THE CREATIVE CURRICULUM®
FOR INFANTS, TODDLERS & TWOS

Child Planning Form

Teacher(s):	LaToya
Group:	Twos
Week of:	November 4–8

Child: Samuel

Current information:
Had two toileting accidents this week during outdoor play.

Plans:
Halfway through outdoor time, remind him to use the bathroom.

Child: Valisha

Current information:
Collected leaves on the playground with Annemarie.

Plans:
Bring baskets outside for the children to use for gathering leaves.

Child: Donovan

Current information:
His aunt and baby cousin have moved in with his family.

Plans:
Continue to observe Donovan for changes in his behavior. Talk with him about what it is like to have a baby in his house. Continue to talk with his mom at drop-off time.

Child: Jonisha

Current information:
Pretended to read books to two children in the library. Asked questions about leaves on the playground.

Plans:
Add some books about leaves to the library and read them with Jonisha.

Child: Marcus

Current information:
Painted with water on the playground, three days in a row.

Plans:
Set up easels and paint outside.

Child: Josie

Current information:
Chased leaves on the playground with Donovan.

Plans:
Bring in streamers and encourage Josie to move like falling leaves.

Here is the *Group Planning Form* that LaToya completed for her group after the brainstorming session.

Group Planning Form

THE **CREATIVE CURRICULUM**®
FOR INFANTS, TODDLERS & TWOS

Teacher(s):	LaToya
Group:	Twos
Week of:	November 4–8

Changes to the Environment:

Bring baskets outside for leaves gathered on the playground.
Add easel to the playground.
Introduce magnifying glasses.

Changes to Routines and Schedule:

Remind children during outdoor play to use the bathroom.

Family Involvement:

Ask for volunteers to go on a walking trip around the neighborhood.

Special Experiences I Plan to Offer This Week					
	Monday	**Tuesday**	**Wednesday**	**Thursday**	**Friday**
Indoor Experiences	Music & Movement: move like leaves Read *Red Leaf, Yellow Leaf* and discuss leaves on playground	Read *Red Leaf, Yellow Leaf* and discuss the colors of the leaves on the playground	Read *A Simple Brown Leaf* Use magnifying glasses to look at leaves at the sensory table	Read *A Tree is Nice* Use magnifying glasses to look at leaves at the sensory table	Prepare for the walking trip
Outdoor Experiences	Collecting leaves on the playground	Easel Painting	Easel Painting Raking leaves	Raking leaves	Walking trip around the neighborhood to look at and collect leaves

Adapting Your Plans

When you work with children from birth to age 3, you must always expect the unexpected. Each infant has a personal schedule and style. As you zip the last jacket and head for the door, an infant may begin crying to tell you he is tired or hungry or needs his diaper changed. Toddlers and twos also have an amazing ability to capsize the best-laid plans. You cannot be sure about when a toddler will decide to flush her socks down the toilet or try to feed his leftover lunch to his teddy bear.

Remember, being responsive is more important than sticking to your plan. Always keep in mind that your positive interactions with children are more important than particular activities. You will need to adapt your plans as you respond to the children's changing needs and interests. Here are some steps to follow.

Review your weekly planning forms. Think about the day before the children arrive. Try to imagine how all the parts of the day will fit together.

Assess the realities of the day. Will an infant need extra time and attention because she is teething? Did a family bring in a bag of freshly picked apples, tempting you to make applesauce for a snack? Are you feeling a little tired and not up to taking the walk you planned?

Remain flexible and adapt your plans as necessary. No matter how carefully you prepare, you must always be ready to change your plans. For example, a toddler might throw a tantrum and need some extra attention, requiring you to postpone the large chalk activity you had planned. Perhaps a bulldozer will begin working at the end of your road, giving you a new purpose for neighborhood walks.

Be responsive to individual children's needs and interests. For example, if you know a child needs you to be ready to step in to keep her from biting another child, you might decide to postpone your plans for making playdough with the children. Instead, you would bring out the playdough you made a few days ago or spend extra time singing and reading with the children. You can make new playdough tomorrow or next week.

Conclusion

This chapter discussed the second component of *The Creative Curriculum for Infants, Toddlers & Twos:* creating a responsive environment. It explained how the physical environment promotes the developing abilities and interests of infants, toddlers, and twos; how the environment supports responsive relationships; and how to plan a structure that gives you direction but allows flexibility. When you thoughtfully organize your room and plan for each child, you create a responsive environment in which children can flourish and learn. The learning component of the curriculum is discussed in the next chapter, *What Children Are Learning.*

inside this chapter

Knowing Infants, Toddlers & Twos

Creating a Responsive Environment

Experiences

Playing with toys

Imitating and pretending

Enjoying stories and books

Routines

Hellos and good-byes

Diapering and toileting

Eating and mealtimes

Sleeping and nap time

Getting dressed

Connecting with music and movement

Creating with art

Tasting and preparing food

Exploring sand and water

Going outdoors

Partnering With Families

What Children Are Learning

Caring and Teaching

Theory and Research

3

What Children Are Learning

Watch an infant, toddler, or 2-year-old interacting with others or exploring the environment. You can tell that important things are happening. Every interaction and every impression a child receives by seeing, tasting, touching, smelling, and hearing affects the development of the child's brain and builds new abilities. What and how children learn during the first 3 years become the building blocks for successful lifelong learning.

The relationships you build with children and the experiences you provide for them build the foundation for school success. From birth, young children begin developing language and literacy skills. They are communicators, eager to let you know what they need and think, and eager to engage you in interactions. Young children think mathematically, comparing who has more, putting things in order by size, noticing different shapes, matching, and sorting. They are also scientists, examining and manipulating everything that comes within their reach and trying to figure out how things work, how they grow, and what people do. They develop these abilities and understandings more readily when they have positive and trusting relationships with the important adults in their lives.

The third component of *The Creative Curriculum* describes what infants, toddlers, and twos are learning. This chapter covers four main topics:

The Foundation for All Learning discusses the social/emotional characteristics and attitudes that influence the way children learn.

Building Language and Literacy Skills describes how children acquire skills to communicate, learn to hear and produce the sounds of language, engage with books and stories, and explore writing.

Discovering Mathematical Relationships discusses children's emerging understandings about number concepts, patterns, geometry and space. It also explains how children gain some understandings about the world by sorting and classifying.

Exploring Like Scientists describes what young children are learning about the physical world of objects, the natural world of animals and plants, and the social world of people.

The Foundation for All Learning

School readiness is an important issue today. Children who enter school ready to learn have strong social/emotional skills and positive attitudes toward learning. How children feel about themselves and how they relate to others influence what and how they learn. School readiness actually begins in infancy.

For very young children, learning depends on the trusting relationships they build with the important adults in their lives. The research on relationships, especially the importance of secure attachments, explains how young children develop strong social and emotional skills when their needs are consistently met by trusted adults and when they have positive interactions with those adults. When they know that they are safe, loved, and cared for, children are ready to venture out to explore everything around them. When adults encourage these explorations and share children's excitement about new discoveries, children gain confidence in themselves as learners.

ZERO TO THREE: National Center for Infants, Toddlers, and Families identifies seven social/emotional characteristics that are essential for school-readiness. These traits are more fundamental to children's success than knowing letters and numbers.[18] They are listed here with definitions and examples of how children show these characteristics.

1. **Confidence:** a person's sense of control over his own behavior and environment; children's expectation that they will be able to succeed and adults will help them if necessary. Children with confidence are eager to try new things; show pleasure when they make a discovery or complete a task by clapping their hands, smiling, and looking at you; know their own names and use words like "my" and "me."

2. **Curiosity:** a desire to find things out, knowing the process will be enjoyable. Children demonstrate curiosity when they actively explore and investigate objects and materials using all of their senses; notice new things in the environment; ask questions about what, why, and how things happen, and try to figure out how things work.

3. **Intentionality:** the drive to make things happen and a determination to persist and not give up. Children show intentionality when they choose what they want to play with, take an interest in sounds and sights around them, stay with an activity for a period of time and complete it, and try different ways to solve a problem.

4. **Self-control:** children's ability to control their actions in age-appropriate ways. Children demonstrate self-control when they are receptive to redirection, increasingly behave in ways that are expected by adults, and learn to express and manage their feelings.

5. **Relatedness:** children's ability to engage with others, knowing they will be understood. Children who have acquired this characteristic trust familiar adults and have secure attachments, enjoy playing games such as peek-a-boo, take an interest in what other children are doing, are increasingly aware of the emotions of others, and enjoy playing with other children.

6. **Capacity to communicate:** the desire and ability to exchange ideas, feelings, and thoughts with others. Children communicate, first through crying, coos, gestures, and facial expressions, and eventually with words or signs. They are able to express ideas and feelings verbally or by signing, ask and answer questions, and converse.

7. **Cooperativeness:** the ability to engage with others in an activity or task, balancing their own needs with those of others to accomplish something. Children who are cooperative may imitate others and then join in, participate in small-group activities, begin to follow simple classroom rules, help put away toys or wipe a table, and offer to help another child.

Young children develop these characteristics when they are with adults who genuinely care about them, talk with them in calm and respectful ways, take joy in their discoveries, have appropriate expectations about what they can do, and guide their behavior in positive ways. Every interaction you have with a child is an opportunity to nurture these seven characteristics that are essential to children's success as learners. The next chapter, *Caring and Teaching,* offers specific strategies for helping every child build a strong foundation for learning.

Building Language and Literacy Skills

A baby's brain is primed for acquiring language. When young children are around caring and responsive adults who talk with them, engage them in conversations, read to them every day, and teach them songs and rhymes, they are eager to communicate. Because infants, toddlers, and twos are very motivated to engage with others and communicate, you can make a difference that will last a lifetime.

Infants, toddlers, and twos need you to offer intentional experiences every day in order for them to acquire the building blocks of language and literacy. These include experiences that enable children to acquire vocabulary and language skills, hear the different sounds and rhythms of language, enjoy books and stories, and explore writing.

Vocabulary and Language

One of the greatest achievements in the first 3 years of life is the development of oral language. This includes the ability to understand the words that they hear (receptive language) and to put their own ideas and feelings into words so they can communicate with others (expressive language). A child with a good vocabulary and language skills can engage in conversations, share ideas and feelings, ask and answer questions, and work through problems.

From the time they utter their first word around their first birthday, until they are about 3 years old, children learn words and how to put them together at an astounding rate. Their language learning is supported by caring and responsive adults who talk to them, label and describe experiences and objects, and engage them in conversations.

People once thought it is not important to talk to babies because they do not understand what is being said. We now know that adults should use every opportunity from birth to talk to babies, describe things, reassure them, and sing to them.

Some children come from homes (and programs) where they hear 215,000 words every week (around 30,700 words a day). Compare that with children who hear only 62,000 words each week (around 8,800 words a day).[19] By age 3, the difference in the vocabularies and language use in these two groups of children is tremendous. Children who have rich language and literacy experiences usually have about twice the vocabulary of children who do not.

Researchers have found that language experiences in the first 3 years are one of the most reliable ways to predict reading ability by third grade.[20] Reading, after all, is getting meaning from the printed text. The more words a child knows, the more he understands when someone reads to him and, later, when he learns to read, himself. Once children fall behind, it is very hard for them to catch up. In school, they fall further and further behind. You can make sure that the infants, toddlers, and 2-year-olds in your care hear and learn to use a lot of language.

Children will show you in many ways that you are helping them develop vocabulary and language skills.[21]

A **young infant** might…

- calm down when you sing a favorite lullaby or talk to him in a quiet, reassuring voice

- turn her head toward you and smile when you speak to her

- make sounds directed to you, listen intently when you imitate the sounds, then repeat the sounds again and again

- lift his arms up when you come to his crib and ask, "Do you want to get up?"

- make sounds like "Ma-ma" and "Da-da"

A **mobile infant** might…

- understand some words: wave her hands when you say, "Bye-bye," or point to a ball when you ask, "Where's the ball?"

- string sounds together and repeat the sounds in a sing-song voice that begins to sound like speech: "Ba-ba-BA-BA-BA-ba-ba-ba"

- point toward and look at an object he wants, saying, "Uh, uh"; then look at you and back at the object, repeating the sound until you hand him what he wants

- respond when you ask, "Where is your nose?" by pointing to her nose

- use 10–50 single words that refer to people, objects, and events, simplifying some words (for example, *ba* for *bottle*, *ma* for *more*, *bow-wow* for *dog*)

- communicate with signs or pictures if he is unable to speak

A **toddler** might…

- point to different body parts as you sing a song like "Head and Shoulders, Knees and Toes"

- combine words into two-word sentences: "Daddy car." "More milk."

- use a questioning intonation to ask questions: "What dat?" or "Go out?" or "Where mommy?"

- answer simple questions: respond when you ask, "Where is your coat?" by showing you her coat

- understand and respond when you say, "Let's put the blocks in the box."

- learn 50–200 words by age 2

- use signs or pictures in a sequence to express an idea: *baby + cry*

A **2-year-old** might…

- begin to use language to get information by asking *who, where, what,* and *why* questions: "Why you going?" "What this?" "Where teddy?"

- use language to express ideas and feelings: "No go outside."

- use 2- to 5-word sentences to communicate

- begin to use prepositions (*in, on*), pronouns (*me, he, we*), negatives (*can't, don't*), and conjunctions (*and*)

- understand and follow directions and simple stories

The Sounds and Rhythms of Language

The ability to hear and distinguish the sounds and rhythms of language is a very important skill for reading. During the preschool years, most children develop *phonological awareness,* the ability to hear the small units of sound in spoken language. They notice rhyming words in songs, poems, fingerplays, and stories. They enjoy playing with words, such as saying "Banana-fana-fo-fana." Preschoolers begin to hear and clap the syllables in their names: Son-ya; Ty-rone. They also notice that some words start with the same sound: *cat* and *cake*; *Denise* and *Danny*.

During the first 3 years of life, the brain is very receptive to learning the sounds that make up language. Every language has its own set of sounds that are used to form words. These sounds are called *phonemes.* If children are with adults who talk and sing with them, they pay attention to the sounds and rhythms of the languages they hear. By around 6 months of age, infants have learned to babble and repeat the sounds that make up the languages they hear.

Children under age 3 can develop *sound awareness,* the ability to notice and recognize different sounds, which is the first step in developing phonological awareness. Newborns have the ability to distinguish their mother's and father's voices from other voices or noises they hear around them. You may have noticed that young infants pay particular attention to the type of speech called *parentese.* When you talk slowly in a high pitched, sing-song voice, face-to-face with an infant, he is likely to pay attention to you long before he understands what you are saying. You may feel a bit silly, talking this way, but it is very effective in getting infants to listen to your voice.

Everyday experiences help children develop sound awareness. When you talk with children, play songs and sing the lyrics, recite nursery rhymes, and do fingerplays, you are helping children become aware of the sounds and rhythms of their language. When you make such experiences a part of your everyday work with young children, they will develop this very important awareness.

A **young infant** might…

- recognize his mother's or father's voice before he sees them
- put sounds together ("ba-ba-ba"), listen intently when you imitate them, then repeat the sounds again and again
- calm when she hears you sing the same lullaby she hears at home

A **mobile infant** might…

- string sounds together in a sing-song voice
- anticipate the part of a song where you do something interesting: "Trot, trot to Boston. Trot, trot to Lyn. Watch out, Jeremy! Don't fall…IN!"
- make the sounds of animals and things: "Baa-baa"; "Choo-choo"

A **toddler** might…

- repeat the refrain from a song she has heard many times: "E-I-E-I-O"
- fill in the rhyming word in a predictable refrain when you pause before saying the word
- recognize familiar sounds in the environment: the siren on a fire truck, a chirping bird, a car horn, the ring of a phone

A **2-year-old** might…

- play with the sounds in words you have taught her, for example "Nanabana"
- make up their own word games: "Silly, Willy, Billy"
- repeat words they enjoy hearing, "Pop, pop, pop"
- repeat familiar phrases from songs and rhymes

Enjoying Books and Stories

Reading books and sharing your pleasure in language and stories are among the most important gifts you can give to infants, toddlers, and twos. Children who regularly hear stories read aloud develop a foundation for literacy, including the motivation to learn to read. That is a key ingredient for success in school. Most children who enjoy being read to develop a love for books that will last throughout their lives, enriching their experiences and stretching their imaginations.

Long before infants can focus their eyes on the pictures, turn the pages, and understand the words you are saying, they can begin to associate books with the pleasant feelings they have when you hold them on your lap and share a book. Sharing books with infants, toddlers, and twos also builds other important literacy skills.

Vocabulary and language—Children learn new words as you share books about a variety of objects, actions, events, and places; link ideas in books with events and objects in children's lives; and repeat words from books during daily routines. Books for twos contain words that are less commonly heard, and they often include more complex sentences than the conversational language used with very young children in daily life. The descriptive language in books and the synonyms for familiar words help stretch children's language skills. Rich vocabularies and background knowledge are essential for children's later comprehension of school texts.

How print works—Toddlers and twos begin to learn about print when you point out words and letters, run you finger under print, and talk about what you are doing as you handle a book (for example, "Let's turn to the next page"). They begin to realize that pictures and print are meaningful and that books in English are read from front to back, one page at a time.

Letters and words—Some twos are beginning to recognize a few letters, usually the first letters of their names and some letters in environmental print, such as the M in the McDonald's logo or the S in a stop sign. They may enjoy finding these letters in simple alphabet books.

Comprehension—This is the ability to make sense of what is heard or read. Infants take their first steps toward comprehending print when they point to pictures in a book. Toddlers and twos begin to relate events in a story to their own lives, and older twos begin to retell familiar stories.

Understanding books and other texts—As you read stories to young children, they become aware that stories have beginnings and endings. They begin to understand that the phrase "Once upon a time" starts some stories and "The End" signals the end of some stories.

Phonological awareness—The types of books you read to children help them become aware of the sounds of language. Sound awareness, which is the first step in the development of phonological awareness, is discussed in the previous section.

As you share books and stories with young children, you will be rewarded by how much they are learning from these experiences.[22]

A **young infant** might...

- gaze at the bright pictures in a book you are holding or one that is propped up where she can see it

- wave, suck, chew, and manipulate the pages of a cardboard or cloth book

- vocalize as you read a book with simple, repetitive language

A **mobile infant** might...

- play with the moving parts of a book (for example, tabs to push, open, or pull)

- help you turn the pages of a book as you hold it and read

- hand you a book; then snuggle against you for as long as ten minutes as you read and talk about the pictures

- laugh or smile when he sees a familiar picture in a book you are sharing

- make sounds and point to pictures as you read each page

- point correctly to the picture of a familiar object when you ask where it is (for example, "Where's the dog?" "Can you show me the baby's eyes? Where are the baby's ears?")

- shake his head when you read a book like *Is Your Mama a Llama?* and you say, "No-o-o. My mama's a..."

A **toddler** might also…

- turn a book that is upside-down until it is rightside-up; then look at each page, turning one page at a time

- make animal noises or other appropriate sounds, such as "Moo, moo" or "Choo, choo," in response to pictures or something you read

- pretend to read the story, babbling as if she is reading the text

- point to a picture and ask, "What dat?"

- make connections between the content of a story and what he sees around him (for example, get a truck after seeing one in a book)

- fill in the next word when you pause before a rhyming word; repeat the words in a familiar predictable book

A **2-year-old** might also…

- select books on her own and pretend to read a familiar story, repeating phases accurately, especially from predictable books

- talk about the events or characters in a story: "Grandpa and me went to zoo. We saw tigers. And lions too!"

- protest when you misread a familiar word or leave out a word

- ask to read you a favorite book again and again

- retell some of the details of a familiar story

- comment on the characters in a book (for example, "That cat'pillar is hungry.")

See chapter 13, *Enjoying Stories and Books,* for ideas about selecting books and making reading experiences enjoyable for infants, toddlers, and twos.

Exploring Writing

Reading and writing go together. A group of letters is a symbol for a word, just as letters are symbols for sounds. Long before children can recognize letters and read or write letters and words, they begin to understand that one thing can represent something else (for example, a picture of a banana can represent a real banana; a block can stand for a car; particular golden arches mean McDonald's).

Children learn about writing if they see print in their environment, hear it read aloud, and see you writing for different reasons. Toddlers and twos are fascinated when they see you writing. They want to imitate what you do. At first, they have no idea what you are doing; they simply notice that you are taking an object, moving it across a piece of paper, and leaving marks. Over time and with experience, they begin to understand the purposes of writing.

Older infants, toddlers, and twos can begin to learn about and experiment with writing if they see pictures and print and if you give them drawing, painting, and writing tools.

A **mobile infant** might…

- watch as you write a note
- make random marks on paper with large crayons

A **toddler** might…

- grasp a large crayon and bang it on a piece of paper to make marks
- draw horizontal and some vertical lines, and circular marks
- move a paintbrush across a large sheet of paper until it is almost completely covered with paint
- make lines and circles in finger paint; then cover them up and repeat the process

A **2-year-old** might…

- experiment to see what kinds of marks she can make: lines, dots, zigzags
- make a series of looped scribbles and tell you, "This my mommy."
- tell you he wants to write a letter and then scribble all over a piece of paper
- point to her name on her cubby and tell you, "My name."
- begin to recognize common symbols in the environment and some letters, especially the first letter in his name
- draw lines and make marks that begin to look like letters
- ask you to write something for her, such as a story or letter that she dictated or her name on a picture

Promoting Language and Literacy Learning

Children gain language and literary skills when you offer them rich experiences and materials and talk with them. The chart that follows summarizes what you can do and say to promote their learning.

Language and Literacy Learning	What You Can Do and Say
Vocabulary and Language	• Explain what you are doing during routines: "I'm going to change your diaper now. You will feel much better when we're finished. First I'm going to…" • Use a high-pitched, sing-song voice and talk face-to-face with infants to get their attention. Speak slowly, and use short sentences and simple speech. • Converse by listening attentively and engaging in back-and-forth exchanges. Use gestures, facial expressions, or other cues to increase their understanding. • Describe what a child is doing: "You like those nesting cups, don't you? You like banging them together. Now you're banging them on the floor. Look! You put one inside the other, and it fit!" • Expand on what a child says: When he says, "Go out," you can say, "Do you want to go outside to play?" If she says, "More milk," you can say, "You finished all of your milk. You must have been thirsty. Now you want more milk. Here it is." • Share picture books with photos or objects that children can point to and name. • Ask open-ended questions to encourage children to verbalize their ideas. If a toddler points to her shoes and says, "New shoes," you can say, "I see that you have new shoes. They are blue. How did you get those shoes?" • Listen carefully and wait patiently as children express themselves. Do not rush them. • Label storage containers and shelves with picture and word labels. • Describe and talk about what children see, hear, feel, taste, and smell, for example, on a walk outdoors. ▶

Language and Literacy Learning	What You Can Do and Say
◀ Sounds and Rhythms of Language	• Imitate an infant's babbling and encourage her to imitate the sounds you make: "I hear you saying, 'Ma-ma-ma-ma.' Now you're saying it back to me." • Recite nursery rhymes, clapping along with the beat: "Patty cake, patty cake baker's man. Bake me a cake as fast as you can." • Talk about the sounds animals make: "What does a cow say? Moo. What does a dog sound like? Woof-woof." • Sing songs that encourage children to listen for and anticipate an action: "Ring around the rosie....Ashes, ashes, we all fall DOWN!" "Open, shut them....but DO NOT PUT THEM IN." • Sing, recite nursery rhymes, and do fingerplays with children, emphasizing the words that rhyme and words that start with the same sound. • Read stories with rhymes and lots of repetition, such as *Is Your Mama a Llama?*, *Good Night Moon*, and simple Dr. Seuss books. • Read stories with rhyming refrains and pause when you get to the rhyming word so children can fill it in: "Brown Bear, Brown Bear, what do you see? I see a red bird looking at …." • Play with words: "See you later, alligator." "Let's comb your hair, you little bear." • Call attention to similarities of words: "*Tanya* and *Timmy* both start with the same sound: /t/. I'm going to tap, tap, tap, Timmy's toes, toes, toes. I'm going to tap, tap, tap, Tanya's nose, nose, nose."
Enjoying Stories and Books	• Provide cloth and soft plastic books that young infants can grasp, chew, and manipulate; cardboard books for mobile infants; and a range of story and content books for toddlers and twos. Display them attractively where children can reach them. • Hold infants on your lap as you read and show them books with simple, bright pictures. • Talk about the pictures. Label pictures a child points to: "That's a bottle, just like yours." Ask the child to find a picture, and ask questions about it: "Does he look happy?" • Let children play with and manipulate the book as you read, and encourage them to help you turn the pages. • Encourage children to chime in as you read a predictable book with repeated phrases. • Read books to children and tell stories every day, one-on-one and with small groups. ▶

Language and Literacy Learning	What You Can Do and Say
◀ Exploring Writing	• Let infants and toddlers see you writing and talk about what you are doing: "I'm making a list of what I need to buy so we can make pancakes tomorrow." • Point out print in the environment, such as letters on alphabet blocks, children's clothing, or displays. • Make picture and word labels for materials in the room, and label children's cubbies and belongings with their names. • Show and talk about pictures: "This is a picture of your mommy and daddy." "Can you find the picture of the puppy on this page?" • Provide large crayons, water-based markers, paint and brushes, and large chalk for toddlers and twos. Offer plenty of plain paper so they can use these tools to make marks, scribble, paint, and explore writing.

Discovering Mathematical Relationships

Mathematical thinking involves noticing similarities and differences; organizing information; and understanding quantity, numbers, patterns, space, and shapes. Learning the concepts and language of math—*more, less, smaller, the same as, how many*—gives children a sense of order and a way to make predictions and comparisons and to solve problems.

Infants, toddlers, and twos discover mathematical relationships every day when they explore space, compare amounts, and sort and match objects. As Jean Piaget and Lev Vygotsky explained, young children need many opportunities to explore and manipulate interesting objects in their environment and to be with adults who take an interest in what they are doing and talk to them about their discoveries.[23]

As you promote children's mathematical thinking, it helps to know what math concepts are important and what experiences are appropriate. The building blocks for understanding mathematics include experiences with number concepts, patterns and sequence, geometry and spatial relationships, and sorting and classifying.[24]

Number Concepts

Basic number concepts involve three different abilities: the ability to repeat a sequence of numbers in a particular order; to match each number with one of the items being counted; and to compare groups or quantities to determine relative amounts, that is, to know which has *more, less,* or the *same.*

Older infants, toddlers, and twos can begin to develop some understandings about number concepts when adults use numbers in everyday activities, sing songs that involve numbers, invite twos to help set the table for lunch, and provide materials they can explore in a variety of ways.

A **young infant** might…

- look at you intently as you put on her socks and say, "Here's one sock for this foot, and one sock for your other foot. Two feet, two socks."

- smile when you bring more cereal and ask, "Do you want *more* cereal? You must be hungry!"

A **mobile infant** might…

- place a lid on each container with which he is playing

- reach for more objects with which to play

- make a sign for "more" after finishing a cracker

A **toddler** might…

- stomp around the room, singing, "One, two, one, two, five."

- help you place one brush in each container of paint at the easel

- put a cup on each plate or a napkin next to each chair at the lunch table

- notice that another child has a larger lump of dough and ask you for more

A **2-year-old** might…

- line up a set of cars and place one block next to each car

- build a tower with blocks and announce, "Mine bigger."

- hold up two fingers when you ask, "How old are you?" and say, "I two."

Patterns and Relationships

Patterns are regular arrangements of objects, colors, shapes, numbers, or events. The ability to figure out a pattern involves recognizing the relationships that make up the pattern. It might be a pattern of sizes (large, small, large, small). It could be a pattern of colors (red, blue, red, blue) or a pattern of daily events ("After my cereal, I get a bottle.").

To begin to develop the ability to recognize patterns and relationships, young children first need many opportunities to explore and manipulate objects and notice similarities and differences.

A **young infant** might…

- focus on the color or texture of your dress
- wave her arms in anticipation when you arrive with her bottle
- stroke a rough carpet; feel the smooth tile floor

A **mobile infant** might…

- open his mouth when you lift a spoon toward his face
- play with nesting cups, trying out different sizes until she finds one that fits inside another
- place several small blocks in a line, scatter them around the floor, and then collect and line them up again

A **toddler** might…

- beat a drum, imitating the way you are doing so
- use a small cup to fill a larger one with sand
- say a repetitive phrase from a story book while you read it aloud
- point to the Papa Bear in a book when you ask, "Which bear is bigger?"

A **2-year-old** might…

- line up cars of different sizes, grouping the big ones together and the little ones together
- group all the green pegs together and the red pegs together in a pegboard
- place rings on a graded stacking toy in order of size
- beat a drum after hearing you shake a tambourine

Geometry and Spatial Relationships

An understanding of geometry and spatial sense
begins with the ability to recognize similar shapes
and body positions in space. Children gain spatial
sense as they become aware of themselves in relation
to objects and structures around them. They learn
about location and position (*on, off, under, below, in, out*)
and about distance (*near, far, next to*).

By playing with objects of different shapes, young
children learn that some objects are similar to other
objects. When you describe what they see ("The
orange looks like a ball"), you help infants, toddlers,
and twos begin to develop an understanding of
geometry. Opportunities to build and explore
structures of various sizes enable toddlers
and twos to develop understandings about
spatial relationships.

A **young infant** might…

- place his hands around a bottle,
  feeling its shape

- experience being wrapped in a blanket

- run her hands back and forth along the
  edge of a table

A **mobile infant** might…

- crawl through a tunnel, enjoying the feeling of
  being enclosed in a space where she can see
  out both ends

- bang blocks against different slots in a shape-sorting
  box until they fall through

- drop a ball into a basket

A **toddler** might...

- try to put a teddy bear into a box that is too small; then find a larger box and put the bear into it

- handle 3-dimensional shapes and put all the cubes in a bucket

- know whether to go *around, in,* or *through* a structure in order to get to an object

A **2-year-old** might...

- blow bubbles outdoors and say, "Look! Balls. Lot of balls."

- learn the names of some shapes: "This a circle. It's like a pizza."

- bend down to look when you say, "Your shoes are under the table."

Sorting and Classifying

Every day, we think mathematically when we organize information in a logical way in order to make comparisons. Preschoolers, for example, might make a collection of leaves, sort them into piles according to type, and then compare how many they have of each type. Sorting and classifying involves the ability to notice similarities and differences. It also involves the ability to organize a collection of objects according to one attribute, such as size, color, shape, or function.

Infants, toddlers, and twos become familiar with similarities and differences by using all of their senses as they explore. They learn by watching, listening, touching, smelling, and tasting. By manipulating objects, they learn how objects are the same and different. When you describe what they are discovering, you help them become aware of different characteristics.

A **young infant** might...

- recognize your voice when he hears you say, "I'm coming. I hear you calling me."

- distinguish between familiar and unfamiliar adults

- show a preference for a particular soft blanket and enjoy stroking it

A **mobile infant** might...

- hit a xylophone with a wooden stick but shake a rattle

- pick out all the oranges pieces from a fruit salad

- collect wooden blocks and put them in a box

A **toddler** might…

- see a picture of a donkey and say, "Horsie."
- place a blue block next to another blue block
- place differently shaped blocks into the matching openings in the shape-sorter box

A **2-year-old** might…

- put all of the yellow blocks in a bucket
- pick out all of the round beads from a pile of assorted beads
- select all of the cubic blocks from a pile of different shapes and then build a tower

Helping Children Discover Mathematical Relationships

The experiences and materials you provide for infants, toddlers, and twos can help them begin to discover mathematical relationships. The next chart lists important mathematical concepts and skills and shows what you can do to encourage children's mathematical thinking.

Discovering Mathematical Relationships	What You Can Do and Say
Number Concepts: Counting	• Recite nursery rhymes that include numbers, such as "One, Two, Buckle My Shoe." • Sing songs and fingerplays that use numbers, for example, "1-2-3-4-5, I caught a fish alive," and "Three little ducks that I once knew…" • Read stories that include numbers. • Count with children: "Let's see how many trucks we have. One, two, three. We have three trucks."
Number Concepts: Noticing Relative Sizes and Amounts	• Provide toys that engage infants and toddlers in exploring different sizes, such as nesting cups and stacking rings. • Use comparison words: "You picked out the *biggest* ball." "You're telling me that you want *more* peaches." • Put containers of various sizes in the sand and water tubs. ▶

Discovering Mathematical Relationships	What You Can Do and Say
Patterns and Relationships (Recognizing repeated patterns)	• Sings repetitive songs. • Read predictable books with a repeated language pattern, for example, *Brown Bear, Brown Bear, What Do You See?*. • Point out patterns so children become aware of them. "Look at the stripes on your shirt: a red stripe, and then a yellow one. Red, and then yellow again." "You lined up the cars: a big car; then a little one; then a big one, and then a little one." • Provide toys that children can use to make patterns, such as colored wooden blocks, large beads and laces, large peg boards and pegs.
Geometry and Spatial Relationships (Recognizing shapes and positions in space)	• Provide large cardboard boxes and tunnels so children can crawl in and out, and over and under, and experience different positions in space: *inside, outside, over, under*. • Talk about 2- and 3-dimensional shapes and link them to common objects: "That block is shaped like a train car." • Use positional words: "Let's put all the balls *in* the box." "Keisha is sitting *next to* Tyrone." • Include materials that children can use to build structures, such as Duplos® and blocks.
Sorting and Classifying (Matching by one characteristic)	• Organize toys on the shelves and in containers labeled with pictures and words. • Point out groups that children have made: "You put all the red pegs in a row." "You seem to like the blue cars best." • Provide older toddlers and twos with collections that they can organize in different ways, such as large plastic bottle caps, plastic animals, pinecones, and shells.

Exploring Like Scientists

Science involves finding answers to interesting questions. What does this feel like? How does this work? Why did this happen? What would happen if we tried it another way? How can we make this work better?

Scientists are curious and eager investigators. They wonder about what they see, try their ideas, observe what happens, and draw conclusions. A new discovery often leads them to investigate more. Opportunities to explore and investigate are everywhere.

Young children are born scientists. They are curious about everything. Infants investigate their surroundings by using all of their senses. They spend a lot of time gazing at things, but, once they are mobile, they are off on their own to find out how things also feel, taste, smell, and sound. Toddlers and twos experiment, trying to discover how things work, what things do, and what they can make happen. They are fascinated by animals and people and what makes plants grow. Like scientists, young children are curious about and want to investigate the physical, natural, and social worlds around them.

The Physical World

Physical science involves exploring the physical properties of objects and materials. Children gather information about the physical world by using all of their senses to explore and investigate. What does this feel like? Slimy, squishy, hard, or sticky? How does this smell? Is it loud or quiet? Is it fast or slow? How can I make this move? Can I roll it, twist it, blow on it, or push it? What will happen if I drop this on the floor?

Throughout the day, you will see young children touching, tasting, looking at, listening to, smelling, and manipulating objects to learn about the physical world around them.

A **young infant** might...

- grasp and mouth a teething ring you offer
- mouth and then shake a rattle you place in her hand
- bat at a hanging toy to make it move (testing cause and effect)
- pull a string attached to a toy to make it come closer
- raise his bottle when the milk level drops and continue sucking

A **mobile infant** might...

- pull aside a blanket after watching you hide a toy because she expects it to exist even when she cannot see it (object permanence)

- repeatedly drop objects on the floor to see what happens

- push the buttons on a pop-up toy to make different things appear; then push them down and start over again

- watch you make a soft toy squeak; then squeeze it to reproduce the sound

- open drawers and cabinets to investigate what is inside; then take everything out

A **toddler** might...

- push a chair across the room and stand on it to reach a toy

- experiment to see what sounds he can make on a xylophone and with musical bells

- pick up acorns in the play yard, drop them on the slide, and watch them roll down and across the ground; then run to collect them and repeat the whole process again and again

A **2-year-old** might...

- try using different tools at the water table: watering cans, cups of different sizes, funnels, scoops, sponges, basters

- use a plastic screwdriver and hammer on a toy workbench to turn bolts and pound pegs

- mix paint colors to make new colors

- use words to describe the properties of objects: *hard, smooth, heavy, sticky*

The Natural World

Life science involves exploring the natural world of living things, including both plants and animals. What does the rabbit like to eat? How loud can I make my voice? What will happen if I pick this flower? Where did all these leaves come from?

A **young infant** might…

- discover her toes, grab her feet, and try to put them into her mouth
- touch your mouth as you sing, to investigate where the sound is coming from
- play with your hair as you hold him
- observe a fish in a bowl with interest

A **mobile infant** might…

- look into a tree when she hears birds chirping
- play with the grass and dandelions in the play yard
- enjoy the sound of crunching leaves as he crawls on the playground
- reach to pet a friendly dog

A **toddler** might…

- get excited when he sees a squirrel scamper across the yard and up a tree
- collect leaves and play with them inside
- pretend that a doll is a baby and take her for a walk in a stroller
- fill a pail with damp sand, pat it down, and turn it upside down to make a cake

A **2-year-old** might…

- watch a line of marching ants and try to figure out where they are going
- ask you, "Where snow go?" after observing that the snowman she helped build the day before had melted
- help you water the plants in the outdoor garden and understand that water helps plants grow
- hold a carrot for the class rabbit to eat and say, "He hungry."

The Social World

Infants are more fascinated by people than anything else. They learn very quickly to distinguish familiar people from strangers. Before long, they can identify the people in their families and people who belong to other families. They are curious about who people are, what they do, and where they live.

Daily living teaches infants, toddlers, and twos about their social world.

A **young infant** might…

- get excited when she sees familiar people enter the room
- gaze at photographs of family members you have mounted on the wall
- watch other babies with great interest

A **mobile infant** might...

- play alongside another child, sometimes imitating what she is doing

- point to himself in the mirror when you ask, "Where is the baby?"

- stop playing to watch an unfamiliar person who entered the room

A **toddler** might...

- recognize that the face she sees in the mirror is her own

- join a group as you read a story

- act out simple life scenes, such as going to the doctor, talking on a phone, or feeding a baby

- offer a toy to another child

A **2-year-old** might...

- understand the sequence of routines (for example, remember where things are stored, get his special blanket when you say it is nap time, or go to wash hands when you announce that lunch is ready)

- pretend to be a firefighter when playing with a fire truck

- show an understanding of the rules (for example, say "No!" when another child tries to take something from her)

- identify himself as a boy

- show a great deal of interest in young babies and what they can and cannot do

Encouraging Children to Explore Like Scientists

To encourage infants, toddlers, and twos to explore like scientists as they engage with the physical, natural, and social worlds, the most important thing is to provide interesting things for them to observe, manipulate, and explore. Watch, appreciate, and talk to them about what they are doing and learning. Your interest and enthusiasm reinforces their desire to find out more and gives them confidence to continue to explore and experiment as scientists do.

Scientific Explorations	What You Can Do and Say
The Physical World	• Place objects in infants' hands that they can hold, manipulate, and mouth safely. • Give a baby a spoon to hold while you feed her with another spoon, explaining, "You can hold a spoon, too. Soon you will feed yourself." • Offer a basket with colorful fabric scraps of different textures for children to examine. • Provide collections of objects for children to explore and play with, such as large plastic bottle caps, plastic containers, and balls. • Show interest in children's discoveries: "That dough feels soft and squishy, doesn't it?" "You figured out how to make music with those bells. You just shake, shake, shake them."
The Natural World	• Take children outdoors each day to experience plants and animals, the weather, and an entirely different environment. Point out what is happening: "I see that you are watching the clouds move in the sky." "What did you find? Those are acorns. Do you want to put them in a bucket?" • Provide natural materials for toddlers and twos to explore and examine: shells, pinecones, feathers. • Plant a small garden outdoors or have indoor plants that toddlers and twos can help care for. • Have a fish tank with a covered top and place it where children can watch the fish. For older toddlers and twos, have a class pet like a rabbit or guinea pig that they can help care for. ▶

Scientific Explorations	What You Can Do and Say
◀ The Social World	• Assign a primary caregiver to each child so children develop secure attachments and learn to trust adults. • Keep group sizes small and help children learn to relate positively to others. • Talk about the different jobs of people in the program: cooks, drivers, teachers, the director. • Read stories about people and what they do. • Provide simple dress-up clothes, dolls, cars and trucks, and people figures. Engage children in imitating and pretending to do what other people do.

Conclusion

This chapter explained how the experiences you provide for infants, toddlers, and twos support learning in language and literacy, math, and science and prepare children for success in school and in life. You will find many more suggestions for selecting materials and nurturing children's learning and development in chapters 6–18, which discuss routines and experiences. Positive relationships and social/emotional skills were described as the base from which infants, toddlers, and twos acquire cognitive and language skills and knowledge about the world around them. The next chapter, *Caring and Teaching*, begins with this important topic.

inside this chapter

Knowing Infants, Toddlers & Twos

Creating a Responsive Environment

Partnering With Families

What Children Are Learning

Experiences

Playing with toys

Imitating and pretending

Enjoying stories and books

Routines

Hellos and good-byes

Diapering and toileting

Eating and mealtimes

Sleeping and nap time

Getting dressed

Connecting with
music and movement

Creating with art

Tasting and
preparing food

Exploring sand
and water

Going
outdoors

Caring and Teaching

Theory and Research

4 Caring and Teaching

Teaching and caring for infants and toddlers is interesting, fun, joyful, rewarding, and sometimes challenging and exhausting. You soothe a crying baby by snuggling in a glider, watch a mobile infant's first tentative steps with fascination, and laugh as she dumps big beads on the floor again and again. You gather a small group of toddlers to listen to a story, and sing and dance in front of the most nonjudgmental audience you will ever have. Children change so much during the first 3 years of life!

This chapter describes the fourth component of *The Creative Curriculum for Infants, Toddlers & Twos* and examines the many different aspects of your role.

Building Relationships explains how to use your knowledge of child development and individual children's strengths and needs to build trusting, responsive relationships with and among children. Program policies and structure can help facilitate your efforts to build relationships.

Promoting Children's Self-Regulation suggests ways to help young children express their feelings and regulate their behavior in acceptable and appropriate ways. The section describes positive guidance strategies, including ways to organize the environment and adjust daily routines.

Responding to Challenging Behaviors offers strategies to manage children's inevitable challenging behaviors. Physical aggression, temper tantrums, and biting are discussed.

Guiding Children's Learning explains why everyday routines and experiences are important parts of your work. You help children learn as they play by paying attention to the ways you talk with them and encourage them to try new skills. This section also provides information and strategies for guiding the learning of children who are dual language learners and children with disabilities.

Assessing Children's Development and Learning describes how assessment is an ongoing process in which information is collected in order to make decisions. You use what you learn about each child to build responsive relationships; determine each child's strengths, needs, and interests; promote learning; and communicate with family members.

Building Relationships

Young children's development flourishes when they have close, supportive, and trusting relationships with the adults in their lives. Such relationships between children and teachers are the core of quality care. Knowing that you will meet their physical and social/emotional needs, children are able to explore and get to know the other people and objects in their environment. Your relationship fuels children's curiosity and desire to learn. Their connection with you allows them to feel safe enough to move, to explore, to experiment and, thereby, to learn.

Strategies for Building Trusting Relationships

Every interaction you have with children is an opportunity to build relationships that help them thrive. Here are some strategies to try.

Delight in the children who are in your care. Greet them affectionately each day. Show that you enjoy them. Laugh with them as they take their first halting steps, fall, and get up again. Smile at the toddler's emerging sense of humor. Celebrate each new accomplishment as you watch a child learn to roll over, sit up, walk, run, and jump. Delight as they coo and babble, speak their first words, and string words together to form sentences. Enjoy the closeness of holding a young infant in your arms and the special time you have reading a favorite story to a 2-year-old.

Relate in ways that build trust. Be dependable. Let children know that they can count on you. Be at the door to greet them each morning. Respond promptly to a child who is crying. Tell children when you are going to leave the room. Keep your promises: "Yesterday I said you could help make playdough today. Are you ready?" Remember that building relationships is a central part of your work. Slow down and spend time with children individually, every day.

Use caring words to let children know that they are respected, understood, and valued. Think about what you say and how you say it. Even infants who cannot yet talk and who do not know the meaning of your words are sensitive to the tone and volume of your voice. Use the child's home language whenever possible. Practice using caring words and a caring tone. For example, when comforting an upset child, you might say, "You are having a hard time. I can tell by your tears that you're feeling sad. Let's sit in the rocking chair together and figure out how to help you feel better."

Build relationships with all children, including those with whom you have more difficulty building positive relationships. As a professional, you need to figure out why you do not bond with some children as easily as with others. Perhaps you and the child have very different temperaments and personalities. As a first step, look for and focus on the positive characteristics of each child. Share your feelings with a colleague if you think this might help, or even ask a colleague to observe you and a child together.

Adapt daily routines to meet individual needs. Offer an infant a bottle when she is hungry, regardless of whether it is time for a scheduled snack or meal. Give a toddler time to finish his puzzle before you change his diaper. Handle children's bodies respectfully, even if it means that a routine will take longer. Explain to an infant, "I'm going to pick you up now so I can change your diaper." Ask a toddler, "Will you please help me take off your wet shirt?" Make daily routines into learning times.

Offer children opportunities to make decisions, whenever possible. Give children clear alternatives when a choice is theirs to make. For example, at snack time, ask children to choose among slices of banana, peach, or pear. This shows that you respect their tastes and their developing decision-making skills. You can even talk with young infants about choices: "Do you want to be rocked or rubbed? Let's see."

Be careful not to overstimulate children. Watch for signs that children are becoming overwhelmed, such as when an infant turns his head away during a conversation or a toddler is not able to sustain attention the way he usually does. Respond by changing your behavior or adjusting the environment so that the child can become calm and engaged.

Observe children closely to help you decide how best to respond. Give a child your full attention. Observe the child's facial expressions and body language. Learn to distinguish an infant's cries, so you will know whether the child is hungry or needs comforting. Learn how to calm an upset toddler. Use the *Developmental Continuum* to help you get to know and appreciate individual children and to decide how to respond to each child. Be aware of each child's personal style and how it might be culturally based. Respect each child's style of interaction. Some children jump into activities immediately and enthusiastically. Others need time to watch and may need some gentle encouragement.

Know yourself. Self-awareness requires a willingness to ask questions such as, "Why am I acting this way?" For example, you would want to identify why you are becoming overly involved with one child or shying away from another. Recognize that your feelings shape your interactions. Being aware of your feelings will help you form relationships and respond to children individually. Take a few minutes each day to take care of yourself so that you will have the focus and energy you need to give the children your full attention.

Helping Children Get Along With Others

The trusting relationships you build with each child help form the foundation for other relationships. When you treat children in loving, respectful, and consistent ways, you promote their positive attitudes toward others. Nevertheless, life in group care can be stressful for children. Interacting with individual children and with very small groups of children will give you and the children a break from the intensity of a larger group. One-on-one and small-group interactions also allow you to give each child more attention and to make more intimate connections than are possible in a large group.

Limit group activities for infants and always be flexible to respond to individual needs. Although they still need you to respond to their individual needs, toddlers in groups may begin to follow the same schedule for meals and naps. Toddlers and twos tend to group and regroup themselves throughout the day as they play at the water table, enjoy a painting experience that you organize, play in the rocking boat, or listen to a story. Twos often enjoy the addition of a very short morning greeting time.

Here are some strategies for helping children get along with others and manage life in a group setting.

Remember that children look to you as a model. The infants, toddlers, and twos you care for are very aware of what you do. The way you interact with each child, with colleagues, and with families teaches children more powerfully than anything you might say directly about how to get along with other people.

Arrange your environment so that children have opportunities to be in small groups when they want. Time away from the whole group offers a chance for social interactions that might not take place when everyone is together. Physical spaces that give children a break from group life and promote one-on-one interactions include a large cardboard box or a comfortable chair with room for two persons. You and one or two children can enjoy being together as you play peek-a-boo or prepare a snack.

Mirror the behavior of infants and toddlers. When you smile at an infant who is smiling at you or imitate the funny expression on a toddler's face, you acknowledge his experience and confirm that relating to others is worthwhile.

Acknowledge children's positive interactions. Comment when you see children engaging positively with each other. For example, when two 8-month-olds are sitting on a blanket together, you might say, "You are getting to know each other. You touched her face very gently."

Matthew (22 months) is drawing a picture for his new sister. Mercedes comments, "You are drawing a picture for your sister. You must be thinking about her."

Give children opportunities to help you. Children begin to understand how to contribute positively to group life when you invite them to help you.

Barbara asks **Leo** *(18 months) and other children to carry a letter to the mailbox. She also asks them to help set out their mats at nap time. She encourages their understanding that these are ways to help other people.*

Encourage children to help one another. Throughout the day, offer children opportunities to assist each other. For example, you might have occasions to invite one child to help look for another's missing sock. Acknowledge when a child uses words or gentle acts to comfort another child.

Read books about helpfulness and friendship. There are wonderful books for toddlers and twos, such as *The Enormous Turnip* and *Bear's Busy Family*. Children also love homemade books about familiar events and people they know, such as *Valisha Helps Jonisha Find Her Sweater*.

Offer interesting materials and experiences throughout the room. Purposeful room arrangement and thoughtful displays of toys and materials will help avoid the inevitable pushing and shoving that happens when too many toddlers are together in a small space.

Include equipment and materials that promote interaction and cooperation. Provide a wooden rocking boat that two or more children can rock together, offer large sheets of butcher paper for children to color or paint on together, and provide opportunities for group water and sand play.

Arrange the environment to help children begin to experience turn-taking and sharing. Placing three chairs around a small table helps children figure out whether there is a place for them or whether they have to come back when fewer children want to sit there. Providing duplicates of toys minimizes conflict over sharing, which is an unreasonable expectation for most toddlers and twos.

Allow children time to work out their differences, but be ready to step in if you are needed. For example, when you wait a few minutes before stepping in, you give two toddlers a chance to discover that there is room for both of them to sit on the sofa together. Watch closely so you can intervene if you see that one is about to be pushed off!

A Structure That Supports Relationships

Program policies and procedures can promote the ability of staff members to develop trusting, responsive relationships with children. Three factors help support relationship building.

Group sizes and teacher-child ratios are key to implementing high-quality programs. Small groups allow teachers to interact with children individually, take the time needed for daily routines, observe and respond to each child, and follow the child's lead. Group care can feel chaotic and overwhelming to very young children. Small group sizes help them feel safe and more secure.

The National Association for the Education of Young Children (NAEYC) recommends limiting group size to no more than eight infants ages birth–15 months. If there are six infants in the group, there should be at least one teacher for every three children. If there are eight infants in the group, there should be at least one teacher for every four children.

NAEYC also recommends limiting group size to no more than 12 children ages 12–36 months. For children ages 12–18 months, there should be 1 teacher for every 3 children when there are 6 children in the group and 1 teacher for every 4 children when there are 8–12 children in the group. For children ages 21–36 months, there should be 1 teacher for every 4 children when there are 8 children in the group, 1 teacher for every 5 children when there are 10 children in the group, and 1 teacher for every 6 children when there are 12 children in the group. The term *teacher* includes teachers, assistant teachers, and teacher aides.[25]

When a **primary caregiver** is assigned to each child, children and families benefit. This person has the major responsibility for a child's care and education, although other teachers participate as well. He or she is often the family's primary contact with the program.

By providing regular and consistent care, a primary caregiver becomes a child's secure base in child care. Children learn that they can trust this person to comfort them when they are tired, upset, or frightened and to help them as necessary as they explore and learn. Their relationship with a primary teacher helps children feel secure enough to relate to other adults.

Continuity of care refers to a program philosophy that supports children's staying with the same teacher for all—or at least most—of their first 3 years. Children under age 3 need continuity of care to feel safe and secure. It takes time for a child and teacher to form a secure attachment. They are less likely to form secure attachments when children change teachers frequently. Despite this knowledge, program policies often require that infants and toddlers move to new groups and new teachers when they reach a certain age or begin to walk. This transition is often very difficult for the child, as well as for teachers and families.

Here are some ways that programs can promote continuity of care:

- Children of the same age and teachers stay together in the same space until the children are 3 years old.

- Children are cared for in mixed age groups and remain with the same teachers and children until they are ready for preschool.

- Children and teachers move together to a new space as children grow older.

- Groups divide. Some children from one group move with one teacher to another room, where they join a new teacher and a few children from her original group.

- Children remain with the same teacher until they are 18 months or 2 years old. They then move to a toddler or twos group.

- Children change teachers but visit their previous teachers whenever they wish.

Helping Children Transition to a New Group or Preschool

While infants, toddlers, and twos make many transitions throughout the day, major transitions occur when children move to a new group within your program and when they move to a new program, perhaps to go to preschool. By making these major transitions as smooth as possible for children and families, you help children build on their successes in your setting as they move to a new one. Change is harder for some children than for others, but some additional support is helpful for everyone. Children, families, and teachers may all feel sad about leaving the strong relationship you have built together over time. Introducing a child and family to new arrangements before the actual change gives them the opportunity to experience the new situation from the base of trust and security they have established with you.

Separation can evoke children's deep feelings. You may find that, during the last weeks or days before the change, a child becomes restless or more easily upset, tests limits more than usual, or may even get angry or frustrated with you. A child may cling to you or want to spend all of his time by your side. Even challenging behaviors show how much the child cares for you. Here are some ideas for making transitions easier for children, families, and you.

Think about transitions ahead of time. Develop program-wide plans for handling internal transitions. When possible, forge relationships with external preschool programs. Share information with the new program about your center, about *The Creative Curriculum,* and the *Developmental Continuum.* Lay the groundwork for a new teacher to get to know a child by sharing information and the insights you gained by using the *Developmental Continuum.* Be sure that your program's director and the child's family approves of taking this step.

Talk to families about how their child handles change and about the strategies that they use to help their child cope with change.

Plan to have the child and family visit the new group or program. Encourage them to visit more than once if possible. Invite the new teacher to visit the child in your setting so she can observe the child in a familiar place. If a child is changing teachers and rooms within a center, it is easy to make numerous visits. During these visits, take photos of the child in the new setting and with the new teacher. Make a book with photos from the new and old settings.

Talk about the change, beginning about 2 weeks before the transition. Take care not to convey your sorrow or concerns or to make too much of a planned change. Integrate your mention of the new setting or new teacher into your everyday interactions.

Celebrate the child's last day with a special snack or by singing a song you made up about the child. This gives you an opportunity to acknowledge the change through a small, low-key ritual. Be sure to say good-bye. Your acknowledgment is a sign of respect to the child, family, and the relationship you have worked so hard to build during the time you spent together.

Promoting Children's Self-Regulation

Developing self-regulation, the ability to control one's own feelings and behavior, is a primary task of early childhood. It takes time. Infants, toddlers, and twos have immediate and intense feelings of joy and excitement, as well as feelings of anger and frustration. They do not yet have the ability to stop and think about how to express their feelings in acceptable ways. They may not have the verbal language to express their feelings. Learning to self-regulate is a slow process that requires your patience and understanding of what each child is able to do at given stages of development.

Setting the Foundation for Young Infants' Self-Regulation

Self-regulation begins when you and a child's family gently establish patterns for routines and respond to the child in respectful, caring ways. You help an infant begin to learn to manage her feelings and behavior when, for example, you pick her up to comfort her or encourage her to sleep by following the same ritual. Here are some suggestions for setting the foundation for self-regulation as you care for young infants.

Establish and follow rituals, providing as much continuity with a child's home as possible. Singing the same songs or rocking a tired baby before laying her down helps her begin to learn how to organize her own behavior.

Use your face, voice, touch, and motion to help a young infant manage his feelings and other responses to stimulation. Holding a young infant, looking in her eyes, and talking to her quietly may help her calm herself and focus briefly on something that catches her interest. Observe and take steps throughout the day to ensure that children are not overwhelmed by the noise and confusion of group life.

Stay nearby when babies are lying or sitting close to each other. Be sure that everything within their reach is safe for children to play with and mouth.

Helping Mobile Infants Begin to Control Their Behavior

Mobile infants are movers who want to explore everything. While you do not want to discourage their eagerness to investigate and try their ideas, you do want to keep them safe. The goal is to set limits that they can understand and to set them in ways that show respect and help children be competent. Here are some suggestions.

Use simple, clear language to communicate which behaviors are acceptable. Let your facial expression and tone of voice emphasize your message: "You may use the crayons on the paper."

Use the word *no* sparingly. Save this for dangerous situations so it will be effective.

Give children many opportunities to move and be active throughout the day. Children who are happily engaged are less likely to get into dangerous situations and conflicts. Practice also helps children master new skills.

Plan the day so there are no long waits between routines and experiences. If children have to wait for a few minutes, then sing, do a fingerplay, or tell a story to help pass the time in an interesting, relaxed way.

Think about the situation from the children's perspective before intervening. For example, be aware that what looks like one child's grabbing a toy from another child may be a "taking away and giving back" game.

Give children the chance to work things out themselves if no one will be hurt. For example, a child may briefly react and then decide she does not care when someone picks up a toy with which she had been playing. In such a situation, your involvement would create unnecessary tension.

Promoting the Self-Regulation of Toddlers and Twos

The behavior of toddlers and twos can sometimes stretch your patience. It is also exciting to watch confident toddlers take the initiative to learn about themselves and their world by testing limits. Try to retain your sense of humor, keeping in mind that testing limits is developmentally appropriate behavior for children this age.

Here are some suggestions for promoting the self-regulation of toddlers and twos in positive ways so they are competent to learn rules and how to follow them.

Encourage their growing sense of independence. Invite them to participate in daily routines. Give them many chances to make choices. Organize the environment so children can hang up their coats and reach the sink to wash their hands.

Understand that toddlers and most twos are not yet ready to share. This does not mean that they are greedy or mean. They need time to develop a sense of ownership and learn first to take turns and then to share. Model and encourage taking turns and sharing, but do not insist on it. To help avoid conflicts, provide duplicates of favorite toys.

Share your feelings about particular behaviors. "I know that you are angry, and that's okay. I don't want people to hurt each other, though. I'm going to help you so you don't hit."

Give children alternative ways to express their anger. "If you feel angry, tell us. Say, 'I'm mad!' so we will know how to help you."

Ask toddlers silly questions so they have lots of opportunities to say *no*.

Matthew (22 months) loves when Mercedes asks questions such as, "Do we eat a shoe for dinner?" or "Is it time to go to sleep after breakfast?"

Pay close attention to a child who is likely to hit or bite. Help the child stop the behavior before another child gets hurt.

Acknowledge children's actions when they show some self-control.

Barbara saw Leo (18 months)—who was about to throw a block—catch her eye. He then put the block on the floor. "That was a good idea, Leo. You put the block down. You did not throw it."

Use familiar signals to let children know when it is time to move from one activity to another. For example, give a 2-minute warning when it is time to clean up. Dim the lights and play soft music when it is time for a nap. When children have a sense of what to expect, they tend to feel more secure and calm during transitions. With less confusion, challenging behaviors are less likely.

Avoid talking with other adults about a challenging behavior in front of the child whose behavior is a problem. Toddlers and twos are very aware of when they are the topic of conversation. Being talked about can be uncomfortable.

Toddlers and twos can begin to understand and follow a few simple, clear rules. Rules such as, "Sit at the table when you cut with scissors" give children a sense of order and security as well as the opportunity to develop self-regulation. Over time and after many reminders, children will learn to take their scissors to the table.

Think about what rules are absolutely essential. Rules should be as concrete as possible, few in number (no more than three or four), simple, and stated in positive terms. Rules generally fall into three categories:

- maintaining physical safety (*We care about each other.*)

- not hurting others (*We treat each other gently.*)

- caring for the room (*We use materials carefully.*)

Using Positive Guidance Strategies

Positive guidance can take many forms. For example, you arrange your environment to prevent dangerous or unacceptable behavior before it occurs. You prevent *dangerous behavior* when you cover an outlet or remove materials and equipment that are too difficult to use. You prevent *unacceptable behavior* when you adjust your daily routines to minimize noise, confusion, waiting, and large-group activities and to increase the time children can run and play outdoors. Here are some strategies for guiding children's behavior in positive ways as you help infants, toddlers, and twos learn to manage their feelings and behavior.

Give the big rule and the little rule. The big rule/little rule strategy for rules and limits involves stating one of your three or four main rules (the big rule) and pairing it with the very specific behavior in which you want the child to engage (the little rule).

Brooks says to Abby (14 months), "Be safe. Keep your bottom in the chair when you are sitting." "Be safe" is one of Brooks' four main rules, and "Keep your bottom in the chair when you are sitting" is the specific behavior she wants Abby to do.

Redirect children's behavior. Redirection provides children with an acceptable alternative to the unacceptable behavior they are engaged in. For example, give an infant a rubber toy to chew on when he picks up the piece of paper that was on the floor. Remind a toddler to climb on the climber instead of the table.

Offer two acceptable choices. Choices support a toddler's desire to be independent. They give children some control over what is happening. Make sure that both choices are acceptable to you and reasonable for the child. Do not offer an unrealistic or unacceptable choice, such as, "You may come with me now or you may stay alone on the playground."

Barbara tells Leo (18 months), "You may walk to the door by yourself, or you may hold my hand and we can walk to the door together."

Change the environment. This can involve moving a child to a new location. For example, you might gently pick up a baby who is crawling on a rough sidewalk and place him on the grass to crawl. As you do so, explain why you are moving him. Changing the environment can also mean changing something about the child's location. For example, when an infant starts rolling over, you might move some objects out of his way so that he can continue his activity. By observing children carefully, you will be able to determine what additions or changes you need to make to your room to support positive guidance.

Be specific. When you see children behaving appropriately, comment specifically. Rather than simply praising children by saying, "Good job," encourage children by explaining exactly what they are doing and why it is appropriate.

Abby (14 months) hands a cracker to Michael. Brooks says to her, "You are giving Michael a cracker. That makes him happy because he is hungry, too."

Model specific language. Help children who are beginning to speak by giving them the language they need. Telling children to "Use your words" is not helpful to toddlers and twos. They need you to give them the words to use and model how to use them.

Matthew (22 months) grabs a truck from a child who is holding two trucks. Mercedes coaches Matthew. "Say, 'I want a truck too, please.' Now you say it."

It is all right if his version sounds like "Truck, too, p'ease." The important thing is that he is learning to use words to convey his wants and needs.

Say, "When…then…" These statements explain to children the expected sequence of behaviors. It lets them know the appropriate next step.

LaToya says to Jonisha (33 months), "When you put on your shoes, then you may go outside."

Use the "tell and show" strategy. *Tell and show* involves telling children what they should do while showing them by using gestures and other visual cues.

Grace says, "We need to put our coats on before we can go outside," while she holds up the coat for Willard (11 months) to see.

You can also use this strategy to draw children's attention to other people's feelings.

Ivan says to Gena (30 months), "Look at Keisha's face. She is showing you that she doesn't like it when you take her teddy."

Make a reflective statement that begins with "I see…" This shows children that you are paying attention to what they are doing. Simply say exactly what you see happening. Letting children know that you notice them can sometimes be enough to stop challenging behaviors. Reflective statements can also encourage children's play and exploration.

LaToya approaches Valisha (33 months) in the block area, where Valisha has built a structure. LaToya says, "Valisha, I see you have used all of the square blocks. You have stacked them very high."

Say how you feel and why you feel that way. Use "I" statements. Such statements explain to a child what is happening, your feelings about the situation, and the reason for your feelings. They help children understand that their actions affect others. By labeling your own feelings, you help children learn names for feelings and support children's developing ability to empathize with others.

Brooks tells Abby (14 months), "I feel scared when you climb on the shelf, because you could fall and get hurt," as she helps her climb off the shelf.

Use your sense of humor. You can use humor to deflect tension, energize a child, and win his cooperation.

Mercedes makes a silly face and pretends to be a giant by taking large steps, on a day when Matthew (22 months) is whining and walking slowly back from the park.

When you take a positive approach to guiding children's behavior, you help children learn self-control and promote their self-esteem. However, some behaviors challenge your patience or upset you.

Responding to Challenging Behaviors

Physical aggression, temper tantrums, and biting are among the most common challenging behaviors. Many caring teachers struggle to deal with these behaviors every day.

The first step is to try to determine the cause of the behavior. Challenging behaviors are often cries for help. Children who use these behaviors may not know how to express their feelings in other ways. Toddlers and twos may not be able to use verbal language to express their anger or frustration. Focus on what the child needs, rather than on what she is doing. Try to imagine what the child might say if she could. Record your observations.

- What time of day did the behavior occur?
- Who was involved?
- What preceded the unwanted behavior?

As you collect and analyze your observations, you may find a pattern that will help you understand the cause of the behavior. You do not have to handle particularly challenging behaviors on your own. Talk with others who know the child well. A child's family and your co-teachers may have information to help you understand the child. A co-teacher may have noticed a pattern of behavior that you missed. The child's family may know about events at home or in the neighborhood that may be upsetting their child. Talking with families about challenging behaviors allows you to collaborate with them in providing the best care for their child at school and at home.

Physical Aggression

Physical aggression must be stopped immediately, and the victim must be given immediate attention. Intervene by positioning yourself on the aggressive child's level and clearly stating the rule about physical aggression. Involve the child in comforting the one who was hurt (if the hurt child permits this). When a child is physically aggressive and has lost control, you may need to hold her until she calms. Children are frightened when they lose control. Your firm hold can help the child feel safe because you have taken charge of the situation.

When children lose control, you can help them compose themselves by modeling calm behavior. Keep in mind that you cannot help children develop self-control if you are out of control. Screaming at children, isolating them with a time-out system, taking away privileges, and making them feel incompetent rarely produce positive results. **Physical punishment is never, ever acceptable**, nor is using food as a punishment (or reward). Use positive guidance strategies to avoid power struggles with toddlers and twos.

Remember that both the aggressor and the victim need your positive attention. When adults pay too much attention to the victim, the aggressive child feels isolated and guilty, and may continue to be aggressive in order get attention.

Temper Tantrums

Temper tantrums are not fun for anyone. They can leave children feeling exhausted and frightened at their loss of control. They can also make adults feel angry, incompetent, and even embarrassed.

If children could tell us what a tantrum feels like, they would probably describe it as a storm of frustration that sweeps in and overwhelms them. Remember that life can be very frustrating for toddlers and twos. Developmental theory suggests that they are learning about limits. They often struggle to accept the limits you set for them as well as the limits of their own abilities. In addition, they frequently find themselves caught between wanting to be a "big kid" and wanting to be a baby. One minute, they want you to hold them in your arms. The next, they become upset because they cannot put on their own shoes, carry a heavy bag of groceries home from the store, or get you to understand their words verbally.

Once a tantrum begins, there is often little you can do except keep the child from hurting himself or someone else and assure the child that you will help him. After he has calmed down, acknowledge his feelings in ways that show you accept him and his feelings: "Not being able to finish that puzzle really frustrated you! It is scary to be so angry." Suggest other ways to deal with the frustration: "Next time you are frustrated, you can ask me to help you." It is best to focus your energies on preventing tantrums.

Planning ahead to minimize temper tantrums will help avoid what can be a very stressful experience for children and for you. Here are some strategies to minimize their occurrence.

Give toddlers and twos plenty of opportunities to be competent. A competent child is less likely to have tantrums. Invite children to help you with everyday chores, such as setting the table. Offer them many opportunities to make choices about what to play with, wear, and eat. Label shelves with pictures so children can find what they want and help put materials away. Read children's cues to help you understand what they want to communicate and respond accordingly.

Minimize frustrations. Create an environment that is as free of frustration as possible. Set up an interesting, safe space that children can explore freely without constantly having you say, "No." Offer toys, games, and puzzles that match the changing abilities of the children in your care. Always make available familiar materials that children have played with successfully in the past.

Give children a chance to be comforted. Very young children need hugs and cuddles. Offer them when they are needed.

Anticipate children's physical needs. You can often prevent tantrums by doing such things as serving lunch before children get too hungry, helping children take naps before they become overly tired, and giving them a chance to play outdoors when they are ready for active play.

Biting

Biting is very common in groups of young children. It is always upsetting and can be frightening for children, parents, and teachers alike. As with tantrums, focus your energies on prevention. Observe so that you can anticipate when a child might bite, and redirect the child to a more appropriate situation or behavior. Understanding the reasons for biting will help you use effective strategies to prevent the behavior.[26]

Why Children Sometimes Bite	Strategies to Help Prevent Biting
Teething causes their mouths to hurt.	Offer children teething toys to mouth.
They are experimenting. An infant or young child may take an experimental bite to touch and taste other people and learn more about them.	Provide a wide variety of sensorimotor experiences to satisfy their curiosity, such as fingerpainting, playing with dough, preparing and eating food, or engaging in water and sand play.
They are exploring cause and effect, and they want to make something happen. Young children like to have an impact on their world. Biting is a sure way to do so.	Provide different activities and toys that respond to children's actions and help them learn about cause and effect. Show them other ways to affect their world by modeling verbal language.
They are trying to approach or interact with another child.	Give children many opportunities to interact with one another. Guide their behavior as necessary to encourage positive interactions.
They feel frustrated. Some children lack skills to cope with situations and feelings. When frustrated or angry, they bite.	Watch for signs of increasing frustration and potential conflict. You can often prevent harmful incidents by responding to children's needs promptly.
They are overwhelmed by too much noise, confusion, or excitement. Too much going on around them and intense emotion can make children feel out of control.	Be aware when noise, confusion, and excitement begin to escalate to the point that children feel out of control. Calm the situation and individual children as necessary.
They are asking for attention. They know that biting is one way to have people focus on them.	Reinforce positive social behavior. If children get attention when they are not biting, they will not have to use this negative behavior to feel noticed.
They are imitating behavior.	Model loving, supportive behavior. Offer children positive alternatives to negative behavior. **Never bite a child to show how it feels to be bitten.**
They feel threatened or feel that their possessions are being threatened. When some children feel that they are in danger, they bite in self-defense. When some children feel unable to protect their things, they bite.	Provide support and assurance so that the child recognizes that he and his possessions are safe.
They sense the increasing tension of their teachers and family members. As adults' tension increases, they are not as accessible to children. Children sense a loss of their secure base, and that sense makes them more likely to bite.	Recognize and explain to families that biting is an unfortunate fact of life in group care. Agree on steps you are taking to prevent biting. Help adults see how children quickly pick up their tension, making a bad situation worse.

Unfortunately, no matter how attentive you are, it is likely that a child in your program will bite another child sooner or later. Here are suggestions for that moment.

Respond to the situation promptly. As soon as an incident takes place, you must take immediate action.

- Comfort the child who was bitten.

- Wash the wound. Apply an ice pack to help keep bruising down. If the skin is broken, follow the universal precautions for handling blood, which include wearing nonporous disposable gloves and recommend that both sets of parents notify their pediatrician and follow his or her advice.

- State clearly that biting is not all right. Speak firmly and seriously. However, avoid being overly dramatic to ensure that your response does not make the act of biting more interesting and appealing. Do not use your voice to punish the child by making her feel guilty.

- Invite the child who bit to help you care for the bitten child (unless the child who was bitten seems afraid of the child who bit). This gives the child the opportunity to help and to leave the role of aggressor. Use these moments to offer the biter support and to teach caring behavior. Remember, from the biter's point of view, it is scary to be so out of control that he hurts someone.

- Help the child who bit understand that there are other ways to express anger and frustration, such as using words or growling like a tiger.

Document biting injuries. Include the name of the child who was bitten, as well as the date, time, and location of the incident. Describe how the injury occurred and the actions you took. This information will be helpful in identifying patterns. It will also help you keep the situation in perspective.

Acknowledge your own feelings so you do not add more tension to the situation. Of course you are upset when a child is hurt, but children are quick to notice your feelings. Biting can be particularly frustrating for you, because it can occur despite your preventive measures. Talk with colleagues about biting and help one another maintain emotional balance.

Hold onto your positive vision of the child. When a child is biting, adults tend to focus solely on the negative behavior. They may refer to the child as "The Problem" or even "The Mouth." A child who is biting is a child in distress. He or she needs your care and support.

Make and carry out an ongoing prevention and intervention plan. Here are some positive steps you can take.

- Observe carefully to identify patterns of instances when biting occurs. For example, is the child more likely to bite before lunch? Does the child bite when things get very loud and confusing?

- Ask the child's family about what might be going on at home. Find out if there have been any recent changes. Talk together about how you might help the child stop biting.

- Decide on a plan. For example, if you notice that a child tends to bite when things get hectic, plan to spend extra one-on-one time with her before she is overstimulated.

- Have someone focus on the child who is biting, ideally someone who knows and enjoys the child. This person should be available to the child all day, to provide support, encourage positive behavior, and, of course, to be ready to step in quickly and to keep the child from biting.

- Observe. Keep track of what is happening. Adapt your plan as necessary.

Help parents understand the situation. Because biting can upset all parents in a program, address this issue before it occurs. Discuss with parents the many reasons why children might bite and describe the various preventive steps. Share strategies that families can use at home to prevent and deal with biting. Invite families to share their strategies with you. Always remember that biting the child back "to see what it feels like" is never an option. If biting does occur, talk with parents directly and openly. Acknowledge their feelings. Consider inviting a community health specialist to meet with parents to address health concerns.

Seek help if biting continues or grows more intense. Although a child's biting usually does not continue long, biting sometimes signals that a child needs special assistance. If you become concerned, call in a community resource person, such as a developmental specialist, to help you explore interventions.

While guiding children's behavior may sometimes appear to be taking up too much of your time, it is an important part of your work with infants, toddlers, and twos. As you help children learn to control their behavior, you build a solid foundation for their positive interactions with others. Keep in mind that there is a reason underlying all behavior. Children who misbehave may not feel safe or connected to others. They may lack a foundation of trust. They need adults who care for and form positive relationships with them. They need opportunities to express their fears and anger appropriately, through dabbling in art, imitating and pretending, storytelling, and talking with caring adults. They need you to remain calm and helpful.

Guiding Children's Learning

Infants, toddlers, and twos are naturally curious. Sometimes they pay attention to what you want them to notice, but sometimes they do not. Sometimes they learn what you intend for them to understand, but they often follow their own interests.

Willard (11 months) *is more interested in how the oatmeal box drum rolls down the slide—a lesson in physics—than in playing it during a music experience Grace offered last week. During a walk to a nearby park,* **Valisha** *and* **Jonisha** (33 months) *are so interested in the squirrels that they pay little attention to LaToya's suggestion that they collect leaves of various colors.*

Working with infants, toddlers, and twos means guiding their learning in ways that let children experience the pleasure, excitement, and sense of competence that accompanies exploration and making discoveries. Positive experiences motivate children to continue learning.

As they engage in routines day after day, children collect, organize, and reorganize information about themselves, other people, and things. That is how they develop understandings that help them make sense of the world. Chapters 6–9 provide extensive information about guiding learning during routines.

In addition to the learning that occurs during daily routines, you promote learning as you offer a variety of experiences to the children in your care.

Barbara notices Leo's (18 months) *fascination with the water as he washes his hands. She guides him to the water table, where he can pour water over his hands and arms. That is an experience in exploring sand and water. When* **Janet** *offers Jasmine a sheet of waxed paper to crumple during lunch and says, "You've crumpled the paper into a ball," she is providing an experience in creating with art.*

As children become more skilled, you will offer more planned and more small-group experiences that you initiate and guide. Chapters 11–18 offer ideas about appropriate materials and experiences for young infants, mobile infants, toddlers, and twos.

Learning Through Play

Children play throughout the day during routines and experiences. Their play takes many forms, for example, dropping a spoon off the table again and again, crawling in and out of a cardboard box, exploring the way different fabrics feel, climbing in and out of a chair, and singing a simple song. Play is filled with opportunities for children to develop and learn new skills.

Play offers children opportunities to

- make choices

- make decisions

- solve problems

- interact with one another

- interact with you

- pursue their interests

- experience learning as fun and exciting

- experience themselves as capable, competent, successful learners

- build language and literacy skills, discover mathematical relationships, and be a scientist

As you interact with children throughout the day, think about ways to encourage their efforts and when and how to intervene thoughtfully to support their learning. Follow each child's lead as you decide when to watch, when to step in, and how to lead the child to the next discovery.

Julio (4 months) is reaching for a colorful toy with his right hand. Linda puts a similar toy just within reach of his left hand. *Willard* (11 months) pulls to standing at a cruising rail. Grace encourages him to side step along the railing. *Matthew* (22 months) says, "Me want milk." Mercedes responds, "Oh, you want some more milk. Here it is."

Sometimes, though, the best option is to watch, listen, and give children the time and space to explore on their own. Learning requires attention, time, and practice. In their efforts to help children, teachers sometimes interrupt, distract, and assume control of children's activities. Watching and listening helps ensure that you do not unintentionally interfere with a child's learning. Here are some questions to help you determine when to step in and when to step back.

Are children engaged? If children are focused and busy, your intervention is probably not needed. When children begin moving frequently from toy to toy, wandering aimlessly, or interfering with others' activities, your assistance is required.

Are children stuck? Are they repeating the same activity with little or no variation for an extended time? Young children gain mastery by repeating activities. Yet, when the same activity is repeated in the same way for too long a time, it can be a sign of boredom that may be interfering with learning.

Are there information and skills that require explicit teaching? Sometimes direct teaching makes the most sense.

Ivan shows Gena (30 months) how to sit more steadily by putting her feet on a wooden step. *LaToya* shows Valisha and Jonisha (33 months) how to put on their coats by flipping them over their heads.

Are children in danger? Balance concerns for children's safety with their need to explore. Evaluate whether you frequently say *no* to children in an effort to protect them. While children's safety should never be compromised, children need opportunities to experiment, explore their surroundings, and take reasonable risks.

Talking With Infants, Toddlers, and Twos

Chapter 3, *What Children Are Learning*, discusses the importance of promoting children's language and literacy skills. Through the back-and-forth verbal and nonverbal interactions you have with children every day, you help them build their receptive and expressive language skills and learn to have conversations. (You might take turns acting and speaking.) Here are some strategies to use as you talk with children and examples of what you might say when it is your turn to speak.

Describe what a child is seeing or doing: *You dropped the ball, and it rolled onto the rug.*

Verbalize children's emotions: *You are smiling. Digging in the sand makes you happy.*

Use words to show the value you place on learning and problem solving: *You had a good idea. Blowing on the hot noodles makes them cooler.*

Express ideas that children will come to understand over time and with experience: *The dog is barking really loudly.*

Provide vocabulary: *That flower is called a* chrysanthemum. *That word has lots of sounds! Say it with me: chry-san-the-mum.*

Build their confidence as learners: *You are learning where those puzzle pieces go.*

Ask children open-ended questions to extend their thinking. For example:

- To promote exploration: *What do you see, hear, feel?*
- To stretch their thinking about causes and effects: *What do you think will happen if you drop this spoon into the water?*
- To help them think about similarities and differences: *How are these two things the same? Which of these go together?*
- To apply knowledge to solve a problem: *How can we fix the torn page in the book?*

Extending Children's Knowledge and Skills

Each of the children in your group has already acquired knowledge and skills. Using the *Developmental Continuum* will help you identify what each child knows and can do. Building on this base will help children be competent, successful learners. Here are a few suggestions to keep in mind.

Use the *Developmental Continuum* to help you see the next steps in the development of children's knowledge and skills. Knowing the sequence of developmental steps guides your decisions about how to help each child progress.

Barbara observes that Leo (18 months) often uses objects in pretend play as they are used in real life (Objective 15, Step 3). She sees that Step 4 is "Substitutes one object for another in pretend play." Barbara therefore substitutes a block for a cell phone and a cup for a boat when she pretends with him.

Balance the familiar with the new and interesting. Small changes or additions to familiar materials and activities enhance children's experiences and often lead to new discoveries and learning.

Matthew (22 months) loves to paint. To give him and others a new experience with painting, Mercedes gives children buckets of water and large brushes to use on the side of the building. This gives Matthew a chance to handle a large brush, make large strokes, and gain a new understanding of the word big.

Plan experiences and interact with children on the basis of what they know and are able to do and what they are ready to try. Offering an enthusiastic word, changing the environment, or gently assisting are ways you can encourage children to something new.

Janet puts out her hands for Jasmine (8 months) to use to pull herself up. She supports Jasmine in her desire to be upright.

Including All Children

All of the children in your care will benefit from the teaching and caring approaches discussed in *The Creative Curriculum*. Some children will need a little extra support from you because they are learning more than one language or because they have a disability.

Dual Language Learners

Language learning is an amazing process, and it is even more astonishing when a child under age 3 is learning more than one language. Children may come from a home where they are exposed to two languages. Perhaps one family member speaks to them in Spanish or Chinese, while another always speaks to them in English. Some children hear one language at home and a second language in your program. In both instances, the children are learning two languages at the same time. In simultaneous dual language situations, it is best if each person consistently uses the same language with the child—for example, always Spanish or always English—rather than switching back and forth between the languages.

Children who are learning two languages go through several stages in their learning. Initially, they may mix the languages together, weaving words together from both languages. This use of both languages in one phrase or sentence is called *code-switching*. This stage continues until children are about 30 months old, when they learn to separate the languages, addressing each person with whom they talk in the appropriate language. Children at this stage learn and repeat common phrases that they hear frequently, such as "wanna play," or "gimme the ball." These imitative patterns of speech help children interact with others and are some of the building blocks of language learning.

It is important to support the child's first language in your program, if possible. If some teachers in your program speak the child's home language (other than English), you can adopt the "one person, one language" strategy in which one teacher always speaks the home language while the other always uses English. This strategy is less confusing for children than if each teacher uses multiple languages. It also ensures that children have good language models in each language.

You and your co-teachers should not interpret for each other. For example, when the English-speaking teacher announces that it is time to put on jackets and get ready to go outside, the Spanish-speaking teacher should not repeat the directions in Spanish. Simultaneous interpretation encourages children to ignore English because they know they will soon hear the same information in their primary language. A more effective method is for the teacher to use gestures, body language, and other visual cues that will help the child understand the verbal message. (See chapter 13, *Enjoying Stories and Books*, for information about reading books to children who are dual language learners.)

You can do a number of things if you do not have teachers who speak children's home languages. First, help the child feel comfortable in your program. Communicate nonverbally. Use gestures and simple language. Find out if a family member or other adult who speaks the child's first language can volunteer in your program. Help children know that you value their language by learning caring phrases and common words in the language even if you are not able to speak more of it. Try to provide books and music in the languages of the children in your room. Foster conversations among children in their home languages. Teach English-speaking children some words in another language as well. Assure families that continuing to speak their first language at home will help their children become bilingual.

Children With Disabilities

All children need to be included and successful. Much, if not all, of what you have learned in this chapter can be applied to your work with children who have diagnosed disabilities or other special needs. For this to happen, you must look beyond the specific diagnosis to see what effects it has on a particular child. You must be careful not to generalize about children on the basis of their diagnoses.

See children as children first. Learn about each child's strengths and interests first, and then consider the child's special needs. Use language that reinforces your understanding of this. For example, speak about a child with autism, rather than an autistic child.

Learn about the effects of a specific disability to decide what, if any, adjustments you need to make. For example, a child with a visual impairment relies more heavily on her senses of hearing and touch for communication. When offered choices, it will be helpful for her to touch each item and hear about the choices. A child with a hearing impairment relies heavily on his sense of sight for communication. It may be useful for you to learn sign language and to use cards with pictures of routines, experiences, and materials so that you can communicate with him. A child with a brain injury may need more time to think about what you are saying and to transition from one activity to another. Slowing your conversations and actions may help engage this child. A child with physical limitations needs you to remove physical barriers that might limit her mobility. When you help her move, she will feel respected if you explain what you are doing and why.

Work closely with children's families. The parents of a child with a disability are your greatest sources of support and information. Ask them to share what they know about their child's condition. Invite them also to share tips and strategies they use at home.

Gena's parents helped Ivan learn to position Gena (30 months) in ways that give her the best possible control over her body.

Ask parents about their involvement with the local early intervention program. If they are unaware of local services, give them the necessary information. See chapter 5, *A Partnership With Families*, for more information about supporting families of children with disabilities.

Set goals and work with a specialist. Use the goals and objectives from a child's Individual Family Service Plan and from the *Developmental Continuum* to guide your work with the child. (See chapter 1, *Knowing Infants, Toddlers, and Twos*, for more information about this.) Many objectives will be the same as those you have for all children, so many ways of supporting the child will fit easily into your regular planning and daily schedule. For other objectives, you might need to add special toys and adaptive equipment, or you might need to change strategies (such as blinking the lights to catch the attention of a deaf child). These adaptations and strategies should be included in the child's plan. As with all children, you should observe continually and assess the goals and objectives that have been identified, adapting them as necessary. With parental permission, work with the child's specialist(s) to develop strategies that will work in your program.

Encourage, but do not force, appropriate independence. Some children need extra support to develop skills and self-confidence. Competence is important for all children. Recognize, however, that some children may have needs beyond your experience and expertise. If this is the case, seek the help of specialists in your community. Your willingness to learn about various disabilities and reach out to experts will set a good model for the children and adults in your program.

Help children with disabilities engage in play with other children. Remember that sometimes children with disabilities do not initiate play as often as other children. They may need more support to begin playing and more help while they play.

Assessing Children's Development and Learning

Assessment is the process of gathering and analyzing information about children in order to make decisions. In *The Creative Curriculum*, caring, teaching, and assessing are linked.

Assessment works best when it is tied closely to curriculum goals and objectives. *The Creative Curriculum Developmental Continuum for Infants, Toddlers & Twos* was designed specifically for this purpose. Using the *Developmental Continuum* will help you observe children in the context of everyday routines and experiences. You will be able to assess each child's current level of development and to think about likely next steps. Then you can plan for each child and the group. As you learn about each child's strengths, interests, and developmental timetable, you can use the information and strategies in *The Creative Curriculum* to build responsive relationships and to offer experiences that promote each child's development and learning.

If you are using the *Developmental Continuum* Assessment System, refer to the *Teacher's Guide* that comes with the Assessment Toolkit, either as a printed document or the online version. The *Teacher's Guide* explains the system and how to use all of the forms that help you link assessment with guiding children's development and learning.

If you are using a different assessment system, be sure that it is compatible with *The Creative Curriculum*'s goals and objectives for children. Your assessment system should be based on your ongoing observations of each child. You therefore need to have systems for taking and organizing observation notes and for collecting items for children's portfolios. Once you have established your systems for observation notes and for maintaining portfolios, you can proceed through the four steps in the assessment process: (1) collecting facts, (2) analyzing and evaluating the collected facts, (3) using what you have learned, and (4) sharing information about a child's progress.

Setting Up Systems for Observing and for Creating Portfolios

Having a system in place for taking and managing observation notes is essential. It will keep you organized and save you time. Keep your system as simple as possible so it works well for you. Here are some ideas that have worked for other teachers.

Use mailing labels or sticky notes to record your observations. At the beginning of the day, place three or four notes or labels on a clipboard with the names of the children whom you wish to observe. Keep the clipboard handy. At the end of the day, transfer the completed notes or labels to each child's file.

Draw a grid on the inside of a folder. Include 3–6 boxes or as many as the number of children in your primary care group. Write a different child's name in each box on the grid. Keep sticky notes in your pocket or near the folder. After writing an observation note about a child, place it in the box with that child's name. Make duplicate folders for various areas of the room.

Develop your own system of shorthand so you can record information quickly. Write brief notes, using short phrases and abbreviating whenever possible. You can emphasize words by underlining them.

You do not need to write an observation note for every child, every day. You may find it easiest to focus on one or two children per day. Remember that you do not need to record everything that happens and everything that a child says and does.

You also need a system for organizing your observation notes. While there are a variety of ways to organize them, many teachers find the following approach useful:

1. Purchase a large loose-leaf notebook and include a tabbed divider for each child in your group.

   In the front of the binder, place a copy of the *Goals and Objectives at a Glance* inside a protective plastic cover.

   Next, insert a copy of the *Developmental Continuum* to use as a reference.

2. Behind each tab in the notebook, insert an *Individual Child Profile* and four blank pages.

   Head each blank page by writing one of these goals: *To learn about self and others, To learn about moving, To learn about the world,* or *To learn about communicating.* You may want use a different color of paper for each goal.

   Later, you will use these pages to sort and store your observation notes for each child.

An *Observation Tracking Form* will help you record which children you have observed and the related objectives. It includes space for the children in your primary care group. Updating it on a regular basis will enable you to focus your observations and to follow children's progress.

In addition to documenting your observations by keeping written records, another major way to collect information about children over time is to keep a portfolio for each child. A portfolio is a collection of items that document a child's interests, skills, accomplishments, and approaches to learning. These create a profile of the child and his learning over time. Portfolios for infants, toddlers, and twos contain items such as photographs, scribbles, paintings, and video- or audioclips.

Next, consider storage. Pocket folders are fine for photographs, drawings, and scribbles, but you might want to use accordion files or shallow boxes for items such as paintings or video- and audioclips. You can even create a large file folder by folding and stapling tagboard.

Collecting Facts

Once you have your systems in place for taking and organizing observation notes and for collecting and storing portfolio items, you can begin documenting what you observe. This is the first step in using the *Developmental Continuum* for ongoing assessment. You collect facts by observing children and writing notes about what they do and say, by maintaining a portfolio for each child, and by exchanging information with families.

How, When, and What to Observe

There will be many opportunities to observe and learn about children every day. Most of your observations occur during daily routines and experiences. Take a moment to think about what you notice. You are likely to see behaviors that relate to specific *Creative Curriculum* objectives. For instance, you might be sitting on the floor, singing and gesturing with two mobile infants. As you sing, you note how children interact with one another (Objective 5) and whether children imitate your actions (Objective 15). Keep some file cards or sticky notes handy so you can record what you see and hear at the time.

In addition to spontaneous, informal observations, try to schedule regular formal observation times. Formal observations involve watching one or more children systematically and recording what you see and hear. This way of observing allows you to slow down and notice things you might otherwise miss. Try to arrange with your co-teacher or a family volunteer to be with the children so you can be free to observe.

You may follow one child for a period of time and record all of the behaviors you observe. Another approach is to observe a group of children and document the behavior of several children. Later you can identify which objectives apply. There may be times when you want to observe a child with a particular objective in mind. Your observation notes yield rich information that will help you in your later analysis and evaluation.

To be useful, observation notes must be objective and factual. When your notes include words like *fussy, shy, aggressive, hyperactive,* or *angry,* they reveal your interpretation of what a child did or said, not simply the facts. Judgmental words may or may not accurately record what took place. Interpretations, impressions, or assumptions include

- labels (for example, *shy, vivacious, creative*)
- intentions (for example, *wants to…*)
- evaluations (for example, *good job*)
- judgments (for example, *beautiful, sloppy*)
- negatives (for example, *didn't, can't, won't*)

Objective, factual observation notes collected over time provide a picture of a child's development and learning. Objective notes include only the facts about what you see and hear. Factual observations include

- descriptions of actions
- quotations of language
- descriptions of gestures
- descriptions of facial expressions
- descriptions of creations

Compare the two following examples of observation notes about an infant during drop-off time.

Example 1
Jasmine is being so fussy and manipulative. Every time I put her down, she starts crying again to get her way.

Example 1 is not an objective note. It uses labels (*fussy* and *manipulative*) and includes an intention (*to get her way*).

Now consider another note about the same event.

Example 2
Jasmine cried for 30 minutes after arriving. She gradually stopped crying when I held her and we sat in the glider.

Example 2 is an objective note. It includes only the facts about what Jasmine did (*cried for 30 minutes after arriving*) and what happened (*stopped crying when I held her*). Accurate notes include all the facts about what a child did and said, in the order they happened.

Writing objective notes takes practice. The more aware you are of what objective notes are like, the more skilled you will become at writing them.

Here are two examples of objective observation notes.

<u>Valisha— 9/8</u>

V picked up scissors; began to cut paper. Moved scissor blades back and forth. Couldn't get paper to cut; scissors crumpled paper. V frowned and dropped scissors on table. V stared at scissors; said nothing. Picked up same piece of paper. Began tearing it with hands.

<u>Willard—10/30</u>

Crawled to bookshelf. Put both hands on shelf; pulled himself to standing. Pulled two books off shelf. Turned around and looked at me. I shook my head, "No." Then W lowered himself to floor and crawled to nearby truck.

To use observation notes for later analysis and evaluation, teachers need multiple observations about each of the objectives. For example, you will need several observation notes that document how a child shows his trust of known, caring adults (Objective 1). If observations are recorded during hellos and good-byes, eating and mealtimes, and during pretend play, you can draw valid conclusions about which developmental step a child has reached. You can also examine your notes to see whether or not a particular behavior on a particular day indicated the child's general level of development.

Maintaining a Portfolio for Each Child

While you do not need a large number of items to complete the child's profile, you do need a variety. Each sample can reveal a great deal of information about the child's development. For example, if you include a photo of a child washing baby dolls in a tub of water, you will know that the child

- knows what a bath is
- knows how to wash a doll's face and body
- can do some things on his own
- persists with a task

When you collect photographs and other samples for children's portfolios, be sure to write a note about what was occurring at the time. Also remember to date the note. For example, the photo of the child washing dolls does not show that he carefully wiped the doll's eyes and said, "No soap." It also does not show that, when he finished washing the doll, he got a towel and patted the doll dry. You need to supplement the portfolio sample with a written note that completes the documentation.

To show a child's development and learning, it is important to collect similar samples over a period of time. For instance, comparing what a child does with crayons over time is one excellent way to identify development. However, it is hard to document development if you compare a single sample of scribbling, a photograph of a block construction, and a video of the child preparing carrots for a snack.

At the beginning of the year, think of two or three types of items that would be good for documenting growth in each goal area. Plan to collect similar samples periodically throughout the year. For example, you might include dated photographs of a child when he is watching and interacting with other children and dated samples of a child's paintings.

If you are comfortable with and have access to the necessary tools, you can photocopy or scan children's scribbles; take photographs to capture a child's involvement in an activity; audiotape a child's use of language; or videotape a child engaged in pretend play, reading a book, or, as in the earlier example, giving a doll a bath.

Date the items you have collected and then file them by the same goals as you use to file your observation notes: *To learn about self and others, To learn about moving, To learn about the world,* and *To learn about communicating.* This will make reviewing your documentation easier when it is time to evaluate the child's progress.

Analyzing Facts

The next step in the assessment process is to sort the observation notes you have collected and to organize your notes for each child by goal area. At the end of each day, or at least several times a week, take out the group loose-leaf notebook you created and follow these steps:

1. Collect all the notes you have about one child.

2. Review the notes about the child and decide to what goal each observation note most closely relates. Make a copy of the note if it applies to more than one goal.

3. Affix the notes to the appropriate pages in the child's section of your notebook.

Now you are ready to analyze the facts. Regularly ask yourself, "What does this observation tell me about the child's development and learning?" Refer to the *Developmental Continuum* and decide which objectives apply. Record the numbers of the objectives on the note or on the back of the portfolio item. Here is how you might analyze the sample observation notes that were presented earlier.

Valisha—9/8

V picked up scissors; began to cut paper. Moved scissor blades back and forth. Couldn't get paper to cut; scissors crumpled paper. V frowned and dropped scissors on table. V stared at scissors; said nothing. Picked up same piece of paper. Began tearing it with hands.

#9, #3, #10, #11, #14

This observation note about Valisha is related to Objective 9, "Demonstrates basic fine motor skills." You would write #9 on the note and place it in Valisha's section of the notebook, on the page headed "To learn about moving."

The note also gives information about Valisha's emotional development, particularly about Objective 3, "Manages own feelings." You would also record #3, and file a copy on Valisha's page headed "To learn about self and others."

Then you would add *#10, #11,* and *#14* and file another copy on Valisha's page headed "To learn about the world." This is because the behavior you documented is also related to those objectives ("Sustains attention," "Understands how objects can be used," and "Uses problem-solving strategies").

Willard—10/30

Crawled to bookshelf. Put both hands on shelf; pulled himself to standing. Pulled two books off shelf. Turned around and looked at me. I shook my head, "No." Then W lowered himself to floor and crawled to nearby truck.

#8, #2, #16

The observation note about Willard also provides information about at least three objectives. It gives you information about Objective 8, "Demonstrates basic gross motor skills"; Objective 2, "Regulates own behavior"; and Objective 16, "Develops receptive language." You might place the note in the observation notebook under physical development, but it can also be used to evaluate Willard on Objectives 2 and 16.

Evaluating Each Child's Progress

Evaluating a child's progress means thinking about all 21 objectives and deciding which developmental step describes the child's level of development for each. You need to consider all the documentation you have collected, including your observation notes and the child's portfolio. Examine the information for each objective. Using the *Developmental Continuum,* think about what the child did and said, and decide which of the five steps best represents the child's skill level for the objective. If you are in a group setting with co-teachers, you may want to do this together or at least discuss your findings.

To understand the evaluation process, consider the observation note about Willard that was presented previously. This note gives you information about Objective 2, "Regulates own behavior." The note reminds you that Willard looked at you after taking books from the shelf. He did not pull more books off the shelf after you shook your head, "No." In terms of Objective 2, this note records an example of a Step 2 behavior, "Uses others' facial expressions, gestures or voices to guide own behavior."

You would not make a final determination about Willard's developmental step on the basis of this single observation. You would review several observation notes and any portfolio items related to Objective 2. If the additional notes and items show Step 2 behaviors, you would choose Step 2 of Objective 2.

Evaluate each child's development on all 21 objectives in this way. While a child's skill level is likely to be the same for many objectives, children may be more advanced in one developmental area than another. For example, a particular child may be at Step 1 for one objective and Step 2 for another.

At your program's checkpoints, use the *Individual Child Profile* to record your decisions about the steps that describe the child's development. Although you observe children every day, you complete the *Individual Child Profile* for each child three or four times a year, coinciding with your parent conferences.

Assessing the progress of a child with a disability requires careful consideration of the objectives and steps. Consider how the child is progressing toward achieving the objective while using whatever modifications, adaptations, assistive devices, or assistive technologies are necessary.

Using What You Have Learned to Plan

The Developmental Continuum outlines important aspects of the amazing progress a child makes during the first 3 years of life. You collect a wealth of information that you can use to consider the next steps in the child's development. This knowledge informs the many decisions you make as you implement *The Creative Curriculum* and plan for each child. Here are some examples of how three teachers use what they learn to plan.

> When Jasmine (8 months) raises her bottle as the level of milk drops, she is doing much more than getting a drink. She is starting to show a beginning understanding of cause and effect. She is discovering that repeated actions yield similar effects (Objective 12, Step 2). To help her explore cause and effect, I will provide toys that she can use to make something happen. I will also talk with her so she hears the language that describes what she is doing. — *Janet*

> Leo (18 months) insists on staying in my lap when a maintenance worker comes into the room. He is using me as a secure base around new people (Objective 1, Step 3). I can build on his trust in me by continuing to be available to him when he needs me, by learning more about him, and by responding in ways that help him to be safe and competent. — *Barbara*

> Based on my observations, I know that Matthew (22 months) is making connections between the stories in books and in his own life (Objective 19, Step 4). Tomorrow we are therefore going to make a book together about his new goldfish. Finding and writing books about people, animals, and events that Matthew knows and cares about will encourage him to keep exploring books. — *Mercedes*

As you can see, teachers' purposeful observations of children help them make daily decisions about what an individual child might need. Even more valuable is the comprehensive picture of development you obtain when you summarize all of your observations for each child in relation to the 21 curriculum objectives several times a year. Because the *Developmental Continuum* covers all areas of development, it gives you a developmental portrait of the whole child.

> LaToya is summarizing all of her observations of Jonisha in order to prepare for a conference with her family. She begins by reviewing Jonisha's progress in relation to Goal 1, "To learn about self and others" (Objectives 1–7). She thinks about Jonisha's strengths and challenges in terms of these seven objectives. Her summary gives her insight into how to further Jonisha's social/emotional development.
>
> Next, LaToya looks at what she learned about Jonisha in relation to Goal 2, "To learn about moving" (Objectives 8–9). She notes what Jonisha is able to do and where she needs extra support. Then she does the same for Goal 3, "To learn about the world" (Objectives 10–15) and Goal 4, "To learn about communicating" (objectives 16–21). For each developmental area, LaToya summarizes Jonisha's development in three or four sentences.
>
> Together, the summaries of Jonisha's development in each of the four areas give LaToya a good idea of Jonisha's overall development. She has a picture of what Jonisha has accomplished and where her skills are emerging. This knowledge will help LaToya think about daily interactions and experiences that will promote her continued development and learning. Chapter 5, *A Partnership With Families*, discusses ways to share this information with families and to develop a plan together.

Weekly planning forms, including the *Child Planning Form* and the *Group Planning Form* are explained in chapter 2, *Creating a Responsive Environment*. *The Creative Curriculum for Infants, Toddlers and Twos Developmental Continuum* Assessment System includes additional forms to help in the assessment process. Teachers who are using a different assessment system will need to summarize the information they have collected by using other forms.

Conclusion

The essence of caring for and teaching infants, toddlers, and twos is building responsive and caring relationships with each child. What makes your work so satisfying and enjoyable is being able to appreciate and find joy in the everyday discoveries that delight a child. As you observe and get to know each child, you reflect and respond to his strengths, needs, and interests; purposefully guide his behavior; support his learning; and use ongoing assessment to document his progress and to plan. Families are your partners in caring for and teaching infants, toddlers, and twos. We turn to this topic in the next chapter.

inside this chapter

Knowing Infants, Toddlers & Twos

Creating a Responsive Environment

Experiences

Playing with toys

Imitating and pretending

Enjoying stories and books

Connecting with music and movement

Creating with art

Tasting and preparing food

Exploring sand and water

Going outdoors

Routines

Hellos and good-byes

Diapering and toileting

Eating and mealtimes

Sleeping and nap time

Getting dressed

Partnering With Families

What Children Are Learning

Caring and Teaching

Theory and Research

5 Building Partnerships With Families

Very young children come to your program with their families. To serve them well, you must develop meaningful partnerships with their families. In a true partnership, families and caregivers bring equal value to the relationship, and they do so to benefit the child.

Taking care of children under age 3 means that you are *sharing the care* with families. The issues you must discuss and agree upon with families are rooted in strong beliefs and practices. The partnership you create together is an essential factor in how infants, toddlers, and twos experience child care and how much they gain from the experience.

This chapter explains the fifth component of *The Creative Curriculum for Infants, Toddlers & Twos* and offers practical ideas for working with families to develop partnerships based on trust and mutual respect. It has six sections:

Special Concerns of Families With Children Under Age 3 discusses the stress of parenting an infant, conflicting feelings about sharing care, and the desire of family members to be part of their child's day.

Getting to Know Families explores differences between families and the influence of culture upon child-rearing practices.

Welcoming Families to Your Program suggests ways to create a welcoming environment and to orient new families to the program. It also explains how to develop an *Individual Care Plan* and the importance of reaching out to all family members.

Communicating With Families show how mutual trust is built through daily interactions with families. It suggests ways to make the most of daily exchanges, more formal communication, conferences, and home visits.

Involving Families in the Program explains a variety of ways to encourage the involvement and participation of family members.

Responding to Challenging Situations presents a partnership approach to resolving differences with families, working through conflicts, supporting families who are under stress, and assisting the families of children with disabilities.

Special Concerns of Families With Children Under Age 3

Think about what it means for new parents to be considering your program for their infant, toddler, or 2-year-old. If they put their thoughts into words, they might ask you these questions:

Will my child...

- be safe and free from harm?
- receive a lot of attention?
- feel comfortable and happy in this child care program?
- be with adults who are warm, loving, and responsive?
- still love me best?
- miss me when we are apart?
- have interesting things to see and to do?
- learn to get along with other children?
- hear lots of language?
- be with adults who know and respect our family?

These questions reflect the uncertainties and fears that parents often experience when they seek child care for their infant, toddler, or 2-year-old. Everything you do to assure families that you and your program will respond positively to their concerns will encourage the trust and confidence essential to building a partnership. Begin by thinking about what parents are feeling during this exciting but vulnerable period of their lives.

The Stress of Parenting an Infant

Being the parent of an infant takes energy. Not only are new parents often confused by their child's behavior and unsure of what to do, but they are also very, very tired. Lack of sleep makes it easy for new parents to lose perspective and to despair that they can ever learn as much as they need to know. When a parent is very young, single, or worried about having enough money to provide essentials, the tension is significant. The stress that parents experience as they prepare for a day of work, get their children ready for the day, and cope with traffic is a major challenge. They sometimes arrive at child care feeling anxious and exhausted.

Some families are comfortable about sharing their feelings and asking you for the support they need. Others are not. They may be too overwhelmed with the changes in their lives. They might not yet trust you, or they might view asking for help as a sign of failure. You can be helpful because you communicate with families every day. If you listen carefully, you may be able to figure out how best to offer help. For example, sometimes your help will be to reassure parents that what they are experiencing is very common and that things will become easier. Sometimes you will offer parents places to sit and read with their children before leaving for work.

Conflicting Feelings About Sharing Care

Placing an infant, toddler, or 2-year-old in a child care program often involves conflicting feelings. Some parents feel relieved when they find a high-quality child care program with a professional and trustworthy staff. At the same time, it is not unusual for new parents to feel sorrow, guilt, or even fear about sharing the care of their child with people they do not know well. They may regret their need to return to work and worry about all they will miss each day. They may even worry that their child will like you better than she likes them. These feelings can be stressful for parents.

You may also have mixed feelings about sharing care. Because working with infants, toddlers, and twos is such passionate work, it is natural to feel deeply protective and attached to young children. You may begin to feel a bit competitive with a parent.

Parents and teachers each play an important but different role in a child's life. Children know who is who. Parents are the most important people to a child. Their relationship is forever. It is built upon a deep trust and a love unlike any other. No matter how skilled and experienced you are, you can never take the place of a parent.

With these conflicting feelings in mind, you can understand how vital it is to reassure parents who have young children in child care that they are the most important people in their child's life and that their role is primary.

Wanting to Be a Part of Their Child's Day

Children change so quickly during their first 3 years that many parents wonder if they will miss important events in their child's life. For this reason, the conversations you have with their families are often personal and intense. You can expect them to want to know all that happens during the time their children are in your care. They want details about what and how much they ate, how well they slept, when they had diaper changes, what toys they played with, and how they related to other children and adults.

However, there is one major exception to your need to share information. No one wants to miss one of his child's "firsts." For example, if you see the first time a child sits up or takes first steps, you may not want to share this information fully. Instead, consider saying something like this: "Tyrone pulled himself up a lot today! I have a feeling that he is about to take his first step. I'll be curious to know what happens over the weekend. I'm going to remember to ask you on Monday morning." Then write yourself a note so you do not forget to ask what happened.

Getting to Know Families

Just as you get to know each child and use what you learn to build a relationship, you begin building partnerships with families by getting to know the most important people in each child's life. By being familiar with the unique characteristics, strengths, and issues important to each family, you can find ways to build the necessary trust and respect. Begin by recognizing the many ways families differ and the profound influence of each family's culture.

Appreciating Differences Among Families

Every family is different. The traditional family—two parents and their children—is not as common as it once was. Many children are growing up with one parent. Some are being reared by grandparents or other relatives. Other children live with two mothers or two fathers. To appreciate differences among the families you serve, start by keeping an open mind about what constitutes a family. Remember, to children, their families are the most important people in the world.

Some families are easy to get to know. They are open to meeting new people, feel comfortable in a new environment, and they are eager to communicate with you about their child and the program. Others are uneasy and unsure of themselves. This may be their first experience using child care and they do not know what to expect, or they may have had a negative experience with child care in the past. Their communication style may differ from yours. For example, they may be uncomfortable with direct questions and reluctant to answer them. They may view you as an authority figure and wonder why you are asking for their advice when you are the expert. Try to understand these differences and not to assume that the same approach will work with each family.

Families bring a wide range of life experiences that shape who they are and how they relate to others. The level of education that family members have achieved, socioeconomic status, health issues, and length of time in this country also account for differences among families. Some are new parents and are very young. Others are caring for elderly or ill family members as well as their infant. Some are facing challenging circumstances such as unemployment, substance abuse, low literacy skills, unstable or unsafe housing, depression, or lack of access to a phone or transportation. Others are experiencing long separations from loved ones who are away for military service or in prison. You may have families who have only recently come to this country, do not know the language, and are trying to understand how to fit in. They may expect to be here permanently or plan to return to their country of origin.

The parents in your program may have jobs that are very demanding. They may be struggling to balance the demands of work and finding that they have little time for their child. Your sensitivity to these different life circumstances influence how families relate to you, and it can help you build the partnerships that are essential to providing high-quality care.

Understanding the Influence of Culture

Culture involves the customary beliefs, values, and practices people learn from their families and communities, either through example (watching what others do) or through explicit instruction (being told what is expected). Cultural background affects how people communicate and interact with others, and it shapes their expectations of how others will respond. Because every culture has its own set of rules and expectations, different cultures interpret what people do and say differently. Culture has a very strong influence on child-rearing practices, beliefs, and goals. Your belief system was probably influenced by those directly responsible for rearing you. Think about your own beliefs and how they influence your practice.

It will help you to learn as much as possible about the different cultures of the families in your program, keeping in mind that every family is different. Try not to generalize about any group's characteristics. Consider the many factors that influence the practices and values of an individual family, including the family's country of origin, its social class there and here, the parents' educational background, and whether extended family members live in the home.

It is easy to misinterpret what families do or say if you do not understand something about their culture. However, you also must avoid assigning cultural labels to families. Rather than making assumptions about cultural influences, it is better to keep an open mind and consider the values behind each family's beliefs. Seek to discover answers to questions such as those that follow, keeping in mind that not all families will be comfortable responding to direct questions.

Observe how family members interact with their child, and be selective about the kinds of questions you ask each family.

- Who are the people in the child's immediate family?

- Who are the decision makers in the family? Are decisions made by one person or several people?

- Do all family members live in the same household?

- Who is the primary caregiver of young children in the family?

- How are children's names chosen?

- How does the family balance children's independence with doing things for them?

- When should toilet learning begin, and how should it be handled?

- What, when, and how are children fed?

- How is discipline handled?

- Do family members have different and distinct roles in rearing children?

- Are boys and girls treated differently?

- Is it acceptable for children to be noisy and to get dirty?

- What kinds of questions are children asked?

- How do adults respond to children's questions?

- How do people interact with one another? Do they look each other in the eye? Are they taught to pause and think carefully about a response before giving it? Do they touch each other as they communicate?

- How do families show respect for elders? For children?

Welcoming Families to Your Program

To develop partnerships with families, take the time to help all families feel comfortable and respected in the program setting. You can create a welcoming environment by thoughtfully organizing spaces and materials. Your initial contacts with families are the first opportunities to begin to get to know them and to learn from them. By involving families in developing a plan for their child, you show that you are sharing the care of their child and that their ideas are invaluable. Remember to think about the possible need to reach out to multiple members of a child's family.

Creating a Welcoming Environment

Your program's environment conveys messages to families. It can say, "Leave your child with us. We're in charge here," or it can say, "We care for your child together. You are always welcome here." Look around as if you were a parent. Does the physical environment welcome families and invite them to participate in the program? Here are some ideas to consider.

Make the **entranceway** attractive, neat, and inviting. Include items such as plants, photographs of the children with their families, and displays of children's work. Arrange space near children's cubbies where family members can undress and dress a child and sit together briefly before saying good-bye. A place that says, "Saying good-bye can be difficult; take your time," helps to ease the transition from home to your room.

Provide a **mail/message box** for each family. To help you sort messages easily by language, color code the mailboxes according to the home languages of the families. This practice will make it easy to put the messages in the right place. Do not assume, however, that every family wants to receive messages in their home language. Although their home language might not be English, the family may want to receive messages in English.

Post a **whiteboard** at the entrance to your room and write a daily message about what happened that day.

Keep a **bulletin board** with up-to-date information about program activities, upcoming meetings, and community events that are of interest to families.

Display **objects that families have brought** for the children to explore, such as handmade quilts, weavings, musical instruments, photos, cooking tools, and ceremonial items.

Mount an attractive display of **photographs** of the children in your class and their families. Either put them on the wall where children can see them or place them in durable photo books that can be handled by the children.

Offer **books and pictures** for children that honor the diversity of the families who are served by your program.

Provide **places for family members** to hang their coats and store their belongings during their visits. Be sure that purses and tote bags are stored out of children's reach, because they often contain unsafe items.

Place a comfortable **rocking chair or glider** in a private space where mothers can nurse their babies. Be cautious about using a rocking chair in an area where crawling infants might injure their fingers.

Offer easily accessed **resources** that parents may read and check out. Juggling daily transitions from home to your room with small children is a challenge. When resources are readily available to families, it is more likely they will use and benefit from them. Locate them inside your room, just outside your door, or at the entrance to the building.

Place a **suggestion box** in a prominent place and provide slips of paper and pens. Be sure to take time to read the suggestions and follow up.

Orienting New Families

Initial contacts with children's families are opportunities to begin building partnerships. Welcome families, introduce your program, and get to know a little about each child and his family members. Depending on your program's procedures, your first contact with families may be at enrollment.

The program director or a parent liaison usually makes the initial contacts with parents, but sometimes teachers are asked to help with enrollment and orientation. Think about what will make families feel comfortable from the start. How can you convey that you are eager to get to know them and their child? Ask yourself whether it is appropriate to serve something to eat or drink. Do you need to arrange for someone who speaks the family's home language to be present?

Collect items to give and list things to do to orient families to the program:

- enrollment form
- health history or medical form
- *Individual Care Plan—Family Information Form*
- brochure, flyer, or handbook
- tour the facility and introduce staff members
- schedule a transition visit for the child, family members, and primary teacher

An enrollment form with specific questions about the child's history and about the family is one way to gather information. Explain how the information requested on the form will be helpful to all staff members who will care for the child. Open-ended questions will help you begin to learn about the child and family.

- What would you most like us to know about your child?
- How is your child comforted best?
- What does your child enjoy doing?
- What are your hopes and dreams for your child?
- What do you most want your child to learn in our program?
- Are there any special traditions, celebrations, stories, or songs that are especially important to your family and your child?
- Are there any special concerns that we should know about as we care for your child?
- How would you like to participate in the program?

A brochure or flyer with some of the basic information that family members need to know is helpful. Some programs give each family a booklet that introduces the program's philosophy and goals for children, describes the kinds of experiences children will have, and outlines policies and procedures.

A transition meeting or home visit before the child begins coming on a regular basis is important for you, the family, and the child. Such a visit helps all of you begin to get to know one another. Visiting the program gives the family and child a chance to become familiar with the new surroundings. As you watch the child interacting with a familiar person, you will learn how to make the child feel comfortable. As you chat with the family, you gain information for the *Individual Care Plan* that is explained in the next section.

As you converse with each family, find out what language the child hears at home. If it is not a language you speak, ask the family to help you learn a few words so you can use them with their child.

You might also use these initial meetings to begin sharing information about child development, routines, experiences, and the curriculum. When the child begins coming to the program, encourage a family member to plan to stay for a while, to help the child feel comfortable with you.

Developing an *Individual Care Plan* for Each Child

The people involved in a partnership share responsibility and the power to influence what happens. In your program, you share the care of each child. You and the child's family have different but important roles to play, as well as the skills and knowledge needed to plan for the child's experiences in child care.

An *Individual Care Plan* (ICP) summarizes information about how best to handle daily routines for an individual child. It helps you care for each child in ways that are consistent with the child's home experiences. The plan is developed *with* the family when the child enters your program, and it is updated as the child's care patterns change. Developing an ICP with the child's family lets them know that you intend to share the care of their child. It also sends the message that you recognize families as experts on their children and that you want to benefit from their knowledge. A sample form for writing an ICP is included in the *Appendix*. Keep the ICP where it is accessible to everyone who cares for the child, including substitute teachers.

In order to develop an ICP, you need detailed information about how the child is cared for at home. The *Individual Care Plan—Family Information Form* (see the *Appendix*) includes questions about arrival and departure times, breast-feeding or bottle-feeding, food preferences and allergies, diapering or toileting needs, and sleeping habits. It will help you get the information you need to collect by talking with the child's family. Use the information to complete the child's *Individual Care Plan*.

Julio (4 months) will enter the program tomorrow. At the transition meeting today, Maria, his mother, shares information with Linda about his sleeping patterns. Linda learns that Julio is a fitful sleeper. He likes to be rocked to sleep, loud noises startle him, and singing soothes him. Linda listens, asks questions, and then records Maria's responses on the Individual Care Plan—Family Information Form. *She collects information about Julio's preferences, and she will accommodate them as much as possible in the child care environment.*

Reaching Out to All Family Members

Parents are not the only family members who should feel welcome in your program. Other members of a child's family may be sharing the care of the child and might want to be involved in the program. Grandparents, for example, might have more free time to share than parents and may have a great deal of patience with young children. Their participation in the program is valuable; they can feed an infant, read to a child, play games and sing, help a child settle for a nap, and more.

Identify special projects or events that interest different family members. For example, you might invite grandparents or special friends to read or tell stories and invite those interested in construction projects to help with a "fix-it" day. Ask family members about topics of interest to them and arrange special speakers or activities.

You might need to make a special effort to welcome and involve fathers, who sometimes feel uncomfortable in an early childhood setting where more women are involved than men. Once fathers discover that their presence and their contributions are appreciated by the program staff and are important to their child, they are more likely to take an active role. By *father* we do not necessarily mean only the child's biological father. A father figure may be another significant male who is a steady influence in the child's life: the mother's partner or husband, an uncle, older sibling, grandfather, another relative, or a family friend.

The most important thing to keep in mind is that all children need caring adults in their lives who take an interest in their development and learning. Find out which adults are important in a child's life and think about how you can welcome them. Learn about their interests, jobs, hobbies, and what they would like to share with the children. Describe what others have contributed to the program. Some adults are more likely to participate in an activity that involves the whole family than in one that is designed solely for parents.

Communicating With Families

Good communication is essential to partnerships. Families want to know all the details about their children's experiences during the day, everything from what and how much they ate to what and with whom they played and how they reacted to experiences. Families often have information to share as well. Informal daily exchanges are just as valuable as the more formal methods you use to communicate with families. You may need to use several different forms of communication, especially if a child lives in more than one home or has a noncustodial adult who wants to be fully involved.

Building Trust Through Daily Interactions

Every day that a child is in your care, you have opportunities to interact with family members and build the trust that is essential to a partnership. Trust develops only over time and is based on many positive and respectful experiences.

Here are some of the positive messages you can convey to families through your daily interactions.

Message to Families	Daily Interactions
You are always welcome here.	Greet each family member and child by name and say something positive about the child, the family, or the program. Learn at least a few words in the family's home language to use when you talk with the child. (Be aware that some family members might not want you to address them in their home language if you only know a few words of greeting.)
We can learn from you.	Acknowledge the insights and information parents have about their child and how valuable these are to you and other staff members who care for the child.
You are entitled to know what is happening in the program.	Set up systems, such as journals or daily notes, to share what has happened each day. Use simple language and translate the information if necessary. Avoid the use of jargon in both written and spoken communication.
We will share the care of your child.	Complete the *Individual Care Plan—Family Information Form* with the family of each infant and update it regularly. Communicate daily with parents or other family members about their child. Use daily logs to share information about each child's day and hold daily conversations, either in person or by phone.
We can work together to resolve differences and conflicts.	View differences as opportunities to learn more about the family's views and work toward a better understanding. Use the steps for handling conflicts (discussed later in this chapter) to support your partnership.

Every positive interaction you have with a family member builds trust. If you do need to discuss a difficult issue at some time, it will be easier and more productive if you have already built a positive relationship with the family.

Making the Most of Daily Exchanges

When you are caring for very young children, daily exchanges are the primary way to communicate with family members and keep everyone informed about what is happening at home and at the program. Respectful and sincere interactions between families and teachers show children that home and the program are connected. Here are some suggestions for daily exchanges with families.

Greet each child and family personally. Use their names; observe indications of how they are faring, and say something specific about the child, the family, or your plans for the day.

Share information about something the child has accomplished or about an event that concerns the child. News can be shared in the morning, but the end of the day is often a good time to talk with families about what their child has done and to explain its significance. "Let me tell you about the building Janelle made with our blocks yesterday. The way she solved the balancing problem was pretty amazing. She tried several ways of stacking the blocks so they wouldn't fall down." However, leave the announcement of important "firsts" to the parent and child.

Solicit their insights and advice about their child. "I can see that Parker doesn't want to say good-bye to you today. Can you think of any particular reason?"

Give support to families when needed. "Perhaps Maya just needs an extra hug. I know she'll be fine once she gets busy. We have lots planned for today."

Be a good listener. Active listening skills convey that parents' concerns and ideas are taken seriously. "I understand how upset you are about the biting incident. I can assure you that we are taking steps to prevent more biting."

Make sure you understand what is being said. If there is uncertainty about a family member's statement, clarify your understanding. "Tell me whether I understand what you are saying. I think I heard you say. . ."

In communicating with families, try to be specific and factual. Vague or subjective comments can leave family members uncertain about what you mean or make them defensive. Notice the difference between the subjective and objective comments in the two examples that follow. Think about how the parent might feel in each case.

Subjective Comments	Parent's Thoughts
When Julio's mother, Maria, comes to get him at the end of the day, Linda tells her, "Julio was very crabby today. He fussed with everyone who tried to comfort him."	What did he do? How did Linda try to comfort him? Why didn't they call me? He is not crabby at home. I'm not sure they know how to take care of my baby. Maybe something is wrong with him or with me as a parent.

Objective Comments	Parent's Thoughts
At lunchtime, Linda calls Maria to discuss Julio's fussiness. She tells her, "Julio cried when he drank his bottle this morning. I tried holding him the way you showed me, but it didn't help. Do you have any suggestions for me?" Then, when Maria picks him up at the end of the day, Linda tells her, "Julio was still a bit fussy this afternoon when he ate. I am wondering if his ears are bothering him, or if he is still just adjusting to me. What do you think?"	I wonder what's wrong. I appreciate Linda's asking me for my advice and ideas. I think that Linda is doing all she can to take care of him. Perhaps he is not used to Linda yet, but maybe he is getting sick. If this continues, I'll take him to the clinic for a checkup. I feel good about leaving Julio with Linda. I know she will call me if she has trouble with him.

Subjective Comments	Parent's Thoughts
When Matthew's father comes to pick him up at the end of the day, Mercedes tells him, "Matthew was such a good boy today. He just loves everyone."	That's a surprise. Matthew is a real challenge at home. He makes his sister cry, and he won't cooperate when we ask him to do things. If he is so good here but challenging at home, are we doing something wrong?

Objective Comments	Parent's Thoughts
When Matthew's father comes to pick him up, Mercedes tells him, "Today Matthew helped us clean up the blocks and trucks, and we only asked him one time! I handed him the basket and asked him to help put the blocks away, and he did. This afternoon, we had a volunteer in our room. Matthew sat on her lap while she read two books to him. She told us she really enjoyed him."	I have a pretty wonderful son. He is learning to clean up. I think we will encourage that at home. Also, the bedtime stories we read to him at night must be helping him listen to stories. I guess my wife was right about how important it is to read to him every day. I feel good about the way he is growing.

Communicating in More Formal Ways

In addition to informal daily exchanges, there are more formal ways to communicate with families. Some can be accomplished easily; others take more time and planning.

Daily communication form—Create a form for families to record information about their child when they arrive at the program each day. Request information that is basic to the child's daily care and explain that it helps you meet each child's current needs more effectively. You may need to encourage parents to take the time to complete this form when they bring their child. Request any information that you find necessary, such as when the child last ate, when her diaper was last changed, her general mood that day, how well she slept last night, when she will be picked up, and who will be picking her up.

Electronic mail—More and more families—and programs—have access to e-mail. Sending e-mail is an excellent way to stay in touch and to share specific information about a child.

Internet—Introduce families to CreativeCurriculum.net if you are using that system. They can participate in a parent-to-parent message board, view their child's portfolio, and add comments or upload pictures.

Journals—Provide each family with a journal that is sent between home and school. You can each write entries to share information. While the families may or may not provide you with objective, specific, and factual information, it is essential that you do so. From time to time, you can include specific questions for families.

Newsletters—Periodically provide families with newsletters about what the children in your group have been doing. When you tell them about experiences and discoveries that the whole group has engaged in, parents can better understand their child's life at the program.

Letters to families—At the end of each of chapters 6–18, you will find a letter to families. Each sample letter describes why a particular routine or experience is an important part of the program, how you support children's learning and development, and how you hope to work together with families. Adapt the letters for your own program and send them home over a period of time—perhaps one letter a week—so that families do not feel overwhelmed with too much information. Sometimes you will want to distribute the relevant letter at a meeting during which you are talking about a routine or experience, such as how you handle hellos and good-byes.

Articles of interest, community resources, and relevant Web sites—These are resources that you can share with parents. Invite families to share the resources that they have found helpful.

Notices—Written notices are a way to give every family the same information at the same time. You might want to explain a policy change, a special event, or the contagious disease of a child or staff member. Use the **mail/message boxes** for these notices.

Holding Conferences With Families

A formal conference with each family is a time to sit down together, uninterrupted, and talk as partners about caring for their child. Conferences are opportunities to share information, observations, and questions. You can solve problems together when necessary and celebrate the uniqueness of each child. If a child has a diagnosed disability, a family conference will involve the team of people who develop goals for the Individual Family Service Plan. Preparation and the many positive interactions you have already had with the family help ensure a successful conference.

Here are steps to take as you prepare for a family conference:

- Arrange a time that is convenient for families and find out whom they would like to include in the conference.

- Let families know what to expect. When you set up the conference, explain that conferences are a time to focus entirely on their child. Find out what the family's goals are for the conference. Ask what they are interested in learning about and whether there are any special issues they want to discuss.

- Review your observation notes and ask co-workers whether they have any information and insights about the child to contribute. Sharing stories and observations will help families get clear ideas about their child's experiences at the program.

- Be prepared to share what children are learning. The information in chapter 3, *What Children Are Learning*, will help you explain the significance of what each child is able to do.

- If language differences may be a barrier, arrange for someone to interpret. Many families know someone who can serve as an interpreter. If they do not, try to make other arrangements.

The first family conference is usually a time to get to know each other, to share information you each have about the child, and to discuss your goals for the year. If you have not already explained how *The Creative Curriculum Developmental Continuum for Infants, Toddlers & Twos* helps you get to know and plan for each child, this is a good time to do so. During future meetings, their familiarity with the *Developmental Continuum* will help you discuss their child's progress, what you are expecting next in terms of development, and how you can work together to support the child in taking his or her next steps.

Start the conference by sharing your observation of something new, interesting, or delightful that their child has done or said. You may also want to ask parents questions such as "What activities do you and your child enjoy doing together now?" or "What interests your child?" Questions of this sort show your appreciation of their child and encourage families to share some of their own observations.

Next, share the *Family Conference Form*, which is available in *The Creative Curriculum for Infants, Toddlers & Twos Developmental Continuum Assessment Toolkit*. Under the appropriate goal heading on the form, highlight the child's new discoveries and the skills she has mastered. Offer specific examples from your observation notes. Instead of presenting a random list of the child's recent accomplishments, this form helps you present examples in the context of the curriculum goals. This organization makes the examples meaningful for the family. For example, a parent may be upset that her son is still sucking his thumb. On the *Family Conference Form*, in the section "To Learn About Self and Others," you would record the explanation that this is how their child is learning to comfort himself (Objective 3, "Manages own feelings"). It may help the parent think about the child's thumbsucking in a new and helpful way.

Throughout your discussion, encourage the family to share their observations, questions, challenges, and joys. Confirm that this is a time for an exchange of information and that combining what each of you knows will give both of you the clearest possible understanding of their child. In addition to recording your own ideas, ask the family for their ideas when you discuss the other sections of the form: "Favorite Activities and Special Interests," "Situations or Experiences that Cause Distress," "Family Comments and Special Circumstances," and "Next Steps at the Program and at Home." Any additional information that the family shares can be recorded in the "Family Comments and Observations" section. Family conferences are also good times to update the *Individual Care Plan* you have for each child.

Talk together about expectations for the child's development and complete the "Next Steps" section of the *Family Conference Form* with the child's family. This will become your blueprint for working with the child during the next 3 months or so until the next assessment checkpoint and conference. Keep it where you will have ready access to it, so you can remind yourself of areas you want to focus on during the next few months. At the next conference, the form can serve as a starting point for your discussion.

Making Home Visits

Home visits are another way of communicating with families. They provide a unique opportunity to see a child and family in their most comfortable setting. Some programs require home visits, but others do not. In either case, families should be given some choice about whether they want a home visit. When a home visit is too stressful for a family, it will not achieve its purpose.

Talk with families about the purpose of the visit. Let them know ahead of time why you are coming. Arrange a time that is convenient for both of you. Families may be anxious or excited about your visit. Reassure them and help them feel comfortable about your presence in their home.

When you make home visits, follow your program's established policies and procedures. Here are some general guidelines to keep in mind.

- Decide ahead of time what you want to accomplish. Is it simply to introduce yourself and meet the family or do you have additional goals?

- Ask the family about their goals for the visit. Address as many of their requests as possible.

- Review the enrollment materials before going on the visit, so that you are familiar with the names of family members and information about the family.

- Develop and use a home visiting plan to help you prepare for the visit.

- Contact the family to set up a good time for the visit. Agree on a date and time and give them an idea of how long you will be staying.

- Get directions to the home. If you feel unsafe going alone, take a colleague from the program with you or arrange for the family to visit you at the program.

- Gather the materials and information you will need before making the visit.

- After the visit, record any information or observations that you want to remember.

These approaches to communicating with families will help you obtain the full benefits of a true partnership. You will have the information you need to care for the child, families will gain confidence in you, and children will be more likely to thrive in your care.

Involving Families in the Program

Most families want and need to be involved in their child's life at the program. For some, this is the first time they have left their child in the care of someone other than a family member. For infants, toddlers, and twos, their families' presence at the program is the best way to help them experience the connection between their home and your program.

Offering a Variety of Ways to Be Involved

While some families are able to arrange their work schedules to feed or eat lunch with their child, join the group for a neighborhood walk, or assist in the room for a morning, many are not able to participate in these ways. They may feel lucky if they have a few extra minutes to spend when dropping off and picking up their children. Offer a variety of options that match families' interests, skills, schedules, and other responsibilities so that family members feel welcome and competent when they come. During the enrollment process, ask families how they would like to participate.

Families are more likely to participate if you let them know how much you value their involvement and how much it benefits their child and the program. A grandmother who comes to hold her grandson and who reads and talks with him and another baby will see how much her help is appreciated. She may even offer to come regularly. However, the parent who sews two covers for the bouncing mattress might never see the children use them. Be sure to thank her and explain the advantage of having two covers: "Bouncing is one of the children's favorite activities. Now we can wash one while the other is in use." Show her some photographs of the children using a new cover. Similarly, acknowledge the parent who produces the newsletter by listing his name in every issue.

There are many ways for families to be involved in the program. Consider some of the following suggestions.

Jobs—On index cards, list program-related needs that families can fill at home. Jobs could include repairing broken toys, shopping at yard sales for water toys such as measuring cups and spoons, and making books or other materials for the room.

Projects—At an evening or weekend session, families can work together to improve the program by such things as painting walls, making a new sandbox, or preparing a garden plot. Some projects can be completed by families at their convenience over a period of time. Celebrate when a project is completed.

Useful junk—Every home has disposable items that the program can recycle as play materials. Empty food containers, ribbons, wrapping paper, and paper towel tubes are among the items that a program can use. Try asking for one or two specific items at a time.

Book reviews—Invite families to read and review children's books or books on child development and parenting. Provide a book review form to record the title, author, publisher, price, and comments. For children's books, leave space on the form for the family to record the ages for which the book is appropriate, what the book is about, and why they and their child liked it. Use these recommendations to select books for the children. Families can also review music CDs and tapes.

Family dinner night—Plan an event that encourages families eat dinner together before going home. Dinner might be a meal planned and prepared with the older children or something simpler, such as pizza.

Family playtime—Open the center for an evening or a weekend afternoon so that families can come with their children and participate in program experiences together.

A room for families—If space is available, consider creating a resource area for families. Include comfortable places to sit, resources of interest to families, and, if possible, computers with Internet access. Some programs find that family involvement increases dramatically when families are invited to use the washer and dryer that are reserved for them.

Class photo album—Provide an album and ask a volunteer to insert photographs you have collected of the children in your group. Display the photo album prominently and include a cover page thanking the person who made it. Include it in the family lending-library.

Participating in the Program

When families are encouraged to spend time at the program, they see how you interact with their children and learn new ideas to try at home. You gain extra help, and their presence shows children that their homes and the program are connected.

Keep in mind that a setting for infants, toddlers, and twos can be an intimidating place for some family members. They may be unsure of what you expect and what they should be doing. Sometimes children behave differently when family members, especially their parents, visit the program. They may act out or insist on their parent's full attention. It is important to prepare parents for these possibilities and to assure them that such behavior is to be expected. Advise them to pay special attention to their child, even as they interact with other children.

Here are some suggestions to make participation a positive experience for families.

Speak personally with each family member. Greet families when they arrive. Offer a quick update about their child and what you have planned for the period of time they will be with you.

Explain the procedures you want them to follow. If a family member will be helping out with routines such as handwashing and feeding, explain the procedures you follow to keep children healthy. If possible, post charts illustrating the steps so you do not have to explain them each time. If the family member is helping in an infant room, be sure to have enough shoe covers available. Shoe covers help keep the floor clean for the infants who spend some of their waking hours on it.

Provide guidance clearly and respectfully. You are responsible for the program environment, and you have an overall sense of what is needed to keep things running smoothly. If two parents who came for lunch are standing in the corner talking with each other while their children are seeking their attention, you might say, "Your children are so excited to see you here, it's hard for them to wait to show you what they are doing. Why don't you join them until we are ready for lunch?"

Offer concrete suggestions about what to do. Plan activities that family members can enjoy with children. "I'm going to bring out some new balls. I think the children will enjoy rolling them back and forth with you." Invite their help when you need it. "We're getting ready to go outside in a few minutes. We could really use your help with putting the children's jackets on."

Avoid lengthy conversations. Explain that lengthy conversations must be postponed until a time when you are not directly responsible for the children. "Let's set up a meeting to talk about this later. Right now I need to be with the children, and I want to be able to give you my full attention when we talk."

Make the physical environment manageable. Labeling shelves and drawers will help families find the supplies they need without having to ask you. If possible, take families on a short tour of the room to explain what goes on in each area.

Share information about how children develop and learn. Display the curriculum goals and objectives and explain how children are developing and what they are learning at the program.

When family members participate in the program, the steps you have taken to make it a positive experience will make them more likely to want to continue.

Responding to Challenging Situations

Despite all of the positive steps you take to build a partnership with each family, you will encounter challenging situations. Even in the best relationships, you will find that misunderstandings and conflicts emerge. Some families are struggling with meeting basic needs, and the ongoing stress makes it difficult for them to be available to their children. You may also have children with disabilities in your program, and their families require special understanding and support. Challenging situations must be handled carefully and positively in order to maintain a partnership with every family.

Resolving Differences: A Partnership Approach

If you work with families who share your values and beliefs and have similar life experiences and personal characteristics, you are more likely to interpret what they say and do in the same way as they do. If you work with families who are very different from you—and if you know little about their beliefs and practices—miscommunication and misunderstandings can easily take place. Understanding and respecting practices that are different from your own help you build positive relationships with all families.

When the adults in their lives share a consistent approach, children gain a sense of continuity that helps them feel safe and secure in child care. This does not mean that you have to agree about everything. There will probably be times when you and a family have different points of view about caring for their child. The question is this: "How can we work out our differences in a positive way?"

Here are examples of how misunderstandings can occur because your views about a situation differ from that of a family member. Following each example, a resolution that respects the partnership is suggested.

Situation	Your View	The Family's View
After careful observations over time, you are concerned that a toddler's language is delayed. You suggest an evaluation by a speech specialist. The parents fail to make an appointment with a specialist.	If a problem exists, it should be identified as early as possible. Parents should want to get all the help they can get for their child.	My child is fine. There's nothing wrong.

For a number of reasons, parents might resist a recommendation to have their child evaluated by a specialist. It is not unusual for parents to deny that there might be a problem. (See the section of this chapter on "Supporting the Families of Children With Disabilities.") If you suspect that this is the reason for their reluctance, provide information, suggest that all of you observe the child more carefully for a few weeks, and keep in touch about what you learn. It is also possible that the family lacks transportation to get to a specialist, or they might be uneasy about managing an unfamiliar system of services. You might offer to have someone from the program go along or arrange to have the specialist observe the child at the program.

Situation	Your View	The Family's View
The mother of a toddler unzips her daughter's coat and hangs it in her cubby near her mittens and boots. Knowing that this child is able to do that herself, you say, "Keisha, you know how to unzip and hang up your coat. Tomorrow, show your Mommy how you can do things for yourself."	Developing personal care skills and developing independence are important objectives for children. I don't want to have to do everything for every child. Keisha's mother is treating her like a baby.	Helping my child is one way I show her how much her family loves her. I want to care for her, especially just before I have to say good-bye for the day. There's plenty of time for her to learn to take care of herself.

You might want to encourage children to do as much for themselves as possible, but some families do things for their children as a sign of love even when the children can do them independently. With this understanding, you can support a mother's practice of unzipping, removing, and hanging up her child's coat. At the same time, you might share with the parent that, when she is not available, her child is learning to care for herself, which is an important life skill. Explain how helpful this is to you because you are responsible for a whole group of children.

Situation	Your View	The Family's View
A family requests that you continue their practice at home of toilet training their 12-month-old child. They explain how they are aware of when their child has to urinate and defecate and that they manage to take him to the potty in time.	"Catching" a child in time to bring him to the potty is not toilet learning. Children let us know when they have the muscle control and awareness to use the toilet. That is the most appropriate time to begin the process of toilet learning.	It is important for us to train our children to use the toilet at this age. We did it with our other children, and it works just fine.

Toilet learning is a topic about which you and families are likely to have strong feelings and perhaps different approaches. It is helpful to discuss the family's approach to toilet learning when they are first considering enrolling their child in your program. You should also explain the program's philosophy and the steps that you typically use when helping children learn to use the toilet. This may prevent some problems before they arise.

When toileting practices differ, it is important to listen to the family's perspective and find some aspect of their approach to affirm. "As you can imagine, it's more challenging with a group of children. I think there is something we can do, however. We check every child's diaper regularly each hour. We could take your child to the toilet at that time and see how that works." This approach conveys your appreciation of the family's preference without making a commitment that you might not be able to honor.

Situation	Your View	The Family's View
When you first meet the grandfather of a toddler, he tells you that he doesn't understand why you do not spank his grandson for hitting other children.	You teach children to be gentle with others by modeling gentleness and guiding their behavior in positive ways. You stop children when they hit others and show them how to verbalize their thoughts and feelings instead of hitting.	The grandfather believes in using a strong-hand approach to raising children. His philosophy is "Spare the rod, spoil the child." It worked for him with his children. He is concerned about his grandson's behavior.

When a family member you do not know well comes to discuss a concern, it is helpful to begin by taking a few minutes to get to know the person better before attempting to address the issue. Explain that you understand his concerns: "It sounds like it's very important to you that your grandson learn to behave well. Is that right?" Then take the time to discuss your program's approach to promoting positive behavior. Share the social and emotional goals and objectives of *The Creative Curriculum Developmental Continuum* and the steps children take in developing self-control and prosocial behaviors. Then explain how you support their learning.

Working Through Conflicts

If you do not try to resolve an issue that is bothering you, you will probably become annoyed. The children will sense that something is not quite right. Avoiding an issue rarely solves the problem and sometimes makes it worse. It is worth making the effort to find a resolution.

Matthew (22 months) has been at the center for just one month, but each week his parents come later and later to pick him up. The program closes at 6:00 p.m., and Grace needs to leave on time to attend a class. She is becoming annoyed with Matthew's parents because her reminders have not made a difference. Finally, she arranges a conference to explain to them how difficult it is for her when they are late. Matthew's father says they did not know they were causing a problem. If they know they will be late from now on, Matthew's parents will have a cousin pick him up.

When a family member is clearly upset about a problem, you want to respond in ways that lead to a positive resolution. It is helpful to know what steps to follow to resolve the conflict. Because conversations about children can sometimes be emotional, they are better handled away from the children and other families. If you are working with children when an upset family member approaches you, suggest delaying the conversation until you can find someone to take over. Then you can give the family member your full attention in a more private place.

Here are the steps of conflict resolution and examples of how they can be applied.

Remain calm and help others to remain calm. When emotions are strong, the first step is to defuse the situation. A good way to remain calm and help others remain calm is to seek to understand the family member's position and validate their feelings. By asking open-ended questions, you can gather details that enable you to understand the significance of what is being said. This approach helps reduce any defensiveness that you and the parent might be feeling. When feelings have been defused, conversations are more likely to be rational. To be sure that you have heard and understood correctly, restate what you think you heard them say. This also lets them know that you are listening.

What a Parent Says	How You Respond
"I'm very upset, so I need to talk to you right now. My son Jerome is afraid to come here, and it's all because of another child in your group."	"You do sound upset. Let me call someone to take my place for a few minutes. Then we can talk where it is quiet." After the director comes to take over, you find a quiet room to meet with Jerome's mother and say, "I'd like to have a better understanding of the problem. What seems to be troubling Jerome?"
"Jerome is afraid of that new child. I think his name is Steven. He says that Steven hits other children and that he has hit Jerome. I want you to keep my child away from this bully."	"You are telling me that you don't care for the way that Steven behaves around other children. You want us to keep him away from your child. Is that correct?"
"Yes, that is what I am saying."	"That is a problem. We certainly don't want Jerome or any child to feel unsafe here."

Clarify the problem and agree on goals. In order to come to an agreement *together,* the problem needs to be clarified and discussed. It is important to allow family members to explain their perspective and for you to share your program policies regarding the issue. Be careful not to attempt to solve the problem too quickly, yourself, without asking for the family members' ideas. Without negating their request or getting into a discussion about another child, talk about your shared vision for all children. You might also find it helpful to share the specific objectives of the *Developmental Continuum* that relate to the issue. Explain the developmental steps that are related to the relevant objectives and discuss the examples. Describe the way your program supports children in acquiring the skills that are related to the issue being discussed.

What a Parent Says	How You Respond
"How can Jerome feel safe here when he is worried about Steven's hitting him? He's starting to have nightmares, and I know it's because he is afraid. What will you do to keep Steven away from my child?"	"We both want Jerome to know he is safe here. I can assure you that one of our goals is to teach all of the children to express their feelings in acceptable ways, without hitting others."
"Well, it doesn't seem like you are doing a very good job with Steven. He only knows how to hit."	"Let me share the goals and objectives of our curriculum with you. Here are the objectives for helping children learn about themselves and others. You can see the steps that children take in relation to each objective. This is how we know what support and guidance each child needs to learn to relate positively to others."
"How do you guide them?"	"One of the ways is by modeling what we want the children to do, how we want them to relate to each other. We also talk with the children when they hurt other children."
"That's all well and good, but, while you are teaching the children to relate positively, my child is still afraid."	"I respect your request to keep Jerome safe. What I hear you saying is that you want us to keep the children apart. Am I right?"
"Well, yes, it is. That's the only way I'll know my child is safe and comfortable here."	"We want you and your child to know that this is a safe place. We can certainly agree on that goal."

Together, generate solutions. Once feelings have been calmed, the problem clarified, and there is some agreement about goals, you will want to resolve the problem in a way that satisfies both you and the family. One way to start finding a solution is to ask for their ideas. You may have an idea of how to solve the problem, but your goal is to involve the family in the problem-solving process. By being willing to share control in the process, you send messages that the family's opinion and ideas count and that you are *partners* in caring for their child.

What a Parent Says	How You Respond
"So what are you going to do?"	"As you can imagine, keeping children apart is hard. Toddlers move around a lot and are free to choose where they want to play. What can we do to help Jerome feel safe?"
"I am not sure. I think that Jerome needs to know you will be watching out for him."	"My co-teacher and I plan to stay close to Jerome and Steven whenever they are playing near each other. Will that help Jerome feel safe?"
"Yes, that would help."	"We will also focus on helping all of the children relate positively to each other. I can give you an update each day. What if we try this for a week and make a point of talking again?"
"All right."	"Good. We'll try this for a week and see if our plan makes a difference."

Continue the dialogue. Once a possible solution is identified, plan to check with each other to discuss whether it is working for you and the family. If the solution is not working well, you will want to talk with the family again and come up with another solution. Reassure them that you will continue to look for solutions with them until the problem is resolved. Use the *Developmental Continuum* to help you and the family better understand children's abilities and needs, and to identify what all of you can do to continue to support the child.

What a Parent Says	How You Respond
"I think Jerome is feeling better now. He's not so afraid any more."	"That's wonderful news. Why do you think that is?"
"For one thing, we've been talking with him at home, reassuring him that his teachers will keep him safe. I've also been telling him that, if anyone hits him, he should tell them to stop!"	"I'm sure that what you are doing at home has helped. We have seen a lot of progress here since we began emphasizing positive ways of playing together. Your concern really helped everyone."
"That's good to know. I was a little afraid to bring it up at first, but I'm glad I did."	"I hope you will always feel free to bring up any concerns. It's the only way we can resolve them. After all, this is a partnership."

Conflicts are a normal part of sharing the care of a young child. Recognizing this fact helps you to think about conflicts as opportunities to understand a family's point of view and find ways to partner with the family. The more you know about children and families, the better you will be able to determine the best approach to handling conflicts.

Supporting Families Who Are Under Stress

Families experience different kinds of stress, and they may have difficulty coping. Ongoing and unrelenting stress can come from many sources. Here are just a few examples:

- living in a violent community
- seeking employment or job training without knowing whether they will be able to continue bringing their child to the program
- long commutes to a job
- a job that does not allow flexibility in work hours to accommodate family needs
- a family member with a physical disability, chronic illness, cognitive delays, low literacy skills, or mental illness
- domestic and/or substance abuse
- adapting to a new culture and/or language
- substandard, overcrowded housing or living in a shelter
- barriers to health care

Parents who are under stress from these or other situations do not always have the emotional energy or physical resources to nurture their children. Sometimes they cannot meet their children's most basic needs. They may not be able to solve problems, communicate with their children, or give them the attention and affirmation they need. Their discipline may be inconsistent, overly punitive, or nonexistent. For many children in these circumstances, life is unpredictable and dangerous, and their confusion may manifest itself in anger, withdrawal, or fearfulness in your program.

While you are not expected to try to solve a family's problems, you can take steps to help when you notice that a family is under stress. Recognize that everyone handles stress differently and that you should not make assumptions about how a family member is coping. Be as supportive as you can. Avoid adding to the stress by being overly critical, such as when a parent forgets to bring boots for her child despite several reminders. Also be mindful of parental stress when you need to discuss a problem you are having with their child. Sometimes it is wise to wait for a better time. Seek ways to affirm the family member.

Your program might have social services and family support workers who can conduct a family assessment to learn about a family's situation and then help find the resources they need. At a minimum, every program can put together information for families, including

- an up-to-date list of community agencies and hot lines for referrals

- brochures and resources for families to borrow

- a list of support groups that deal with family issues

Parenting is one of the most important jobs in the world, yet there is very little training for this critical role. Adults who were fortunate enough to have caring, nurturing experiences when they were children have a solid foundation for becoming supportive parents. Those who had less constructive experiences still want the best for their children and are doing what they think is needed. Although some parents do things that distress you, hold to the belief that most are doing the best they can. Learn as much as you can about the strengths and needs of each family so that you have realistic expectations and can individualize your approach to your partnership. Your way of working with one family will not necessarily be the same as with another.

Supporting the Families of Children With Disabilities

It is very possible that some of the children in your program will have special needs. Many of these children and families will already be receiving early intervention services for a diagnosed disability. Others may have special needs that have not yet been identified. Your factual observations and the *Developmental Continuum* can play a role in helping the family and specialists identify the child's special needs and obtain the needed services.

When parents realize that their child is not developing typically, they often experience a mix of emotions that is unique to dealing with this new reality. Knowing the emotional stages experienced by many families of children with disabilities will help you offer appropriate support.[27]

1. **Denial**—Initially parents may deny the child's special needs or disability. Recognize that this is a first step in coming to terms with their child's disability and do not put any pressure on the family to accept what may be obvious to others.

2. **Projection of blame**—A common reaction to learning that their child is not perfect is for families to want to blame someone else. There may or may not be any basis for the accusations some families make. You might hear family members say things such as, "If only they would have…." You may even become a target of blame. Again, patience and a willingness to listen without taking sides will help you and the family through this stage.

3. **Fear**—At this stage, the family is still learning about the special needs of their child. The information is probably new to them, and they may question it. You or someone in your program can offer support by helping them sort through the information and by learning about the disability, yourself.

4. **Guilt**—Some families worry that they did not do all they should have to prevent the disability. Their thinking might or might not be rational. Remember that this is a difficult time for the family. At this stage, the family may find it helpful if you offer ideas about channeling their energy into activities to support their child.

5. **Mourning or grief**—The reality of a disability often brings tremendous grief, pain, and disappointment. Families must work through many emotions before being able to accept their child's disability. You can help by listening and showing that you care.

6. **Withdrawal**—Withdrawing in order to manage their powerful emotions is often a healthy and essential step for families. You may become concerned about family members as you see them withdraw and become isolated. Continue to communicate with them, and offer your understanding and respect for what they are experiencing.

7. **Rejection**—At this stage, the family member may show some signs of rejecting their child's disability. This can mean failing to recognize the child's capabilities and strengths or setting unrealistic goals for the child. The *Developmental Continuum* and your objective observation notes can help the family member realize their child's strengths and capabilities and set realistic goals for the child.

8. **Acceptance**—At this stage, the parent is able to accept the child with his disability and offer the support that helps him develop and learn.

Recognize that there is no set timetable for how quickly or slowly family members progress through these stages. Not all families go through each stage, and sometimes family members cycle through the stages more than once. An event, such as seeing another child who is developing at a typical pace, can trigger feelings all over again. It may be painful for you to observe families while they are experiencing the powerful emotions involved during these stages.

It is important to recognize the limits of your own time, energy, knowledge, and skills with regard to a child's disability and the family's needs. You can encourage family members to seek additional support from specialists who are more familiar with their child's disability than you are. A list of available resources may be helpful, but they will probably need the assistance of a social worker or someone who knows how to negotiate the maze of special services. This person should be someone who can guide them through the process of getting help and support for themselves and their child.

Conclusion

When you achieve partnerships with children's families, everyone benefits. Children feel more secure and comfortable when their families and teachers share their knowledge respectfully and interact positively. Children are more likely to experience consistency in the care they receive when families are invited to share what they know and what they want for their child. Families feel more secure when they leave their child in the care of someone who makes the effort to build a relationship with them. When you share your knowledge of child development in a way that helps families understand the importance of what their very young children are able to do, families gain confidence in their parenting. You gain the families' valuable insights about their children, and that enables you to provide more individualized care. As partners in the care of their child, families are more likely to feel as though they are an important part of your program and to offer their support.

Part 2

Routines

Daily routines are one of the most important ways to put research and theory into practice. By responding consistently to children, you meet the basic needs identified by Abraham Maslow, T. Berry Brazelton, and Stanley Greenspan. Their work focused especially on the physical and social/emotional needs that are discussed in the theory and research section of this book. The way you handle routines also enables you to help children build trust and autonomy, as explained by Erik Erikson. Your consistent and responsive care helps children develop secure attachments with the important people in their lives.

Some of your attitudes and personal beliefs may conflict with what you are learning about good early childhood practices. As your program implements *The Creative Curriculum,* consider these questions with your colleagues and program director:

- How does *The Creative Curriculum* align with your beliefs and values?

- Do you disagree with any of the practices described in this section? How and why do your practices differ?

- Will you have to adapt your personal values and beliefs to fit curriculum guidelines? What specific adaptations will you have to make?

Each of the chapters on routines includes questions to encourage you to think about your views about a particular routine. Information on safety and health is included because many routines require attention to those concerns. Because partnerships with families enable you to provide consistent care for each child, each chapter ends with a sample letter that invites families to be your partners in making routines rich learning opportunities for children.

inside this chapter

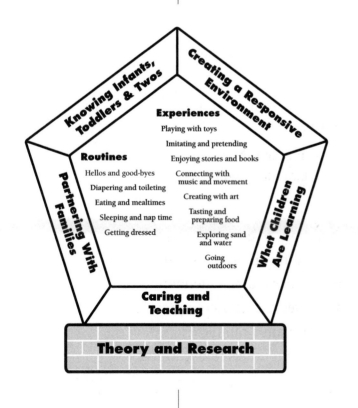

6 Hellos and Good-Byes

Matthew *(22 months) begins to cry when his mother says good-bye and reassures him that she will return. Mercedes kneels, puts her arm around Matthew, and says, "You are sad because your mommy left." She pauses and gently pats his back. "It's hard to say good-bye. Mommy will be at work, thinking about you. She will be back later. Let's look at our family picture album together." When Mercedes shows the page with photographs of Matthew's family, he smiles and points to his parents, saying, "Mama, Daddy." Mercedes responds, "Yes, that's Matthew's mama, and there's his daddy. They know that you will be here with me until they come to take you home."*

Every day begins as families and children say hello to you and good-bye to one another. Every day ends as children reunite with their families and say good-bye to you. Children, their families, and you all experience strong feelings during these times. These times of the day deserve your attention.

Arrivals set the tone for day. A painful farewell is sometimes harder on parents than on children, who often recover quickly once they feel secure in your care. Parents often feel anxious and guilty when their children are crying as they leave. Because every child is different, you have to be flexible and responsive to what each child and family needs from you.

Reunions at the end of the day can be just as emotional for children and families. A child who said good-bye easily or who adjusted well after a painful good-bye may greet her father joyfully or ignore him. She also might have a temper tantrum or begin to cry because she saved her strong feelings for her family, the people she trusts most. The happy response delights her father, but the others might make him feel rejected, sad, or guilty. Departures need your attention as much as arrivals.

Learning to separate is a lifelong process and an important part of growing up. When you help children learn to manage separations from and reunions with their loved ones, they feel understood and gain self-confidence.

Supporting Development and Learning

A child's stage of development influences the way he or she reacts to hellos and good-byes. In part because they involve such strong feelings, hellos and good-byes are opportunities for valuable learning that affects all areas of young children's development.

Learning about themselves and others: As children learn that they can trust you to take care of them and to be their secure base during the day, hellos and good-byes become easier. With your help, children learn to manage the strong feelings evoked by separations and reunions, and, as they develop empathy, they learn to comfort other children. The hello and good-bye rituals that you help young children develop also ease the transitions between home and your program. Family pictures and books connect them to family members who are not immediately present, and they assure children that their families will return at the end of the day.

Learning about moving: Hellos and good-byes provide opportunities for children to develop physical skills. You say, "Wave bye-bye," and model waving for a young infant, who raises her hand to wave good-bye to her mother. You chant, "Peek-a-boo, I see you," as you and the baby cover and uncover your eyes, enjoying this game of disappearing and reappearing. As they make pretend calls to their families, toddlers use their small muscles to push the buttons on toy phones. Twos also practice their fine motor skills when they scribble a note for a handmade book about saying good-bye.

Learning about the world: Young children show important cognitive development when they understand that, although their families disappear for a while, they return at the end of the day. Pretend play allows them to practice hellos and good-byes with dolls and stuffed animals, and to pretend to talk with their absent families on toy phones.

Learning about communicating: It is no wonder that *bye-bye* is often one of the first words in an infant's vocabulary. Saying good-bye is a frequent experience for a young child. Children continue to develop vocabulary and language—both receptive and expressive—as you label their feelings during separation, reassure them that families will come back, and comfort them by reading stories of babies and mothers who find each other.

Creating an Environment
for Hellos and Good-Byes

Special materials in an organized environment make arrivals and departures easier.

Encourage families to bring their child's comfort item from home, such as a special blanket or stuffed animal. Familiar objects help young children feel secure when they are away from those they love. Respect the children's needs and wishes to hold their special objects. Label these items to prevent them from getting lost, and have a place to keep them when children are not using them. Check your safety regulations so that you know when children are old enough to have stuffed animals and untucked blankets in their cribs.

Include pictures of children and their families in your room. Ask families for photographs or take pictures of them with their children. Make an attractive wall display at children's eye level. Consider filling a basket with family pictures so children can carry them around, or make an album or book of family pictures.

Place an interesting toy or material where it can be seen when children arrive. A flowering plant, a photo you took during a neighborhood walk, or a new toy gives parents and children something to explore together as children begin the day. Because arrivals are transitional times, adults and children are sometimes unsure of what to do next. Having something to focus on can be comforting.

Photograph family members in your setting. Take photographs of family members playing and reading with their children. Place the pictures where children can see them easily. These photos show that families are an important part of your program. They are also another way to help children feel connected to their families during the day.

Place toy phones or disconnected real ones near family pictures. Invite children to make pretend calls to their parents. Make pretend calls, yourself, to show them how.

Offer quiet places where toddlers and twos can retreat when they need some quiet time after saying good-bye. Children may choose to go to a special place until they are ready to join the group. These areas can be any quiet places: a comfortable chair, a cozy corner of the room with pillows, or a loft or window seat.

Caring and Teaching

Caring and teaching involves not only managing hellos and good-byes, but also helping children feel connected to their families during the day. The more comfortable children feel in your care, the better they are able to cope with these times of the day.

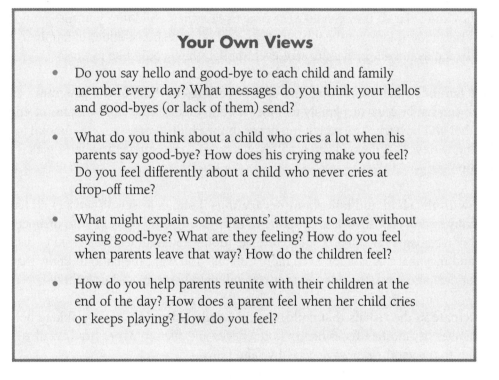

Your Own Views

- Do you say hello and good-bye to each child and family member every day? What messages do you think your hellos and good-byes (or lack of them) send?

- What do you think about a child who cries a lot when his parents say good-bye? How does his crying make you feel? Do you feel differently about a child who never cries at drop-off time?

- What might explain some parents' attempts to leave without saying good-bye? What are they feeling? How do you feel when parents leave that way? How do the children feel?

- How do you help parents reunite with their children at the end of the day? How does a parent feel when her child cries or keeps playing? How do you feel?

Supporting Children and Families During Hellos and Good-Byes

Hellos and good-byes offer opportunities to build positive, trusting relationships with children and families. Families have different ways of approaching separations and reunions. In some cultures, people believe that very young children should be able to function separately from their families. Other people believe that a mother should never be separated from her infant. As you work with families, try to get to know each family's beliefs and values so that you can support them during hellos and good-byes. Here are some ideas.

Allow sufficient time for hellos and good-byes, to meet individual needs without rushing. For example, a child with a disability may need extra time to adjust. A child learning English as a second language may be comforted by your speaking a few words or singing a simple song in her home language. A child who usually transitions easily may need extra comforting on a particular day.

Spend time with each child and his or her family before the child is left in your care for the first time. As parents get to know you, they will feel more confident about leaving their child in your care. Children will feel more comfortable when they see you interacting positively with their families.

Arrange a transitional period with families. Children need time to get to know you and to feel comfortable in their new setting while a family member is present. Let families know this so they can take the time to ease their child into your program. However, understand that the job situations and other responsibilities of family members may not allow them to stay, even though they would like to do so.

Have families leave something that clearly belongs to them at the program. An object that belongs to a family member is a reminder to the child that his mother or father will be back. The parent might say to the child, "I'm leaving the book I'm reading with you. Will you keep it with your things so we can get it when I pick you up?"

Stay with the child and talk about her feelings if she is upset. When a child has difficulty saying good-bye, it is tempting to rush through the process or to distract the child while a family member leaves. However, doing so might lead the child to distrust you and may make separation even more difficult. You want the child to know that you understand how she feels and that you will help her manage her feelings.

Participate in the rituals that children and families develop. Be available to hold an infant after her mother kisses her on both cheeks and the top of her head. Walk a toddler to the window to wave good-bye and blow kisses. Rituals help children—and adults—feel more secure, because they know what to expect.

Reassure families after a difficult departure. Try to call or e-mail family members during the day to let them know that their child is fine and to explain what you did to comfort the child after they left. This kind of communication is reassuring and builds trust.

Supporting Children Emotionally Throughout the Day

When good-byes are over and children are in your care, they often miss their families and ask about them. An infant might be cranky without an obvious reason. A toddler might ask, "Go home?" only 10 minutes after his father left. There is no reason to ignore or distract children from thinking about their families during the day. In fact, helping children feel connected to their families makes them feel more comfortable in your program. Here are some other things you can do to support children emotionally.

Make daily routines an important part of each day. When children learn that they can depend on consistent routines, it gives them a sense of security that enables them to cope better with separation.

Offer experiences that allow children to express and manage their feelings about hellos and good-byes. Respect children's feelings and provide soothing activities. Music can calm a child's anxiety and make her want to dance. Singing, exploring sand and water, and playing with stuffed animals and dolls are all experiences that help children manage their feelings.

Encourage play that helps children master separating and reuniting. Play games such as peek-a-boo. Offer other opportunities for children to appear and disappear, such as by playing in tunnels, cardboard boxes with doors that open and close, or tents made by draping a blanket over a table. Provide props for toddlers and twos, such as hats, briefcases, cloth bags, and empty food boxes. Encourage them to pretend that they are leaving for work or the store and coming home again. Toddlers and twos also enjoy playing hide-and-seek.

Read books with children about separations and reunions. Books such as *Are You My Mother?* (*¿Eres tu mi mamá?*), by P. D. Eastman, and *The Runaway Bunny*, by Margaret Wise Brown, can help children understand separation and reunion as they hear about the experiences of others. In the first book, a little bird falls from the nest and asks everyone, "Are you my mother?" until he finally finds her. In the second book, a bunny plays an imaginary game of hide-and-seek with his mother. He imagines that he will run away, and she assures him that she will always find him. Also consider writing your own books.

Recognize that children are competent. Children sense when you have confidence in their ability to separate from family members and function well. Your interactions with them help children recognize their own abilities.

Responding to What Children Need

Infants, toddlers, and twos behave differently during hellos and good-byes, depending on their developmental level, temperament, what is happening at home, their physical health, or even the weather.

Young infants who come to your program before they are 6 months old may not have difficulty separating from a family member. During these early months, most babies adjust well to new situations and teachers if their needs are met promptly and consistently. If your care is loving and responsive, very young infants are unlikely to have difficulty during good-byes.

Julio's father is rushed today. He hands Julio (4 months) to Linda quickly, puts the clothes he brought from home on the shelf, kisses Julio's head, and says good-bye. Julio begins to cry, and Linda feels his muscles tense.

Linda's Thoughts and Questions	Julio is feeling uncomfortable because his morning routine has been rushed. He is learning to communicate his feelings. I wonder if he is reacting to his father's mood. How can I comfort him?
How Linda Responds	"My pequeño bebé," Linda says as she rubs Julio's back. His crying calms to a soft whimper, and his body begins to relax. Linda gets Julio's favorite stuffed animal. "Would you like your soft perrito?" Julio reaches for the stuffed dog, holds it, and snuggles up to Linda.
What Julio Might Be Learning	To recognize and reach out to familiar adults (*Objective 1, Trusts known, caring adults*) To express a variety of emotions and needs, using facial expressions, body movements, and vocalizations (*Objective 3, Manages own feelings*) To use his whole hand to grasp objects (*Objective 9, Demonstrates basic fine motor skills*)

Mobile infants typically show more of a preference than young infants to be with family members and special adults. Around the age of 8–12 months, children often develop anxiety about being separated from the special adults with whom they have bonded. While helping a child through difficult separations may be challenging for both you and the child, remember that the difficulty is a sign that the child has a secure, healthy attachment with his parents. Your job is to build a trusting relationship with him so that he can develop a secure attachment with you as well.

Willard (11 months) returns to child care after a family vacation. Grace greets him warmly, but he clings to his mother. Grace suggests that she stay for a little while. When Grace joins them, Willard looks at his mother, puts his hands on her leg, and looks at Grace. Grace smiles and says, "Hi, Willard. I see that you are looking at me." Willard smiles slightly and turns, burying his face in his mother's arm. When Willard looks at Grace again, he is smiling. Grace says, "Oh, Willard, I missed your smile. I'm so glad you are back!" Willard reaches out and puts his hand on Grace's hand. She gives it noisy kisses. Willard squeals with laughter. His mother gets up to leave. Willard grabs her legs and screams. His mother says, "I'm sorry, Willard, but I have to leave."

Grace's Thoughts and Questions	Willard has not seen me for a couple of weeks. He wants to stay with his mother, but I know his mother has to leave. How can I comfort him and help him feel safe with me again?
How Grace Responds	Grace gently helps Willard let go of his mother's legs and lifts him into her arms. "It is very hard to say good-bye to Mommy. You are sad to see her go." Willard continues to cry loudly, and he screams as she leaves. Grace rubs his back and continues to talk to him in a soothing voice. "Oh, you love your mommy very much." She walks around with Willard, gently rocking him in her arms. Willard continues to cry and buries his face in Grace's shoulder. Grace gently strokes Willard's head and says, "I'm so glad that I'm getting to hold you right now."
What Willard Might Be Learning	To find security in being with familiar people (*Objective 6, Learns to be a member of a group*) To use others' facial expressions, gestures, or voices to guide his feelings (*Objective 3, Manages own feelings*)

Toddlers and twos may cheerfully wave good-bye to their families on some days. On other days, they may cling so tightly to their parents that you have to pull them off gently so that their parents can leave. The same clingy child may ignore a family member who comes to pick her up. If you have established a nurturing relationship with children and if they have a consistent routine, then, even on the most challenging days, children will know that they can trust you to ease them through difficult times.

When his father arrives, Matthew (22 months) is playing happily on the slide. Matthew ignores him and continues playing. Mercedes talks to Matthew's dad about how Matthew has become skilled at going up and down all by himself. Mercedes then walks over to Matthew and says, "Matthew, it is time to go home with your daddy." Matthew shakes his head and says, "No."

Mercedes' Thoughts and Questions	I don't want Matthew's father to feel badly because Matthew is acting as though he doesn't want to leave. I should explain how hard transitions are. Children need our help to switch from one activity to another. What can I say to help Matthew transition to going home?
How Mercedes Responds	Mercedes says, "Matthew, you're having fun on that slide." Matthew smiles and says, "Slide down." Mercedes explains, "You may go up and down the slide two more times. Then it is time to go home." Matthew goes up and down the slide. Mercedes cheers and says, "One." When he heads up the stairs again, Mercedes says, "Last time, Matthew. Make it a good one!" After Matthew slides down, Mercedes scoops him up and kisses him on the cheek. As they walk to the gate, Mercedes explains to his father the challenge of toddler transitions.
What Matthew Might Be Learning	To follow simple directions and sometimes test limits (*Objective 2, Regulates own behavior*) To balance while moving arms and legs in active play (*Objective 8, Demonstrates basic gross motor skills*) To understand simple directions and explanations (*Objective 16, Develops receptive language*) To speak in two-word phrases (*Objective 17, Develops expressive language*)

SHARING THOUGHTS ABOUT HELLOS AND GOOD-BYES

Dear Families:

Every day, you and your child say good-bye to one another in the morning and hello again in the afternoon. These hellos and good-byes are children's first steps on a lifelong journey of learning how to separate from and reunite with the important people in their lives. Learning to say hello and good-bye to people we love is a process, not something to be achieved in the first week, month, or even year of child care. Indeed, after many years of experience, we adults sometimes find it difficult to separate and reunite. We give special attention to hellos and good-byes in our program because they are such a major part of your child's life—now and always. Being able to separate is necessary if children are going to develop as confident and capable individuals. Learning to reunite is equally important.

How We Can Work Together

- **Try to spend some time here with your child, when you arrive and before you leave each day.** Your presence will help make the transition between home and child care easier for your child.

- **Never leave without saying good-bye to your child.** It is tempting to leave quietly if your child is busy and not noticing you. By saying good-bye, you strengthen your child's trust in you. Your child knows that you will not disappear without warning. When you are about to leave in the morning, I will be happy to help you and your child say good-bye.

- **Create hello and good-bye rituals.** A good-bye ritual might be as simple as giving your child a giant hug before you leave. A hello might be to come into the room, kneel near your child, smile, open you arms wide, and softly call his name. Having rituals offers both of you the comfort of knowing what to do.

- **Every day is different.** Be aware that, on some days, good-byes and hellos will be harder than on other days. Your child's stage of development and other factors, such as being hungry, tired, or upset by a change in your schedule, can make saying good-bye and hello difficult.

- **Bring familiar items from home.** We welcome family photos and other reminders of home that we may keep where your child can reach them. Seeing these special objects will help your child feel connected to you throughout the day.

By working together, we can help your child feel comfortable, secure, and confident in child care.

Sincerely,

inside this chapter

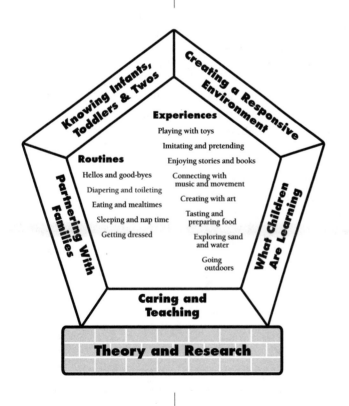

7 Diapering and Toileting

Grace explains, *"I'm going to change that wet diaper,"* *before gently picking up Willard (11 months). As she places him* *on the changing table, she invites conversation by saying, "You* *are wearing bright blue pants today. Did your Daddy put them* *on you this morning?" Willard says, "Dada." Grace continues,* *"We're going to put those bright blue pants right back on as soon* *as we're finished, okay?" As Grace pulls off Willard's pants, he* *touches his tummy. "That's your tummy," she explains. "Are* *you giving your tummy a little pat?"*

If a child's diaper is changed six times a day until he is 30 months old, he will have had his diaper changed more than 5,400 times. Anything a child experiences 5,400 times is an important part of life for him and for those who create the experience.

Diapering offers a chance to focus all of your attention on a single child. You can talk with each other, sing, or play a game of "Where are your toes?" When you approach diapering as an opportunity for meaningful interactions rather than a task to hurry through, you teach children important lessons: that bodily functions are a normal, healthy part of everyday life and that interactions with others are rewarding.

Between 2 and 3 years of age, children typically become physically, cognitively, and emotionally ready to begin using the toilet. If you and the child's family follow the child's lead, are supportive, work together, and avoid power struggles, you can help make mastering the skill of using the toilet a pleasant learning experience. Their child will also develop the self-confidence that comes with gaining self-control.

Supporting Development and Learning

Perhaps you have found yourself racing through diaper changes or wishing that all the children you care for had already graduated to underpants. However, diapering and toileting are times for caring and learning, and, as always, what you say and do make a difference in what children learn and how they feel about themselves.

Learning about themselves and others: When young infants begin needing a diaper change at about the same time each day, they have taken an important first step in regulating their own behavior. As 2-year-olds, children continue learning about themselves as they take the giant step of toilet learning. Being able to use the toilet helps 2-year-olds feel good about their bodies, delighted with their new personal care skill, and proud to say, "I flushed! I'm big now!" As 2-year-olds gather in the bathroom, they learn that everybody pees and poops! Children's trust in teachers is built gradually through such care as having wet diapers changed consistently and having toileting accidents handled in a matter-of-fact way.

Learning about moving: As infants, toddlers, and twos develop, they become more active participants in diapering. They practice gross motor skills as they walk up the steps to the diaper-changing table, and they develop fine motor skills as they help you take off or put on their pants, snap the snap, and button the large button. Learning to use the toilet requires children to control an important muscle in their body, the sphincter.

Learning about the world: Young children are curious about everything. Diapering and toileting hold many mysteries. How does my body work? Where does the water come from when I turn on the faucet? Why does the toilet make a loud sound when I push the handle? What happens to my poop when I flush? Diapering and toileting help infants, toddlers, and twos learn about how things can be used, and they provide many opportunities to explore cause and effect.

Learning about communicating: Diapering is a time for one-on-one conversations. Infants learn that you are listening and understand what they are communicating when you respond to the special cry that means that they are wet and uncomfortable. Children's vocabularies and language skills grow when you talk about what you are doing as you change their diapers and name body parts and clothing. Books about toileting, such as *Everyone Poops* by Taro Gomi, delight mobile infants, toddlers, and twos.

Creating an Environment for Diapering and Toileting

You and the children will spend lots of time at the diapering table and in the bathroom, so it is important to make the diapering and toileting areas pleasant and attractive. When a space is inviting, you are more likely to relax. The children will sense this and be more relaxed, too. You can add special touches, such as a shatterproof mirror (out of children's reach) or pictures of children.

Remember that convenience is important as well. You will need to have all of your supplies nearby: diapers, wipes, clean clothes, gloves, and bleach solution. Diapering and toileting go smoothly and safely when the area is well-arranged area and has ample room for storage.

The Diaper-Changing Station

Choose the right location. A diaper-changing station should be next to a handwashing sink and away from food preparation areas. This space should be used only for diapering.

Make sure the area is safe and sanitary. Changing surfaces should be nonporous and kept in good repair. They should be surrounded by railings or barriers at least 6 inches high. (Avoid straps. They are easily contaminated and do not keep children safe.) Provide a commercial-grade, step-on, foot-pedaled, or other type of hands-free diaper can. Follow procedures for cleaning and sanitizing the surface after each diaper change.

Make it easy on your back. Most people find that a convenient height for the changing surface is 28–32 inches from the floor. Step-up stairs save you from lifting heavy toddlers and twos. Toddlers often prefer to be changed while they are standing up. Try letting them stand on a mat or use a platform with handholds while you are changing their diapers. Be sure to clean and sanitize the area as you would a changing table.

The Toileting Area

Make it as easy as possible for children to use the toilet independently. Child-size toilets and sinks are ideal. If your program does not have child-size equipment, the American Academy of Pediatrics and the American Public Health Association recommend that you use modified toilet seats and step aids for toilet learning.[28] They discourage using potty chairs because they are difficult to clean and sanitize. If you use potty chairs, be sure to follow the guidance on cleaning and sanitizing them. Arrange the environment so children can be successful and feel competent. If toilets and sinks are not child-height, provide a step stool to help children reach them. Place paper towels within the children's reach, close to the sink. Display photographs of children washing their hands, brushing their teeth, or tossing a paper towel in the trash can.

Adapt the area as necessary for toddlers and twos with disabilities. Many different types of potty seats are designed to meet the needs of children with various disabilities. Families and therapists can advise you about appropriate equipment. If a child uses a wheelchair or walker, be sure to allow enough space in the bathroom. You will also need handrails to make it easy to transfer between the wheelchair and toilet.

Caring and Teaching

Infants, toddlers, and twos can tell how you feel about diapering and toileting by your tone of voice, body tension, and facial expression as they experience these routines with you. Because you are so important to the children in your care, it is important to view diapering and toileting positively.

Your Own Views

- How do you feel when you are changing diapers? How do your feelings about diaper changing influence your interactions with children during this routine?

- How do you feel when a child has a toileting accident? What do you say or do? How does this makes the child feel?

- What do you want to teach children about their bodies while they are learning to use the toilet?

Keeping Children Safe and Healthy

One of your most important responsibilities as a teacher is to keep children safe and healthy. Diapering involves germs that may spread if you are not careful. Stools sometimes carry germs that can cause illnesses with diarrhea and vomiting, as well as serious diseases such as hepatitis A. For this reason, procedures for diaper changing and handwashing must be followed carefully. Follow these guidelines to make diapering and toileting as safe and healthy possible:

Learn your program's policies. For instance, does your program use disposable or cloth diapers? What are your program's policies on the use of gloves or diaper creams? While you must follow universal precautions and wear gloves when blood is present, some programs also recommend or require gloves for routine diapering. If you do use gloves, you have to know when to put them on and how to take them off to avoid contamination.

Follow a recommended procedure for changing diapers. Practice diaper changing until it becomes second nature to you. While you are diapering, remember to talk with the child and take advantage of this time to be together one-on-one.

Schedule regular times to check children's diapers and change diapers between times as needed. The American Academy of Pediatrics and the American Public Health Association recommend that diapers be checked at least hourly for wetness and feces.[29] Following a schedule will enable you to guide other children to activities that do not require your active participation, so you can pay attention to the child whose diaper you are changing.

Have everything you need nearby before you start diapering. This way, you can focus on the child, and you will not have to ask a busy colleague to assist you.

Keep a hand on the child at all times. That is the only way to guarantee the child's safety. Never leave a child alone, even for a moment.

Remain aware of the rest of the group as you change a diaper. Watch, listen, and use your good sense to recognize when you are needed by other children. Try to arrange the diaper-changing table so that you are facing toward, rather than away from, the room. If this is not possible, hang a mirror behind the table so you can watch the rest of the group.

Responding to What Children Need

Depending on their developmental levels and personal characteristics, infants, toddlers, and twos react to diapering and toileting very differently. Your responses will change according to what a child needs from you.

Linda smiles at Julio (4 months) and sings to him while she is changing his diaper. He gazes into her eyes and relaxes.

Young infants interact with you individually during diapering. They also begin exploring and learning about their bodies and things around them. They vocalize back and forth, pausing to listen as you converse together.

Julio (4 months) has been lying on a blanket, smiling at Linda, waving his arms, and kicking his legs. He begins to grimace, whimper, and squirm. Linda smells an odor. "You have a poopy diaper, Julio," she explains. "Let's get you changed right away!" Linda picks him up, takes him to the diaper table, and lays him down. Julio looks at Linda as she chats with him. "Look, you're all clean," she says as she puts on a fresh diaper. She continues talking to him as she gets him dressed and washes his hands.

Linda's Thoughts and Questions	Julio's way of letting me know that he has a wet diaper is to make faces, whimper, and squirm.
	I think he needed to be changed around this time yesterday. I wonder if he's beginning to need a diaper change at the same time every day.
How Linda Responds	Linda changes Julio's diaper as soon as she notices his cues. She talks to Julio, explaining what she is doing. "First we have to take the messy diaper off, and then I will clean your bottom. All clean!" she says, looking back at him as he looks at her. "Time for the dry diaper." After the diaper is on, she washes Julio's hands, smiles, and says, "All done!" Julio smiles back.
What Julio Might Be Learning	To recognize and reach out to familiar adults. (*Objective 1, Trusts known, caring adults*)
	To develop a routine pattern for when he needs his diaper changed. (*Objective 2, Regulates own behavior*)
	To show interest in the speech of others (*Objective 16, Develops receptive language*)
	To use facial expressions, vocalizations, and body movements to communicate (*Objective 17, Develops expressive language*)

Mobile infants participate increasingly in the diapering routine. They lift their legs so you can take off the diaper, hold their hands out to be washed, tug on wet pants, and bring you a clean diaper. They begin to learn new words, such as the names of body parts and clothes, and concepts such as up–down, wet–dry, open–close, and cool–warm.

Brooks lifts Abby (14 months) onto the changing table, explaining, "It's time to change your wet diaper, Abby." As soon as Brooks lays her down, Abby quickly rolls over and begins to crawl. Brooks keeps her hand on Abby's back and acknowledges, "Abby, you want to move."

Brooks' Thoughts and Questions	Abby really enjoys practicing her motor skills. She wants to move, not lie still, but she needs to have her very wet diaper changed. I wonder how to engage her in this routine. How can I acknowledge her desire to move and still change her diaper?
How Brooks Responds	Brooks tells Abby, "I know you want to get down. As soon as I change your diaper, you may get down." "Dow," repeats Abby, recognizing the familiar word. Brooks continues, "Yes, up and down. Abby, now it is time to roll over so that we can change your diaper," She helps Abby roll onto her back and begins to change her diaper, talking to her throughout the process. Abby reaches in the direction of the stack of diapers. "Thank you, Abby. You do need a clean diaper. Will you please hold it for me?" She hands the diaper to Abby.
What Abby Might Be Learning	To begin to be receptive to verbal redirection (*Objective 2, Regulates own behavior*) To begin to move from place to place (*Objective 8, Demonstrates basic gross motor skills*) To understand simple multiword speech in familiar contexts (*Objective 16, Develops receptive language*) To use word-like sounds to communicate (*Objective 17, Develops expressive language*).

Toddlers are becoming very interested in their bodies and bodily functions. They are able to participate more actively in diapering. They can get their own diapers from their cubbies, pull down their own pants, and often try to take off their wet diapers.

Matthew (22 months) looks at Mercedes, points to his diaper, and says, "Wet." Mercedes reaches for Matthew's hand and says, "Thank you for telling me that you are wet, Matthew. Let's go change your diaper." Matthew shakes his head, clenches his hands into fists, frowns, and insists, "No! Me do!"

Mercedes' Thoughts and Questions	Lately Matthew has been letting me know when he is wet. However, this is the second time that he has protested when I've thanked him and then tried to change his diaper. He wants to be more involved in the diaper-changing process. How can I give Matthew the opportunity to participate in diaper changing but still follow all of the diapering steps needed to maintain a safe and healthy environment?
How Mercedes Responds	"Matthew, would you like to help me change your diaper?" Matthew nods his head up and down. As Mercedes points to the cubby where his diapers are kept, she asks, "Will you please get a clean diaper for us to use?" Matthew gets a diaper and hands it to her. "Thank you, Matthew. Will you please take your shorts off now?" Matthew pulls at his shorts. It takes him a few tries, but, with some help, he is able to pull them down and step out of them. He smiles at Mercedes and exclaims, "Did it!" As she helps him walk up the steps to the changing table, Mercedes acknowledges, "You took your pants off all by yourself! Okay, let's change that diaper."
What Matthew Might Be Learning	To follow simple directions (*Objective 2, Regulates own behavior*) To try more complex personal care tasks with increasing success (*Objective 7, Uses personal care skills*) To demonstrate understanding of simple directions and questions (*Objective 16, Develops receptive language*) To speak in two-word phrases (*Objective 17, Develops expressive language*)

Twos are about to accomplish a special task—toilet learning—and you have an important role to play. Here are some of the ways that children show that they are becoming more aware of their bodily functions and that they will soon be ready for toilet learning:

- staying dry for long periods of time

- wanting to sit on the toilet with their clothes on

- telling you that they are wet, had a bowel movement, or are going to (although usually too late to get them to the bathroom in time)

- saying that they want to use the toilet and talking about their urine and bowel movements, using whatever words are used at home

To help a child learn to use the toilet, follow these steps:

- Watch for the signs that children are ready. Remember that 2-year-olds do not automatically become ready for toilet learning on their second birthday. While some twos show signs of readiness, many children are not ready to undertake this big step until they are at least 30 months old.

- When they seem ready, encourage children to use the toilet. Talk with them consistently and calmly, but without undue pressure or shaming them.

- Frequently remind children to go to the toilet. That way, they might not get so involved in what they are doing that they forget and have an accident. Take advantage of group potty time so children can see and learn from one another.

- Acknowledge children's successes.

- Allow children to see their urine and bowel movements and invite them to help flush them away if they choose.

Expect twos to have toileting accidents as they learn to control when and where they go to the bathroom. If you treat their toileting accidents matter-of-factly, children will develop positive attitudes about using the toilet.

Gena (30 months) is busy building a farm for a new set of animals that Ivan put out this morning. All of a sudden she begins to cry. Ivan walks over and asks "Gena, what happened? I saw you playing with the new animals, and now you're crying." Gena points to her wet pants. "I forgot," she says. Ivan responds, "That's okay. Accidents happen. Let's get you into some dry clothes so you can be comfortable. Then you can finish your farm."

Ivan's Thoughts and Questions	Gena is beginning to understand that she is expected to use the toilet, and she feels embarrassed when something goes wrong.
	She sometimes gets so involved in her play that she forgets to use the bathroom.
	How can I help her remember to go to the bathroom, even while she's absorbed in play?
How Ivan Responds	Ivan helps Gena change into dry clothes and seals her wet ones in a plastic bag for her family to take home and wash.
	Later in the day, Ivan talks with Gena. He suggests that he help her use the toilet each day after snacks, so she can play without worrying. Gena agrees to the plan.
What Gena Might Be Learning	To understand what behavior is expected, with increasing regularity (*Objective 2, Regulates own behavior*)
	To continue an activity, despite distractions (*Objective 10, Sustains attention*)
	To understand increasingly complex and abstract spoken language (*Objective 16, Develops receptive language*)

Working in Partnership With Families

Family members and you are likely to have strong feelings about, and perhaps different strategies for, toilet learning. For example, some people think that teaching a child to use the toilet means that the adult should take responsibility for getting the child to the bathroom at the right time. With this in mind, they may begin toilet learning when children are as young as 6 months. Others think that learning to use the toilet should begin when a child is ready to assume responsibility for his or her own use, typically around 30 months of age.

Here are some strategies to help you work with families on diapering and toileting.

Complete the *Individual Care Plan—Family Information Form* (see the *Appendix*) when families enter the program. It includes questions about the type of diapers the family uses, how often the child's diaper is changed at home, times that the child usually needs a diaper change, and any special instructions for diapering.

Ask parents whether and how they are helping their child learn to use the toilet at home. Listen carefully and try to understand families' perspectives when they do things differently from you. Ask questions to help you understand their approaches.

Discuss the signs that indicate that a child is ready for toilet learning. Share with families the steps you take to help a child learn to use the toilet. Offer this information at a meeting or workshop for families whose children are starting to use the toilet.

Help families be realistic in their expectations for toilet learning. Remind them that accidents are inevitable and should be treated matter-of-factly. Explain that even children who use the toilet successfully during the day may need to wear diapers at night for a time or may regress temporarily in response to stress. Explain that girls often achieve success sooner because they can more easily control urination. Finally, remind families that each child is different.

Offer resources to families who may be confused or overwhelmed by toilet learning practices. Display books and articles. Encourage family members to share their experiences with each other.

Negotiate differences between your approaches, if necessary. Things do not have to be done exactly the same at home as in child care, but children need to know what to expect. For example, a child may wear diapers in your program, even though he goes without diapers during weekend days at home. His parents assume responsibility for getting him to the toilet at the right time at home, but you might not be able to do so in your group setting.

SHARING THOUGHTS ABOUT DIAPERING AND TOILETING

Dear Families:

If your child's diaper is changed six times a day for 2 1/2 years, he or she will have had a diaper change more than 5,400 times. Anything experienced 5,400 times is an important part of your child's life—and of yours. Over time, your child will become physically, cognitively, and emotionally ready to begin using the toilet. We will celebrate this milestone together!

While diapering may not be your favorite task, it can be a special time for you and your child. It offers a chance to focus all of your attention on your child. You can talk together, sing, or play a game of "Where are your toes?" When you approach diapering as an opportunity to spend time with your baby, rather than as an unpleasant task to hurry through, you teach your child an important lesson: that bodily functions are a normal, healthy part of everyday life.

How We Can Work Together

- **Let's share information about diapering and toileting.** Tell us how you approach diapering at home. How often do you change your baby's diaper? How do you know that the diaper needs to be changed? Are there any special instructions for diaper changes? Here, we keep track of when we change your child's diapers every day. Be sure to take a look at our daily log and let us know if you have any questions.

- **Please make sure that we have changes of clothing so we can keep your child clean and dry.** Don't be surprised or upset when we send home soiled clothing in a tightly closed plastic bag. Germs can be spread easily during diaper changing, and experts tell us not to rinse soiled clothing at the center. This procedure helps keep your child healthy.

- **Let's talk about approaches to helping children learn to use the toilet.** We'll look together for the signs that your child is ready to learn to use the toilet. We'll also talk regularly about your child's progress. Then we can then decide together about ways to support your child and resolve any differences we may have.

- **Remember that toileting accidents are normal.** Learning to use the toilet takes time. Even children who can use the toilet successfully sometimes have toileting accidents. Having realistic expectations allows us to respond to toileting accidents matter-of-factly. We have some great books that you can read to your child about going to the toilet. *Everyone Poops*, by Taro Gomi, is sure to become a family favorite!

By keeping a sense of perspective and a sense of humor, we can give your child the time and support needed to learn to use the toilet.

Sincerely,

inside this chapter

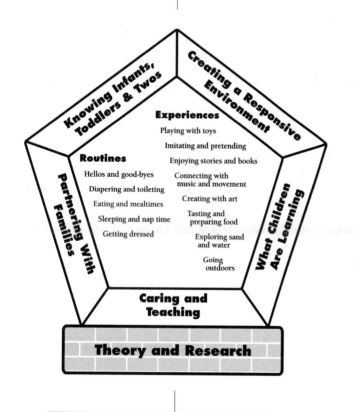

8 Eating and Mealtimes

Valisha *(33 months) has just finished washing her hands. LaToya, who is getting ready for lunch, says, "Valisha, I need some help. Will you please carry these spoons to the table? We need them to eat our lunch." Valisha takes four spoons from LaToya, places one on each placemat, and exclaims, "I did it!" "Thank you," responds LaToya. "What else do we need?" "Napkins," answers Valisha, getting them from the lunch cart. She sits on one of the chairs and distributes the napkins, admitting, "I'm tired." LaToya smiles. "You've been a big help, Valisha. Today we're having one of your favorite lunches: rice and beans." Valisha responds, "Yea! Mommy makes that."*

Mealtimes and related activities, such as setting the table, washing hands, talking with others at the table, and brushing teeth, are all learning opportunities. During these activities, you interact with children and help them get to know one another. Through your involvement, they also develop good nutrition and health habits. During mealtimes, infants, toddlers, and twos explore the tastes, colors, textures, and aromas of foods and enjoy a sense of caring and community.

When Linda cradles Julio (4 months) in her arms to give him his bottle, she gives him the message, "You can trust me to take good care of you." When Brooks puts a spoon and a dish of mashed sweet potato on (14-month-old) Abby's plate, her actions say, "Go ahead. Here's a chance to practice feeding yourself." LaToya teaches concepts and social skills when she talks with children about the fact that the green beans are the same color as the playdough they made, reminds them to use the chairs for sitting, and helps them brush their teeth. She also supports their development of healthy habits.

Supporting Development and Learning

Here are some of the many things children learn during eating and mealtimes.

Learning about themselves and others: When a mobile infant somewhat successfully guides a spoonful of applesauce to his mouth, his expression suggests his pleasure in feeding himself. As infants learn to regulate their behavior, they develop routine patterns for eating. By the time they are toddlers, they participate in group routines, such as family-style dining. Toddlers not only develop food preferences, but they discover their friends' likes and dislikes, too. Eating and mealtimes are filled with opportunities for infants, toddlers, and twos to develop a range of personal care skills. Invite twos to join in when it is time to clean up after meals and snacks.

Learning about moving: As they use their fingers and spoons to bring food to their mouths, children practice fine motor skills and refine their eye-hand coordination. Imagine a young infant who curls his fingers around your hand as you give him his bottle. Soon he will use a pincer grasp to pick up the tiny Cheerios® on his plate. Drinking from a cup, beginning to serve food, pouring milk from a very small pitcher, and cleaning up the inevitable spills are some of the everyday activities that promote children's small muscle development and coordination.

Learning about the world: During mealtimes, infants, toddlers, and twos continue to learn how things work. Children use all five senses to see, smell, taste, touch, and listen to the foods, related objects, and people involved in mealtime experiences. Young infants learn about cause and effect as they tip their bottles when the level of milk drops. Mobile infants solve the problem of how to eat noodles with their fingers. Twos smell lunch being made in the kitchen and say, "Time to eat." Mealtimes also present opportunities for twos to develop mathematical concepts such as *more* and *less.* They also develop spatial awareness when they do such things as pour drinks and spoon food onto their plates from the serving bowl.

Learning about communicating: Mealtime conversations are opportunities for children to hear and practice using interesting, descriptive language as they munch on *crunchy green lettuce* or taste *smooth* infant *cereal.* As mobile infants, toddlers, and twos sit together during mealtimes, they begin to engage in nonverbal and verbal conversations with you and their friends. Toddlers and twos certainly use their expanding language skills to let you know their food preferences.

Creating an Environment for Eating and Mealtimes

Bottles, breast milk, formula, baby food jars, dishes, and spoons are all necessary supplies in an infant classroom. The environment for eating and mealtimes therefore includes places to prepare and store food and to ensure safe food handling. In addition, you need comfortable places to hold and feed young infants, and inviting spaces where small groups of mobile infants, toddlers, and twos can eat together.

Here are some important considerations.

Observe health and safety guidelines when organizing the food-preparation and eating areas. Locate areas for eating and mealtimes away from diapering, toileting, and laundry areas. An infant room must have a handwashing sink and, ideally, a small refrigerator.

Arrange adequate storage and space for food preparation. Storage cabinets, often mounted on the wall, and a counter for food preparation help make this area functional. You also need a place to warm bottles. Some programs warm bottles under hot running water, while others use a bottle warmer or crock pot. It is not safe to warm bottles or baby food jars in a microwave oven because the contents do not heat evenly. Always make sure that electrical cords are safely out of children's reach.

Have comfortable seating for feeding young infants.
Because you will be holding young infants in your arms when feeding them, have a comfortable glider or soft chair to sit in. Locate these throughout the room. You do not need to dedicate a space only to feeding young infants.

Provide a comfortable chair and a private space for mothers who are breast-feeding. Include a pillow to support her baby on her lap, a foot rest, and a glass of water to drink.

Have appropriately sized tables and chairs. Once they can support themselves, mobile infants can sit in sturdy infant chairs at low tables. Slightly higher tables and chairs are made for toddlers and twos. Children should sit with their feet touching the floor, rather than in high chairs or at tables with bucket seats, where their legs dangle in the air.

Arrange an eating area for mobile infants, toddlers, and twos. Think about how to arrange your tables to make mealtimes manageable. This will depend partly on the number of tables you need. Most likely no more than 3–4 mobile infants and toddlers will be eating at a time. In a class for 2-year-olds, the group will eat together, with four or five children sitting at tables with a teacher.

Use plates and eating utensils that are unbreakable, safe, and easy to handle. Toddlers can learn to serve themselves by using small plastic pitchers for pouring water, juice, or milk and by using plastic serving bowls. When pitchers and glasses are clear, children can see how much they have poured. Never use Styrofoam™ materials or plastic utensils that can be broken easily. Special utensils, deep-sided bowls, and mugs with two handles make it easier for children to feed themselves.

Make cleanup as easy as possible. Locate your eating space in an area with an easy-to-clean floor, have the children wear bibs, place extra napkins and paper towels nearby, and invite children to help clean up spills.

Caring and Teaching

Being with you is an important part of children's mealtime experiences. Model good manners and the pleasures of social interaction. For young infants, who need to be fed on demand and held when you give them a bottle, mealtime is important one-on-one time with you. Mobile infants are also fed according to individual eating schedules.

For a group of toddlers, of twos, or of mixed ages, family-style dining is a good way to organize mealtimes. In this arrangement, everyone sits together around the table—on low chairs or on your lap, depending on children's ages—so they can see and interact with each other. Toddlers and twos serve themselves, with your help. Children may begin eating as soon as they have food on their plates. Although some families expect children to wait until everyone is served, waiting is difficult for hungry toddlers and twos.

During eating and mealtimes, you build positive relationships with young children while you nurture their bodies. Infants are more comfortable when they are fed by their primary teacher as much as possible. Toddlers and twos also like to sit and eat with their primary teacher. Good experiences at mealtimes help children develop positive attitudes toward food and nutrition.

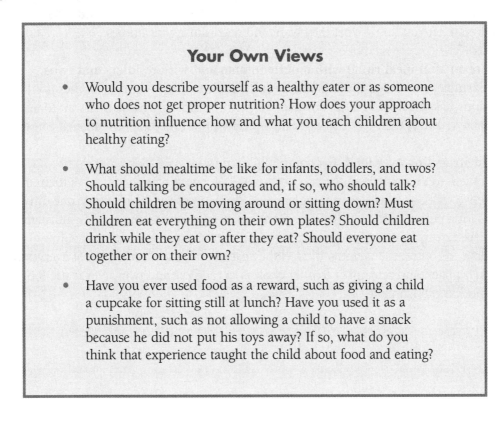

Your Own Views

- Would you describe yourself as a healthy eater or as someone who does not get proper nutrition? How does your approach to nutrition influence how and what you teach children about healthy eating?

- What should mealtime be like for infants, toddlers, and twos? Should talking be encouraged and, if so, who should talk? Should children be moving around or sitting down? Must children eat everything on their own plates? Should children drink while they eat or after they eat? Should everyone eat together or on their own?

- Have you ever used food as a reward, such as giving a child a cupcake for sitting still at lunch? Have you used it as a punishment, such as not allowing a child to have a snack because he did not put his toys away? If so, what do you think that experience taught the child about food and eating?

Here are some strategies to use during eating and mealtimes.

Feed children when they are hungry. Watch and listen for cues that babies are hungry, and feed them as soon as possible. Before becoming so hungry that they cry, infants often show that they are ready to be fed by opening their mouths, making sucking sounds, and moving their hands randomly. Keep waiting times for mobile infants and toddlers as brief as possible, too. Have the food ready when the children come to the table. Be sure to have everything you need, including food, beverages, dishes, and spoons. You do not want to leave the table to look for missing items.

Always hold young infants when feeding them bottles. Sit in a comfortable chair and snuggle with the baby. Enjoy having infants curl their fingers around yours, helping you hold their bottles. Even when they can hold the bottle by themselves, they still want to be held, enjoying your special time together.

Create a calm and pleasant atmosphere. Transitions that help set a relaxed tone include reading a book together or doing another quiet activity. Allow enough time for a leisurely meal.

Encourage relaxed, friendly conversation. Talk together during mealtimes about familiar topics of interest to the children, such as the tastes and smells of the foods you are eating, activities you did earlier in the day, and plans for the afternoon. Encourage children to let you know what they want and need during mealtimes.

Create an after-meal ritual with mobile infants and with toddlers and twos. For example, encourage children to stay at the table and talk with each other until everyone has finished. Be sure, however, to permit children who cannot wait to leave the table to brush their teeth or work on a puzzle until everyone has finished eating.

Avoid struggling over food. Encourage children to try new foods, but do not force them to eat something they do not want. Talk about new foods, serve them in attractive ways, and taste everything yourself. Sometimes toddlers eat just one or two foods for a period of time. If they are given nutritious choices, they get the nutrients they need over the course of a week or a month, even if not at each meal. Allow children to control the quantity of food they eat, do not expect them to eat everything on their plates, and remember to offer choices to toddlers and twos. Never use food as a reward or punishment.

Promote children's growing independence during snack and mealtimes.
Encourage children to participate in whatever ways are appropriate for their level of development. Seat an infant on your lap so he can hear and watch the other children. Offer a mobile infant a chance to use her fingers to feed herself. Provide spoons that are easy to hold for toddlers who want to feed themselves. Invite 2-year-olds to help you set the table and do other mealtime tasks.

Offer experiences that encourage children to practice mealtime skills throughout the day. For example, include plates and eating utensils in the pretend play area so children can enact mealtime events. Provide small pitchers and cups for water play. Children can use these to practice pouring liquids. See chapter 15, *Tasting and Preparing Foods,* for ideas about involving children in cooking experiences.

Recognize children's new skills and accomplishments. Make a positive comment when you see a child just learning to hold a bottle, drink from a cup, or spread cottage cheese on a cracker. Acknowledging their competence encourages them to practice their skills and attempt new ones.

Consult with specialists about a child with a disability that affects eating.
They can advise you about feeding procedures, as well as about appropriate adaptive equipment.

Invite families to join their children for snacks and meals whenever they can.
With their help, each child can be given more attention. Having family members present can also ease separation difficulties and help children enjoy eating at the program as much as they enjoy it at home.

Consider the best time for you to eat. Although you want to be a good model for children, you may find that trying to eat at the same time you are supervising a group at the table is too much. You may prefer to have your lunch during a more quiet time. In some programs, teachers eat a small portion of their lunch with the children and the rest of their meal during their lunch break.

Keeping Children Safe and Healthy

Here are some health and safety points to consider and share with families, whether you or the families provide food for the children.

Learn the rules for handling food safely. Carefully follow the instructions for mixing formula, storing breast milk, serving semisolid and solid baby food safely, and so forth. Clean and sanitize food preparation and eating areas with a surface bleach solution. Your local food service inspector or sanitarian can help you learn how to handle food to minimize the risk of food-borne illnesses.

Promote good health and safety practices. Handwashing is extremely important when preparing foods, and before and after eating. Wash your hands, wash infants' hands, and help toddlers and twos wash their hands. Wipe infants' teeth with a soft cloth, and help older children with toothbrushing. Do not allow children to eat when walking, running, playing, lying down, or riding in vehicles. Store cleaning materials in locked cabinets, out of the reach of children. Do not use microwave ovens to heat bottles or baby food jars.

Learn about good nutrition for infants, toddlers, and twos. The United States Department of Agriculture (USDA) Child and Adult Care Food Program (CACFP) provides guidelines for nutritious meals and snacks for children birth to age 3. The Food and Nutrition Service publishes *Feeding Infants: A Guide for Use in the Child Nutrition Program*, which can be downloaded from the USDA Web site. Model good nutrition practices for children.

Be aware of and follow food safety precautions. For example, do not give honey to infants under 12 months of age because it may carry harmful bacteria. Avoid giving infants under 12 months white table sugar, artificial sweeteners, corn syrup, egg whites, fried foods, shellfish, raw onions, and processed meats. Do not offer tomatoes and pineapple to infants before age one. The high acidity of these foods can harm delicate mouth tissues.

Avoid serving foods that may cause choking. Children under 3 years should not eat certain foods because they are choking hazards. Hot dogs and peanuts are the most frequent causes of choking in children under age three. Other foods that can cause a young child to choke include raw carrots; raisins and similar dried fruit, such as cherries or cranberries; popcorn; whole grapes; blueberries; whole olives; corn; uncooked peas; nuts; peanut butter; crumbly cookies or crackers; jelly beans; and hard candy.

Never prop bottles. Putting a baby to bed with a bottle of milk or juice can cause ear infections, choking, and bottlemouth, a severe form of tooth decay that may cause tooth loss.

Be aware of children's allergies. If you observe or learn from families that a child is allergic to a particular food, make sure this information is circulated and posted where everyone, including volunteers, can see it. Common food allergies include chocolate, strawberries, peanut butter, other nuts, and tofu.

Stop to burp young infants. Stop every 3–5 minutes or when a child has consumed 2–3 ounces of formula or milk. This rest lets the child slow down and prevents her from swallowing too much air. If the child does not burp, place her in an upright position for 15 minutes after the feeding to prevent spitting up. Ask the family what burping technique their baby prefers. For example, you might hold the baby upright on your shoulder and gently pat her back, or sit the baby on your lap and pat her back while supporting her head and neck. Another technique is to rest the baby over your lap, tummy down; lift and support his head so it is higher than his chest; and pat his back.

Work with families to comfort babies with colic. About 10–20 percent of young infants in Western cultures develop colic, a condition that can last through the fourth month. Babies with colic tend to cry loudly, uncontrollably, and for a long time; extend or pull their legs up to their stomachs; have enlarged stomachs; and/or pass gas. There is often no apparent cause for colic, but most children outgrow the condition.

Responding to What Children Need

Babies' mouth patterns and hand and body skills affect the kinds of foods they are able to eat, as well as how they should be fed. Here is general information about what infants, toddlers, and twos are able to do, the kinds of food they can eat, and how to feed them.

Young infants are born with nursing reflexes. A baby turns his head toward an object, such as a nipple, when his mouth, lip, cheek, or chin is touched. When a baby's lips are touched, his tongue moves out of his mouth. This reflex allows feeding from the breast or bottle but not from a spoon or cup. Feeding solid foods is not recommended until a baby is 4–6 months old.

Between about 4 and 7 months of age, babies develop new skills that enable them to eat semisolid foods, such as infant cereal with iron and strained vegetables and fruit. They open their mouths when they see food. They can now move their tongues up and down, and swallow many foods without choking. They can sit with support, have good head control, and use their whole hands to grasp objects. Infants who are eating soft or solid foods but who are not yet able to sit alone should sit in your lap while you feed them. Place the food on a nearby table or counter.

Janet feeds Jasmine (8 months) some applesauce while sitting at a child-size table. As Jasmine opens her mouth, Janet uses the spoon to direct applesauce into it. Janet comments, "I know you like applesauce, Jasmine, because you always finish the bowlful." As Janet feeds her, Jasmine dips her right hand into the bowl, looks up at Janet, and pops her hand into her mouth. Most of the applesauce falls out of Jasmine's hand before it reaches her mouth.

Janet's Thoughts and Questions	Jasmine really wants to feed herself, although she does not always get the food into her mouth.
	It would be so much easier for me to feed her, but I know that it's important to encourage her desire to feed herself and to support her developing self-feeding skills.
	If I let Jasmine feed herself, will she get enough to eat?
How Janet Responds	As Janet wipes up the spilled applesauce, she comments, "It's great that you're feeding yourself, Jasmine. Applesauce is very slippery."
	"Jasmine, I want to be sure you eat enough food. Let's do this: I'll feed you one spoonful of applesauce; then you take a turn feeding applesauce to yourself."
What Jasmine Might Be Learning	To attempt simple personal care tasks (*Objective 7, Uses personal care skills*)
	To use whole hand to grasp and drop objects (*Objective 9, Demonstrates basic fine motor skills*)
	To notice particular characteristics of objects (*Objective 13, Shows a beginning understanding that things can be grouped*)
	To demonstrate awareness of a problem (*Objective 14, Uses problem-solving strategies*)

Mobile infants, from about 8–11 months, learn to move their tongues from side to side. They have some teeth and begin to chew. They use their thumb and index finger to pick up objects, learn to eat from a spoon, drink milk from a cup with less spilling, and begin to feed themselves with their hands. Now they are ready to eat mashed, diced or strained fruit, vegetables, meat, poultry, beans, and peas. They can also eat cottage cheese, yogurt, cheese strips, pieces of soft bread, and crackers. They continue to drink breast milk or iron-fortified formula and can also drink fruit juice, but now they drink from a cup as well as a bottle. At about 11 months, they begin to hold a cup and, with help, begin spoon-feeding themselves. Once infants can sit comfortably, they can sit in low, sturdy infant chairs at low tables.

Barbara is sitting with Leo (18 months) and two other children at a low table as they eat lunch. She says, "M-m-m. These crackers are nice and crunchy." Suddenly, Leo reaches over and grabs two crackers from Wanda's plate. He starts to eat one of the crackers but stops when Wanda starts to scream. Leo quickly puts the crackers back on Wanda's plate.

Barbara's Thoughts and Questions	Wow! Leo actually put the crackers back on Wanda's plate when she protested. I've been trying to help him use other children's reactions to guide his behavior. Maybe it's beginning to work!
How Barbara Responds	"Leo, Wanda was angry when you took her crackers. She's glad you put them back. Would you like some more crackers?" Leo nods his head up and down. As she moves the plate closer to him, Barbara explains, "You may take some from this big plate."
What Leo Might Be Learning	To use other's facial expressions, gestures, or voices to guide his own behavior (*Objective 2, Regulates own behavior*)
	To respond to the emotions of others (*Objective 4, Responds to others' feelings with growing empathy*)
	To participate in group routines (*Objective 6, Learns to be a member of a group*)

Toddlers and twos continue to refine their fine motor skills and eye-hand coordination. This enables them to participate even more in feeding themselves. They learn to hold and drink from a cup, eat with a spoon, and later eat with a fork. They begin serving themselves from bowls and even pour milk from a very small pitcher.

The physical growth of toddlers slows, so their appetites often decrease. As they become more successful at regulating their behavior, they usually stop eating when they are full. They need small servings of food throughout the day. Toddlers and twos often have strong food likes and dislikes, eat one favorite food for a while, and then often refuse to eat the food they used to prefer.

Start family-style meals, with small groups of children sitting at low tables. Provide utensils so they can serve themselves and eat independently. Encourage children to try new foods, but do not force them. They are more likely to try them if you serve foods in an appealing manner. Offer choices and be patient; they may need many opportunities to try a food before they actually eat it.

Valisha (33 months) and Jonisha (33 months) have just finished eating lunch, served family style. Jonisha says, "I want more milk. I can pour it." Then she exclaims, "Oops!" as the milk she is pouring from a small pitcher makes a puddle on the floor. She stands up, goes to the sink, and gets a paper towel. After she tries wiping the spill with the towel, she says, "There's too much. I'll get the mop." She puts the paper towel in the trash can, gets the child-size mop, and, with some help from LaToya, cleans up the spill.

LaToya's Thoughts and Questions	Jonisha thought of a good solution to the problem of spilled milk. When it didn't work, she thought of and carried out another, more effective solution. I think I can find ways to help her practice pouring at the water table and in the pretend play area. I wonder if that pitcher is just too big for the children.
How LaToya Responds	"Milk sometimes spills, Jonisha. You figured out the best way to clean it up. I think that pitcher might be too big. I'll look for a smaller one, to make it easier to pour milk without spilling it."
What Jonisha Might Be Learning	To use eye-hand coordination while doing increasingly complex tasks (*Objective 9, Demonstrates basic fine motor skills*) To continue an activity until her goal is reached (*Objective 10, Sustains attention*) To carry out her own plan for solving simple problems (*Objective 14, Uses problem-solving strategies*) To use simple sentences with three or more words (*Objective 17, Develops expressive language*)

Working in Partnership With Families

The essential role that food plays in family life is influenced by many cultural and family traditions. Eating and mealtimes therefore offer opportunities to strengthen your partnerships with families. Communication with families is necessary to creating familiar mealtimes that are pleasant for children. It is especially important with very young children, because food and feeding practices have to be carefully coordinated between families and the program for health reasons.

For children younger than 3 years, special feeding issues must be discussed with families, preferably at the very beginning of your relationship. These may include nursing, weaning, introducing solid foods, allergies, and, if families provide meals, what food to bring.

Talk with each family about what their child eats at home and in your program. The *Individual Care Plan—Family Information Form* includes questions to guide your conversations with families and to collect specific information about feeding and eating practices at home. Update the form regularly so that you can coordinate closely with the family. When appropriate, discuss the family's plans for introducing solid foods and for weaning. With the knowledge and approval of the child's family, introduce new foods gradually, letting the child try each after the family has first introduced it at home. When you introduce a new food, allow time—usually five days—before introducing another. You need to be sure that the child is not allergic to each new food.

Respect and follow families' preferences and special food requests as much as possible, whether for reasons of health, culture, religion, or personal preference. For example, do not give extra bottles to an infant whose mother wants to continue nursing. If differences arise, discuss them with the family. Be aware that families' viewpoints might be different from yours with regard to such things as self-feeding, messiness at mealtimes, playing with food, and sitting at the table.

Invite mothers to come to the program and nurse their infants at any time. Provide a comfortable place where they can be with their babies without interruption.

Ask families about foods their children eat at home. Share your program's menus. If families provide their children's lunches, suggest safe and nutritious foods. Keep records of what and how much children eat during the day. Give families brief notes with this information, to help them plan their children's meals and snacks at home.

Working with families helps build continuity between home and your program, and it helps children feel comfortable and secure. The following letter to families is another way to communicate about eating and mealtimes.

Sharing Thoughts About Eating and Mealtimes

Dear Families:

Imagine your child eating a meal or snack in child care. What is he or she experiencing? Certainly your child is getting the foods he or she needs to be healthy and strong. Children also experience much more. Snacks and meals—and, for older children, related activities such as setting the table, cleaning up, and brushing their teeth after eating—give your child a chance to feel cared for and to develop personal care, communication, and social skills. Mealtimes also give children chances to begin practicing good nutrition and health habits.

Children's experiences and the attitudes they form now will affect their future eating habits. By modeling healthy practices and making eating a pleasurable and social time, we can lay the groundwork together for nutritious and enjoyable eating for the rest of their lives.

How We Can Work Together

- **Join us for a snack or meal whenever you can.** Your child will love having you with us. So will we! In addition, you will have a chance to see how we do things, and you may ask questions and make suggestions. Of course, if you are nursing your child, please come anytime. We have set up a comfortable place where you can feed your baby without interruption.

- **Let's communicate about changes in your child's diet or eating habits.** For example, please let us know when your pediatrician recommends adding new foods. After you introduce a new food at home, we'll introduce it here at the center. We can also work together when your child is ready to be weaned from the bottle.

- **Give us any information we need to keep your child healthy.** For example, let us know whether your child has allergies or a tendency to gag or choke. Keep us informed of any changes.

- **Please tell us what your child experiences during mealtimes at home.** What does your child eat and drink? What are your child's favorite foods? Do you have special family foods? What do you talk about? How does your child participate? This information will help us give your child a sense of continuity. It enables us to talk about family meals and serve some of the same foods.

- **Please ask us for menus and ideas for mealtimes.** Sometimes it's hard to come up with ideas for lunches. We'll be glad to give you some tips. We welcome your ideas as well.

Together, we can make mealtimes an enjoyable and valuable learning experience for your child.

Sincerely,

inside this chapter

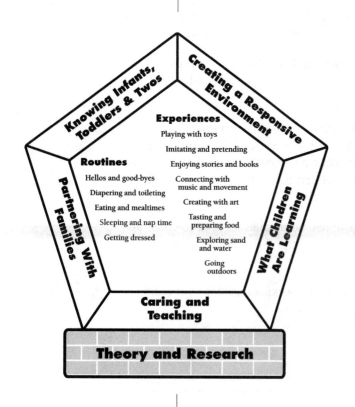

9 Sleeping and Nap Time

Leo *(18 months) is lying on the cushion in the book nook, rubbing his eyes. Barbara remarks, "You're a sleepy boy, even though your mama said that you slept well last night. You usually don't nap until 11:00, but I think you need an early nap today. Would you like to sit in the rocking chair with me before you lie down?" Leo nods, "Yes." He snuggles on Barbara's lap in the chair. Barbara holds Leo and rocks him until he is ready to lie down on his cot.*

Sleep is necessary for healthy growth and development, so sleeping and nap time are important parts of a program for young children. Very young infants sleep most of the day, waking only for diapering, feeding, and other care. Active toddlers and 2-year-olds, by contrast, spend more time awake than asleep, napping for an hour or more to restore their energy. Even a child who does not seem to want to sleep will benefit from a rest time away from group activities. A well-rested child is better able to participate fully in the program.

Because each infant's sleep-wake cycle is likely to be different, meeting the individual needs of the infants in your care can be challenging. Even though toddlers and twos generally sleep on regular schedules and might nap as a group, it is still necessary to look for cues to their individual and changing needs. One child may need to nap earlier than usual on a particular day. Another may sleep for less or more time than he does ordinarily.

Strengthening your relationship with children is as important as meeting their physical needs when you put them to sleep. When you sing a soft lullaby and rock an infant, or read a story and rub a toddler's back at nap time, you show that you care about her well-being and security.

Supporting Development and Learning

Sleeping and nap times are necessary to children's physical, cognitive, and language development, and for their social well-being.

Learning about themselves and others: When infants develop regular sleeping patterns and comfort themselves as they fall asleep, they are showing early signs of regulating their behavior and managing their feelings. Toddlers and twos develop personal care skills as they learn to spread their blankets on their cots and take their shoes off before napping.

Learning about moving: Infants practice large muscle skills when they roll over in their cribs or pull themselves up to show you that they are awake. Toddlers and twos also practice large muscle skills as they walk (or toddle) to their cots or mats, carry their favorite books with them, and sit and lie down on their cots. They also learn that it is important to stop moving and rest during the day. Well-rested children have the energy to move their bodies when they are awake, to explore their environment, and to play.

Learning about the world: Infants, toddlers, and twos begin to develop a beginning sense of time and sequence as sleeping and naps conform to a routine. They learn cause and effect and problem solving when their teacher responds to crying, eye rubbing, crankiness, or slowed activity by saying, "You're sleepy. It's time for you to take a nap." They learn how objects function as they use cribs, cots, sheets, and blankets.

Learning about communicating: Children communicate their sleeping needs both nonverbally and verbally. When infants rub their eyes, turn their heads away, and make their cries of fatigue, they signal their need for sleep. When you respond, they learn that their signals are effective. When you explain what you are doing as you put infants, toddlers, and twos in their cribs or help them onto their cots, you are helping them learn language. When you read the delightful rhymes in Mem Fox's *Time for Bed* or other bedtime stories, or sing a favorite lullaby, you are not only helping a child fall asleep, you are also introducing children to the joys of storytelling, the sounds of language, and the rhythm and pitch of music.

Creating an Environment for Sleeping and Nap Time

By themselves, cribs take up a lot of room in an infant environment. In addition, best practice in health care recommends that cribs be three feet apart. Check with your state and local policies to make sure you know what is required in your area. Finding the best arrangement for cribs so that children can sleep and also have a large enough area to play is a challenge. Because each infant sleeps on a personal schedule, you need to create an environment that is conducive to both sleeping and playing.

Some programs solve the problem by having a separate space dedicated just to sleeping. In fact, some state licensing regulations require this arrangement. The American Academy of Pediatrics and the American Public Health Association recommend that separate sleeping rooms for infants have at least 30 square feet per child.[30] In addition, if the room is walled off, a teacher needs to stay with even one child.

By choice or because space is limited, other programs place infants' cribs throughout the room or set them in a bedroom-like area. Where cribs are in the room, low walls or partial wall dividers may be used to reduce some of the surrounding visual stimulation and sounds that interfere with sleeping.

As infants grow, they begin to sleep on a more predictable schedule. Eventually, the individual schedules of the infants in your room will merge. Toddlers and twos generally sleep at the same time. At a regularly scheduled period, place cots throughout the room. Also remember to have a cot available for toddlers and twos who are sleepy when they arrive in the morning or who need to nap earlier than the group.

When setting up a sleeping area for infants and napping spaces for toddlers and twos, these strategies are very important.

Place nap time supplies close to cribs. The less you move around, the more easily children will fall asleep. A comfortable glider chair lets you rock a sleepy baby and then put him in his crib easily.

Have an individual crib, cot, or mat for each child. Assigning cribs, cots, mats, and bedding helps minimize the spread of head lice and infectious diseases. Labeling cribs, cots, and linens with children's names helps reserve their use for individual children.

Make sure cribs are safe. The National Institute of Child Health and Human Development makes these recommendations to reduce the risk of Sudden Infant Death Syndrome (SIDS):[31]

- Use firm crib mattresses.

- Place babies on their backs to sleep.

- Keep pillows, heavy blankets, comforters, stuffed toys, rattles, and squeeze toys out of cribs.

- If a thin blanket is used, make sure it does not reach higher than the baby's chest and that the ends of the blanket are tucked under the crib mattress.

- Make sure babies' heads and faces are uncovered while they sleep.

- Fasten bumper pads to the crib with at least six short safety straps to ensure a tight fit. Remove bumper pads when children learn to stand up or move around in the crib.

- Watch for strangulation hazards. Make sure that there are no dangling cords from blinds or drapes near cribs.

- Keep side rails up when children are in their cribs. Lower the crib height of the mattress when children begin to sit or stand. Watch for signs that infants have outgrown their cribs, for instance, when they can pull themselves off the crib floor by holding onto the railings. When cribs are no longer safe, move children to cots.

Provide children with clean sheets and bedding. Wash linens whenever they are soiled or wet. Generally, you should wash or send linens home for washing at least weekly. You may need to have linens for infants, toddlers, and twos washed more frequently. Store bedding so that it does not touch the surface of another child's cot. Your local health department can help you learn how to store bedding to help prevent the spread of disease.

Provide evacuation cribs. Having evacuation cribs is an emergency measure. They are special cribs with 4-inch wheels, capable of holding up to five infants. Place an evacuation crib near an emergency exit.

Be sure that each child sleeps in the same place each day. Place cribs, cots, or mats in the same place each day. The regularity eliminates confusion, helps children develop a sense of their own place, and promotes security and trust.

Create peaceful spaces where children can sleep. Absorb noise by using carpeting. Putting curtains on the windows reduces unwanted light. Where lighting is necessary, make it soft. If room barriers are not available, you can move cribs, cots, or mats to places in your room where you can diminish noise and visual stimulation.

Remove all toys, crib gyms, and mobiles from cribs. That helps children understand that cribs are for sleeping, not playing. It also reduces safety concerns.

Provide a place for mothers who are breast-feeding. The sleeping area is generally quiet and private. Many programs allocate a separate section in the area for breast-feeding.

Caring and Teaching

From birth, children differ in how much sleep they need, how soundly they sleep, and the regularity of their sleeping patterns. Children also differ in the length of time they require to fall asleep and wake up. Knowing how each child falls asleep and wakes can help you manage nap time with a group of infants, toddlers, and twos. According to the National Sleep Foundation, when infants are put to bed drowsy but not asleep, they are more likely to soothe themselves, to fall asleep independently at bedtime, and to put themselves back to sleep when they wake during the night.[32] As always, talk with families about how they prefer to help their children fall asleep and follow family practices when possible.

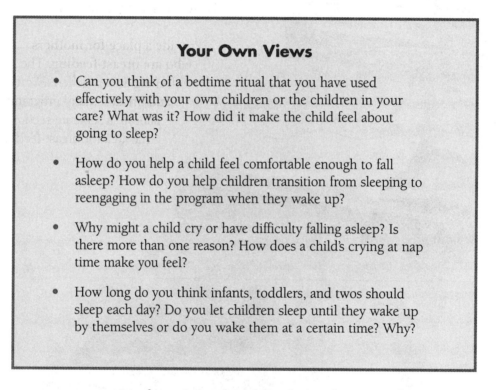

Your Own Views

- Can you think of a bedtime ritual that you have used effectively with your own children or the children in your care? What was it? How did it make the child feel about going to sleep?

- How do you help a child feel comfortable enough to fall asleep? How do you help children transition from sleeping to reengaging in the program when they wake up?

- Why might a child cry or have difficulty falling asleep? Is there more than one reason? How does a child's crying at nap time make you feel?

- How long do you think infants, toddlers, and twos should sleep each day? Do you let children sleep until they wake up by themselves or do you wake them at a certain time? Why?

Here are some suggestions for caring and teaching during sleeping and nap times.

Learn about and follow each child's sleeping pattern. Children may not sleep at exactly the same time each day, but careful observation helps you identify and provide for their patterns. The transition to nap time for toddlers and twos should be quiet, to help them relax. Also plan for when children wake up. Provide activities for toddlers and twos who wake up while the others are still sleeping.

Know how each child in your primary care group falls asleep and wakes up.
Some children fall asleep immediately, while others take longer. Some children wake up ready to go, while others prefer some quiet time before getting started. Learn each child's individual napping style so you can provide adequately for the full range of sleeping and waking styles in your room.

Develop consistent nap time routines with individual children, to help them fall asleep. Learn each child's routine for calming down, relaxing, and falling asleep. Talk with families about what they do at home so you can offer similar routines in your room. Some typical strategies are singing the same lullaby, playing a familiar CD, rocking, rubbing a child's back, or reading a story. Dimming the lights and playing soft, soothing music often help children relax.

Do not put children to sleep with a bottle. Allowing children to have a bottle in their mouths for long periods while they are sleeping may cause the severe tooth decay known as baby bottlemouth. Having bottles during nap time can also cause choking and ear infections.

Respond appropriately to children who cry at nap time. Your response to a child who cries depends in large part on your knowledge of the child. Some children cry to release tension before they fall asleep. Others cry if they are overtired or afraid. A short cry before falling asleep is normal for some children. Others need to be picked up and held in order to settle down.

Keep a sleeping log. A record of the child's active and sleeping periods will help you understand the cause of the crying and respond appropriately. You can also talk with family members, to help you understand why a child cries and to determine the best way to respond. Remember, though, that completely ignoring a crying child is never appropriate.

Take infants out of their cribs as soon as they wake up. Cribs are only for sleeping. Put babies on the floor for tummy time or provide other play experiences.

Avoid making nap time a battle. When children associate nap time with tension and stress, they are more likely to cry when you put them to sleep. Find ways to reduce your own stress and aim to enjoy the napping process with children. Keep in mind that sleeping means being still and that infants, toddlers, and twos—who are learning how to move their bodies—want to use their emerging physical skills. They may not want to be picked up, held, rocked, and placed in a crib to rest. Some children protest by standing in their cribs and crying, or by squirming in your arms as you try to rock them.

Knowing a child's temperament, wants, and needs allows you to create a nap time routine that works for him. Involve families in developing successful strategies for children who resist sleeping.

Encourage families to bring familiar comfort items from home. Giving children items that they use at home to comfort themselves or playing familiar music can help them relax and fall asleep.

Take children outdoors each day. Make sure that infants, toddlers, and twos have both daily exercise and sleep. Time in the fresh air and sunshine also helps to establish patterns of wakefulness and sleep.

Responding to What Children Need

Your plans and methods of managing sleeping and nap time will differ according to the ages of the children in your care and what you know about each child.

Young infants typically develop a consistent sleep-wake cycle between 3 and 6 months of age. This cycle of staying awake when it is light and going to sleep when it is dark is known as *Circadian rhythm*. Infants with an established Circadian rhythm typically sleep 9–12 hours during the night and take 30- to 120-minute naps, 1–4 times a day.[33] By the time they are age 1, they may take fewer and shorter naps during the day. Infants communicate their need for sleep by crying, rubbing their eyes, or simply falling asleep wherever they are. While sleeping, they often appear restless, twitch their arms and legs, smile, and suck.[34] As you respond to their sleep signals, you are helping them regulate their behavior.

Jasmine (8 months) has previously enjoyed being rocked to sleep for her nap. However, when Janet rocks her at nap time today, Jasmine continues to squirm and cry. Janet tries to put Jasmine down in her crib, but she cries even harder.	
Janet's Thoughts and Questions	I know that Jasmine is not hungry and that she has a clean diaper. I think she is just tired and needs a nap, but she seems to be resisting my efforts to help her fall asleep. Even though rocking is usually what she likes, it isn't working today. I wonder if her mother left a note this morning that might give me a clue.
How Janet Responds	Janet carries Jasmine to the bulletin board where family notes are posted. She finds a note and reads that Jasmine might be teething and that, although she needs more time than usual to calm down, she still reacts well to rocking. Janet decides to go back to rocking and to sing Jasmine one of her favorite lullabies. Within 5 minutes, Jasmine's body relaxes and quiets. She looks up at Janet, who is still singing.
What Jasmine Might Be Learning	To express a variety of emotions and needs, using facial expressions, body movement, and vocalizations (*Objective 3, Manages own feelings*) To show interest in the speech of others (*Objective 16, Develops receptive language*)

Mobile infants tend to take fewer naps. They also give verbal or nonverbal signals that they need to rest. For instance, mobile infants may appear drowsy (even if they have just arrived at child care). They may cry or be irritable and difficult to comfort. Sometimes mobile infants protest strongly when you put them in their cribs, even though they are tired. When you respond consistently to their cues, you promote children's learning about nap time routines. Mobile infants begin to regulate their sleep-wake cycle to get the rest they need.

Willard (11 months) arrives at the center this morning at 7:30. He is in a good mood for a while, as he plays with playdough, trucks, and blocks. At 10:15, Grace observes that he cries every time another child comes near him. When she offers a toy or tries to involve him in another activity, he does not engage with it.

Grace's Thoughts and Questions	Willard hasn't napped in the morning for a few weeks, but he seems tired today. I think a nap might help him. Without one, he might become overly tired and unable to eat lunch or play happily. How can I help him to relax and rest for a little while?
How Grace Responds	Grace rubs Willard's back and says, "Willard, you look tired. I think a rest might help." He does not respond. Next she offers him his favorite blanket, saying, "Here's your blankie." He looks up at Grace, raising his arms. She picks him up, takes him to the glider, sits him in her lap, rubs his back, and rocks him. He snuggles to her and closes his eyes.
What Willard Might Be Learning	To use others' facial expressions, gestures, and voices to guide his own behavior (*Objective 2, Regulates own behavior*) To respond to simple gestures and to the intonation, pitch, and volume of simple speech (*Objective 16, Develops receptive language*)

Toddlers and twos usually take one nap a day, lasting 1–3 hours. They communicate their need for sleep both nonverbally and verbally. Sometime during their second year, children change from sleeping in the morning and afternoon to sleeping only during the afternoon. As time passes, they may take longer to calm down and fall asleep, or they may just rest and not sleep on some days. During this time, one nap might not be enough and two might be too many. This transition can be difficult, especially in group care situations. Remain flexible and plan your day to allow for one or two nap periods per day. Plan for a quiet time to help toddlers transition from active play to sleep, and prepare experiences for children when they wake up. As you plan, remember that some children will be ready to play actively while others are still sleeping. Despite changes in their need for sleep, children still depend on you to help them regulate sleep and wakefulness.

Mercedes has put on some soft music and is sitting on the floor between two cots, gently rubbing children's backs to help them relax at nap time. In another part of the room, Matthew (22 months) is rolling around on his cot and babbling. Mercedes hears a thud and realizes that Matthew has thrown a book across the room.

Mercedes' Thoughts and Questions	Every day this week, Matthew has had difficulty relaxing and falling asleep. Even when I put him in a quiet corner alone, he manages to disrupt the other children. How can I help Matthew and the other children in my room at the same time?
How Mercedes Responds	Matthew continues to roll on his cot, so Mercedes walks quietly across the room and softly says to him, "I can see that you are tired of this book, but when you throw books someone might get hurt." She offers Matthew a soft book and a cloth bunny. She tells him that he may play with them until she returns. "When I come back, I will read a story to you," she says. He says, "Yeah, book" and begins looking at the book while he talks to the bunny.
What Matthew Might Be Learning	To respond to simple directions and sometimes test limits (*Objective 2, Regulates own behavior*) To speak in two-word phrases (*Objective 17, Develops expressive language*)

Working in Partnership With Families

Working with families to provide consistency between home and your center is essential for helping children establish good sleeping and nap time habits. Here are some suggestions for working with families to make sleeping a positive experience for children in your room and at home.

Gather information about children's sleeping habits and patterns. Develop an *Individual Care Plan* with families at the time of enrollment. Update it on a regular basis by asking families how many hours a night their children sleep. Find out about children's sleeping schedules. Learn about the families' bedtime rituals and routines.

Share information about sleeping on a daily basis as well. When children do not follow their typical napping schedule and sleep less than usual, be sure to let parents know. The information will enable them to recognize crankiness or other troublesome behavior as a sign of tiredness and adjust bedtime accordingly. When a child has extended her nap time, inform her family that she has had a long nap and is rested. Knowing this, her family member may decide to vary their routine on the way home.

Be aware of families' cultural preferences for putting infants, toddlers, and twos to sleep. Some families may not put children to sleep in a separate room. They may not let children sleep alone and may keep them awake until older children in the household go to sleep. Infants in some cultures may be swaddled or put to sleep on bedboards. Become knowledgeable about the sleeping practices your families follow with their children, and, whenever possible and appropriate, incorporate them into your program.

Work together to resolve differences. Some families may ask you to limit the time their child sleeps at your program. Listen and gather information from family members. Share information about your views and teaching experience, and then work out a plan that is acceptable for both your room and their home. As you strive to reach agreement, keep an open mind about new possibilities that evolve as you talk with each other.

Offer support to families. Be available to support families whose children have sleeping problems. Reassure them that sleeping problems are common, especially during the first years of life. Take time to read and stay current with new information about sleeping issues and practices for young children. Ideas about best practices change over time, and you want to be sure that the information you give to parents is up-to-date. Encourage families to talk with other families whose children are having similar sleeping problems. They might be able to share helpful suggestions. Remind family members that each child has his own style of sleeping and waking, and that differences are natural and expected and are not necessarily signs of a problem.

The letter to families that follows is another way to share information.

SHARING THOUGHTS ABOUT SLEEPING AND NAP TIME

Dear Families:

Every young child needs enough sleep during the day and at night for healthy growth and development. When children are rested, they enjoy and benefit from learning opportunities throughout the day. When your baby was born, you may have expected him to sleep easily. Many babies do, but sleeping is sometimes difficult for others. Your infant needs you to figure out how to comfort him and help him relax into sleep. As his needs and preferences change when he gets older, it will still be very important for you to respond to his changing patterns. Sharing information will help us make sure that the sleeping routine we offer at the program is consistent with the care you provide at home.

How We Can Work Together

- **Let us know your child's preferences.** We are helped by knowing what works or does not work at home. Does your baby fall asleep quickly, or does she take some time? Is there a special lullaby you sing or words your child is used to hearing at bedtime?

- **Keep us informed about any changes in your child's sleeping patterns.** When we know that your child's pattern has changed at home, we can adapt his schedule at the program. We will share the same information with you so we can both plan better. For example, if we know that your child did not sleep well the night before, we can offer an early nap if necessary. If you know your child took a long nap and is well rested, you may decide to vary your routine instead of going straight home. Please let us know if you have concerns about your child's sleeping schedule at our program. For instance, please tell us if you think he is sleeping too little or too much.

- **Bring special items that comfort your child.** If your child has a special blanket or other object that makes falling asleep easier, please bring it to the center. Please label it with your child's name and make sure we have it every day. We will take care that it does not get lost and help you remember to take it home at night.

- **Always put your baby to sleep on his or her back.** This is a recommendation of the American Academy of Pediatrics to help prevent Sudden Infant Death Syndrome, or SIDS. You can check on the latest recommendations of the American Academy of Pediatrics by reading their Web site or asking us for this information. We will be happy to share what we have learned with you.

We appreciate your help. Together, we can help make sleeping and nap time a pleasant and restful experience for your child.

Sincerely,

inside this chapter

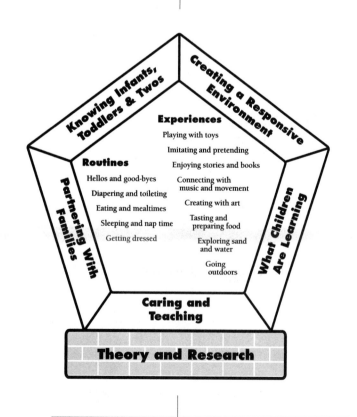

10

Getting Dressed

Brooks *is about to dress Abby (14 months). She starts by playing peek-a-boo with Abby's shirt. Hiding her face behind the shirt, Brooks playfully pretends to worry, "I can't see Abby! Where is Abby?" While Abby giggles in response, Brooks gently slides the shirt over her head and says, "There she is! First we put your head through and then your arms." Abby cooperates by extending her arms, as Brooks offers one armhole and then the other. "Thank you for helping me put your shirt on," Brooks says. Abby then holds up a sock, and Brooks asks, "Where does the sock go?" Abby smiles broadly and touches her foot. "Right, it goes on your foot."*

Infants, toddlers, and twos are totally dependent on adults to provide for their basic needs. One basic need is clothing. Meeting this need includes dressing children in clothes that are clean and dry and that are appropriate for the weather and for both indoor and outdoor play.

Dressing and undressing children are simple yet repetitive activities that can become tiresome when approached as tasks to be completed quickly. Changing clothing may even become a struggle when a child resists you or insists on doing it herself. By approaching dressing and undressing as troublesome chores rather than as learning opportunities, you miss chances to enjoy being with a child and encourage new skills.

Supporting Development and Learning

Dressing and undressing can be rich experiences for children when they are viewed as opportunities to develop social/emotional, physical, cognitive, and communication skills.

Learning about themselves and others: Off go the shoes. Over the head goes the shirt. Down go the pants. Snap goes the jacket. Dressing and undressing routines are chances for infants, toddlers, and twos to begin to learn personal care skills. Competence and pride in accomplishment grow as each new skill emerges. The "do-every-thing-for-me-baby" quickly becomes the "I-can-do-it-myself" 2-year-old who can take over parts of his own care.

Learning about moving: During dressing and undressing, children use small and large muscles. A mobile infant who holds her foot in the air so you can put on her sock, or who pushes her arm through an armhole, is coordinating her body and increasing her physical strength. When a 2-year-old repeatedly puts on and takes off his jacket, he is using a sequence of physical skills. Getting the jacket on with the over-the-head method requires full body movement, while attempts at zipping, snapping, and eventually buttoning involve small muscles.

Learning about the world: For a toddler or two to find his two matching shoes among all of the shoes under the coat hooks, he must see similarities and differences as well as remember, recognize, and classify objects by the characteristics of color, shape, and size. Giving toddlers and twos time to find their shoes by themselves is an early exercise in memory, sorting, and matching. A child who points to his jacket on the coat hook when you say, "It's time to go outdoors," is thinking ahead and planning. When you say, "It's cold outside today," and he takes his mittens out of his pocket and tries to put them on, he is beginning to use problem solving strategies. When you allow enough time for getting dressed, you are inviting children to learn about the world and to increase their ability to function in it.

Learning about communicating: By naming body parts and items of clothing while you are dressing a child, you teach new words. Your conversations with infants while you are putting on their pants, with toddlers while you are helping zip their jackets, or with twos when you are tying their shoes supports their understanding and use of language. Reading books about dressing also helps extend their most basic language skills by introducing details related to dressing and items of clothing. For instance, in *Corduroy*, by Don Freeman, Lisa's stuffed bear loses the button from his overalls, and she sews it back on his shoulder strap.

Creating an Environment for Getting Dressed

The arrangement of your room and the materials you provide can help infants, toddlers, and twos participate in dressing and undressing. A few simple additions can engage children in a variety of motor experiences that support their eye-hand coordination, an awareness of their own bodies in space, and their ability to sequence tasks.

Store children's personal clothing items within their reach. Provide coat hooks, cubbies, and storage containers for items that children can safely get on their own. Storage that is out of their reach may be used for items that children do not need to retrieve regularly. When personal items such as coats, jackets, and spare clothing are accessible to toddlers and twos, they are encouraged throughout the day to dress independently. The American Academy of Pediatrics and the American Public Health Association recommend that coat hooks be placed either slightly above or below children's eye level to minimize risk of injury to eyes, and that the hooks be spaced or put in individual cubbies so that coats will not touch each other.[35]

Bag soiled clothing; do not wash or rinse it. Washing or rinsing clothing increases the risk of contamination for teachers and other children. Put each child's soiled clothing in a separate plastic bag, close the bag securely, and send the clothing home at pick-up time.

Label storage places for personal clothing so that children can begin to find their own things. Putting picture or photo labels of children on cubbies or next to hooks makes it easy for teachers, children, and families to recognize where each child's personal items belong and to put them in the same place each day.

Supply dress-up clothing and other materials for practicing dressing skills. Select dress-up clothing that is easy to put on and take off so children can have fun practicing. To minimize frustration, be prepared to assist when necessary. Items such as vests with snaps, shoes with laces or Velcro®, and jackets and shirts with buttons or zippers encourage children to learn snapping, buttoning, lacing, and zipping. Add an unbreakable mirror so children can see themselves in their fancy vests and oversized shoes and enjoy the results of dressing themselves. The National Association for the Education of Young Children recommends that, unless disposable hats are used, hats be cleaned after each use. They also advise washing dress-up clothing weekly.[36] In addition to dress-up clothing, boards with fasteners and old shoes with buckles or laces give children chances to practice dressing skills. In fact, virtually all items that engage children in small muscle activity are helpful.

Caring and Teaching

Dressing times may seem like the most ordinary of all the daily routines in caring for young children. It is tempting to want to get through the process as quickly as possible, especially when trying to change a squirming, crying baby or a toddler or 2-year-old who wants to do everything by himself. If you take the time to pay attention to each child during dressing times, this routine offers many opportunities to interact with the child and to build a child's sense of competence.

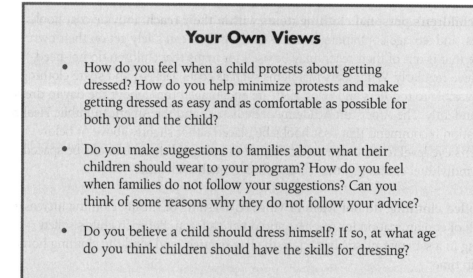

Your Own Views

- How do you feel when a child protests about getting dressed? How do you help minimize protests and make getting dressed as easy and as comfortable as possible for both you and the child?

- Do you make suggestions to families about what their children should wear to your program? How do you feel when families do not follow your suggestions? Can you think of some reasons why they do not follow your advice?

- Do you believe a child should dress himself? If so, at what age do you think children should have the skills for dressing?

Here are some practical suggestions for making dressing routines work well for you and the children.

Handle children's bodies with respect. When you touch or pick up an infant, consider how you handle her body. Do you lift her swiftly into the air and then quickly lay her down on the diaper-changing table? Do you stop, bend beside her, smile, tell her that you are going to pick her up, let her know you need her help, and then pause and wait for her reaction before gently lifting her up? By interacting gently throughout the dressing process, you let infants, toddlers, and twos know that you respect their bodies. When lifting young infants, remember to support their heads and necks.

Talk with children about what you are doing. Use caring words and a calm voice while changing children's clothes. Describe what you are doing as you do it. "I will put your head through this part…Your arm goes in here…There it is! Your clean shirt is right on your tummy!" Be playful. Ask a toddler or 2-year-old, "Where should we put your sock? Does it go on your head? No-o-o. That's silly. It goes on your foot." Learn the words in children's home languages for common articles of clothing so you can use them as you dress or undress the child.

Be aware that children's temperaments influence the way they experience dressing. Some children have intense reactions to wet clothing or any change in the condition of their clothing. Others are more flexible and easygoing and do not seem to be bothered if their shirts are wet or sticky. Some children need you to help them move quickly through the dressing process. Others do better when you slow down and take your time. For children who are sensitive to touch and find certain textures uncomfortable, you will want to have soft, tagless, well-worn cotton clothing on hand.

Let children participate in whatever way they can. An infant may simply lift his arm when you put a shirt on him, while a 2-year-old might put a sweater on with only a little assistance. Observe how each child in your group prefers to participate, and adjust your approach to involve each child as much as possible.

Keep familiar extra clothing on hand for each child. Ask families to bring clothing from home so their children can be changed when necessary during the day. Also keep an ample supply of extra clothing in your room to be shared as needed. You can ask for donations from all parents, shop at garage sales or similar places, or save leftover and forgotten clothing from year to year.

Give children choices whenever possible. Simple choices provide them with a much-needed sense of control and with practice in making decisions. You may ask mobile infants, toddlers, and twos a simple question such as, "Are you ready to go with me?" Then pause to watch for their reaction. Ask 2-year-olds more complex questions and wait for their responses: "Do you want to get dressed here by your cot or over there by your cubby?" "Do you want to wear your green socks with butterflies or the purple ones?"

Engage children with songs, fingerplays, and playful games that encourage learning and cooperation. When you dress a young infant who is lying on his back, lean slightly forward so that he can focus on your face as you sing and talk. One day you can sing a line such as, "This is the way we put on your shirt." Substitute *pants, shoes, socks,* and *jacket* on other days. Involve toddlers and twos by asking them to help choose the game they would like to play, song to sing, or fingerplay to say as they dress. Do not hesitate to repeat favorite games, songs, and fingerplays that children enjoy. Use them as long as they help children participate or remain calm. When you find that they are not helpful, choose another strategy.

Step in to minimize frustration when a child attempts a task that might be too difficult to accomplish alone. Recognize that children are eager to help with dressing and may want to help even when a task is too difficult for them. Stay nearby and offer help as needed. When a child is becoming frustrated, be ready to offer comfort and reassurance. "Buttoning that button is tricky. May I help?" "That zipper seems to be stuck. Maybe we can get it up if both of us try." When a child makes a mistake, offer a new way to look at the situation. For example, when a toddler or 2-year-old has put his shoes on the wrong feet, you might say, "You did it all by yourself! How do those shoes feel? If we switched them, would they feel different? Let's try that and see."

Responding to What Children Need

Depending upon their temperaments and developmental levels, children react to dressing very differently. Vary your approaches according to what you know about each child.

Young infants interact with you one-on-one during dressing. When Linda changes Julio's clothing, he explores his environment by looking around and listening. As she sings and talks to him in gentle tones, he explores his world. He focuses on Linda's face; visually searches the room to identify the sources of sounds; and moves his hands and feet, learning where his body ends and the rest of the world begins. He experiments with his voice, cooing softly, gurgling, and squealing. Before long, he begins to participate in dressing by extending a leg for a sock and by pushing his arms through armholes.

Linda is feeding Julio (4 months) a bottle. When he finishes, she rocks him, and he becomes drowsy. As she lays him in his crib, she notices that the neck of his sleeper is wet under his chin. However, he does not seem to mind and falls asleep immediately.

Linda's Thoughts and Questions	Julio's sleeper is wet. I know that keeping him clean and dry is important. Should I wake him to change his sleeper now, or let him sleep and change it when he wakes?
How Linda Responds	Linda checks to see how much of Julio's sleeper is wet and whether he is chilled. She decides to wait until he wakes up and to change his sleeper when she changes his diaper.
What Julio Might Be Learning	To develop routine patterns for sleeping and other basic needs, with adult's help (*Objective 2, Regulates own behavior*)

Mobile infants may cooperate as you dress them. You may also witness their emerging sense of independence as they take off clothing frequently during the day, especially their socks and shoes. Celebrate their accomplishments before you put their clothes back on. A simple acknowledgment of their success is helpful in supporting their development, as when you say, "You took your socks off all by yourself!"

Brooks hears Abby (14 months) squeal with delight. Brooks looks across the room and sees Abby toddling across the carpet. She has a shoe on one foot. The other is bare. When Brooks notices Abby's sock and shoe nearby, she realizes that Abby removed them.

Brooks' Thoughts and Questions	Abby seems to be enjoying herself and her accomplishments. I realize that learning to dress and undress is important, but one of her feet is bare and the floor is a little cold.
	I know Abby will probably protest and resist my attempts to put her sock and shoe back on.
	How can I help her put them back on without a power struggle?
How Brooks Responds	Brooks picks up Abby's shoe and sock. She approaches Abby with both in hand and playfully crawls beside her on the floor.
	As Brooks crawls, she sings, "Where is Abby? Where is Abby? She's missing her sock and her shoe. Where is Abby? Where is Abby? She's missing her sock and her shoe." Abby laughs. Brooks laughs and cuddles her while slipping on her sock and shoe.
What Abby Might Be Learning	To use others' facial expressions, gestures, or voices to guide own behavior (*Objective 2, Regulates own behavior*)
	To attempt simple personal care tasks (*Objective 7, Uses personal care skills*)

Toddlers and twos are developing the skills they need to put on and take off simple clothing by themselves. They gain confidence in their abilities when you take note of their accomplishments. Toddlers and twos may insist, "Me do it!" when you attempt to help them. They may also try to assert control or independence by playing a game of chase when you want to dress them. Remember that they are not trying to make your life difficult. They are trying to take charge of themselves.

Mercedes helps the children in her room get ready to go outside. They put on their coats, hats, and gloves. Everyone is ready to go except Matthew (22 months), who has his hat and coat on but is struggling with his zipper. Mercedes approaches Matthew, kneels down, and asks, "Matthew, may I help you with your zipper?" Matthew says, "No," and turns away.	
Mercedes' Thoughts and Questions	I know that Matthew likes to do things by himself, but the rest of the group is ready to go outside. I want to support Matthew's desire to do things on his own, but I don't want the other children to have to wait too long. I know that, if I don't do something to gain his cooperation, this situation could turn into a power struggle. How can I support Matthew's independence and avoid a power struggle while helping him get his coat zipped?
How Mercedes Responds	Mercedes gently touches Matthew's arm and says, "Matthew, will you please help me zip my coat?" Matthew turns around and looks at her coat. As she begins zipping, Mercedes says, "I'll start at the bottom. Will you finish zipping it all the way up for me?" Matthew smiles and zips her coat. "Zzzzip!" responds Mercedes, exaggerating the word. Matthew laughs. "Now, how about your coat? I'll start the zipper, and then you can zip it all the way up." Matthew agrees. As he zips his coat, he repeats Mercedes' exaggerated, "Zzzzip!"
What Matthew Might Be Learning	To try more complex personal care tasks, with increasing success (*Objective 7, Uses personal care skills*) To use eye-hand coordination while doing simple tasks (*Objective 9, Demonstrates basic fine motor skills*) To demonstrate understanding of simple directions, questions, and explanations (*Objective 16, Develops receptive language*)

Working in Partnership With Families

At home, families probably experience many of the same joys and struggles you have while dressing their child. Share your ideas for successful dressing experiences and ask for their help. Talk with families about how they manage dressing at home. The *Individual Care Plan—Family Information Form* includes a place to record information that families share about dressing. You can incorporate some of their regular practices into your dressing routine. For example, you might want to follow a mother's practice of dressing her baby while sitting on the floor rather than while at the changing table.

Let families know what they need to provide for their child, such as ample extra clothing that is labeled with their child's name. Request that they dress their children in clothing that allows them to be active and sometimes get messy. Assure families that you will help their children take care of their clothing by providing smocks for art and for water play.

As the weather changes, be sure to remind families which articles of clothing the children will need for safe and active outdoor play. Depending upon the climate where you live, this might mean warm jackets, mittens, hats, and boots in winter, and loose clothing and sun hats in summer. Sending a letter like the sample that follows is one way of engaging families as partners in dressing their children.

SHARING THOUGHTS ABOUT GETTING DRESSED

Dear Families:

Infants, toddlers, and twos are dressed and undressed throughout the day—every day—at home and in our program. Dressing is one routine that adults and children often want to finish as quickly as possible. After all, dressing a squirming infant, a protesting toddler, or a 2-year-old who insists on putting on her own clothes is not a simple task. From the child's point of view, stopping what she is doing and being still while an adult dresses her is not fun, either.

We view the dressing routine as rich in learning possibilities and as an opportunity to focus on one child at a time. As we pull on a shirt or pants, we talk, listen, sing, and play a simple game. We offer children choices, letting them select which shirt to wear or which item of clothing to put on first. By asking rather than telling, we reduce the struggles we might otherwise have and engage the children in helping us instead.

How We Can Work Together

- **Please provide extra articles of clothing.** We want your child to be warm enough or cool enough, dry, and as clean as possible. Spare clothes that your child is used to wearing help us keep your child comfortable. When extra clothing is labeled with your child's name, we have time to interact with your child because we do not need to spend it to figure out which clothes belong to whom. Remember that, as your child grows and as seasons change, you will need to replace the extra clothes you have left with us.

- **Select clothing that is easy to manage.** Pants with elastic waists, shoes with Velcro® fasteners, and overalls with straps that stretch make getting dressed easier for your child and for us.

- **Share ideas with us about dressing your child.** Let us know what works well when you dress your child at home. We will let you know what works for us, too. By sharing ideas, we can learn from one another and strengthen our partnership to benefit your child.

- **Dress your child for active, sometimes messy play.** Also be sure that your child's clothes are appropriate for the weather. That way, playing outside will be healthy and pleasurable. Remember that clothes with a snug fit or that need to be kept clean prevent children from fully enjoying such activities as climbing, food preparation, and painting. If you want to bring your child to our program in clothes that you do not want to become soiled, we'll be happy to help him or her change into play clothes that do not restrict movement or handling messy materials. We will do our best to take care of your child's clothes.

Together, we can make getting dressed a positive learning experience for your child.

Sincerely,

Part 3

Experiences

Children whose basic needs have been met consistently and who have secure attachments are eager to experience the world. According to Jean Piaget, infants and toddlers learn through **sensorimotor activity**. They react to what they experience through their senses and through physical activity. For example, they discover that they can make a noise by banging a toy, that objects fall when they are dropped, and that a ball rolls when pushed. During the **preoperational stage**, which starts around age 2, children continue to explore objects and begin to use them purposefully. They stack blocks until they fall, fit shapes in a sorting box, use a crayon to make marks, and use objects in pretend play.

Caring for infants, toddlers, and twos is deeply satisfying when you appreciate and find joy in the everyday discoveries that delight a child: the sound a rattle makes, a clown that pops up when a button is pressed, the ants marching across the pavement. You plan meaningful experiences for infants, toddlers, and twos by selecting materials that match children's growing abilities and interests, by observing what children do, and by thinking about what you learn. Because you can never predict exactly how children will react and what will capture their attention, you *plan for possibilities*. Your positive interactions make children's experiences opportunities for building relationships and promoting learning. Lev Vygotsky emphasized this social dimension of learning.

The chapters in Part 3 describe how each type of experience supports children's development and learning. Each chapter also suggests appropriate materials for each age group and explains how you can support children's learning by thoughtfully observing and responding to each child. The letter that concludes each chapter will help you explain the value of the experience to children's families.

inside this chapter

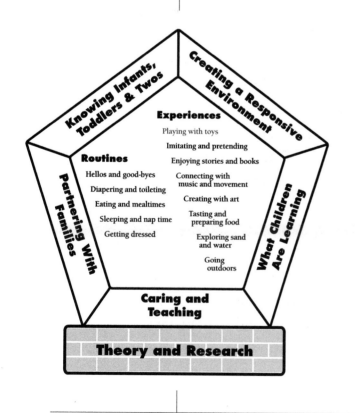

11 Playing With Toys

Brooks *shakes a covered shoe box to show Abby (14 months) that something is inside. Opening her mouth in surprise, Brooks prompts, "I wonder what's making that noise." Abby reaches for the box and pulls off the lid. Inside is a collection of large, colorful, plastic laundry detergent bottle tops that Brooks has saved. Abby reaches in with both hands and picks up two bottle tops. She looks them over, bangs them together a few times, and then tosses them onto the rug. Several more times, she reaches into the box with one hand, grasps another top, and throws it. "You really like to throw those bottle tops," Brooks comments. With a big smile, Abby dumps the rest of the tops out of the box and claps her hands.*

Some of the very best playthings for infants, toddlers, and twos are not commercial toys. They are simply common objects and natural materials that appeal to children and that can be explored safely. Large plastic bottle tops, cardboard boxes, crinkly tissue paper, wooden and plastic kitchen utensils, pinecones, leaves, and shells appeal to young children as much as many toys you can purchase (and sometimes even more). Any object that young children can explore, put together, take apart, push or pull, stack, or bang becomes a toy in a child's hands.

Many toys are designed to entertain children and capture their attention, for example, mobiles that swing and play music and wind-up toys that move across the floor. Other toys are structured to fit together in a particular way: puzzles, nesting cups, and pegboards. Still others are open-ended and can be used in a variety of ways: to build and stack, or to create a pattern or design.

All toys must meet safety standards so that children under age 3 can explore them safely with all of their senses. Effective toys capture children's attention, keep them engaged, and help them acquire and strengthen new skills.

Supporting Development and Learning

Infants, toddlers, and twos develop social/emotional, physical, cognitive, and language skills when they play with toys.

Learning about themselves and others: As young children develop a trusting relationship with you, they become more confident about exploring toys. They experiment and are eager to see your reactions. Toys that can be used successfully by more than one person—such as balls, blocks, and simple matching games—teach children about the give-and-take of relationships and how to recognize the needs of others.

Learning about moving: Toys inspire young children to explore actively. As they grasp, pull apart, fit together, fill and dump, stack, roll, and toss toys, children are strengthening and refining the small muscles in their hands and fingers and developing eye-hand coordination. They develop large-muscle skills as they carry toys, build with blocks, and push and pull toys such as wagons and small brooms.

Learning about the world: Children learn how objects can be used by exploring the toys you provide. They learn that a rattle will make a noise only if they move it and that a round block will only fit through a round hole, not a square one, if the hole is the same size as the block. When an infant pushes a button on a toy and it makes music, and if the child repeats the action again and again with the same result, she learns about cause and effect. Trying several ways to fit the pieces of a puzzle together helps children develop problem-solving strategies. Children's ability to sustain attention grows as they explore what they can do with toys. Beads, blocks, large pegs, Duplos® and other manipulatives provide opportunities for children to explore the many ways that objects can be grouped.

Learning about communicating: Your room is filled with interesting objects, such as a big red block, a soft squishy bear, and a round bouncing ball. As you direct children's attention to toys, name them, and describe their characteristics, you teach children interesting language. Toys that are appealing and fun for children inspire conversations, especially if you show an interest in what children are doing, describe what your senses tell you, and ask questions. When you hear an infant say, "Ba, ba," as he plays with a ball, you know he is connecting the word with the appropriate object and learning to express his ideas.

Creating an Environment for Playing With Toys

There is an enormous variety of toys for infants, toddlers, and 2-year-olds. In general, look for toys with these characteristics:

- simple
- colorful
- safe and washable
- open-ended (variety of uses)

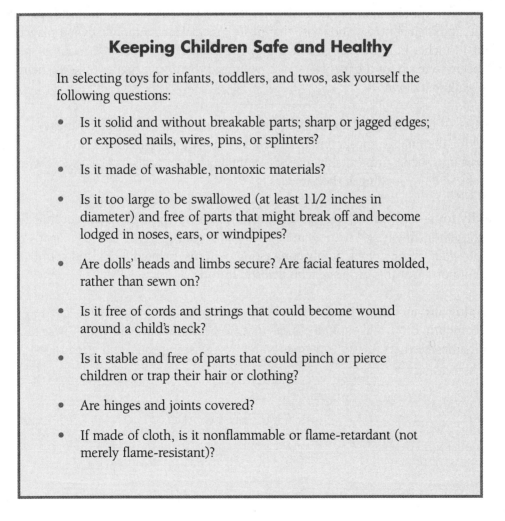

Keeping Children Safe and Healthy

In selecting toys for infants, toddlers, and twos, ask yourself the following questions:

- Is it solid and without breakable parts; sharp or jagged edges; or exposed nails, wires, pins, or splinters?

- Is it made of washable, nontoxic materials?

- Is it too large to be swallowed (at least 1½ inches in diameter) and free of parts that might break off and become lodged in noses, ears, or windpipes?

- Are dolls' heads and limbs secure? Are facial features molded, rather than sewn on?

- Is it free of cords and strings that could become wound around a child's neck?

- Is it stable and free of parts that could pinch or pierce children or trap their hair or clothing?

- Are hinges and joints covered?

- If made of cloth, is it nonflammable or flame-retardant (not merely flame-resistant)?

Selecting Materials for Different Ages

The ages, developmental abilities, and individual interests of children are important considerations in selecting the best toys.[37]

Young infants

Young infants respond to toys they can see, hear, taste, touch, and smell. They focus their attention on toys and other objects that resemble a face, have clear lines, or are brightly colored. Almost every object they grasp goes directly into their mouths. When they can sit up, young infants enjoy toys that they can bat. Here are some good toys for young infants.

Mobiles—Mobiles promote the development of vision and hearing when infants are interested in the sight and sound of them. Infants especially like mobiles with patterns, circles, and high contrast, and those that make music. Hang a mobile over a play area, about 14 inches from their eyes, where they can focus best. At about 4 months, infants will begin to reach for the mobile, so you will need to move it higher to keep them from pulling it down.

Mirrors—From the age of about 4–6 months, children are captivated by mirrors. Watching their image appear and disappear in a mirror helps them learn to focus. You can position stable, unbreakable mirrors on the bottom of walls in play spaces where infants can enjoy looking at their images.

Cuddly toys—Stuffed animals; hand puppets; and soft, washable, one-piece rag dolls delight young infants and help them begin to learn concepts like *hard–soft*, *light–dark*, and *big–little*. Bright colors, boldly contrasting patterns, painted faces, and sounds are more important at this early age than realistic features.

Grasping and mouthing toys—From about 3 months on, young infants love to grasp, shake, mouth, drop, and explore objects that they can hold in their fists. These include small rattles, teethers, plastic key rings with keys, grasping balls, and cloth toys.

Mobile infants

Mobile infants continue to enjoy toys that they can explore with all of their senses.

__Willard__ (11 months) finds that a large stuffed dinosaur is easier to hug than a small rubber one. As __Abby__ (14 months) yanks on large snap beads or inserts a circle into a foam board, she learns how to squeeze, twist, push, and pull.

Puzzles, block towers, and large pegs in a pegboard are great fun to take apart, although a mobile infant may not yet be able to put them together. Here is a list of toys for mobile infants.

Balls—A ball is one of the toys that children love most. They delight in rolling, holding, getting, and throwing balls of all types. Provide a variety of sizes and textures, such as clutch balls with easily grasped, indented surfaces; balls with chimes or visible objects rolling inside; and balls that roll in unpredictable ways, such as weighted balls and oddly shaped ones. When they can stand, mobile infants enjoy the challenge of batting a large beach ball.

Manipulative toys—These are toys that mobile infants can pull apart and fit together, dump and fill, stack and knock down, and shake. Good selections are stacking rings, nesting cups, foam boards, shape sorters, and measuring spoons.

Puzzles—For mobile infants, select puzzles with only two or three pieces and with pieces that can be held by knobs. (You can glue empty spools on the pieces to serve as knobs if they do not come that way.) The puzzles should be colorful and depict objects, people, or animals familiar to the child. By exploring the puzzle pieces and discovering how the shapes fit together, mobile infants develop eye-hand coordination and problem-solving strategies.

Activity boxes—These toys have doors that open, dials to turn, knobs to pull, and buttons to push. They can be attached to furniture and provide practice in wrist control and the use of finger muscles. Examples are busy boxes and surprise boxes that pop up.

Push-and-pull toys—Sturdy carriages and child-size shopping carts are especially appropriate for children who are beginning to walk, because they offer much-needed support. More experienced walkers enjoy such toys as plastic lawnmowers and carpet sweepers. Toys that play music or make other sounds as they move enhance the play experience by encouraging the child to move in order to make the sound. Such toys also help children build understandings about cause and effect.

Transportation toys—Small plastic or wooden cars, buses, trains, trucks, and airplanes delight mobile infants as they turn the wheels and push them across the floor. Ride-on toys that they scoot with their feet are exciting for this age group when they are more balanced and coordinated.

Blocks—At first, mobile infants prefer to pick up, pile, knock down, and even throw blocks. For these reasons, foam, cloth-covered, and small plastic blocks are the best choices. Later, introduce firmer blocks, made of lightweight wood, for stacking. Stacking blocks should be cube-shaped, brightly colored or patterned, and easily grasped (2–4 inches). A selection of 20–25 blocks is sufficient.

Toddlers

Toddlers continue to use all of the toys mobile infants use, but they are likely to use them in different ways.

Matthew (22 months) enjoys stacking blocks to make a tower, knocking it down, and repeating this process again and again. Sometimes he also pretends that a block is something else, like a car zooming along the road.

In order to continue supporting children's development, select toys that stimulate toddlers' understanding of themselves in relationship to the world around them. Here are some suggestions.

Push-and-pull toys—These are ideal for toddlers, who are now steady on their feet. They enjoy pushing a carriage full of dolls, mopping and sweeping with child-size tools, and pulling a wagon. These activities often lead to pretend play.

Animal figures—Soft, fuzzy stuffed animals are popular with toddlers, as are rubber, wood, vinyl, and plastic figures. They like to carry stuffed toys around and to make up scenes using farm and zoo animals and monsters.

Puzzles and matching games—These toys provide opportunities for toddlers to develop and apply thinking skills. Select simple 4- to 5-piece puzzles in which each piece is a complete picture and has a knob for children to grasp. They can be made of any thick, durable, nontoxic material.

Manipulative toys—These include more complex and challenging shape-sorting and activity boxes, nesting cups, pegboards with large pegs, stacking rings (with 5–10 pieces), and large plastic snap beads.

Transportation toys—Plastic, wooden, and metal cars, trucks, buses, trains, and airplanes continue to delight toddlers, who line them up or race them across the floor. Include some vehicles with simple movable parts, such as doors that open and close, and trains that couple easily.

Blocks—Toddlers enjoy building with a variety of lightweight but sturdy blocks. Choose blocks of uniform sizes and of shapes that are easy for children to build with and stack. Here are good choices for this age group:

- rectangular plastic blocks of a variety of colors
- cardboard blocks designed to look like bricks and with a coating that makes them easy to clean
- large interlocking plastic blocks (such as Duplos®)
- large foam blocks
- colored wooden table-blocks of uniform sizes
- alphabet blocks

Gross motor toys and equipment—Toys and space for gross motor play are important, especially on days when children may not go outside. Include tunnels for toddlers to crawl through, doll carriages and child-size shopping carts to push, and ride-on equipment that they can propel with their feet.

Twos

Twos are acquiring many new fine motor skills, so they can manipulate objects with more purpose. They build and create with objects, sort and match materials, fit things together, arrange them in patterns and designs, and use toys for pretending. Most of the toys listed for toddlers are also of interest to twos, although they use them in more advanced ways. In addition, they are ready for more complex materials and equipment. Here are some suggestions.

Puzzles and matching games—Twos who enjoy puzzles may want the challenge of puzzles with 6–12 pieces. As they become more skilled in sorting and matching, they can play games in which they match giant dominoes (2–4 inches in size) or match simple and familiar picture pieces to lotto boards.

Manipulative toys—Twos may enjoy stringing large wooden beads on laces; lacing cards or a wooden shoe; and practicing with personal care boards that have snaps, buttons, laces, zippers, and Velcro® strips. Include more challenging shape sorters, shapes that fit together, and large plastic or wooden nuts and bolts.

Transportation toys—With their increased fine motor skills, twos enjoy handling movable parts: steering wheels that turn; bulldozer shovels that pick up and dump; cherry pickers that they can raise and lower; and knobs, levers, buttons, and wheels of all sorts.

Unit blocks—To build stable constructions, twos need heavier, sturdier blocks. Hardwood unit blocks are the universal favorites because of their weight, durability, and many uses. While twos do not need the specialized shapes that preschoolers enjoy (such as triangles and arches), you should provide at least 40–60 blocks per builder in a group.

Simple props—Enhance the block play of 2-year-olds by including small wooden and plastic animals and people, miniature traffic signs, doll house furniture, and small vehicles. They can use them to decorate their block structures and for dramatic play.

Large blocks—Twos like to build with hollow blocks and those made of heavy cardboard or sturdy foam. They are likely to use their constructions as play settings, climbing on them, sitting inside, and pretending.

Gross motor toys—To provide physical challenges, include climbers and riding toys that children can push with their feet. As they near age 3, some children are even able to manage tricycle pedals. Large cardboard boxes make wonderful spaces for crawling. Balls of varying shapes, colors, textures, and sizes are great for kicking, batting, throwing, and catching.

Including All Children

All children benefit from playing with toys when they are able to use them well. Depending on the disability, some toys present special challenges. You can choose toys and adapt others so that no child spends large parts of the day observing the play of others instead of actively joining in. Simple adaptations can open a world of play and exploration for children with varying types and degrees of disability. You may also find that toys chosen for a child with a disability become favorites of other children in your program.

Some easily implemented, low-technology modifications to materials and your environment can make all the difference. Here are some suggestions.[38]

Handles or built-up knobs—Glue knobs or corks to puzzles and other toys to assist children with limited fine motor skills. Add foam curlers to build up the handles of spoons, brushes, crayons, and markers.

Activity frames—Activity frames are similar to the play "gyms" designed for infants. Hang toys securely from the frame so that the children have easy access to them. These devices allow children with motor impairments to use toys that would otherwise be out of reach or that the children would not be able to retrieve if dropped. The frames can be placed on the floor, attached to a table, or attached to a wheelchair or stander.

Playboards—You can attach toys to a firm surface (such as foam core, pegboard, or carpet) with Velcro®, string, or elastic. Create a variety of playboards that allow children to participate in imaginative play. Examples of simple playboards include a purse (with keys, brush, wallet, etc.); a tea party (with cups and spoons); or a playhouse (with people and furniture). The child can then use his hands or a grasping aid to move the pieces without worrying about dropping them. Other children can also participate in this play.

Other strategies to help children with special needs are to attach play materials to steady surfaces, to select toys with large pieces (such as puzzles), and to simplify the game or toy. Ivan has found that he just needs to provide a wedge for Gena (30 months) so she can reach and play with the toys she enjoys.

Remember that the child's family and therapists are great resources. Invite the child's physical or occupational therapist to visit your program and suggest ways to adapt your space and toys to meet the child's abilities and interests.

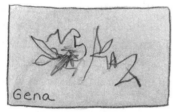

Setting Up and Displaying Materials

Toys should be placed near, comfortable surfaces with enough space for children to play near one another comfortably. Even infants like to watch what other children are doing. Here are some suggestions for toy arrangement.

Put out a few toys at a time. Too many toys can overwhelm young children. Change your inventory as children master each rotation of toys or get tired of them. However, do not remove all of the toys that children have mastered. As in familiar books, children find comfort in favorite toys.

Have duplicates of most toys. Children younger than age 3 have a difficult time sharing. You can minimize conflicts by providing duplicates.

Store toys on low shelves. If toys are stored on the bottom ledge of a bookcase or room divider, children can get them when they want to play with them. Leave ample space between stored toys to make it easy for the children to see each one. Avoid using toy chests. They are safety hazards, and it is difficult for children to find toys in them.

Make a label for each type of toy. Picture and word labels placed on containers and shelves show children where things belong. You can draw a picture of the toy, photograph it, or cut a picture of it from a catalog. This helps children find what they want, and cleaning up becomes a matching game.

Group similar toys together. This helps children locate their favorite puzzles, transportation toys, push-and-pull toys, and so forth. Grouping by type also helps teach children to classify objects.

Provide a protected area for block building. One option is to use a corner of the room with a shelf or couch to protect a space for builders. Children can play with soft blocks anywhere: on a rug, linoleum, or a wooden floor. Small table blocks can be used on a table or on the floor.

Caring and Teaching

It is fascinating to watch what infants, toddlers, and twos do with the toys and objects you provide. By observing purposefully, taking a real interest in what they do, and responding to them, you will learn much about what interests each child and appreciate what each child is doing and learning.

Young Infants

Very young infants are much more interested in watching your face, hearing your voice, and being held than in any toy. Once they can focus on objects better and hold them in their fists, they are ready to respond to the toys you provide.

Linda has a soft play mat with an attached play gym. She lays Julio (4 months) on his back, and he reaches for the dangling toys, batting them with his hand. Linda talks to him as he plays. "You like the play gym, don't you, Julio? You're having a good time. You discovered that the toy moves when you hit it. Now you're watching it go back and forth, back and forth." Linda is careful to observe for cues that Julio is ready to do something else.

Just as an infant lets you know when he is hungry, tired, or in need of changing, his behavior lets you know when he is ready to play or when he is finished with one play experience and ready for another.

Jasmine (8 months) can now sit by herself and scoot around on the floor, so Janet encourages her play by placing a mirror near the floor. When they play peek-a-boo, Jasmine can watch the action in the mirror.

Here are the kinds of things Janet might say to Jasmine as they play together.

- Describe the experience: *There's Jasmine, in the mirror.*
- Verbalize feelings: *That surprised you, didn't it?*
- Play with language: *Peek-a-boo. I see you. Peek-a, peek-a-BOO!*
- Describe actions: *You can see yourself in the mirror. There's Jasmine.*

Mobile Infants

Mobile infants seem to be in love with the world and fascinated by everything in it. They are immediately interested when you place a basket of toys near them and will proceed to pull out every object they can reach, dumping each on the floor and then reaching for another. Filling and dumping are favorite activities of this age group. Any container and object (or objects) will work. They also enjoy tossing things, so give them plenty of space and soft, unbreakable toys.

Abby (14 months) is playing with vinyl blocks. She attempts to stack them, but they keep falling over. Instead of building a tower for her as a model, Brooks works with Abby to help her figure out a solution. She encourages Abby to experiment with placing the cubes. Through trial and error, Abby eventually learns that the more fully the top cube covers the bottom one, the steadier the tower will be.

Take time to watch and think about what a child is experiencing and about how and when you might respond. Here is what you might say and do.

- Describe what the child does and what happens (cause and effect): *Look what happened when you pushed the button. The clown popped out!*

- Encourage the child to solve problems: *Oh, the ball rolled under the table. How can you get it?*

- Build vocabulary by using descriptive words: *You decided to play with the red fire truck. It's the same color as your red shirt.*

- Promote a recognition of group needs: *You put all of the blocks back in the bucket where we keep them. That was a big job, so you and [another child] did it together.*

Toddlers

Toddlers use toys with increasing intention. As they play, they build their physical and language skills, learn concepts, apply thinking skills, explore the world of social roles and make-believe, and learn to be a member of a group. Here are some ways to respond to their play.

- To promote physical skills: *I see that you are using your big muscles today. Thank you for helping me carry these big blocks over to the tree.*

- To support thinking skills: *Can you find the picture on the shelf that matches the snap beads?*

- Encourage perseverance: *It's hard to get that puzzle piece to fit. Why don't you turn it around and see if it fits then? I bet you can get it to fit.*

- Promote a recognition of the needs of others: *You are waiting patiently for your turn with the ride-on toy.*

Twos

It is fascinating to watch what twos do with toys. As long as you do not give them too many choices and you show an interest in what they are doing, their use of materials can be creative and joyful. Engage twos in conversation about what they want to play with and what they intend to do. In addition to the kinds of comments and descriptions explained earlier, invite twos to tell you what they are doing. Use open-ended questions to encourage them to think about what they are doing and to verbalize their thoughts. Here are some ways to interact with twos as they play with toys.

- Invite the child to talk about what he has done: *Tell me why you arranged the cars that way.*

- Describe what you see: *First you used all of the rectangular blocks to build your farm. Then you added animals, and now you are adding people.*

- Support social skills: *Why don't you both take the Bristle Blocks® over to the rug so you can play together?*

- Promote problem-solving skills: *When you put the big block on top of the little one, your building fell down. How can you build it so it won't fall?*

- Ask open-ended questions: *What do you think will happen if you try it another way?*

Responding to and Planning for Each Child

As you observe children playing with toys, think about the goals, objectives, and steps of the *Developmental Continuum*. Consider what each child is learning and how you might respond. Here is how four teachers who are implementing *The Creative Curriculum* use what they learn from their observations to respond to each child and to plan.

Observe	Reflect	Respond
Julio (4 months) lies on his tummy on a play mat. He reaches for a teether, grabs it, and brings it to his mouth. He continues to look around the mat for several minutes, and then he notices two children pushing trucks. He watches them and begins to grunt, moving his head up and down.	Julio is using his whole hand to grasp objects (*Objective 9, Demonstrates basic fine motor skills*). He is beginning to move purposefully (*Objective 8, Demonstrates basic gross motor skills*). He watches and responds to other children (*Objective 5, Plays with other children*).	Linda decides to encourage Julio's interest in the other children by responding to the cues that tell her that he would like to change his position. She says, "You see those two girls playing with the trucks. I'll pick you up, and we'll move closer so you can see them better."
Abby (14 months) fills a purse with small blocks and carries it as she toddles around the room. She approaches Samanda, opens the purse to show her what is inside, and then continues carrying it around.	Abby is walking with increasing coordination (*Objective 8, Demonstrates basic gross motor skills*). She is engaging momentarily with other children (*Objective 5, Plays with other children*).	Brooks provides other objects for Abby to carry, so Abby can strengthen her large-muscle skills and balance. She encourages her engagement with other children by saying, "Abby, I think Samanda wants to look carefully at the blocks you collected. Will you please show them to her again?"
Leo (18 months) takes the top off a shape sorter and dumps out all of the shapes. He brings it over to a bucket of plastic people and begins to fill the sorter with the people. When the sorter is full and no more people will fit, he holds it up to Barbara and asks, "Mo'?"	Leo is using one hand to hold an object and the other hand to manipulate another object (*Objective 9, Demonstrates basic fine motor skills*). He is experimenting with trial and error approaches to simple problems (*Objective 14, Uses problem-solving strategies*). He is using gestures, word-like sounds, and single words to communicate (*Objective 17, Develops expressive language*).	Barbara responds to Leo by describing the problem: "I don't think any more will fit in there, Leo." She encourages him to solve the problem by asking, "What else can you put the people in?" She pauses, giving him time to think about the question, and then offers some suggestions. She asks, "How about using a bigger container so that more people will fit?" Then, as she points to a collection of baskets and a cardboard box, she adds, "We have baskets and a big box." ▶

Observe	Reflect	Respond
◄ Gena (30 months) is playing with the farm animals. She puts three horses next to each other, places two pigs together, and matches two sheep. She looks up and says, "Same, same. All the same."	Gena is grouping objects with similar characteristics (*Objective 13, Shows a beginning understanding that things can be grouped*). She uses simple sentences with three or more words (*Objective 17, Develops expressive language*).	Ivan acknowledges Gena's work, saying, "I see you have put all the horses together, the pigs together, and the sheep together." To encourage her language development, he expands what she said. "All of the horses, all of the pigs, and all of the sheep. The same kind of animal goes together."

Responsive Planning

In developing weekly plans, these teachers use their observations and refer to the *Developmental Continuum*. Here is what they record on their weekly planning forms.

On the *Child Planning Form*, under "Current information," Linda writes about the cues Julio used to tell her that he was ready to do something else. Under "Plans," she writes that she will observe Julio closely so that she can respond appropriately to his cues. She also writes a reminder to share what she learns with her co-teacher.

After reviewing observation notes about the other children, Brooks realizes that two other children have been carrying toys in purses. She decides to add some small baskets for filling and carrying. Brooks adds this task to the *Group Planning Form* under "Changes to the Environment."

Barbara recognizes that Leo was exploring the concept of quantity (how many he can fit into the container). On the *Child Planning Form*, under "Plans," she records that she will provide opportunities for him to experiment with quantity through water play. On the *Group Planning Form*, under "Changes to the Environment," she records, "Add 2 sets of nesting cups to the water table." She also makes a note to use words such as *more, less, same, empty*, and *full* with the children.

Ivan uses the *Child Planning Form* to record his observation of Gena's expressive language. Under "Plans," he writes that he will continue to expand her sentences, offering her opportunities to hear more complex language and new words. He also decides to bring a collection of lids that he can put in small tubs for the children to sort. He adds this to the *Group Planning Form* under "Indoor Experiences" for Monday, Tuesday, and Wednesday.

SHARING THOUGHTS ABOUT THE VALUE OF TOYS

Dear Families:

Toys are designed for children's enjoyment. They are also important tools for learning. When children play with toys, they learn how to move, how things work, and how to communicate with and relate to others. Here are just a few of the ways that toys help your child grow and learn.

When your child does this…	Your child is learning…
• bats a ball to make it move	• cause and effect
• rolls a toy car	• about movement and space
• puts pieces in a form board	• concepts such as shape, size, color
• snaps plastic beads together	• eye-hand coordination
• builds with blocks	• how objects can be used

What You Can Do at Home

Here are some ideas that can help your child make the most of playing with toys at home.

- **You are your child's favorite toy.** Your interest and involvement make playing with toys even more fun and engaging.

- **A few good toys are better than too many.** Too many toys can overwhelm a young child. It's far better to have a few good toys that can be used in a variety of ways.

- **Choose simple toys at first.** Good toys for infants are those that they can explore with all their senses. Plastic rings and rattles that they can grasp, squeeze, and mouth are especially good. Mobile infants enjoy playing with toys that they can push or pull, such as plastic lawnmowers. They also like toys with movable parts, such as doors, knobs, big buttons, switches, and so on.

- **Pick toys that challenge your child.** Toddlers are ready for simple puzzles with 4–5 pieces, plastic and wooden cars and trucks, blocks, shape sorters, nesting cups, and riding toys. Your 2-year-old will enjoy puzzles with more pieces, matching games, large beads and laces, balls, and blocks of all kinds.

- **Common household objects make wonderful toys.** An empty box, large empty thread spools, pots and pans, plastic food containers, and kitchen utensils are just a few of the things that young children use as toys.

Whether you buy or make your child's toys, what's most important is that you take pleasure in watching your child play, talk about what he or she is doing, and respond enthusiastically to each new discovery.

Sincerely,

inside this chapter

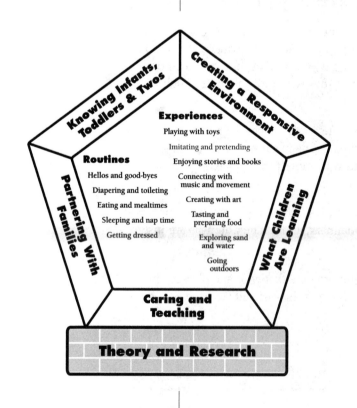

Imitating and Pretending

12

Leo *(18 months) is sitting on the floor with a large pot and wooden spoon. "It looks like you are busy cooking something, Leo," remarks Barbara. Leo continues to stir. "What are you making?" she asks. Leo looks up and smiles. Barbara says, "M-m-m, it smells like pea soup to me." When Leo nods, Barbara says, "I thought so. May I please have some of your soup?" She gets a bowl and hands it to Leo. When he doesn't respond, Barbara says, "Oh, I'm silly. You need a big ladle to serve the soup." She hands a ladle to Leo, who pretends to serve some soup to her.*

Pretending is a way of learning as well as a way of playing, and it requires a great deal of thinking. Pretending shows that children are developing from the sensorimotor thinking of infancy to more mature symbolic thinking. It evolves gradually from the imitation and exploration of infants, toddlers, and twos.

Young infants imitate facial expressions, many of the language sounds they hear, and the immediate actions of others. By about age 15 months, mobile infants can remember the actions on objects that they have previously seen others perform, so they are able to imitate those actions later.[39] Being able to remember and then imitate an action is important to early pretend play, which often takes the form of reproducing the actions children have seen others make. Toddlers and twos remember past experiences and often purposefully pretend to be something or someone else, such as a great big monster or a daddy feeding a baby.

When you show an infant how to wave bye-bye, clap her hands together, and play peek-a-boo, you are encouraging her to engage with others and to imitate speech and actions. When you see a mobile infant imitating a puppy and you say, "What a nice puppy!" you are encouraging him to continue to pretend. When you hold a doll on your shoulder and pat its back, you are showing a toddler how to pretend about real life situations. When you hand a toy phone to a 2-year-old so he can pretend to call the doctor about his sick baby, you are teaching him how to pretend with objects.

Supporting Development and Learning

Children develop social/emotional, physical, cognitive, and language skills when they imitate and pretend. Here are just a few examples.

Learning about self and others: Managing their feelings is one of the most important things that children under age 3 are learning. When they pretend to be a scary dog or an angry mother, they are experimenting with safe ways to express a range of feelings. They also explore emotions when they believe that dolls and stuffed animals have feelings and should be cared for.[40] As the brief play encounters of mobile infants with other children develop into coordinated play as children approach age 2, they begin to develop understandings about friendship. As twos assume pretend roles, you might observe them taking on the roles of important people in their lives by selecting particular items that represent those roles.

Learning about moving and doing: While they explore, imitate and pretend, very young children strengthen their large muscle skills and refine their small muscle skills. Perhaps they pretend to be a kitty cat that is crawling around a box or a father who runs to catch the bus. Maybe they push a doll carriage or a toy shopping cart full of empty food boxes. Such experiences involve large muscles. They practice using small muscles when they press the buttons on the toy phone, dress a doll, or put things in a suitcase or pocketbook.

Learning about the world: Young children use imitation to make sense of their experiences and to interact with others socially. As their physical skills mature and as they gain experience with the world, they begin to act out events and familiar routines. They also begin to explore social roles, especially those of parents and other powerful figures. In your simple pretend play area, children show that they know how objects can be used. The play stove is for pretending to cook, a doll bed is for pretending that a baby is sleeping. The fire hat prompts toddlers and twos to pretend to drive to a fire, first using a realistic steering wheel but later pretending to drive just by turning their hands in space to indicate the motion of a turning steering wheel.

Learning about communicating: As you wave good-bye to a baby's father early in the morning, you say, "Bye-bye, Daddy." Up goes the baby's hand, opening and shutting, imitating your farewell gesture. Gestures and, later, words continue during games of peek-a-boo, as you and the infant pretend to disappear and, to the baby's glee, reappear in a delightful two-way conversation of sorts that encourages children to engage in play. Single words, two-word phrases, and simple sentences appear in pretend play as infants become toddlers and toddlers become twos. "Baby hungry," a toddler says as he feeds a baby doll. A 2-year-old might explain, "My baby likes 'nanas."

Creating an Environment for Pretend Play

A few well-chosen props and materials invite infants, toddlers, and twos to imitate and pretend. As they get older, additional realistic props inspire twos to take on different roles and pretend about situations they have experienced.

Selecting Materials for Different Ages

Young Infants

Materials that allow young infants to use all of their senses and that promote their physical skills are appropriate, such as soft dolls or stuffed animals that they can grasp and hold. Dolls should be washable and have simple facial features with no moveable pieces or detachable parts. Young infants especially like bright colors and objects that have rattles inside and make noise when shaken. Offer play items that allow them to try different actions and to watch what happens as a result.

Your daily interactions are as important as the toys and other items you provide. Babies prefer to play when they are with nurturing adults. As they experiment with toys and other objects, young infants imitate the actions of other people and try new ways to make things happen.

Mobile Infants

These active explorers like to push; pull; shake; bang; fill and dump; and climb in, out, around, and on top of furniture and equipment. Realistic toys are good choices for mobile infants. They respond to lifelike dolls of vinyl or rubber that they can carry, hold, and pretend to feed. Here are suggestions of popular materials:

- carts, baby carriages, and other wheeled toys
- doll bottles, baby blankets, and a cradle
- toy or real telephones
- hats and pocketbooks
- pots, pans, and plastic dishes and utensils
- plastic, wood, or rubber cars, buses, trucks, planes, and trains

Notice what happens when you put out realistic toys and objects. See if a mobile infant picks up a cup and pretends to drink or places a doll in a toy stroller and pushes it around the room.

Toddlers and Twos

Because they take great interest in the details of toys and props, toddlers and twos are intrigued by small cars with doors that open and shut; trucks with movable parts; and dolls with movable arms and legs, hair, and facial features. Provide props that encourage role playing, especially the roles of parents and other powerful figures such as monsters, doctors, and firefighters. Props such as toy household items also encourage children to replay parts of their everyday experiences. Dolls should represent the ethnicities of the children in your program.

As older toddlers and twos develop more small-muscle control, it is possible for them to handle simple doll clothes and dress-up clothes. They might play for long periods of time, for example, arranging people and animal figures in- and outside of a toy barn and talking to them as they play. By regularly rotating the props you make available, you can keep toddlers and twos interested and extend their play.

In addition to the materials listed for mobile infants, consider adding these materials:

- dress-up clothes, such as jackets, hats, and dresses
- work-related props, such as boots, firefighter hats, work gloves, stethoscopes
- suitcases, pocketbooks, and lunch boxes
- doll bottles, baby blankets, and a cradle or small box to serve as a doll bed
- child-size dishes, pots, and pans
- child-size broom and mop
- assorted plastic containers and empty food boxes

For 2-year-olds, prop boxes are a good way to organize a collection of items related to a particular pretend play theme. For example, they may replay firsthand experiences at the doctor's office when they open a hospital prop box containing materials such as these:

- white or green shirts or old scrubs, and nurses caps
- stethoscope
- gauze and adhesive bandages
- pads and markers for prescriptions
- toy syringe

Similarly, a supermarket prop box might contain empty food containers, paper bags, and plastic fruits and vegetables. Think about experiences the children have had and what props might spark their interest and encourage them to pretend.

Setting Up and Displaying Materials

While infants do not need to have an area set aside for imitating, toddlers and especially twos will be drawn to an area arranged for pretend play. In a defined area, you can display the objects and props you know children will enjoy. Because they are most likely to pretend about their own lives, a simple house corner is ideal. A small table and chairs, a doll bed, a carriage, and a sink and stove create a place for toddlers and twos to engage in pretend play.

Place picture and word labels of the items where the materials are stored, so children learn where to find what they need and where to return it when they finish playing. An orderly arrangement of the materials conveys the message that you want children to use the materials and take care of them. Here are some ideas for storing and displaying props and materials:

- Use wooden pegs on a board to hang clothes, hats, and pocketbooks.

- Store shoes and other small items in a shoe bag.

- Hang dress-up clothes on a small coat tree that has been shortened to the children's level.

- Suspend three-tiered wire baskets from a hook to hold plastic food, ties and scarves, costume jewelry, and doll clothes.

- Hang pots, pans, cooking utensils, mops, brooms, and dress-up clothes on a pegboard with hooks.

Avoid displaying too many things at once. Too many choices overwhelm children, and they stop playing. Keep in mind that, while props can be very helpful in extending pretend play, the best way to encourage this type of play is to show your interest in what children do and follow their lead in pretending. Imitating and pretending with young children is another opportunity to build relationships that enable children to thrive.

Caring and Teaching

By observing children carefully, by taking a real interest and delight in what they do, and by playing games and having fun with children, you help them learn how to play and how to interact with other children. You also help them learn through their play. The *Developmental Continuum* will help you determine each child's developmental level for particular objectives. The information will help you decide what each child needs from you and how best to respond in ways that support each child's developing abilities.

Young Infants

Your relationship with young infants builds the foundation for all learning, including their ability to gain the most from imitation and play. Secure relationships make it easier for children to interact with other people, and they encourage children to play. Children's explorations become increasingly purposeful over time.

Julio (4 months) *grasps a doll and immediately puts it into his mouth.* **Jasmine** (8 months) *has more ways of exploring. She may turn the doll over to examine it from different angles and then pat it gently.*

As early as 2 months of age, babies are fascinated by each other. They get excited when they see other infants, and they stare at each other when they have chances to do so.[41] If you work with 6- to 9-month-old infants, notice how they try to get and return the attention of other children by smiling and babbling. Offer safe opportunities for young infants to be together, and encourage their interest in what other children are doing.

As you care for young infants, take time to talk with them about ways they are imitating and socializing. Here are some examples:

- Repeat the language sounds a child makes: *I hear you saying, "Ba-ba-ba." Now I'm going to say it: "Ba-ba-ba." Can you do that again?*

- Describe what a child is doing: *You like watching the other children. I see you smiling at them.*

- Engage a child in repeating actions in a fingerplay: *You clapped your hands together! Let's do it again. Pat-a-cake, pat-a cake, baker's man.*

Mobile Infants

Your playfulness and the various materials you provide become increasingly important as infants become more mobile. At this stage, infants explore objects and find out what they can do with them, sometimes by exploring new ways but often by imitating what they have previously seen others do with them. By about 10 months, an infant's brief action shows that she understands how an object is used, but she is not yet pretending. For example, she brings an empty spoon to her mouth while you are feeding her. Later, a mobile infant shows an awareness of pretending during an activity that only involves himself, as when he closes his eyes tightly and laughs while pretending to sleep.[42]

As they get older, you might observe mobile infants amusing themselves by playing with materials in unconventional ways.

Willard (11 months) takes a hat, puts it on his foot, and looks at Grace with an impish grin. To participate in the game, Grace shakes her head, smiles, and says, "No-o-o, not there! A hat doesn't go on your foot." Willard continues the game, putting the hat on different parts of his body and waiting to see Grace's reaction. He finally puts it on his head and he laughs when she confirms, "That's right. A hat goes on your head!"

As much as mobile infants enjoy playing with you, they are also becoming quite interested in each other. By 9–12 months, they imitate and touch each other. They handle objects together and may play for longer periods. During the next six months, children begin to exchange roles in action games, such as taking turns chasing and being chased. When they have the opportunity to play with familiar peers, children tend to engage in the same kinds of play. Even at this young age, children seem to understand when another person wants to play and what the person wants to do.[43]

Mobile infants are fascinating to watch. Take time to observe what they do and think about what you are learning before you decide how to respond. When you describe what children are doing and ask questions, you help them become aware of their actions. Here are some examples:

- Sing songs and fingerplays that involve simple actions: *Let's sing "The Wheels on the Bus." Can you make your hands go 'round and 'round?*

- Respond to a child who is pretending to be a dog: *Hello little puppy dog. Why are you barking? Are you hungry? Here's a bone for you"*

- Provide multiples of pretend play props, to minimize waiting and conflicts. *Here is another pot so you can make lunch, too.*

Toddlers

The pretend play of toddlers is more complex. Either their play involves another person or object, such as a stuffed animal, or the child acts out an activity that they have seen performed by someone else.[44] They enact simple routines, using objects in play as they are used in real life, such as combing a doll's hair or feeding a doll a bottle. Later they begin to substitute one object for another while they pretend, such as using a ring from a stacking toy as a bagel or a cylindrical block as a baby bottle to feed a doll. You will notice that children use objects that resemble in size and shape the ones they represent.

As toddlers learn more about the world, they typically develop fears about such things as loud noises, large animals, being separated from their families, and going to the doctor. Pretend play is one way that they cope with their fears.

Leo (18 months) *stamps around the room, growling and swiping the air with his arms. He is assuming the role of the scary monster he most fears. By becoming the monster, he can control what the monster does and thereby experience some power over what he fears. Barbara responds, "Oh, my, what a scary monster! I bet that monster is looking for a friend. I'll be your friend, Mr. Monster. Come play with me."*

By accepting this type of play, verbalizing what you think a child is feeling, and joining in, you can help toddlers work through fears that they cannot express directly. For this reason, pretend play is as important to a child's emotional development as it is to cognitive and social development.

Take time to encourage children's interest in pretending. You can do this by talking about what they are doing and by joining their play. Here are some examples:

- Provide props: *Here are some empty food boxes to put in your shopping cart.*

- Pretend along with toddlers: *Will you please take me for a ride in your car?*

- Describe what a child is doing: *I see that you are taking the baby for a ride in the carriage. Are you taking her to the park?*

Twos

The play of 2-year-olds becomes increasingly social and complex. At first, they share a common play theme without combining their activities with each other. For example, they might both pretend to make lunch, but each will pretend to pour milk instead of one child's pretending to serve the other. By about age 30 months, children begin to assume roles that go with another child's role, such as pretending to be a parent when the other child is pretending to be a baby.[45]

Sometimes children get so immersed in their play, you might have difficulty getting their attention for another purpose. Play is also a child's private reality at that moment,[46] so a child who has assumed the role of someone else might correct you when you call her by her given name.

> **Gena** (30 months) tells Ivan, "I not Gena. I Pooh Bear." Ivan plays along, "Okay, Pooh. It's time to eat your honey."

Twos are beginning to plan their play. They reenact events and announce what they are going to do. They also combine a sequence of tasks while they pretend.[47] For example, Jonisha may gather together several items needed to "play baby," and then hold the doll, pretend to feed it, and put it to bed. Two children might put on firefighter hats and pretend to put out a fire together. They may pretend with objects that do not closely resemble what they represent, such as by picking up a piece of string, pretending that it is a hose and using it to squirt imaginary water on an imaginary fire. This is an important achievement and shows that they are able to imagine a hose, fire, and water without relying on realistic props. Their increasing ability to use language to communicate with each other also makes their play more complex and interesting, and it helps them keep their play going.

When twos engage in this type of pretend play, encourage them by providing the materials they need, talking with them, and participating in the play. Here are some examples.

- Provide props to extend children's interests: *Did the car break down? Uh, oh! We'd better get the tool box and see what we can do to fix it.*

- Describe what a child is doing: *I see that you are wearing the firefighter hat and that you have a hose. Is a house on fire?*

- Participate in pretend play by taking on a role: *Hello? Hello? Is this the doctor? I have a sick baby here. We need to see the doctor. Is she in the office today?*

- Encourage a child to pretend without props: As you hand the child an imaginary phone, say, *The doctor wants to talk to you.*

- Ask open-ended questions to encourage imaginative thinking and expressive language: *I see you have packed your suitcase. Where are you going? How will you get there?*

Young children engaged in pretend play have many ideas and are often very imaginative. Take time to observe and appreciate what they are doing. Then take on a role, yourself; join them in their pretend play; and help them interact with other children. Always match the child's pace, recognizing that some children—because of a disability, temperament, or inexperience—may respond more slowly or need more support from you.

Responding to and Planning for Each Child

As you observe children imitating and pretending, think about the goals, objectives, and steps of the *Developmental Continuum*. Consider what each child is learning and how you should respond. Here is how four teachers who are implementing *The Creative Curriculum* use what they learn from their observations to respond to each child and to plan.

Observation	Reflection	Response
Jasmine (8 months) picks up a bright red plastic block and examines it. She looks at Holly, who is banging a wooden spoon on an empty oatmeal box. After watching her, Jasmine starts to bang her block on the floor.	Jasmine is watching and responding to other children (*Objective 5, Plays with other children*). She imitates the actions of others (*Objective 15, Engages in pretend play*).	Janet describes what Jasmine is doing, "You are watching Holly and making a big noise by banging that block. She imitates Jasmine's actions, using a cup: "I think I'll see what noise I can make with this cup. Bang, bang."
Abby (14 months) goes over to Jessie (16 months), who is wearing a hat, and tries to take it off. Brooks says, "Jessie is wearing that hat. I see you want one, too." She hands Abby a hat. Abby accepts it, puts it on her head, and smiles at Jessie.	Abby responds to verbal redirection (*Objective 2, Regulates own behavior*). She has brief play encounters with other children (*Objective 5, Plays with other children*).	Brooks wants to encourage Abby's interest in other children. She tries to involve her in pretending with one or two other children. She says, "Now you each have a hat to wear. Would you like to play with these trucks while you wear your hats?"
Matthew (22 months) is wearing a firefighter hat and holding a paper towel roll. He walks around the room saying, "Shhhh. Out, fire!"	Matthew substitutes one object for another in pretend play (*Objective 15, Engages in pretend play*). He is beginning to express himself in two-word phrases (*Objective 17, Develops expressive language*).	Mercedes expands what Matthew says and asks questions to encourage him to express his ideas verbally and extend his pretend play: "I see you have a hose to squirt the fire. Is it a big fire? Do you need a lot of water? Here, I'll turn on the fire hydrant for you. Is that enough water?"
Valisha (33 months) puts a plastic stethoscope around her neck and announces, "Doctor is here." Jonisha (33 months) holds up a baby doll and explains, "She sick. She needs some medicine." Valisha says, "Okay," as she opens the black bag she is holding. "Here's some," she says as she hands Jonisha a small wooden block.	Valisha and Jonisha are using objects in pretend play as they are used in real life and substituting one object for another in pretend play (*Objective 15, Engages in pretend play*). They are participating in coordinated play (*Objective 5, Plays with other children*). They are using simple sentences with three or more words (*Objective 17, Develops expressive language*).	Deciding not to interrupt their play, LaToya observes the sisters as they continue to play with the doctor props and doll. She pulls a piece of paper out of her pocket and writes a quick observation note describing their pretend play.

Responsive Planning

In developing weekly plans, these teachers will use their observations and refer to the *Developmental Continuum*. Here is what they record on their weekly planning forms.

> On the *Child Planning Form*, under "Current Information," Janet writes that Jasmine is beginning to imitate the actions of others. Under "Plans," she writes that she will involve Jasmine in some new fingerplays and encourage her to imitate the actions. On the *Group Planning Form*, Janet lists the new fingerplays and songs she wants to introduce to the children.

> Brooks makes a note on the *Child Planning Form*, under "Current Information," that Abby is showing an interest in other children. She wants to encourage this, so, under "Plans," she records that she will invite Abby and Jessie to help her make playdough. On the *Group Planning Form*, she writes that she will make playdough with the children on Monday.

> On the *Child Planning Form*, under "Current Information," Mercedes documents Matthew's interest in firefighters and his ability to pretend. She decides that this is something she wants to encourage. In the "Changes to the Environment" section of her *Group Planning Form*, Mercedes writes that she will add firefighter boots and rain slickers to the dramatic play area, fire trucks in the block area, and some storybooks and nonfiction books in the library.

> On the *Child Planning Form*, under "Current Information," LaToya notes that Jonisha and Valisha are acting out more complex pretend play scenarios. Because the group is going to take a walk to a local veterinary hospital next week, LaToya decides that she will add some stuffed animals and blank prescription pads to the doctor props. She records this idea under "Plans." She then lists the prescription pads and the animals she will add on the *Group Planning Form*, under "Changes to the Environment."

Infants, toddlers, and twos engage in imitation and pretend play when they are encouraged by the adults they love. Your ongoing observations of children will enable you to respond to them intentionally and use what you learn to plan experiences that will support their development and learning. Families also play a key role in supporting this type of play. They will be more likely to engage in imitation and pretend play with their children if they understand the importance of play. The letter to families is one way to share this information.

Sharing Thoughts About Imitation and Pretend Play

Dear Families:

Imitation and pretend play are among the most important ways that children learn about the world and relationships with people. The foundation for this type of play begins when young infants form secure attachments with the important people in their lives and explore their surroundings. They imitate other people, in order to understand how objects are used and as a way to get and keep the attention of others. Before long, they make believe with realistic items. For example, a toddler might feed a doll with a spoon or rock a doll to sleep. Two-year-olds learn to use objects to stand for other things, for example, to use a block as a car by pushing it along the floor.

As social pretend play begins, children explore social roles such as being a mother, a father, a doctor, and a baby. Being able to pretend also helps children cope with fears and anxieties. This is why children pretend to go to the doctor or to be a monster. Children who have good pretend play skills are more likely to be ready for school than those who lack these skills, because pretend play benefits every aspect of a young child's development. Children who have good pretend play skills are also often good at making friends.

What You Can Do at Home

Because imitation and pretend play are so important to every child's development and eventual success in school, we hope you will pretend with your child at home.

- **Encourage your child to explore.** The more children learn about objects and people, the more information they have on which to base their pretend play.

- **Talk about real life experiences as they take place.** When you take your child to various places—to the grocery store, post office, or a clinic—talk about what is happening. Explain what people are doing, their jobs, and the names of tools and other objects they use. This helps your child understand and recall experiences.

- **Provide props that inspire pretend play.** Dolls, doll blankets, a cradle, telephones (toy or real), pots, pans, and plastic dishes will inspire your child to explore social roles. Other useful props include plastic people and animals; transportation toys such as cars, trucks, and boats; and various ride-on toys.

- **Let your child dress up.** You can encourage your child's interest in pretending by providing dress-up clothes and work-related props such as firefighter hats, work gloves, and a toy stethoscope.

- **Play make-believe with your child.** This is one of the best ways to encourage your child to pretend. You can also encourage pretend play by asking questions; offering a new prop; and taking on a role, yourself.

Together we can help your child use imitation and pretend play as important ways to learn.

Sincerely,

inside this chapter

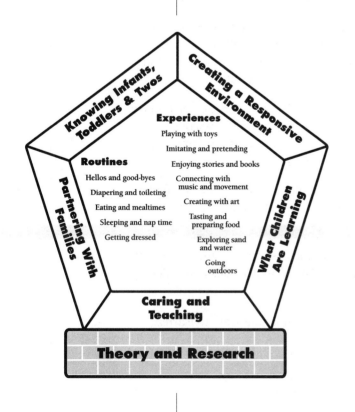

13

Enjoying Stories and Books

Matthew *(24 months) hands Mercedes a book as they sit together in the book area. She asks, "Do you want me to read* Mrs. Wishy-Washy *again?" Matthew opens the book to the picture of the cow in the tub. "In went the cow," says Mercedes. "Wishy-washy, wishy-washy," Matthew responds. "In went the pig," Mercedes reads. "Wishy-washy, wishy-washy," chant Marcella and Deneitra, who have joined them. "Away went the cow. Away went the pig. Away went the duck. Oh, lovely mud," Mercedes reads.*[48] *"Again, again," Matthew urges. "Love mud."*

Sharing stories and books with young children can be among the most treasured times of your day. With so many excellent books to touch, look at, and listen to, children will grow to love books. Even young infants, who do not yet understand the messages found in books, learn from exploring them.

Your interaction as you snuggle together with a book, your enthusiasm, the way you bring a story to life through your dramatic reading, and your interesting questions make the experience special for very young children. Because you know the children in your group so well, you can choose wonderful books for an infant to manipulate and explore, a toddler who is about to acquire a new brother or sister, or a 2-year-old who loves animals.

Supporting Development and Learning

Sharing stories and books with infants, toddlers, and twos supports their development and learning in many ways. Here are just a few examples.

Learning about themselves and others: The comfort of a favorite teacher's lap and the warmth of her voice create enjoyable associations with books and reading. Well before they understand the words, children gain a sense of security from the familiar rhythm of a favorite sleep-time book. As children grow older, they begin to relate to pictures and stories of familiar places and events. Books help children learn about how people are the same and different. They help infants, toddlers, and twos to identify and handle their emotions, and to feel connected to their families throughout the day.

Learning about moving: Looking at books encourages very young children to use their fine motor skills. Infants explore books in the same ways that they explore everything else. They reach for and grab, mouth and chew, shake, turn, and toss books. At 4–6 months, infants learn to grasp objects, including books. Sitting up frees a baby's hands to reach, grasp, and hold books. Mobile infants love to stick their fingers between pages, wave books in the air, point to pictures, and pat the illustrations. Toddlers can hold books with both hands and turn sturdy pages. Twos can turn the book right side up and carefully turn book pages without tearing them, most of the time.

Learning about the world: Books help children make sense of the world and learn new concepts. As they explore the properties of books, children learn about *light-heavy*, *big-little*, and *soft-hard*. As they look at picture books, they also learn concepts about size, number, and spatial relationships such as *up-down*, *in-out*, and *over-under*. Young children get information and learn how to do many things from books.

Learning about communicating: Storytelling and book reading help children build vocabulary and increasingly complex language skills. They enable young children to learn new words for naming animals, objects, actions, experiences, feelings, and ideas. A young infant enjoys the sounds of language as you read simple books. As you point to a picture of a cow, a mobile infant says, "Moo, moo," repeating the sounds you just made. Later, toddlers and twos name pictures and fill in repetitive words and phrases when you pause during readings. They explore book reading is when they pretend to read to their dolls or tell their teddy bears a bedtime story.

Creating an Environment for Enjoying Stories and Books

Books must be a regular part of your program. All you need are books and comfortable places for children to look at them—on their own and with you—and to hear them read aloud. Looking at books is something children can do anywhere in your program. Encourage them to look at books on the floor, on their cots, and in a shady area outdoors.

Have soft, welcoming places for reading near the book display. An overstuffed cushion, covered mattress, carpeted risers, or a glider make book nooks cozy. Your space should be appropriate for reading with a small group of children as well as with one child at a time. Provide an inviting area where a toddler or 2-year-old can sink into a cushion or rock on a child-size rocker to look at a book by himself. Be prepared for the fact that the children's favorite books will migrate around the room, carried by mobile infants or brought to you by toddlers or twos.

Selecting Books for Different Ages

Select high-quality books that you will enjoy sharing with the children. Keep the children's developmental abilities in mind and look for books that respect diversity and promote inclusion. Rotate and add new books to encourage children's interest, but keep old favorites available for repeated (and repeated and repeated) readings.

Include some homemade books, especially for older toddlers and twos who love to see pictures and hear stories about themselves. You can pull out a book with family pictures when a child feels sad about saying good-bye to his mother. You can help children remember the first snowy day with pictures of them when they were frolicking in snowsuits and building a snowman. Digital cameras are a wonderful tool to make bookmaking easier. You can also make "feely" books with fabrics of different textures or with other familiar objects.

A visit to the children's room of your local library can help you supplement your program's book collection, as can organizations such as Reading Is Fundamental. Yard sales and thrift stores are good sources for inexpensive books to expand your collection and replace worn books.

Young Infants

Simple, bold illustrations interest young infants. As babies begin to reach and grasp, they become more active partners in reading. For the 4- to 6-month-old child, "reading" is sometimes book chewing, shaking, banging, sniffing, and observing. Older infants enjoy turning pages. Books for infants should focus on familiar things: bottles and food, clothes, toys, pets, and people. Stories should be simple, rhythmic, and sometimes wordless.

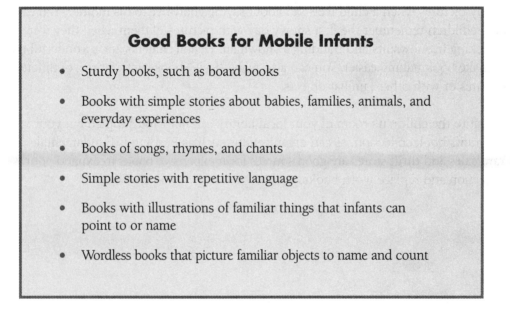

Good Books for Young Infants

- Washable, sturdy, chewable books made of cloth, plastic, or vinyl

- Board books that are easily cleaned, with pages that are easy to turn

- Books with highly contrasting pictures, or simple illustrations or photos, with one or two objects per page

- Books that have things to feel and move, such as tabs, flaps, holes, and a variety of textures

Mobile Infants

Recognizable pictures interest mobile infants. They begin to select books on the basis of content. They also enjoy books with repetition, rhyming verses, and nonsense syllables.

Good Books for Mobile Infants

- Sturdy books, such as board books

- Books with simple stories about babies, families, animals, and everyday experiences

- Books of songs, rhymes, and chants

- Simple stories with repetitive language

- Books with illustrations of familiar things that infants can point to or name

- Wordless books that picture familiar objects to name and count

Toddlers

Toddlers are beginning to follow simple plots. They especially like to hear stories about children and animals whose daily lives are similar to their own. Toddlers identify easily with mice who have grandmothers and with children who learn to use the potty.

This age group enjoys the whole process of listening to a story read aloud. They like books with pages they can turn, illustrations they can point to as you ask questions, and phrases that sound silly and are repeated predictably.

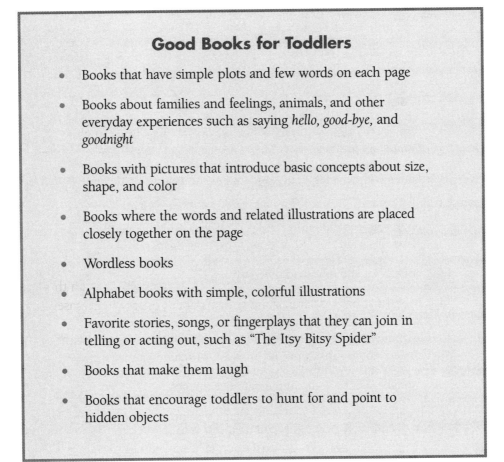

Good Books for Toddlers

- Books that have simple plots and few words on each page

- Books about families and feelings, animals, and other everyday experiences such as saying *hello, good-bye,* and *goodnight*

- Books with pictures that introduce basic concepts about size, shape, and color

- Books where the words and related illustrations are placed closely together on the page

- Wordless books

- Alphabet books with simple, colorful illustrations

- Favorite stories, songs, or fingerplays that they can join in telling or acting out, such as "The Itsy Bitsy Spider"

- Books that make them laugh

- Books that encourage toddlers to hunt for and point to hidden objects

Twos

By the time they are age 2, children who have frequently heard books read aloud bring favorite books to you again and again. They are ready to complete the rhyme or fill in the word you omit as you read a familiar story to them. They may begin "reading" to you, a friend, or a doll by telling parts of a familiar story. Many twos will listen to a whole story, following the simple plot. They participate in book-related experiences, such as seeing what they can spy after listening to *Each Peach Pear Plum*, by Janet and Allen Ahlberg.

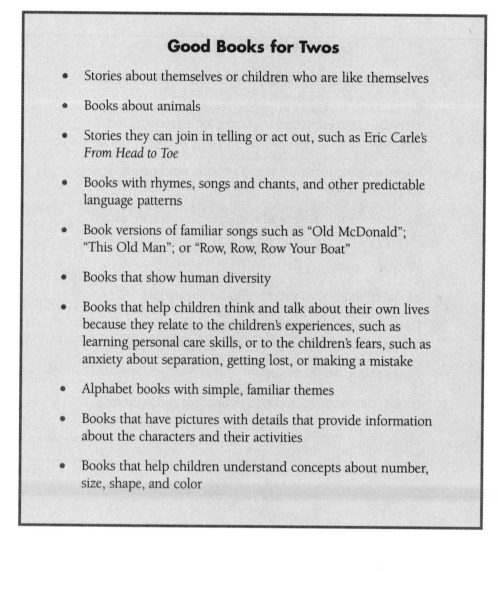

Good Books for Twos

- Stories about themselves or children who are like themselves

- Books about animals

- Stories they can join in telling or act out, such as Eric Carle's *From Head to Toe*

- Books with rhymes, songs and chants, and other predictable language patterns

- Book versions of familiar songs such as "Old McDonald"; "This Old Man"; or "Row, Row, Row Your Boat"

- Books that show human diversity

- Books that help children think and talk about their own lives because they relate to the children's experiences, such as learning personal care skills, or to the children's fears, such as anxiety about separation, getting lost, or making a mistake

- Alphabet books with simple, familiar themes

- Books that have pictures with details that provide information about the characters and their activities

- Books that help children understand concepts about number, size, shape, and color

Setting Up and Displaying Materials

One effective way to display books for toddlers and twos is in wall pockets made of heavy-duty fabric and clear vinyl. A book pocket looks like a shoe bag with one pocket for each book. The clear pockets protect the books while allowing children to see the covers. You can buy book pockets or make them yourself. For mobile infants to be able to get and handle the books, remove them from the pockets and stand them on a low table or on the floor. Thick cardboard books are best.

While book pockets can also be used with older infants and younger toddlers, you may prefer to display books by simply fanning them out on low, open shelves. This arrangement allows children to identify and reach for their favorites. A freestanding display encourages children to pick up a book whenever they are interested. Low shelves and baskets are also good ways to display books. The key is to display books so children can see and reach them.

Put out just a few books at the beginning of the year, but have a minimum of two books per child. Add more books as children develop book-handling skills. Rotate books regularly so that children are excited by new books, but remember to keep old favorites available to the children.

Display books in different places in your room for twos. For example, add books about families to the pretend play area and place books about buildings, farms, trucks, and animals near the blocks. Take books outdoors for reading in a shady, comfortable outdoor spot. Add other interesting props and materials that help support early literacy. Writing tools and paper encourage early scribbling. Include play props that encourage story telling and retelling, such as puppets and felt board pieces. For example, the children can arrange the three bears by size or match felt cutouts to those in Charles G. Shaw's *It Looked Like Spilt Milk*.

Wear and tear on books is inevitable with very young children. Do not let that stop you from making books available. While you expect wear and tear, always model treating books with care. Only display books that are in good repair. Torn books give the message that it is all right to tear books; books in good condition show that we take care of books. Repair torn books before returning them to the bookshelf.

Caring and Teaching

Relationships are at the heart of language and literacy learning. Exploring books and telling stories can be a cozy daily ritual and a way to calm an upset child. Make sure you read to every child, every day, either individually or in a shared reading experience. Reading aloud is one of the best ways to help children become successful readers.

Here are some general tips for reading and storytelling with children.

Become familiar with the book before you read it to the children. Think about what words might be new to the children so you can introduce them. Also think of questions you might ask about the pictures or the story.

Tell stories, as well as read them. The first time you read a story, talk or tell the story, rather than read it word for word. You can also tell stories by using wordless books and other storytelling props.

Make reading interactive. Set the stage. Snuggle. Build anticipation and excitement. Be a dramatic story reader, such as by pitching your voice high for Mama Bear and low for Papa Bear. Involve children in telling the story. Comment and wait for children to respond, ask questions and wait, and offer other prompts. Let children skip to their favorite pictures or pages. Encourage them to chant a book's repetitive phrases or fill in a missing rhyme. Point out when the story has ended, and ask whether they liked the story and whether they want to hear it again.

Follow the child's lead. Be ready to stop when the child loses interest. Watch for infants' cues. When young infants squirm, turn their head away, or push the book away, they are telling you that it is time to stop for now. Do not require children to sit during story time. While you are reading, allow children to crawl, toddle, or walk away and then return.

Be prepared to read the same story again and again. Children have favorites and do not tire of hearing those stories every day.

Link books to the daily routines in a child's life. If you are having difficulty calming a child for a nap, you might recite goodnight messages to some of the objects in your environment, just as in Margaret Wise Brown's *Goodnight Moon*. If you want to encourage children to dress themselves, you might repeat the advice given in Shigo Watanabe's *How Do I Put It On?*.

Provide opportunities for children to share books. One child can read to another or to a doll or puppet. As they develop understandings about stories and books, children retell stories they have heard many times or make up stories based on book illustrations.

Take advantage of storytelling and book reading opportunities as they occur. This can happen, for example, when a child brings you a book to read or comes to listen to a book you are reading with another child.

Extend the children's learning. For example, *Build It Up and Knock It Down* is a book by Tom Hunter, based on the song of the same name. Once you have read the book, you can listen to the song on a compact disc and the older children can sing along. They can act it out, play an opposites game, practice building and knocking down block buildings, and crawl in and out of large boxes that you have added to the indoor gross motor area.

Young Infants

Sitting closely with you makes story and book experiences enjoyable for young infants. Choose a time when the baby is alert and well rested. Find a comfortable position for both you and the baby, perhaps with the baby snuggled on your lap or lying on the floor next to you. Read only a couple of pages and let the child turn the pages if he can. Read books the baby loves again and again.

Here are some more tips for enjoying stories and books with young infants:

- Offer a toy for a child to hold and chew while you read: *Here's a cuddly bear, just like the brown bear in the book.*

- Focus the child's attention by pointing to and naming things in the picture: *There's the baby's nose, and here's your nose!*

- Follow the child's lead: *You like the way that feels. It's soft and fuzzy.*

Mobile Infants

It is exciting when mobile infants recognize and point to pictures in books. They can listen for longer periods as you read very simple stories. You can even try reading to a group of two or three children. These experiences will be successful as long as you have realistic expectations of the children. Be prepared to stop at any point. Lost interest is your cue that the reading activity needs to be concluded. You can pick up the book again when a child shows interest.

Here are some tips for enjoying stories and books with mobile infants:

- Get the children's attention before starting: *Let's look at this book together.*

- Encourage the children to examine the illustrations as you read the text: *Can you find Spot in the picture? Point to the dog.*

- Take cues from the children's gestures, sounds, or words: *Yes, that is a baby, just like you.*

- Ask simple questions to help children understand what is being read, even if they cannot express themselves verbally yet: *They're going bye-bye, aren't they? Can you wave bye-bye like the mommy in the story?*

Toddlers

Reading with toddlers is much more interactive.

Matthew (22 months) *recites simple phrases from books that his parents and Mercedes have read and reread to him. If children are responsive, try reading a simple book all the way through. Toddlers can become caught up in the rhythm of the words and the flow of the plot. You will soon learn which books capture the children's attention and which children are ready to listen to an entire story.*

Here are some tips for enjoying stories and books with toddlers:

- Pause during your reading and allow children time to anticipate the next words: *The child choruses, "E-I-E-I-O," as you read* Old McDonald.

- Respond to the children's verbal and nonverbal cues about the illustrations: *You're pointing to the dump truck. I know that you like big trucks.*

- Relate the story to the children's own lives: *You have a dog, just like the boy in the story.*

Twos

When they have had many chances to explore stories and books during their first two years, children 24–36 months begin to understand that there are different kinds of books. They also have definite favorites. Some books remind them of the things they do every day or of special events in their lives. Some tell stories about things that are not real. Help twos increase their vocabularies by reading books that have more extensive vocabularies than the children's speaking vocabularies. Read books that introduce new concepts through pictures and simple language.

Most twos can sit and be part of a small group of 2–4 children during a more formal, but brief, story time. Remember to let children decide how long they want to stay with the group.

Books with word play or refrains are especially good for small-group reading. You can help twos enjoy books by reading stories in ways that engage their emerging sense of humor. Skip an expected phrase or part of a familiar story from time to time. Switch words or play with words in silly ways. Twos love correcting you and making you read the story right, shouting out a predictable response together, or hearing how silly a funny word sounds when everyone says it at the same time.

While reading books with twos, try these tips:

- Set the stage for story reading by talking about the book cover: The Snowy Day, *by Eric Carle. What do you see in this picture?*

- Help them focus their attention and begin to predict the story: *Poor Corduroy lost his button. I wonder where it is.*

- Encourage children to use the illustrations to understand and explain what is going on and to make predictions: *Where are the children now? What do you think will happen to the little girl now that it is raining?*

- After reading the story through once, ask questions while you read it again: *Do you remember what the caterpillar eats next?*

Including All Children

By making some simple adaptations, you can make sure that all children—including dual language learners and children with disabilities—have enjoyable experiences with stories and books. The following suggestions help make stories and books meaningful for all children.

Dual Language Learners

You can support children who are learning two languages by including, when possible, books and recorded readings in the children's home languages. Invite families to help you find stories to tell or read to the children. Families can also help you make homemade books and recordings. Make sure your collection includes books without words so children can look at pictures and name objects or talk about the pictures in their home languages and in English.

Story reading is an excellent way to help children who are learning English build both receptive and expressive language. Here are some useful techniques.

Read the story in the child's home language before reading it in English, if possible. Perhaps family members can read books in their home language.

Introduce key words and phrases in English and demonstrate the meaning with gestures or larger actions.

Use pictures, props, and other visual cues to help children understand the text. Point out details of the illustrations before you read.

Allow children to respond nonverbally by pointing to, picking up, showing, or giving something.

Read the whole book aloud in one language before reading it later in another language. Children are confused and lose interest when you alternate languages page by page.

Let children respond in their home languages, even when you ask a question in English or simply ask them to point to something.

Read books with repetitive patterns and phrases, encouraging children to complete the phrase when they are ready.

Children With Disabilities

You can adapt many of the strategies that you use for sharing stories and books with all children to build on the skills and interests of children with disabilities.

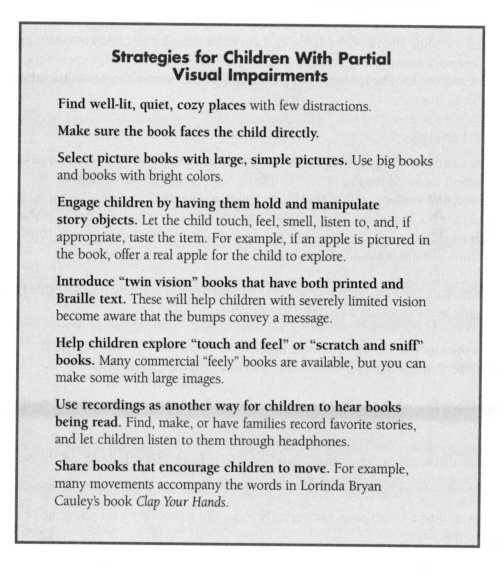

Strategies for Children With Partial Visual Impairments

Find well-lit, quiet, cozy places with few distractions.

Make sure the book faces the child directly.

Select picture books with large, simple pictures. Use big books and books with bright colors.

Engage children by having them hold and manipulate story objects. Let the child touch, feel, smell, listen to, and, if appropriate, taste the item. For example, if an apple is pictured in the book, offer a real apple for the child to explore.

Introduce "twin vision" books that have both printed and Braille text. These will help children with severely limited vision become aware that the bumps convey a message.

Help children explore "touch and feel" or "scratch and sniff" books. Many commercial "feely" books are available, but you can make some with large images.

Use recordings as another way for children to hear books being read. Find, make, or have families record favorite stories, and let children listen to them through headphones.

Share books that encourage children to move. For example, many movements accompany the words in Lorinda Bryan Cauley's book *Clap Your Hands*.

Strategies for Children With Hearing Impairments

Sit close enough to the child so that she can hear you. This distance may be as close as 8–12 inches from the hearing aid.

Speak at a normal speed and articulate clearly. Try not to exaggerate your lip movements. Exaggeration makes lipreading more difficult, not easier.

Read books that encourage children to use all of their senses. Provide concrete objects that match the pictures in the books so that children can explore them as the text is being read.

Learn some sign language that corresponds with book illustrations if the child is learning sign language.

Strategies for Children With Motor Disabilities

Make sure the children are comfortable. They should sit upright, be relaxed, and be able to see the book.

Bring the book close to a child who has difficulty reaching out to touch or hold a book. Support the child's hand so he can grasp the book.

Help a child with limited fine motor skills by taking her hand, guiding it to point to a picture, and then placing her hand on a matching concrete object to feel it.

Responding to and Planning for Each Child

As you observe children interacting with stories and books, think about the goals, steps, and objectives of the *Developmental Continuum*. Consider what each child is learning and how you might respond. Here is how four teachers who are implementing *The Creative Curriculum* use what they learn from their observations to respond to each child and to plan.

Observe	Reflect	Respond
Julio (4 months) and Linda are sitting together in the glider, reading a board book. A different animal is pictured on each page, and Linda tells him what each is called. As she turns each page, Julio squeals with delight and bangs his hands on the book. After a few minutes, he turns his head and pushes the book away.	Julio is showing interest in the speech of others (*Objective 16, Develops receptive language*). He is using his body movements and vocalizations to communicate (*Objective 17, Develops expressive language*). He is actively manipulating books as they are read aloud (*Objective 19, Enjoys books and being read to*).	Linda notices Julio's nonverbal cues and says, "You are all done with the story." She closes the book and follows his gaze to see what caught his attention.
Willard (11 months) sits in Grace's lap as she reads him a counting book about babies. "One, two, three babies are smiling at me." As she reads each number, she bounces Willard gently on her knees. He laughs and turns the page.	Willard is continuing an activity when an adult interacts (*Objective 10, Sustains attention*). He is engaging briefly with books as they are read aloud and finding pleasure in the experience (*Objective 19, Enjoys books and being read to*).	Grace acknowledges Willard's delight. "You like to bounce when we count the babies." She continues to read the book with Willard, bouncing him gently as she counts.
"Let's look at the photo album your mother brought in today," Barbara suggests to Leo (18 months) as they settle down in a comfortable chair. She turns to the first picture and asks, "Where's Mommy?" Leo points to his mother, father, and himself in the picture, identifying, "Mommy. Daddy. Me, me."	Leo is using single words to communicate (*Objective 17, Develops expressive language*). He is recognizing and showing a beginning understanding of pictures (*Objective 20, Shows an awareness of pictures and print*).	Barbara continues to ask Leo questions about the photos to encourage his language development. "What does your dog say?" Leo responds, "Woof, woof." Then Barbara asks "Who is this? Is she your grandma?"
Gena (30 months) is sitting in the book area with her doll, Molly. She picks up a favorite book and turns the pages, pointing at pictures and talking quietly to Molly. She continues even when Sam sits down beside her.	Gena is continuing an activity until her own goal is reached, despite distractions (*Objective 10, Sustains attention*). She is pretending to read a favorite book (*Objective 19, Enjoys books and being read to*).	Ivan observes Gena and writes a quick observation note. He also notices that Sam is interested in what she is doing. To encourage Gena to interact with other children, Ivan says, "Gena, I see that you are reading your book to Molly. Is it all right if Sam and I listen, too?"

Responsive Planning

In developing weekly plans, these teachers use their observations and refer to the *Developmental Continuum*. Here is what they record on their weekly planning forms.

On the *Child Planning Form,* under "Current Information," Linda notes Julio's interest in the illustrations of animals. Under "Plans" she makes a note to bring in other books with animal pictures. On the *Group Planning Form,* in the space for "Changes to the Environment," she lists the books that she will add to the bookshelf and book pockets.

Grace records her observation about Willard on the *Child Planning Form,* under "Current Information." She will focus on Willard's developing motor skills and interest in books by reading other stories that will encourage him to clap and turn the pages. On the *Group Planning Form,* under "Changes to the Environment," Grace lists the books that she will add to the room. Under "Indoor Experiences," she notes that she will focus on adding motions as she reads to the children.

Barbara thinks about how much Leo enjoyed looking at and talking about the photos of his family. On the *Group Planning Form,* under "Family Involvement," she writes a reminder to ask families to bring photos from home. She will use the pictures to make individual books about each child's family to keep in the room.

On the *Child Planning Form,* Ivan records that Gena enjoyed reading to her doll and to other people. He makes a note under "Plans" to borrow a variety of books for the room from the public library. In the "Indoor Experiences" section on his *Group Planning Form,* he writes a reminder to share the books each day during story times. Later he lists the books under "Changes to the Environment" so he will remember to add them to the bookshelf after he reads them to Gena and the other children.

Reading books and sharing your pleasure in language and stories are some of the most important experiences you can offer infants, toddlers, and twos. Children develop a foundation for literacy when they regularly hear books read aloud and have opportunities to explore them firsthand. Their love for books will continually enrich their experiences and stretch their imaginations and dreams. The letter to families is a way to offer ideas about sharing stories and books with their children.

Sharing Thoughts About Enjoying Stories and Books

Dear Families:

Everyone agrees that books are a necessary part of a child's education. Even young infants benefit from having simple books read to them! Looking at books and hearing them read aloud stimulate an infant's brain development in important ways

Before children learn to read, they need to know a lot about language, how a story progresses, and how books work. Children who learn to love books are more likely to become successful learners and lifelong readers. In our program, we offer your child a wide variety of good books, and we read together every day.

What You Can Do at Home

Read and tell stories to your child every day. The words and pictures are important, but, most of all, spending time with you as you read aloud and tell stories lets your child know how much you value these activities. Reading is a wonderful way to be together, whether during your child's bedtime routine or a relaxed daytime opportunity.

Here are some suggestions for reading with your child.

- **Pick a story that you enjoy.** Share rhymes, songs, and stories from your childhood. Your enthusiasm will be contagious. Start by talking about the book's cover or simply by beginning to read.

- **Talk about the pictures.** You do not always have to read a story from beginning to end.

- **Ask your child questions as you read.** Have your child find an object in a picture, for example, "Where is the dog's ball?" Take cues from your child's gestures, sounds, or words, for example, "Yes, that's the baby's Grandma, just like Nona Maria." As your child is able to follow a story, you can ask more open-ended questions. For example, you might ask, "What do you think will happen next?" or "What did you like best about the story?"

- **Be prepared to vary the length of your reading sessions.** Your child might want you to read a story again and again, but you also need to be prepared to stop at any point. There is no need to force your child to be still while you read. Sometimes children want to be more active. Stop when your child no longer seems interested.

Let us share. We can give you the titles of the books your child enjoys here, and you can tell us your child's current favorite books and rhymes at home. We would also love to have you record your child's favorite story or nursery rhyme so we can play it for your child here. We will be glad to help you make the recording.

Together, we can help prepare your child to be a lifelong reader.

Sincerely,

inside this chapter

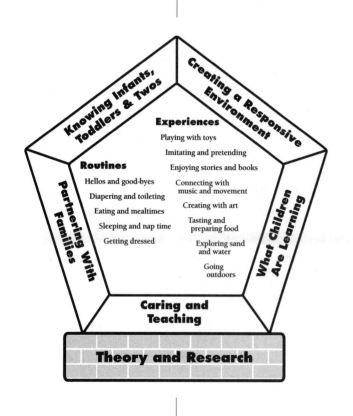

14 Connecting With Music and Movement

Jasmine *(8 months) is sitting on the floor, bouncing to some music. Janet says, "It looks as though you want to dance." She sits next to Jasmine and joins her in moving to the beat. They smile at one another. Then Janet holds out her arms and asks, "Would you like to dance?" When Jasmine reaches toward her, Janet picks her up and begins dancing across the room. Jasmine laughs and bounces up and down in Janet's arms.*

Most people enjoy listening to, creating, and moving to music. Music affects our emotions and inspires movement. Newborn infants can often be comforted by the rhythmic sound of an adult's heart as they are held closely, or by being rocked steadily or bounced gently. By the time they can sit, infants often bob their heads and torsos or move their arms to music.

Just as toddlers and twos want to hear favorite stories again and again, they like to hear and sing favorite songs repeatedly. You may hear toddlers and twos chorus refrains such as "E-I-E-I-O" as they play. They love to make music by hitting a pot with a spoon or by playing real instruments, and they enjoy moving to different tempos and rhythms.

As infants, toddlers, and twos move to music in different ways, they stretch their bodies and imaginations. Whether they move their hands in fingerplays or move their whole bodies as they dance, children respond to the rhythm and beat of music and the related words. You can offer spontaneous and planned music and movement experiences that encourage listening, singing, fingerplay, dancing, and other ways of moving and making music.

Supporting Development and Learning

Children develop social/emotional, physical, cognitive, and language skills as they engage with music and movement.

Learning about themselves and others: As you dance with an infant in your arms; take her to the changing table, singing, "This is the way we change your diaper"; or hum a lullaby to help her fall asleep, you are building a relationship that fosters trust. Familiar songs and songs with children's names can be part of hello and good-bye rituals. They help children feel safe and often help them feel connected to their absent families. Simple songs, such as "If You're Happy and You Know It," can help toddlers and twos label their feelings. As children sing together or parade in a group, banging on drums and shaking maracas, they learn to share music with others.

Learning about moving: When infants, toddlers, and twos hear music, they often respond by moving their bodies. They may kick excitedly, bounce on your knee as you cuddle and sing, or march around the room to a favorite recording. Young children learn to move through space and practice basic gross motor skills as they respond to various kinds of music. Over time, they learn to move their legs, feet, arms, hands, heads, hips, and torsos quickly and slowly, up and down, in and out, and over and under. They also sharpen their fine motor skills as their hands open and shut in simple fingerplays.

Learning about the world: Young children learn about position in space and build memory and sequencing skills as they participate in musical experiences that encourage them to move, change positions, and perform movements in a particular order. When infants shake a rattle or press a button to hear a sound, they are learning about cause and effect. Children also gain important background knowledge through songs. They sing about wheels going 'round and 'round and Old McDonald's farm animals.

Learning about communicating: Music and movement experiences also play an important role in language and literacy development. Infants' early coos and babbles have musical qualities, as do the conversational duets they share with you. Songs can be used to promote an awareness of sounds and to encourage children to experiment with language. You call attention to the features of sounds, such as pitch (high-low), volume (loud-soft), and tempo (fast-slow). Songs, rhymes, and fingerplays are wonderful ways to help children extend language and build vocabulary, such as when you explain the itsy-bitsy spider's waterspout, help children learn that stars twinkle, and anticipate the moment when the players all fall down!

Creating an Environment for Music and Movement

Organize a safe open space for dancing and moving. It must be large enough so that children will not bump into anything or each other. This space may be used for other activities as well.

Choose a carpeted area if possible, because young children like to fall down intentionally. Carpeting also helps to absorb sounds, as do cushions.

Include comfortable adult seating, such as a glider, so you can rock babies to music.

Place a radio, tape recorder, or compact disc player (and cords) close to an electrical outlet and out of children's reach.

Use the outdoor environment as another setting for music and movement experiences. Simple games that involve identifying outdoor sounds help children develop listening skills. There is enough space outdoors for children to move freely and to join simple circle games.

Selecting and Displaying Materials

In addition to your voice and enthusiasm, you need a variety of musical selections, equipment for playing recordings, and materials for children to make their own instruments. Young children tend to prefer music and songs that have a strong rhythm, repetition, and nonsense words; evoke a mood (such as calm or lively); suggest different movements; and tell a story. There are many wonderful recordings of music for children, ranging from traditional favorites to new songs.

Expand your musical choices beyond those selections recorded specifically for children. If possible, introduce a variety of styles: classical, country, folk, reggae, rock and roll, and jazz. Include music from a variety of cultures, as well as other styles you enjoy, so the children hear different melodies and rhythms. Supplement your collection with materials from the library and from families. Many public libraries have selections of tapes and compact discs. Families may also be able to provide music that shares their individual preferences and cultures.

Young Infants

Include toys for young infants that make musical sounds. Hang musical mobiles, and give babies wrist and ankle bells to hold. Babies' random movements soon become intentional as they learn that they can make sounds by moving things. Offer toys that make sounds as children use them, such as balls with bells inside or push-and-pull toys that make musical sounds as they roll along.

Mobile Infants, Toddlers, and Twos

Young children use their bodies as their first rhythm instruments, but you will want to offer other simple rhythm instruments. Possibilities include drums, xylophones, large bells, clackers, rattles and shakers, tambourines, maracas, cymbals, and wood blocks. These allow children to create and respond to music as they bang, ring, swish, and click. Make sure that anything with small objects inside or attached, such as a shaker or a bell, does not present a choking hazard.

You can also make your own instruments. For example, make drums from oatmeal boxes and cymbals from metal pie pans. Make rattles and shakers by filling containers with rice, macaroni, or buttons and fastening them very securely. You can also turn pots and pans upside down, offer wooden spoons, and observe as children experiment with different rhythms and sounds.

Store the instruments in clear plastic containers so children can see them. For variety, rotate the instruments that are available to the children. As with all materials, offer several of each type to minimize problems with sharing. Providing duplicates is more important than having a wide variety.

Add picture book versions of children's favorite songs and fingerplays to your book collection. Some sets include cassettes or CDs. Include books that call attention to indoor and outdoor sounds, tell stories about the joy of singing and dancing, encourage children to clap their hands, or make suggestions about ways to move.

Caring and Teaching

Sharing your own appreciation of music and movement will inspire children to participate joyfully. You do not need to be a great singer to delight young children with music. Focus on the fun of singing together. Sing short, simple, familiar songs. Remember that young children are likely to ask for their favorite songs repeatedly. Make up new songs about the children and about familiar things, people, and events. Children love to hear songs with their names and to laugh at the silly songs you make up about what they are doing. Listen and respond when you hear children singing their own versions of familiar tunes.

Music can be a part of many routines and experiences. Play soft music for children at nap time and sing to them during routines such as dressing, diapering, and toileting. Promote children's attention and listening skills by playing music selectively and inviting a child or two to listen with you for a few minutes. If you play music constantly, it becomes background noise that children tend to ignore after a while. Play music for short periods throughout the day, to remind children that it is time to clean up, to encourage a child's gross motor movement, and to soothe an upset child.

Help children learn concepts through simple games, songs, and fingerplays. As children circle and fall during "Ring a Round the Rosie," or feel their toes when you play "This Little Piggy," they are learning new language, concepts, social skills, and physical skills.

Music is a wonderful way to help children feel connected to their families during the time they spend with you. Ask families about the songs they sing at home and the kinds of music that they like. Learn the lullabies that a family croons at bedtime. Include music from the children's home cultures and in different languages, as possible. Share equipment with family members so they can record songs for you to play while their children are in your care.

Young Infants

Young infants respond to music and other sounds by turning their heads, smiling, laughing, and moving their arms and legs. They are usually calmed by soft, rhythmic sounds, such as lullabies, and by the voices of familiar teachers. They tend to respond in more energetic ways when music is lively. Keep in mind that some infants are more sensitive than others to sounds and may be overstimulated by music that other infants enjoy.

Julio (4 months) is fussy. Linda picks him up and sings softly to him as she sits with him in the glider. He quiets and gazes at her. She smiles and asks, "Are you feeling better, now? Do you want to sing some more?" As Linda continues rocking and singing, she gives Julio a positive experience with music and movement.

- Sing short, simple songs to infants in a high, quiet voice: *Mama's little baby loves shortening, shortening. Mama's little baby loves shortening bread.*

- Comment upon the child's response: *You like it when we dance together. Here we go, back and forth, back and forth.*

- Call the child's attention to interesting sounds: *Those wind chimes are making music for us. Listen.*

- Repeat sounds an infant makes: *Da, da, da. You're singing your da-da song.*

Mobile Infants

To promote children's increasing skills, conduct music and movement experiences with one or two children at a time. These experiences include playing rhythm instruments, dancing, and singing during daily routines and play experiences. Sing while changing a child's diaper or dressing to go outdoors.

Willard (11 months) and Abby (14 months) enjoy the sounds and music that are part of their daily lives. For example, Willard waits for Grace to walk her fingers up his belly while she sings, "The Itsy-Bitsy Spider." Abby beams with pleasure when Brooks sings, 'Where is Abby? Where is Abby?" to the tune of the fingerplay "Where is Thumbkin?"

As their language skills improve, some mobile infants will join you as you sing. Sometimes they repeat sounds over and over, such as "B-B-B-B" or "da-da, da-da, da-da." They may half-babble and half-talk as they sing a familiar song such as "Baa, Baa, Black Sheep." With their increasing balance and physical coordination, they also enjoy playing simple rhythm instruments and moving to the beat.

As you interact with mobile infants, you can promote both their pleasure in and learning from music and movement. Here are some ways to help children focus on their experiences:

- Encourage children to respond to music physically: *You are moving slowly to this slow music.*

- Call a child's attention to common sounds: *Do you hear the clock ticking?*

- Identify different sounds: *The drum is beating in this marching music. It goes "boom, boom, boom."*

- Teach simple fingerplays, such as "Open, Shut Them" and "The Wheels on the Bus."

- Vary the speed at which you chant rhymes. Sing *"Pat-a-Cake"* very slowly and then more quickly, giving the child an opportunity to tap your outstretched hands to the beat.

- Move with the child to the beat: As you gently bounce the child on your knee, sing, *One baby monkey jumping on the bed.*

Toddlers

With your encouragement, toddlers will pay attention to the sounds around them, and you might see them running to the window to listen to a chirping bird or a passing plane. They have learned to discriminate among many sounds, and they can match the sound *moo* to a picture of a cow and the sound *meow* to a picture of a cat. They are also fascinated by the nonverbal sounds that they can produce. Practically anything can become a musical instrument, so toddlers experiment with shaking, tapping, banging, hitting, and pounding a variety of objects.

Toddlers continue to sing and to enjoy music and fingerplays as social experiences. They have discovered songs that they particularly like and want to repeat them again and again. They hum and sing as they play, and they make up simple two-pitch songs.

As their fine and gross motor skills develop, toddlers have more control over their bodies. This allows them to experiment with various kinds of movement.

Here are some ways to interact with toddlers during music and movement experiences and other opportunities to listen.

- Encourage a child's enjoyment of songs: *Shall we play the animal song you like so much?*

- Nurture their interest in environmental sounds: *You hear the rain blowing against the window.*

- Encourage toddlers to sing familiar songs: *Is today your baby's birthday? Are you going to sing "Happy Birthday" to him?*

- Focus children's attention on the way they move: *Can you move quickly to the beat of this drum?*

- Help them discriminate among different sounds: *Listen carefully. Do you hear the bird on the windowsill? Now do you hear a barking dog?*

- Use music and movement experiences to build a positive relationship: *Let's hold hands and stomp through the leaves together.*

Twos

Two-year-olds love rhythm and repetition. They have become good listeners, responsive to music with complex patterns. They move their whole bodies in different ways to various kinds of music, jumping, bouncing, falling, and swaying. They love to twirl and fall like autumn leaves, spinning tops, or tired children. Dance with the children, sometimes holding hands or letting them stand on your feet as you move to the music. Help children focus on rhythm by clapping, stomping, or shaking a tambourine to the beat of songs and rhymes.

Twos begin to sing some of the lyrics of familiar songs. They can fill in words when you pause, just as they complete a sentence in a story, especially when the song includes rhyme and repetition. You may also hear them singing catchy jingles they hear on TV and the radio. Encourage twos to create original songs. Sing along when you hear them singing a made-up song while putting their dolls to sleep. Encourage them to create new verses for their favorite songs. "Daddy's taking me to the zoo tomorrow" can soon be "Daddy's taking me to school tomorrow" or "Momma's taking me to the store today."

Two-year-olds often enjoy singing or listening to music during a brief small-group time. Remember to keep group times short, and expect and allow children to come and go as they wish. Here are some ideas for encouraging 2-year-olds to have fun with music and movement.

- Stimulate their imaginations: *Let's pretend we are pancakes. Let's flip in the pan.*

- Use songs as part of daily routines: *Let's sing your good-bye song to Daddy.*

- Introduce more complicated fingerplays, using hands and two fingers: *Two little ducks went out to play, over the river and far away.*

- Omit a word and let the children fill in the blank: *If you're happy and you know it, clap your_____.*

- Encourage a child to explore ways to make music: *That tambourine made a loud sound when you hit it with your hand. Does it make another kind of sound?*

Responding to and Planning for Each Child

As you observe young children during music and movement experiences, think about the goals, objectives, and steps of the *Developmental Continuum*. Consider what each child is learning and how you might respond. Here is how four teachers who are implementing *The Creative Curriculum* use what they learn from their observations to respond to each child and to plan.

Observe	Reflect	Respond
Linda holds Julio (4 months) as she rocks him in the glider. She sings, "Duérmete mi niño. Duérmete mi sol. Duérmete pedazo, De mi corazón. Go to sleep my baby. Go to sleep my sunshine. You will always be in this heart of mine." Julio gazes at Linda as she sings. His body relaxes, and his eyes begin to close.	Julio is beginning to develop his own pattern for sleeping (*Objective 2, Regulates own behavior*). He is showing an interest in the speech of others (*Objective 16, Develops receptive language*).	Linda continues to sing and rock Julio until she sees that he is ready to go to sleep. She gently lays him in his crib as she continues to sing softly. Julio drifts off to sleep as Linda notes the time on his family's communication log.
Willard (11 months) watches as Grace puts a CD in the CD player. He smiles when the music starts, bounces up and down, and babbles, "Du-du-du."	Willard is discovering that repeated actions yield similar effects (*Objective 12, Shows a beginning understanding of cause and effect*). He is babbling and combining sounds to communicate (*Objective 17, Develops expressive language*).	Grace acknowledges Willard's interest, "Willard, I see you smiling and dancing. You must like the music." To encourage his language development, she imitates his sounds, "Du-du-du. You are singing with the music. Du-du-du."
Leo (18 months) sits on the floor with a xylophone. He hits the colored keys with the mallet, one by one. He looks at Barbara and laughs.	Leo is learning how objects can be used by handling them (*Objective 11, Understands how objects can be used*). He explores ways to make something happen (*Objective 12, Shows a beginning understanding of cause and effect*).	Barbara encourages Leo's interest in the xylophone by saying, "Leo, I hear you making music." As he hits another key, Barbara raises the pitch of her voice and says, "You made a high note." He hits another key and looks at her. "You made a low note," she says, lowering her pitch.

Observe	Reflect	Respond
Jonisha (33 months) sits under a tree on the playground, watching leaves blow in the wind. Later, inside the room, LaToya turns on some music. Jonisha waves her arms around, rocks her body back and forth, and spins in a circle. She says, "Look! I'm a leaf!"	Jonisha is using simple sentences with three or more words (*Objective 17, Develops expressive language*). She is making use of imaginary objects in pretend play (*Objective 15, Engages in pretend play*).	LaToya acknowledges Jonisha's play by saying, "You are moving like those leaves on the windy playground." To support Jonisha's language development, LaToya says, "Those leaves were swirling around and around in the wind. They were and moving just the way you are moving now."

Responsive Planning

In developing weekly plans, these teachers use their observations and refer to the *Developmental Continuum*. This is what they record on their weekly planning forms.

On the *Child Planning Form*, Linda notes Julio's response to the lullaby she sang in Spanish. Under "Plans," she writes that she will ask Julio's mother and grandmother to teach her another Spanish song that she can sing to Julio.

On the *Child Planning Form,* Grace writes a note about Willard's dancing and singing to the music. Under "Plans," she writes that she will play various types of music to find out what he likes and that she will talk to him about the sounds and rhythms he is hearing. On the *Group Planning Form,* under "Family Involvement," she writes a reminder to encourage families to bring recordings of their favorite music so that she can share them with the children.

As Barbara reviews her observation notes for the week, she sees that several children enjoyed using the two new xylophones she added to the display last week. On the *Group Planning Form,* under "Changes to the Environment," she notes that she will add a few small drums and some maracas. Under "Outdoor Experiences," she writes that she will bring the instruments outside for the children to use on Monday and Tuesday.

On the *Child Planning Form*, under "Current Information," LaToya writes about Jonisha's creative movement experience. Under "Plans," she writes that she will bring in some long streamers and scarves that Jonisha might enjoy waving while she dances.

Chapter 14: Connecting With Music and Movement

Music and movement are joyful experiences for children. As you rock babies to a gentle lullaby, sing a favorite song from your own childhood, or dance around the room with a toddler, you share special moments with children. The letter to families is a way to offer ideas about sharing music and movement with their children.

354

The Creative Curriculum for Infants, Toddlers & Twos

SHARING THOUGHTS ABOUT MUSIC AND MOVEMENT

Dear Families:

Listening and moving to music are important for children. Newborns are comforted when they are rocked or gently bounced to a steady rhythm. Older infants, toddlers, and twos have favorite songs and love making music by banging a pot with a spoon. In addition to being pleasurable, these experiences are important to children's overall development. Here are some examples of what children learn.

When your child ...	Your child is learning...
• is soothed when you play soft music	• to comfort himself
• holds hands and dances with another child	• about playing with other children
• stomps around the room to a march	• to use his large muscles
• joins a fingerplay	• fine motor skills

What You Can Do at Home

It's easy to make music and movement a part of your child's life. Here are some suggestions to try at home.

- **Call your child's attention to a variety of sounds.** Listen to the ticking clock and a singing bird, and talk about them.

- **Sing to your child.** Start with simple songs, including those that you particularly enjoy.

- **Make up songs with your child.** To start, use a familiar tune and just substitute a few words, such as a person's name or an event. For example, you might sing, "Sarah had a little doll, little doll, little doll..."

- **Play different types of music.** In addition to children's music, your child may enjoy listening to a variety of melodies and rhythms: folk songs, reggae, jazz, classical music, popular music, and so on.

- **Move and dance together.** It's fun to take giant steps and then tiny steps during a walk. You can even try to hop like a frog or wiggle like a worm!

- **Offer your child simple rhythm instruments.** You can make a drum from an oatmeal box, cymbals from metal pie pans, and shakers by filling containers with rice or buttons and fastening them securely. Your kitchen is a child's orchestra. Listen as your child bangs on your pots, pans, and unbreakable bowls.

It doesn't matter whether you can carry a tune or play an instrument. Sharing your enjoyment of music and movement with your child does matter. We'll be happy to share the songs we sing, and we'd love to learn some of your family's favorites.

Sincerely,

inside this chapter

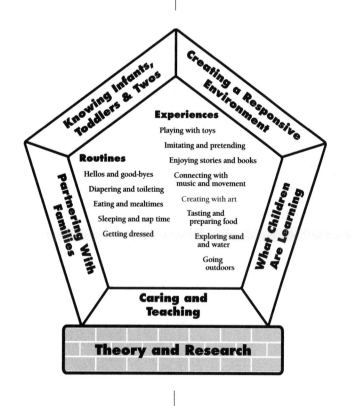

Knowing Infants, Toddlers & Twos

Creating a Responsive Environment

Experiences
Playing with toys
Imitating and pretending
Enjoying stories and books
Connecting with music and movement
Creating with art
Tasting and preparing food
Exploring sand and water
Going outdoors

Routines
Hellos and good-byes
Diapering and toileting
Eating and mealtimes
Sleeping and nap time
Getting dressed

Partnering With Families

What Children Are Learning

Caring and Teaching

Theory and Research

15

Creating With Art

Brooks *helps Abby (14 months) put on a smock and says, "Abby, I see you are ready to help me make some squishy Cloud Dough today." Abby nods, and Brooks places a bowl of flour along with plastic pitchers of pre-measured salad oil and water on the table. Abby, who is familiar with the process, looks up at Brooks expectantly. As Brooks begins to pour the flour into the mixing bowl, Abby extends her arm into the stream of flour and squeals with delight. Brooks encourages, "Doesn't the flour feel cool and soft? It's going to feel very different when we finish making the dough."*

Art for infants, toddlers, and twos is largely a sensory experience. A young infant strokes the fringe on a stuffed animal and relaxes contentedly. A mobile infant joyfully tears colored tissue paper and waves the pieces in the air. A toddler squeals with delight as she moves her fingers through smooth finger paint. Twos are beginning to understand that pictures, models, and constructions represent people and things. A 2-year-old pokes, pounds, and then rolls out a lump of playdough and proudly shows you how he mixed two colors together to make marbled dough. Young children are interested in what different materials are like and what they can do with them. They are not intent on making a product (as older children can be). Painting lines on paper with a brush and tearing paper into pieces are satisfying experiences by themselves.

When you provide a variety of art experiences for young children, they discover that certain materials feel interesting and are fun to use. They also learn that they can control and make marks with a variety of tools and materials. Older twos are beginning to understand that the pictures, models, and constructions they make can represent people and things. The everyday art experiences you offer infants, toddlers, and twos build a foundation for both appreciating and creating through art.

Supporting Development and Learning

Art experiences are a wonderful way for infants, toddlers, and twos to develop their social/emotional, physical, cognitive, and language skills.

Learning about themselves and others: Art materials give children a safe, constructive way to express their feelings, as when they pound dough with their fists or swirl their fingers through paint. Older twos feel a sense of accomplishment when they triumphantly make their first snips with scissors or tell you that their drawing is a picture of a cat.

Learning about moving: When you provide a wide variety of tools and materials for art experiences, young children build their fine motor skills. Holding a crayon and making a mark is a sign that mobile infants are learning to control their small muscles. When toddlers paste a feather on a collage, they are demonstrating eye-hand coordination. As children's small muscles and eye-hand coordination develop, they are able to use smaller and more refined tools for art experiences.

Learning about the world: The world is full of surprises for infants, toddlers, and twos, and experimenting with art materials is another way to learn about objects. Put a sheet of clear adhesive paper on the wall and let children find out that some objects stick. Let a toddler dip a comb in paint and notice that it makes a print on paper. Give twos a large paint brush, a bucket of water, and an outside wall to paint, and watch their surprise as the wall darkens. All of these discoveries help children learn about objects and about cause and effect. When a 2-year-old scribbles on a page and decides afterward that he made a picture of a puppy, he is beginning to understand that he can use art materials to represent something.

Learning about communicating: As you talk with children about what they are doing, seeing, and feeling during an art experience, you help build their understanding of language and give them interesting new words. You might say, "That *goop* is *sticky*," "fingerpaint is *smooth*," and "playdough is *squishy*." The vocabulary of textures is vast: *rough, smooth, bumpy, itchy, velvety,* and so on. Art is related to stories and books as well. Many books for very young children focus on naming colors, animals, people, and common objects. As you read a variety of books with children, talk about the illustrations so that they begin to understand that pictures are meaningful.

Creating an Environment for Art

The materials you select should correspond to children's interests and abilities. Beginning art experiences are a part of everyday explorations for young infants, so they do not need a special place for art. Mobile infants and young toddlers need some bare floor space or a child-size table on which to draw, paint, print, mold, tear, and paste. Older toddlers and twos are ready for a protected space where they can choose and use art materials.

Selecting Materials for Different Ages

The best art materials for infants, toddlers, and twos are those that invite exploration and experimentation.

Young Infants

With common materials, you can give young infants the kinds of experiences that nurture an interest in exploring and experimenting. All the sensory experiences you offer are a foundation for later art experiences. Place some fabric scraps within their reach, such as swatches of flannel, corduroy, satin, silk, taffeta, netting, knits, hosiery, denim, fleece, lace, fake fur, and burlap. Once infants are able to sit, they enjoy playing with various types of nontoxic papers that they can crumple, tear, shred, and wave in the air. Pieces of waxed paper, butcher paper, parchment, rice paper, tissue paper, and cellophane provide different experiences.

Mobile Infants

These additional materials will be of interest to mobile infants.

Finger painting—Have a slick table surface on which infants may paint directly with their hands, or you can cover the table with oilcloth or vinyl. They can also paint directly on cafeteria trays.

Painting with water—Children can use stubby-handled brushes (5–6 inches long) to paint with water on the outside walls of buildings, sidewalks and blacktops, or tree trunks.

Drawing—Give mobile infants jumbo crayons and chalk. Provide large sheets of sturdy paper. Outdoors, children can use chalk on blackboards, sidewalks, and blacktops.

Molding—Substances like Cloud Dough or Basic Playdough work best because they can be squeezed easily.

Cloud Dough

6 cups flour

1 cup salad oil

water to bind (approximately 1 cup)

Knead ingredients together. Final product will feel oily and very smooth. Store in an airtight container.

Basic Playdough

3 cups flour

1 cup salt

1 cup water

1/4 cup salad oil

Knead all ingredients together. Form into balls. Store in an airtight container.

Baker's Clay

4 cups flour

1 cup salt

11/2 cups warm water

Mix all ingredients together. Shape into a ball. Store in an airtight container.

Toddlers

The same materials used by mobile infants will interest toddlers, who also enjoy some additional materials.

Painting—Provide flat bristled brushes (5–6 inches long) with nylon hair and stubby handles. Large paper (about 24 inches x 36 inches or larger) allows toddlers to paint with broad, pumping motions. Include newsprint, manila, and butcher paper of various sizes and shapes. Try covering an entire table with butcher paper to give children a broad canvas. Most toddlers prefer to paint as they stand at a table or sit on the floor.

Tempera Paint for One Child

2 1/2 ounces water

1–2 teaspoons Tempera paint (any color)

3 drops liquid dish detergent such as Ivory®

Pour all ingredients into an empty juice can. Stir with tongue depressor.

Finger painting—Use cafeteria trays, mirrored surfaces with protected edges, or plastic wrap taped to table and floor surfaces. Children can also finger paint directly on a table as younger children do. In addition to commercial finger paint, consider making your own with liquid starch. You can also try making Goop or vary the experience by offering nontoxic shaving cream.

Goop

3 cups corn starch

2 cups warm water

Gradually add water to corn starch. Mix ingredients together with hands. Goop is ready to use when it changes from being lumpy to satiny.

Goop hardens in the air and turns to liquid when held. It resists punching, but a light touch causes a finger to sink in.

When you first offer tempera, water paint, and finger paint, limit children's color choices to one or two colors. A greater variety of colors can be introduced later.

Drawing—Toddlers can use all the materials already listed for mobile infants, plus water-based felt-tip markers. Provide both white and colored papers.

Molding—Toddlers enjoy dough of different textures and colors. They can use an eyedropper filled with liquid food coloring to add color to the dough and then work the color in with their fingers and fists. Provide a few utensils to extend the molding experience for children, such as a potato masher or blocks of different shapes.

Twos

While 2-year-olds enjoy the same materials as younger children, they use them with greater skill and in new ways. Encourage their explorations by adding a few additional tools and materials.

Molding—Offer children basic tools, such as wooden mallets, tongue depressors, plastic rods cut to 6-inch lengths, a wooden dowel for rolling out dough, and a garlic press. You can also involve twos in helping to prepare the dough. Once cooked playdough hardens, children can paint what they created.

Cooked Playdough

2 cups corn starch

1 cup baking soda

1 cup water

Mix all ingredients together and cook over medium heat. Stir constantly until mixture forms a ball. Allow to cool slightly and knead. Store in plastic wrap in the refrigerator.

Drawing and painting—Give twos different types of papers. Each type provides a different experience. You might offer several of these:

- poster paper of various colors, sizes, and shapes
- tissue paper of various colors, sizes, and shapes
- crepe paper of various colors, sizes, and shapes
- corrugated cardboard of various colors, sizes, and shapes
- finger painting paper coated with buttermilk, liquid starch, or sugar water (great for chalk)
- butcher paper

You can also offer a variety of objects and tools, in addition to paint brushes:

- feathers
- twigs or leaves
- eyedroppers
- foam rubber brushes
- toothbrushes
- vegetable and pastry brushes
- sponges

Vary the texture and smell of paint for a variety of painting experiences. As you prepare tempera and finger paint, try changing its quality by adding one or more of the following items.

Adding this...	Makes paint...
flour	lumpy
Karo™ syrup	shiny and sticky
sand or sawdust	rough and gritty
Epsom salt	sparkly
liquid soap	slimy

Printing—This may be a new activity for twos. Make pads by fastening a piece of firm foam rubber or a sponge onto a Styrofoam™ meat tray. Then pour tempera paint onto the foam or sponge. Collect tissue paper, butcher paper, newsprint, and a variety of colored and textured papers for children to use for printing. Provide objects such as rubber stamps, sponges, and corks leaves to dip into the pad and press onto the paper.

Collage Making—Collect colorful yarn; ribbons; papers with assorted textures and colors; magazines and catalogs; scraps of material; leaves, dried flowers, and weeds; and recycled gift wrapping, greeting cards, and post cards. To assemble the collage, use library paste and, if appropriate, give children small, blunt-nosed scissors (4 inches and 4 1/2 inches long).

Setting Up and Displaying Materials

Organize the environment to minimize messes while encouraging children's exploration and creativity. Here are some suggestions for setting up.

Locate the area near a sink. If no sink is available nearby, you can bring buckets of water to your art area for preliminary cleaning up. Fill empty hand lotion or liquid soap dispensers with water for initial handwashing and later help children wash their hands thoroughly at the sink. Eventually, twos can help wash paint brushes and wipe off the table surface where they have been finger painting.

Protect the floor and other surfaces. Use an old shower curtain or a painter's drop cloth to protect the floor from spills and drips. Cleaning equipment such as mops, paper towels, a broom, and a dust pan should be within close reach. Squeegees like those used to wash windows are also helpful for removing finger paint from tables.

Protect children's clothing. Children should wear smocks to protect their clothing from messy materials. You can purchase smocks or make them from old shirts or oilcloth.

Provide surfaces at different heights. Mobile infants and toddlers can explore materials on the floor, as well as while sitting or standing at a low table. Toddlers and twos also enjoy painting at a large low easel.

Keep some materials out of reach. Certain types of materials should be stored on high shelves or in storage cabinets where children cannot reach them. These include materials that you need to prepare (paints and collage items) or that require close supervision (paste and scissors).

Display art materials for toddlers and twos on a low shelf. Materials like playdough, paper, crayons, and chalk can be displayed in containers on a low shelf where children can choose what they want. Label containers and shelves with pictures and words so children can find and return materials.

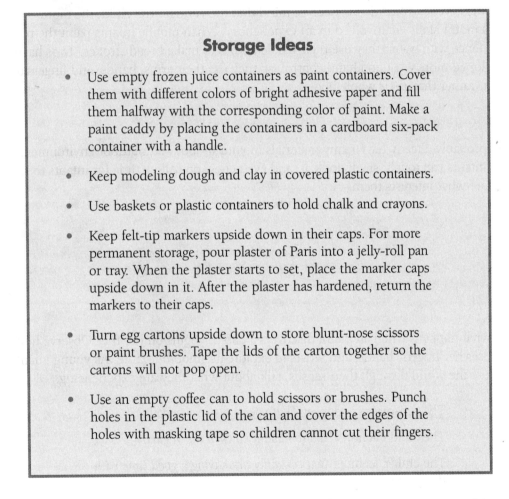

Storage Ideas

- Use empty frozen juice containers as paint containers. Cover them with different colors of bright adhesive paper and fill them halfway with the corresponding color of paint. Make a paint caddy by placing the containers in a cardboard six-pack container with a handle.

- Keep modeling dough and clay in covered plastic containers.

- Use baskets or plastic containers to hold chalk and crayons.

- Keep felt-tip markers upside down in their caps. For more permanent storage, pour plaster of Paris into a jelly-roll pan or tray. When the plaster starts to set, place the marker caps upside down in it. After the plaster has hardened, return the markers to their caps.

- Turn egg cartons upside down to store blunt-nose scissors or paint brushes. Tape the lids of the carton together so the cartons will not pop open.

- Use an empty coffee can to hold scissors or brushes. Punch holes in the plastic lid of the can and cover the edges of the holes with masking tape so children cannot cut their fingers.

Display children's artwork. Even though toddlers and twos are more interested in exploring what they can do with art materials than in finishing a painting or drawing, save some of their work for portfolios and to display in the room. Post selected works where the children will see them, for instance, on the bottom of a wall or room divider. To protect their work, you can buy clear Plexiglas® frames or sheets.

Caring and Teaching

While there are some differences in the kinds of art experiences you offer infants and those you plan for toddlers and twos, the process of using art materials is more important than what children produce with them. The goal is to make it possible for children to explore and experiment freely with a variety of materials.

To plan art experiences, review what you know about the children in your group. What do they most enjoy? What new skills are they developing? Who enjoys messy activities? Who avoids them? Keep in mind that the younger the child, the more gross motor skills are involved in art experiences. When mobile infants paint the play yard fence with water, they use their whole bodies to make broad strokes. Twos have developed more wrist and hand control, so they use their arms, hands, and fingers to paint, rather than their whole bodies.

Young Infants

You probably already have many materials in your indoor and outdoor environments that infants can touch, smell, look at, and even chew on. Allow time for infants to explore what interests them.

Julio (4 months), while sitting on Linda's lap, becomes fascinated by the texture of her scarf. Noticing this interest, Linda allows him to play with it as long as he likes.

See what happens when an infant discovers a dab of yogurt on her tray. Observe how she uses her fingers, hands, and wrists to explore its smooth texture. As young infants explore the world through their senses, talk about what they are experiencing.

- The sensory experience: *That yogurt feels so smooth.*
- The child's actions: *You're making lines in the yogurt.*
- The child's feelings: *You certainly are having a good time with that yogurt!*

Share joyful moments of discovery together and focus on what the child is doing. You will gain insight into the infant's developing skills and interests, and this information helps you plan future experiences for the child.

Mobile Infants

Mobile infants can grasp a crayon or brush, and paint with water on a chalkboard, wall, or fence. Begin by offering fat, stubby crayons that mobile infants can grasp with their whole hand. Do not expect an infant to hold the crayon with thumb and fingers or to be able to draw using wrist movements. At this stage of development, drawing usually involves a lot of arm movement and sometimes whole body movement.

Offer the child a crayon or let her select one. She will probably be as interested in the way it feels and smells as she is interested in its color and what she can do with it. Tape a large piece of paper (at least 24 x 36 inches) to the floor. Then gently show the child how to use the crayon by guiding his hand.

Introduce older mobile infants to painting with water in much the same way, because children go through the same developmental steps in painting as they do in drawing. They paint with bold arm movements, using their entire arms and bodies.

For molding experiences, children need the freedom to poke, pound, and squeeze the dough. Handling molding materials is both soothing and filled with learning opportunities about the use of objects and about cause and effect.

When you make dough with children, notice what intrigues them and build on their interests.

- Comment on their actions: *You sure can squeeze that Cloud Dough hard.*

- Help them solve a problem: *Looks like it's getting sticky. Should we add some more flour?*

- Talk about their reaction: *You like it better when the dough isn't so sticky.*

- Engage the child's cooperation: *What a big helper you are in cleaning up.*

Toddlers

Many of the same art experiences you offer mobile infants are appropriate for toddlers. Because they have more control over their small muscles, they can begin to paint and draw with a variety of tools. Toddlers are more aware of what they are doing and understand you when you talk with them about their experiences.

Organize experiences so that toddlers can experiment and use materials without having too many constraints. Then interact in ways that show you are interested in what they are doing and make suggestions to extend their ideas.

- Describe what the child is doing: *You painted lots of lines on the ground with your water and paintbrush.*

- Make suggestions to extend the experience: *Do you want to paint anything else? I see a fence and a table. They might need some painting.*

- Provide choices: *What color should we make our dough today? We have red, yellow, and blue food coloring.*

- Reflect a child's feelings: *I thought you would enjoy the feel of that Goop we made! It's kind of sticky, isn't it?*

Twos

Twos happily use the same materials in different ways, but they also begin to take an interest in what they are producing. Because they have developed greater wrist control, they can control their scribbling. Their lines become curves, spirals, ovals, and eventually circles. They may start making designs, repeating them, and sometimes seeing patterns in what they made. While the patterns may be totally unplanned, they are exciting for a child to discover. These experiences also affect children's thinking. For example, they learn about predicting ("If I use paste, the object will stick"); about space ("If I squeeze this much paint out of the bottle, the paint runs off the paper"); about transformation ("If I add yellow paint to red paint, it looks different"); and about cause and effect ("If I rub the paint brush against the edge of the bottle, paint will not drip down the brush").

Some twos have enough muscle control to use paste and scissors.

Jonisha (33 months) proudly tears magazine pages into tiny pieces with great concentration, and she snips other pages with scissors. Then she pastes the scraps on a piece of construction paper. She loves the creative process and is satisfied with her three-dimensional creation.

If you make a few simple adjustments, children who are physically challenged can also have fun with art experiences.

Ivan found some egg-shaped markers that have caps with animals on them. They are the perfect size for Gena (30 months) to grasp and use. She can even grasp the cap and get it on and off the marker. When Ivan brought them out for Gena, other children gathered and wanted to play with "Gena's markers." Gena became the focal point of a play activity in which she could participate fully with her classmates. Ivan also used these markers to talk about colors, different animals, and animal sounds.

Enjoy your interactions with twos as they explore and experiment with art materials.

- Describe the child's actions: *First you rolled out the dough. Then you pounded it flat. Now I see you are making circles in the dough by using the paper towel roll.*

- Talk about the sensory experience the child is having: *When your fingers move through that Goop, does it feel slippery?*

- Ask open-ended questions: *How did you make those wavy lines in the finger paint?*

- Encourage problem solving: *How can you keep the paint from dripping down the paper on the easel?*

Your interest in what a child is doing makes any experience, including art, both more enjoyable and an opportunity for the child to learn.

Inappropriate Art Activities

Any art activity that focuses on a finished product rather than on the creative process is inappropriate for infants, toddlers, and twos. Young children are not yet developmentally able to create representative art. The following experiences would therefore *not* be part of a developmentally appropriate art program for children under age 3:

- using coloring books

- providing patterns or models for children to copy

- activities where teachers do most of the work (e.g., cutting, taping, stapling, drawing)

- telling a child what to draw, paint, or make

- expecting that a child will produce something recognizable

- "finishing" a child's work to make it "better"

Always keep in mind that, for very young children, art is a sensorimotor experience that builds a foundation for creativity and an appreciation of beauty. The process is more important than what is produced.

Responding to and Planning for Each Child

As you observe children during art experiences, think about the goals, objectives, and steps of the *Developmental Continuum*. Consider what each child is learning and how you might respond. Here is how four teachers who are implementing *The Creative Curriculum* use what they learn from their observations to respond to each child and to plan.

Observe	Reflect	Respond
Julio (4 months) nestles into Linda's shoulder, rubbing his cheek on her soft sweater. He smiles and lays his head and hand on her shoulder, patting the sweater.	Julio recognizes and reaches out to a familiar adult (*Objective 1, Trusts known, caring adults*). He is exploring an object, using his senses (*Objective 11, Understands how objects can be used*).	Linda talks to Julio in soothing tones to help build a trusting relationship with him. She comments on what he is doing, "Feel how warm and fuzzy the sweater is, Julio."
Willard (11 months) dips his fingers into paint and begins to push his finger across the paper in the tray. He makes a few small marks, dips his fingers in again, and makes a few more. He smiles, dips his whole hand in, and smears it across the entire paper.	Willard is learning how objects work by handling them (*Objective 11, Understands how objects can be used*). He is noticing particular characteristics of objects (*Objective 13, Shows the beginning understanding that things can be grouped*).	Grace encourages his exploration of the paint and says, "Willard you covered your whole paper." She points to a blank sheet of paper and asks, "Would you like to paint another?"
Matthew (22 months) holds a marker in each hand, scribbling up and down on a large piece paper. He looks at Jenna (24 months), who is also drawing with markers. Then he reaches over and draws a line across her paper. Jenna scowls. Matthew quickly pulls his hand away.	Matthew is showing awareness that others' feelings are separate from his own feelings (*Objective 4, Responds to others' feelings with growing empathy*). He is experimenting with scribbling (*Objective 21, Experiments with drawing and writing*).	To support Matthew's understanding of others' feelings, Mercedes explains, "Jenna didn't like it when you wrote on her paper. She made an angry face, and you stopped." "Here is your paper, Matthew," she says as she points to his paper. "You can make lots of lines on this one."
While playing outside, Valisha (33 months) picks up a piece of stubby chalk and begins scribbling on the blacktop. She tells LaToya, "I drawing hopscotch."	Valisha is scribbling with the intention of communicating (*Objective 21, Experiments with drawing and writing*). She is coordinating her eye and hand movements to complete increasingly complicated tasks (*Objective 9, Develops fine motor skills*).	To promote Valisha's positive feelings about her writing, LaToya says, "Oh, I see that you are drawing a hopscotch board with that chalk. We can play hopscotch when you are finished?"

Responsive Planning

In developing weekly plans, these teachers use their observations and refer to the *Developmental Continuum*. Here is what they record on their weekly planning forms.

As Linda reads her observation notes, she realizes that a couple of the children have been interested in fabric textures. She decides that she will bring fabric swatches with different textures to put out for the children to explore on Wednesday, Thursday, and Friday. She records this on the *Group Planning Form*. Under "Family Involvement," she makes a note to ask families on Monday to bring in any fabric that they are willing to donate.

On the *Child Planning Form*, under "Current Information," Grace writes a brief note about Willard's experience with finger paint. Under "Plans," she notes that she will offer finger painting again the following week but provide larger sheets of paper for him to experiment on.

On the *Child Planning Form*, under "Current Information," Mercedes writes about Matthew's interaction with Jenna. Under "Plans," she writes that she will set up a group art activity so Matthew has the opportunity to share an art experience with his peers. On the *Group Planning Form*, under "Wednesday," she records that she will bring a large sheet of butcher paper to the playground for the children to paint a group mural.

LaToya records her observation of Valisha on the *Child Planning Form*. Under "Plans," she writes a note to add some more writing tools to the art area. On the *Group Planning Form*, under "Changes to the Environment," she makes a list of the writing materials she will add. She also writes, under "Monday," that she will introduce small chalk boards and stubby chalk as an indoor experience for the children to explore all week.

With your support and interactions, young children learn and grow through art experiences. You can also help families appreciate all of the learning that occurs through art. On the following page, you will find a letter that you can send home to families explaining the role that art plays in your program.

SHARING THOUGHTS ABOUT ART EXPERIENCES

Dear Families:

When you think about art experiences, do you imagine a child with crayons or a paint brush in hand? Painting and drawing are just two of the many ways young children enjoy art. In fact, art experiences begin early in life as a baby enjoys stroking the fringe on her blanket or finger paints with the blob of yogurt that falls on her tray. As they get older, they enjoy scribbling with a crayon and squeezing playdough with their hands. Art experiences allow children to have wonderful sensory experiences and to experiment with a variety of materials. They also help children develop thinking and physical skills. Here are some examples.

When your child does this...	**Your child is learning...**
• covers paper with paint	• about cause and effect
• pokes a hole in playdough	• how objects can be used
• tears paper for a collage	• eye-hand coordination
• uses paste successfully	• to solve a problem

What You Can Do at Home

Young children like to explore and experiment with art materials. They are more interested in feeling, seeing, smelling, tasting, and controlling tools and materials than in making something. Here are some ideas for offering art experiences at home.

- **Offer your baby different textures to explore.** Place a basket with a collection of different fabrics near your child and encourage her to play with them. Talk about how they feel.

- **Make simple art materials together.** You can make playdough for your child to squeeze and pound, or make Goop for another wonderful sensory experience. We have several recipes for making art materials that we'll be glad to share with you.

- **Keep plain paper and crayons available for your toddler.** Encourage your child to draw freely and to experiment. Do not expect her to draw something you will be able to recognize.

- **Encourage your child to use art materials freely.** For young children, the process of creating is important, not the finished product. Show your interest in what your child is doing by describing his actions: "You made lots of different marks on the paper. These are round circles, and these are lines."

Together, we can give your child the kinds of experiences that encourage exploration and an appreciation of art.

Sincerely,

inside this chapter

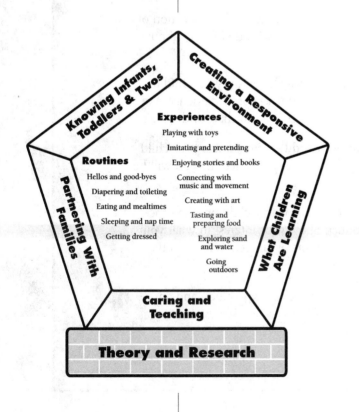

16

Tasting and Preparing Food

LaToya *tells the children in her group, "We have an exciting snack today. We have carrots right from our garden! After we scrub them, we can taste the vegetable we grew." LaToya asks Valisha (33 months) to help her set vegetable brushes and water bowls on the trays in front of the children. She then hands each child two carrots to scrub. As Jonisha (33 months) displays her washed carrot for the other children to see, LaToya exclaims, "I don't think it could be any cleaner!"*

When you invite children to taste and otherwise explore a new food or include them in helping you prepare a snack, you are promoting more than good nutrition. Food and related conversation and activities encourage development and learning in all areas. They evoke feelings of security because children associate them with family and home. They also provide a wealth of sensory experiences and promote the development of fine motor, cognitive, and language skills.

Tasting and preparing food are part of everyday living with infants, toddlers, and twos. Children become aware of the tastes and textures of various cereals, fruits, and vegetables as you and their families gradually introduce new foods. They begin to express their personal preferences and start to learn the names of different foods. At first, they are primarily interested in squishing, mashing, and smearing food. Before long, they become eager and able to help prepare some of the foods they eat, especially because they like to participate in activities that are important to adults. Whether it is scrubbing a carrot or dipping a slice of apple in melted cheese, children enjoy and are proud to help you with meaningful tasks.

Supporting Development and Learning

While they are tasting and preparing food, children have opportunities to strengthen their social/emotional, physical, cognitive, and language skills.

Learning about themselves and others: Infants are eager to practice the skills that enable them to feed themselves. Toddlers and twos learn to work cooperatively with others in preparing simple foods. They also develop other personal care skills, such as washing their hands, serving themselves, and cleaning up after themselves.

Learning about moving: Children strengthen their small muscles by such activities as tearing lettuce for a salad and scrubbing vegetables. They coordinate their eye-hand movements when they pour water into a cup or spread apple butter on a cracker. Their whole bodies are involved as they help with cleanup, sweep the floor with a child-size broom, or walk to the trash can with a banana peel in hand.

Learning about the world: Children build a foundation for mathematical thinking when they sort fruit by color and fill a quart pitcher with cups of water. They learn problem-solving skills when they fill a muffin tin only halfway so the batter does not overflow as it bakes. They observe scientific principles as they shake cream until butter forms and as they watch cheese melt. They learn how objects are used when they mix pancake batter with a wooden spoon, help you spoon muffin batter into pans, and experiment with using a rubber spatula.

Learning about communicating: Children learn the vocabulary of cooking when they *knead* dough, *chop* pieces of fruit, and *stir* pancake batter. As twos follow simple picture and word recipes, they learn that pictures and print convey messages. They also learn to follow simple directions and to have conversations with children and adults.

Creating an Environment for Tasting and Preparing Foods

Food experiences are best when they take place near a sink, because then cleanup goes more smoothly. If you are going to use an electrical appliance, make sure your space includes an outlet where you can plug it in safely. A washable floor makes it easier to clean up the inevitable spills.

Selecting Materials for Different Ages

Young infants

Most food experiences for young infants are seeing, tasting, smelling, and touching experiences, so you don't need to do anything special. They only need their eyes, mouths, noses, and hands. A teaspoon of rice cereal for a 4- to 6-month-old is a new taste and texture sensation. By 8 or 9 months, you and the young infant can take turns directing food to his mouth. You might wish to give an infant a cracker to hold and nibble between the bites of cottage cheese that you spoon into her mouth.

Mobile infants

Spoons, training cups, and new foods are interesting challenges for mobile infants. They can also begin to participate in food preparation activities. Wooden spoons, plastic mixing bowls, and rubber spatulas are important tools for this age group.

Toddlers and Twos

Toddlers and twos can participate more fully in food preparation activities. Provide utensils that children can use on their own. As much as possible, offer children real utensils rather than toy ones. Real gadgets and utensils not only make the experience more authentic, but they are less frustrating to use than toys that are not intended to work. Utensils that toddlers and twos can learn to use include mixing spoons and spatulas, plastic measuring cups, vegetable brushes, wire whisks, and potato mashers.

You can help children who have physical disabilities participate in cooking activities by providing adapted cups, utensils, and dishes. Suction cups provide a stable base for both eating and mixing bowls. Rubberized nonslip material can also be used under utensils and bowls to prevent sliding. Ask the child's parents for suggestions about what adaptations work well. Adaptive aids can sometimes be found at hardware and kitchen stores, and specialty items are sold at medical supply outlets that carry aids for daily living.

With your supervision, twos can prepare simple snacks. You can make simple picture recipe cards that show the steps. Recipe cards not only teach children about following directions, they also help children learn that pictures and print carry meaning.

Selecting and Displaying Materials

Here are some considerations for planning food-related experiences.

Think about the equipment you will need. For example, if an oven is not available, a toaster oven or a wok might do nicely.

Provide a child-size table and chairs. To enjoy food preparation experiences fully, children need to be able to work, move about, and observe freely. A child-size table can be used as a work station as well as for eating. Chairs enable children to sit while they observe, thereby minimizing children's getting in each other's way.

Store safe cooking tools and utensils in low cabinets. If materials are stored on low shelves, the older children can get what they need on their own. Picture and word labels show toddlers and twos where these materials belong, so they can find what they need and help clean up.

Provide smocks. When their clothing is protected, you do not have to worry about stains and the children can participate fully. If you do not have smocks, you or a parent can easily make them from old shirts or pieces of oilcloth.

Store nontoxic cleanup supplies where you can reach them easily. Invite children to help you wipe up the spills that are sure to occur.

Keeping Children Safe and Heathy

Pay careful attention to food safety when planning food experiences. Refrigerate all perishable foods, especially milk, milk products, eggs, and mayonnaise. Do not leave them out of the refrigerator for more than an hour. Before and after handling food, wash your and the children's hands well. Help children remember not to return their tasting spoons to a common bowl.

Food preparation experiences that involve using real utensils, tools, and appliances require close supervision. Preventive measures will eliminate many potential problems. For example, by choosing nonbreakable materials, you guard against injuries. Storing adult items, such as egg beaters and electrical appliances, out of children's reach or in a locked cupboard also minimizes injuries.

Before beginning food experiences with children, it is vitally important to know whether any children have food allergies. Many young children are allergic to egg whites, soy, wheat, and peanuts. Children who are lactose intolerant have to avoid milk and milk products such as yogurt and ice cream. Ask parents about food allergies when you complete the *Individual Care Plan—Family Information Form*. Not only do you want to keep children from eating anything that might harm them, you want to plan food-related learning experiences in which children are able to participate fully.

Before children begin to prepare food, you need to talk with them about basic safety rules. Consult your local health department for the latest health and safety information. Helpful resources are available from the United States Department of Health and Human Services' Maternal and Child Health Bureau and from the Department of Agriculture's Food and Nutrition Services.

During any tasting and food preparation experience with children, there is always the possibility that, despite every precaution, a child might gag or choke. Because it is often difficult to think clearly in an emergency, it makes good sense to post the first-aid guidelines for choking in the area where you will be providing food experiences. Make sure your first-aid and CPR training and certification are current.

Caring and Teaching

As you offer children food tasting and preparation experiences, think about what they are learning. Observe children as they try a new food or help you peel an orange for a snack, and note how they are mastering physical, cognitive, social/emotional, and language skills.

Young Infants

Food experiences for young infants involve both tasting foods and building relationships with those who feed them. When you hold an infant and feed him his bottle, he tastes the milk, gets nutrients, and, equally important, he feels safe and secure.

Janet gives Jasmine (8 months) opportunities to explore her food, and she talks with Jasmine about what is happening. She also takes advantage of opportunities to introduce the names of foods, adjectives that describe them, and verbs that explain what the child is doing.

When Jasmine tries to pick up applesauce with her fist, Janet comments, "You're having a hard time picking up the applesauce. It is very slippery." When Jasmine pounds a slice of banana with her fist, Janet asks, "You like mashing that squishy banana, don't you?"

Mobile Infants

In addition to food-tasting experiences, mobile infants enjoy being involved in the preparation of their snacks. Food experiences for children of this age involve shaking, dabbing, dipping, stirring, and mashing. Here are some examples of appropriate learning experiences:

- shaking grated cheese on macaroni or vegetable purees (squash, green beans, peas, carrots, beets, cauliflower, or zucchini)

- dropping cheese cubes onto rice or mashed potatoes

- dabbing apple butter on bread or toast

- shaking cinnamon on cottage cheese, yogurt, cooked cereal, or applesauce

- dipping banana chunks, steamed apple, or pear wedges into yogurt

- mixing cottage cheese with macaroni, kasha (roasted buckwheat), or bow-tie pasta

- making dips for snacks by mixing grated cheese or spices (such as powdered cinnamon and nutmeg) with sour cream, yogurt, or mashed chick peas

As you help mobile infants prepare food, observe them carefully so you will know how to respond. Stretch children's thinking as you interact with them.

- Encourage vocabulary development by modeling complete language: *We're going to use the avocado to make a dip called* guacamole.

- Encourage children to think about cause and effect: *Let's see what happens to the avocado when we mash it.*

- Promote children's understanding of how objects can be used: *Abby, will you please hand me the potato masher so that we can mash the avocado? Come here, and I'll show you how it works.*

Toddlers and Twos

Toddlers and especially twos can take an even more active role in preparing foods. On the basis of the children's interests and abilities, you can plan activities that involve spreading, pouring, slicing, whisking, squeezing, and garnishing. Here are typical favorites:

- preparing finger foods by topping cucumber slices, toast strips, or crackers with cheese, cottage cheese, or fruit wedges

- using a plastic knife or a small icing spatula to spread fruit butter on crackers, bread, or toast

- stirring together the ingredients for hot cereal, and pouring milk or maple syrup into the bowl

- whisking eggs in a bowl

- dipping bread slices in beaten eggs, cinnamon, and milk to make French toast

- scrubbing raw potatoes or yams; mashing cooked potatoes or yams

- mixing gelatin in water; cutting shapes from firm gelatin

- squeezing lemons, oranges, and limes for fruit drinks

- snapping the ends of green beans

- shelling peas

- arranging food decoratively on a plate, tray, or table

As children help prepare food, encourage them to think about what they are doing. Here are some suggestions:

- Describe what you see them doing: *You are using the masher to mash the yams, Gena.*

- Encourage children to think about the effects of their actions: *How do the mashed yams look different from the whole yams? Is it easier to eat mashed yams or whole yams?*

Observe the children in your care to see what skills they are developing. Then use the information to plan experiences that will extend their learning.

Jonisha (33 months), like several of the other children, enjoys helping prepare her own morning snack. Knowing this, LaToya prepared recipe cards for banana dip. The first card shows a banana being broken into pieces. The second card shows cinnamon being sprinkled into a bowl of plain yogurt. The third card shows a hand dipping a banana chunk into the dip. LaToya shows the cards to Jonisha, explaining each step. When they finish, she tells Jonisha, "I'm going to sit next to you as you make banana dip for your snack. If you need any help, I'm right here." Jonisha smiles broadly as LaToya moves the plate of peeled bananas closer to her.

LaToya made sure that Jonisha had a successful experience by thinking about what needed to be done ahead of time. She peeled the bananas and set out all of the ingredients. She made and reviewed the recipe cards with Jonisha before the child tried to make her snack. She stayed nearby to lend support. While Jonisha made the dip, LaToya described what Jonisha was doing and commented on how it was just what the recipe cards said to do.

To extend the learning experience, LaToya later brought out some other fruits (apple slices and a strawberry) and some vegetables (carrot sticks and seedless cucumber slices). Then she asked Jonisha to try them and to think about the different tastes. Jonisha did not much like the carrot or cucumber, but she was very happy to eat the fruits. Encouraged by LaToya's questions, Jonisha concluded that fruits are better for dipping than vegetables.

In order to document this learning experience, LaToya photographed the activity. She then put copies of the photos in a homemade book and noted what Jonisha is doing in each picture. By doing this, she will enable Jonisha's parents to see what their daughter has been learning. She knows that Jonisha will love looking at the book *Jonisha Dips a Banana.*

As you begin to plan food preparation activities, start with the snacks you serve to the children. Think about how you might involve the children in preparing them. Choose recipes that have a limited number of steps and require only beginning physical skills, such as dipping, shaking, or mashing. More complex skills, such as pouring, spreading, and squeezing, can be added as children's mastery of fine motor skills improves.

For special projects, you might want to consult some of the published books for preparing foods that toddlers like. Simplify recipes that you think children will enjoy into two or three steps. Then make picture and word recipe cards that illustrate the steps.

Although there are a number of excellent cookbooks for young children that make use of recipe cards, most will be too complicated for your needs. These books are more appropriate for use with preschoolers and older children, even if they claim to be for infants, toddlers, and twos. Others include the preparation of foods that are nutritionally inappropriate. To use cookbooks effectively with infants, toddlers, and twos, you will need to rethink the recipes in terms of children's skills and special dietary requirements.

Families are another good resource for cooking ideas. Invite parents to share recipes for foods they prepare for their children at home. By preparing and serving these foods at your program, you strengthen the bond between home and the program. Including family recipes is one way for your program to acknowledge the backgrounds of the children and families you serve.

Responding to and Planning for Each Child

As you observe children during tasting and food preparation experiences, think about the goals, objectives, and steps of the *Developmental Continuum*. Consider what each child is learning and how you might respond. Here is how four teachers who are implementing *The Creative Curriculum* use what they learn from their observations to respond to each child and to plan.

Observe	Reflect	Respond
Jasmine (8 months) drinks from a cup as Janet holds it for her at snack time. She lifts her hands and bangs the sides of the cup.	Jasmine is attempting a simple personal care task (*Objective 7, Develops personal care skills*).	Janet describes what Jasmine is doing, "You are drinking from the cup." Then she asks, "Would you like to hold the cup?"
Abby (16 months) sits at the table when she sees Brooks setting it for snack.	Abby is expecting to participate in group routines (*Objective 6, Learns to be a member of a group*).	Brooks says, "Abby, you know it is time to eat snack because you see me putting out the bowls." She holds her hand out to Abby and says, "Let's go wash our hands so we may eat."
Matthew (22 months) is helping to make pancakes for breakfast. He pours milk from a small pitcher into the mixing bowl, spilling some on the table. He exclaims, "Uh-oh!" and gets a wipe to clean the table.	Matthew is using eye-hand coordination while doing simple tasks (*Objective 9, Demonstrates basic fine motor skills*). He is planning ways to use objects to perform one-step tasks (*Objective 11, Understands how objects can be used*).	"Accidents happen," Mercedes says. "Thank you for cleaning it up so quickly. Give it another try! We still need milk in the bowl."
Valisha (33 months) pulls LaToya toward the toaster oven. She smells muffins baking and says, "Muffins are ready. I'm hungry."	Valisha is carrying out her own plan for solving a problem (*Objective 14, Develops and uses problem-solving strategies*). She is using simple sentences with three or more words (*Objective 17, Develops expressive language*).	LaToya acknowledges Valisha's presence and interest by saying, "I smell those muffins, too. You are hungry and ready to eat them. They are almost done baking." To encourage Valisha's problem-solving skills, she asks, "What should we do to get the table ready for snack time?"

Responsive Planning

In developing weekly plans, these teachers use their observations and refer to the *Developmental Continuum*. Here is what they record on their weekly planning forms.

> On the *Child Planning Form,* under "Current Information," Janet writes that Jasmine is beginning to be interested in feeding herself. Under "Plans," she notes that she will offer Jasmine more opportunities to feed herself finger foods and that she will offer her a spill-proof cup. Janet also makes a note about this on the *Group Planning Form,* under "Changes to Routines."

> After reviewing her observation notes, Brooks realizes that a few of the children are beginning to participate in mealtimes as a group. She decides that she will take photographs of the children as they prepare for mealtimes and create a book that she can share with them and that illustrates the steps of the routine. On her *Group Planning Form,* under "Indoor Experiences" for Monday, Tuesday, and Wednesday, she writes that she will share the book with the children.

> On the *Child Planning Form,* under "Current Information," Mercedes records Matthew's interest in cooking and his increasing eye-hand coordination. Under "Plans," she notes that she will add small pitchers and bowls to the water table and that she will offer two food preparation experiences next week. On the *Group Planning Form,* under "Indoor Experiences," she records her plan for the children to help prepare their snacks on Tuesday (cut vegetables and yogurt dip) and Thursday (pear bunnies).

> LaToya records Valisha's interest in preparing food on the *Child Planning Form.* Under "Plans" she writes that she will make pancakes with the children next week.

Tasting and preparing foods is a good way to promote development in all areas. The letter to families is a way to offer ideas about sharing food-related experiences with their children.

SHARING THOUGHTS ABOUT TASTING AND PREPARING FOOD

Dear Families:

Perhaps the idea of involving very young children in food preparation seems strange to you. However, one of the reasons that preparing food appeals to children is that it is a meaningful, grown-up activity. Participating in activities that your child observes you doing every day is exciting for them.

In our program, we build on the children's interest in food experiences because they help your child develop many concepts and skills. For example, what do you think your child might learn from a simple task such as snapping the ends off green beans? Did you think about these concepts and skills?

- shape
- color
- part and whole
- cause and effect
- sustaining attention
- eye-hand coordination
- fine motor skills

As you can see, preparing food is educational as well as practical and fun!

What You Can Do at Home

At home, children can be involved easily in food preparation. Here are some ideas.

- **Let your child help.** Because you probably already cook at home, it's easy for you to involve your child. You can even include a young infant. Let her sit where she can watch you as you describe what you are doing. Older infants, toddlers, and twos can participate more actively. When you let your child help you prepare and serve foods, you show that you value his contributions to family life.

- **Talk about the foods and what each of you is doing.** Here are some topics to discuss as you prepare and taste foods together:

    - the names of different foods and how they look, smell, feel, taste, and sometimes sound
    - what different utensils are used for and where you keep them
    - why you serve a variety of foods with each meal

Maybe you'd like to help the children cook at our program. We'd love for you to supply a recipe or help the children make their snack. Also, please send us your ideas for food preparation experiences. We especially welcome your family favorites. We want your child to have wonderful food-related experiences both here and at home.

Sincerely,

inside this chapter

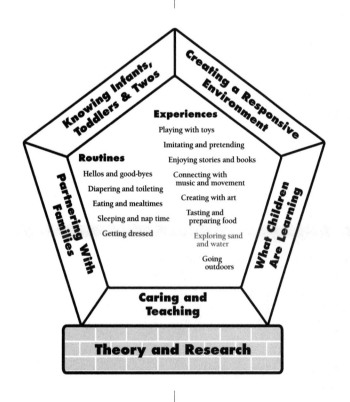

17

Exploring Sand and Water

Willard *(11 months) waves the rubber animal he has just washed. "That has to be the cleanest dinosaur I've ever seen! Look how shiny it is when it's wet," Grace exclaims. Willard babbles in reply and flashes a smile as he hands the dinosaur to her. He turns around and points at the shelf with the other rubber animals. "I bet you want to wash another animal," Grace prompts. "How about this giraffe? He really needs a bath."*

Sand and water are readily available and provide wonderful sensory experiences. There is something about the cool water and the sensation of sand sifting through fingers that almost everyone finds appealing. Sand and water are soothing materials that can calm children and keep them happily engaged.

Most young infants thoroughly enjoy simple water play. Being held by someone they love and the effects they get by kicking and slapping the water are satisfying experiences. Adding a few props, such as cups and rubber animals, can extend the play of mobile infants for long periods of time. Sand and water play are usually among the favorite activities of toddlers and twos, who purposefully explore and experiment with tools and other objects.

Sand and water play can take place outdoors or indoors. It all depends on the weather and your setup.

Supporting Development and Learning

Children develop social/emotional, physical, cognitive, and language skills as they play with sand and water. Here are some examples.

Learning about themselves and others: When you interact with children as they play with sand and water, they use their trust in you as a secure base from which to explore the materials. Playing near other children, they take an interest in what others are doing and start to imitate their actions. If there are plenty of props for everyone, children will be more likely to start playing together.

Learning about moving: Children strengthen their hand muscles and improve eye-hand coordination when they scoop and sift sand, pour water or sand from one container to another, and squeeze water from a baster. They build large muscles when they chase bubbles and carry a bucket of sand from one side of the yard to another. Eye-hand coordination also improves as they practice using simple tools.

Learning about the world: Children make exciting discoveries as they experiment with sand and water. They find out that they can hide things in sand but not in water. They see how sand moves when it is sifted, raked, and shoveled, and how water can be poured and splashed. They learn that sand and water can be stored in containers. Playing with sand and water offers many opportunities to learn about cause and effect and to solve problems.

Learning about communicating: As adults model relevant language, children learn to describe their experiences. As children experiment with sand and water, they ask and answer questions during their play. Sand and water also support the development of pretend play that involves increasingly complex conversation.

Creating an Environment for Sand and Water Play

Because sand and water play are somewhat messy, prepare your environment in advance. If you are not worried about spills, the children will be free to explore and have fun. An uncarpeted area is the logical choice. If this is not available, protect carpeted floors by spreading a plastic tablecloth, shower curtain, or tarp on the floor. To make cleaning up spilled water even easier, spread old towels on top of the plastic.

As always, children's health and safety is a primary consideration. You will need to review and follow the health and safety standards that apply to sand and water.

Keeping Children Safe and Healthy

- Supervise children who are playing with sand and water closely. Be ready to step in to prevent injuries.

- Teach toddlers and twos a few simple rules, such as "Keep the water in the basin."

- Use individual trays or tubs to reduce the spread of germs.

- Use only fresh water in water tubs and empty the tubs after each use. Standing water is a drowning hazard and an ideal environment for bacteria to grow.

- Sanitize water tubs and props after each use, using a mild bleach solution of 1 tablespoon of liquid chlorine bleach to 1 gallon of water or 1 teaspoon of liquid chlorine bleach to 1 quart of water.

- Cover outdoor sandboxes when they are not in use, to keep animals out of them.

Selecting Materials for Different Ages

Sand and water are satisfying materials for very young children. As children develop, they also discover the fun and possibilities that props and toys add to their play.

Young Infants

Sand is not recommended for young infants because they put it in their mouths. Instead, begin with water play. Feeling and splashing water usually delight young infants. Once they can sit on their own, a small basin with about an inch of water and a few very simple props like plastic cups and rubber toys will keep them engaged.

Mobile Infants

Both sand and water play are appropriate for mobile infants. Their play is likely to involve filling and dumping cups and pails. When you add floating toys for water play and various scoops for sand play, children discover what they can do with them. Each discovery is a wonderful surprise.

Toddlers and Twos

By age 2, children become more purposeful in their explorations of sand and water. In addition to the props you provide for mobile infants, gradually introduce more that will inspire toddlers and twos to experiment and pretend. Here are some suggestions for additional props:

- plastic or rubber animals, people, boats, and other vehicles
- wire whisks
- rakes and shovels
- small watering cans
- sieves
- water/sand mills
- plastic cookie cutters
- slotted spoons
- squeeze bottles, basters
- pie tins (with and without bottom holes)
- ladles
- scoops
- muffin tins
- straws
- bubble-blowing solution and supplies
- collectibles that are not choking hazards, such as large shells, feathers, and pinecones

Setting Up and Displaying Materials

When you offer **water play** to infants, begin with no more than a cafeteria tray of water. As children become more mobile, you can use a plastic basin with 2–3 inches of water. Toddlers and twos can use a water table of an appropriate height. A table on wheels can be pushed outside on warm days. Consider placing individual basins inside the water table, to limit the spread of germs and give each child a defined space in which to play.

For **sand play**, sterilized, fine-grained sand (sold at hardware and home improvement stores) is best for health reasons. A sand table works well for older infants, toddlers, and twos. You can put a small amount of sand in individual basins to be used on a table or inside a large sand table. When using individual basins, pick smaller props such as coffee scoops, small rakes, funnels, plastic animals, and vehicles.

Props for sand and water play should be kept where children can reach them easily. Make sure that they are attractively displayed and readily visible, so children can find what they want to use. Here are some ideas for displaying materials.

Place props at children's eye level so they can see what is available.

Use baskets or plastic boxes to hold collectibles such as shells.

Store props in baskets or plastic containers by function. For example, one basket might have props for filling, such as scoops, measuring cups, and shovels. Another basket might have props for making bubbles, including bubble solution, wands, straws, and homemade bubble frames.

Tape a picture and word label on the outside of the container and on the shelf where it is kept. Cover the labels with clear contact paper or tape, to protect them from wet fingers.

Caring and Teaching

Observe and talk with children as they play with sand and water, and show them how delighted you are with their discoveries. You will learn a lot about each child's temperament, interests, and developing skills. Then you can use what you learn from your observations to plan ways to extend their learning.

Young Infants

Your positive relationships with young infants provide a secure base from which they can explore new materials and sensations.

Julio (4 months) *sits in Linda's lap while she makes a game of dripping water on his feet. He squeals with delight and presses his back against Linda. As Linda observes Julio's reaction, she is happy to see how comfortable Julio is with her. Julio now trusts her to keep him safe and help him manage new sensations. She sees water play as an opportunity to build their relationship by sharing an enjoyable experience.*

Babies who are a bit older enjoy making their own discoveries. They can play more independently.

Jasmine (8 months), *is much more active physically than Julio. Rather than sit on Janet's lap during water play, she likes to sit on the floor and conduct her own experiments with water. She especially likes to pat and slap the shallow tray of water that Janet places near her.*

As you help young infants play with water, talk about what they are experiencing and doing.

- Describe the child's reaction: *That water felt cool on your skin. It surprised you, didn't it?*

- Talk about what a child does: *You slapped the water with your hand, so it splashed.*

- Sing about water-related activities: *Row, row, row your boat...*

Mobile Infants

By the time they are mobile infants, children explore sand and water more intentionally. They like to use their hands as tools, and simple props enhance their play. Filling and emptying containers with sand or water are satisfying for them. As they play, mobile infants develop eye-hand coordination and begin to learn about cause and effect, and about the properties of sand, water, containers, and other props.

Abby (14 months) discovers that water and sand feel different, and she begins to understand the meaning of wet and dry. She finds out that sand changes when it is combined with water. Brooks makes a habit of introducing new vocabulary to Abby during sand and water play. She uses new words as she converses with Abby: "Look. The wet sand is darker than the dry sand, and it sticks together when you pat it."

Here are some ways to promote the learning of mobile infants as they play with sand and water.

- Describe changes the child can observe: *The sand became wet and dark when we added water.*

- Encourage children to appreciate designs: *You made wavy lines in the sand with the rake.*

- Help children become aware of their feelings: *Playing with water is so much fun!*

- Talk about what you and the child are doing: *I'm going to dip the wand in the bubble solution. Let's see what happens when you blow on it.*

Toddlers and Twos

Most toddlers begin applying what they have learned about the properties of sand and water. For example, instead of simply scooping wet sand in and out of pails, they now use tools to mold shapes. They are still experimenting, however. They want to see what will happen when they deliberately do something with these materials, and they predict the effects of their actions. Children also begin to engage in pretend play as they explore sand and water.

Leo (18 months) pushes a toy boat through a basin of water, saying, "Toot, toot."

Jonisha (33 months) tells LaToya, "Need more water." Then she pours a little water into a pail of sand, turns the pail over, and announces, "I made a house."

When they have many opportunities to explore sand and water and to use different props, children discover that some objects float on water but some sink, and that sifted sand forms a mound. They enjoy filling a bucket with damp sand, turning it over to make a cake, and then smashing it. They will do this repeatedly, just as they love to build towers with blocks, knock them down, and build them again.

To promote their learning during sand and water play, talk with toddlers and twos about what they are doing. Here are some examples:

- Point out cause-and-effect relationships: *What happened to the sand when you poured it in the colander?*

- Encourage children to solve problems: *How can you get this sand into the bucket?*

- Encourage children to make predictions: *What will happen if you drop the block in the water?*

- Support pretend play: *Your baby doll is getting nice and clean because you are giving her a bath. I think she's going to be hungry when you finish bathing her. Do you have some food for her?*

Props help 2-year-olds explore sand and water in new ways. As they experiment, twos learn new concepts.

Introduce props gradually, making sure that twos have plenty of time to try them. One all-time favorite for young children is blowing bubbles.

Bubble Solution

2/3 cup of liquid detergent (Joy® or Dawn® work best)

1 quart of water

1/3 cup of glycerin

Dip empty frames into the solution to make large bubbles. To make foamy bubbles, use empty shampoo bottles.

Provide a variety of frames to dip into the bubble solution and then wave or blow on. Empty eyeglass frames and plastic berry baskets make wonderful bubbles. Show children that bubble blowing works best when both their hands and the frames are completely wet. A dry surface often causes bubbles to burst on contact.

Here are other activities you might try with toddlers and twos:

- painting a building, sidewalk, fence, or tree with water
- playing music to set the tone for children's sand and water play
- reading stories about going to the beach and about boats and earth-moving equipment

Get to know children's temperaments, likes, and dislikes so that you can offer appropriate sand and water experiences.

Barbara knows that Leo (18 months) occasionally has emotional outbursts and temper tantrums. She finds that sand and water play calm Leo when he loses control of his emotions. "You may take away our books and balls," says Barbara, "but if you take away our sand and water tubs, Leo and I won't make it through the day."

Responding to and Planning for Each Child

As you observe children playing with sand and water, think about the goals, objectives, and steps of the *Developmental Continuum*. Consider what each child is learning and how you might respond. Here is how three teachers use what they learn from their observations to respond to each child and to plan.

Observe	Reflect	Respond
Jasmine (8 months) holds both of Janet's hands as she takes a few steps around the playground. Jasmine stops to watch two toddlers who are digging in the sandbox.	Jasmine watches and responds to other children (*Objective 5, Plays with other children*). She is beginning to gain balance and to move from place to place (*Objective 8, Demonstrates basic gross motor skills*).	Janet sits with Jasmine on the ground near the children who are digging. She talks to Jasmine about what they are doing: "Tyler and Shontelle are having a great time, digging with their shovels."
Willard (11 months) picks up a large plastic snap bead from the sand tray where he has been playing and hands it to Grace.	Willard uses his thumb and index finger to grasp and drop objects (*Objective 9, Demonstrates basic fine motor skills*). He continues an activity when an adult interacts (*Objective 10, Sustains attention*).	To encourage Willard, Grace smiles at him and says, "Thank you for the bead, Willard. May I have another one?"
Matthew (22 months) tries to take a small toy boat out of the water table by using a wooden spoon. The boat falls off the spoon. He tries again, but the boat falls. He looks around, chooses a small fishnet, and lifts the boat out. He looks at Mercedes and smiles.	Matthew plans ways to use objects to perform one-step tasks (*Objective 11, Understands how objects can be used*). He persists with trial-and-error approaches to solving a problem (*Objective 14, Uses problem-solving strategies*).	Mercedes acknowledges Matthew's accomplishment, "Matthew, you found a way to get the boat out. You used the net to solve the problem." She challenges him: "What else can you pick up with the fishnet?"

Responsive Planning

In developing weekly plans, these teachers use their observations and refer to the *Developmental Continuum*. Here is what they record on their weekly planning forms.

> On the *Child Planning Form,* Janet notes Jasmine's interest in watching the other children. Under "Plans," she writes that she will continue to observe Jasmine when she is playing near other children and encourage her engagement with them.

> Grace records Willard's use of the pincer grasp on the *Child Planning Form.* She decides that she will bring out a collection of large plastic keys so that he can continue to practice grasping. She records this under "Plans." On the *Group Planning Form,* under "Indoor Experiences," Grace also makes a note about offering the keys on Thursday and Friday.

> On the *Group Planning Form,* under "Changes to the Environment," Mercedes records that she will add new tools and small toys to the water table. She plans to add two pairs of tongs, a sieve, and a ladle, as well as several small floating fish and ducks. On the *Child Planning Form,* under "Current Information," she records Matthew's problem-solving experience. Under "Plans," she writes a note to encourage him to use the new materials at the water table.

Sand and water play provide infants, toddlers, and twos with wonderful opportunities to explore and experiment. Sometimes families are unaware of the many benefits of this type of play, thinking mostly about the potential mess involved. The letter to families is one way to explain how sand and water play contribute to their child's development.

SHARING THOUGHTS ABOUT EXPLORING SAND AND WATER

Dear Families:

Sand and water play is messy, no doubt about that. Children love it, though, and they learn a lot from it. When an infant splashes water, he learns that slapping it makes the water move (cause and effect). When a toddler pours a cup of sand into a bucket, she begins to learn about size, shape, and quantity. When a 2-year-old makes a birthday cake with sand and puts sticks in for candles, he is pretending with objects.

In our program, the children play with sand and water both indoors and outdoors. Young infants splash water in a tray. Older infants wash dolls and rubber toys, and they dig and pour sand. Toddlers and twos squirt water with basters, blow bubbles into the breeze, and make designs in sand with combs and molds.

What You Can Do at Home

We encourage you to enjoy sand and water with your child. Of course, close supervision is needed to keep your child safe. Here are some suggestions to consider.

- **Fill a tray or plastic tub with an inch or so of water.** A small amount of water is all your child needs to have fun. Place the tub on the floor, on top of some towels, and then let your child splash! If you have an older infant, toddler, or 2-year-old, also offer plastic measuring cups, squeeze bottles, and perhaps a funnel or a sieve.

- **Talk with your child during bath time.** Ask questions to encourage observation and thinking: "What will happen if you drop your rubber frog in the water?"

- **Fill a dishpan halfway with clean sand.** That way, your child can play with sand both indoors and out. The dishpan will keep the sand contained. To vary the experience, add a shovel, funnel, coffee scoop, and small plastic animals.

- **Pretend with your child.** When you add a few simple props, sand and water are wonderful materials to encourage pretend play. You and your child can have a tea party, drive boats through the water, and build sand castles and tunnels.

One wonderful benefit of sand and water play is that they are both soothing materials. They can calm a child who is having a hard time. This helps you as well. We will be happy to suggest more ideas for sand and water experiences that you can offer at home.

Sincerely,

inside this chapter

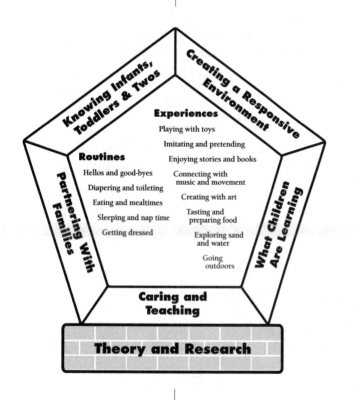

Knowing Infants, Toddlers & Twos

Creating a Responsive Environment

Experiences

Playing with toys

Imitating and pretending

Enjoying stories and books

Routines

Hellos and good-byes

Connecting with music and movement

Diapering and toileting

Creating with art

Eating and mealtimes

Tasting and preparing food

Sleeping and nap time

Getting dressed

Exploring sand and water

Going outdoors

Partnering With Families

What Children Are Learning

Caring and Teaching

Theory and Research

18

Going Outdoors

Ivan *walks over to Gena (30 months), who, from her adaptive stroller, is admiring the fat pea pods growing in the wheelbarrow garden. "Those peas have really grown," he says. "We'll be able to eat them soon." Gena nods and says, "Sun. More sun." Ivan responds, "I think you're right, Gena. We need to move our wheelbarrow garden to a sunny spot." Gena watches Ivan move the garden and then turns her attention to some children who are chasing bubbles. Noticing that Gena is now more interested in what the children are doing, Ivan asks, "Do you want to go over and blow bubbles?" Gena smiles and exclaims, "Yes!" Ivan pushes her to join the other children, opens another jar of bubble solution, and holds the wand so Gena can blow. The other children run over to chase the bubbles, and Gena laughs.*

The outdoors offers an entirely different environment for children to explore. There are fresh air and weather to experience: sun, clouds, rain, snow, fog, wind, and hot and cold temperatures. Outdoor environments offer more open space in which to run and stretch. There are different landforms and structures to master: hills, boulders, platforms, tires, swings, and slides. There is also wildlife at which to marvel: caterpillars, worms, birds, bugs, and plants.

Infants, toddlers, and twos should go outdoors every day, unless the weather is extreme or the air quality poses a health risk. All young children need natural spaces that encourage sensory, physical, and social exploration. By the time they are mobile, children enjoy such experiences as splashing water and crawling over a path created with blankets, tires, and floor mats. As toddlers and twos, they cannot resist the challenges of running in open space, climbing on low tree stumps, and propelling themselves on riding toys.

Supporting Development and Learning

Outdoor play can contribute to children's overall development by giving them chances to explore with all of their senses, practice fine and gross motor skills, develop language and social skills, and begin to appreciate the world around them.

Learning about themselves and others: Depending on the weather, the children might need to put on jackets, hats, mittens and boots before going outside. Dressing and undressing are personal care skills that children develop with practice. Spending time outdoors, especially in natural environments, improves children's mental health and emotional well-being. Children also learn to play with others through such interactions as taking turns with sandbox tools, using the outdoor rocking boat, chasing each other, and pulling each other in a wagon.

Learning about moving: Outdoor play spaces and equipment provide children with many opportunities to build their gross and fine motor skills. Lying on a blanket, young infants can move their heads toward the sound of wind chimes, roll over, and reach for streamers. Mobile infants can pull up to standing by holding onto an outdoor cruising rail and take their tentative first steps on a cushion of grass. Toddlers and twos roll, throw, kick, and sometimes manage to catch balls. They walk, run, jump, slide, pedal, and climb. Small muscles get used as children dig and dump in the sandbox, paint the wall with water, or show you the tiny ladybug that they picked up with their thumb and forefinger and carried carefully so they could delight you with their discovery.

Learning about the world: Curious infants, toddlers, and twos investigate and explore the natural world when they play outdoors. They begin to understand cause and effect and make connections. For example, they learn that we wear raincoats when it rains and that the snow melts on warm days. They watch how the wind moves tree branches and listen as birds and airplanes fly overhead. They explore the objects they find outdoors, for example, learning how a shovel can be used in the sandbox and the garden. They notice the differences between dry sand and wet sand. They solve playground problems, such as how to retrieve a ball that rolled under the climber. Sometimes they experiment with more than one solution.

Learning about communicating: There are many outdoor sounds, and children learn to name what they hear. Noticing and discriminating sounds will later be important to the development of literacy skills. Children talk about what they see. Is it a worm, a caterpillar, or a slug? As people converse with them, they learn to describe objects: *fuzzy, fast, shiny, slimy, striped,* and *colorful.* They connect ideas in books, such as reading about fictional animals, with their experiences in the outdoor world, such as finding live animals on the playground.

Creating an Environment for Outdoor Play

To create an interesting and appropriately challenging outdoor space for infants, toddlers, and twos, think about the experiences you want them to have outdoors. Do you remember playing outdoors when you were a child? What appealed to you most? Did you like observing butterflies, catching insects and frogs, watching cloud formations, jumping in piles of leaves, collecting seeds, and building forts? Did you enjoy swinging on swings, moving up and down on a seesaw, climbing to new heights, and throwing and kicking balls?

Recalling your own positive experiences outdoors can help you identify the experiences very young children enjoy outside and how much they benefit from a well-designed environment. Whether your program is urban, suburban, or rural, you can set up interesting structures, offer enjoyable experiences, and help children explore nature.

Keeping Children Safe and Healthy

Ensuring children's safety and health is always a primary consideration. Advanced planning and watchfulness will help you meet the challenges involved in taking children outdoors. Here are some important considerations.

Teacher supervision—Watching and being prepared to intervene when necessary are the primary ways to keep infants, toddlers, and twos safe and healthy outdoors. At all times, you must have enough adults outdoors so that every child is continually supervised.

Conflict prevention—You can reduce hitting, pushing, and biting incidents by offering plenty of interesting things to do. Provide duplicates of favorite outdoor toys such as balls, buckets, shovels, and riding toys. Be alert and ready to step in when necessary.

Developmentally appropriate equipment—Equipment should be designed to match the sizes and skills of infants, toddlers, and twos. A general rule for equipment height is one foot for every year of a child's age (for example, a 2-year-old should use equipment that is no higher than two feet). An average-size adult should not be able to make a structure to wobble or tip. All equipment must meet the standards of the Consumer Product Safety Commission with regard to exposed surfaces, spacing, design, location, and installation.

Layout—The layout of your play area can make it manageable, interesting, and safe. Of course, children who are not yet mobile need to be protected from being bumped by children who are already crawling, walking, and running. Defined areas with clear pathways help control children's traffic and help children choose what to do. Fixed play equipment should be arranged so that the children playing on one piece of equipment will not interfere with children playing on or running to another piece of equipment. To avoid injuries, locate swings and riding toys away from areas where children run.

Shock-absorbent materials—All playground equipment must be surrounded by shock-absorbent material that meets the standards of the Consumer Product Safety Commission. There should be a 6-foot fall zone around the equipment. Shock-absorbent material needs to be raked regularly and checked monthly to determine whether it needs to be replenished. Avoid using rubber and do not use sand if animals are a problem. Also be cautious about using material that children might choke on, such as pea gravel or small wood chips.

Protection from too much sun—In hot weather, sunhats, long-sleeved shirts, and pants provide sun protection. Families must provide sunscreen and written permission for you to use it on their child. Be sure to offer children extra water on hot days. If you do not already have shady places where children can get out of the sun, you can create them. Set up large umbrellas, drape a sheet from a fence, put up a tent, or use an awning.

Nontoxic landscape—Soil should be analyzed for lead content and for other harmful substances when there is reason to believe a problem may exist. Be sure all vegetation is nonpoisonous, in case a curious child takes a taste. Be on the lookout for fire ants, spiders, snakes, and mushrooms, which can sprout up overnight. Check with your regional Poison Control Center or Cooperative Extension Service for complete information.

Water safety—According to the American Academy of Pediatrics and the American Public Health Association, drowning is the third leading cause of the unintentional injury of children younger than age 5.[49] In some states, it is the leading cause of death. To prevent drowning, outside play areas should not include swimming and wading pools, ditches, canals, excavations in which water can collect, fish ponds, and other bodies of water. When providing water play, be sure to empty the containers, because germs collect easily in standing is water. In many areas, standing water is also a breeding site for mosquitoes.

Daily monitoring and maintenance—Outdoor play areas should be checked daily for broken glass, needles, trash, and other hazardous materials such as animal feces, garden chemicals, and paint. Follow your program's procedures for requesting maintenance and repairs.

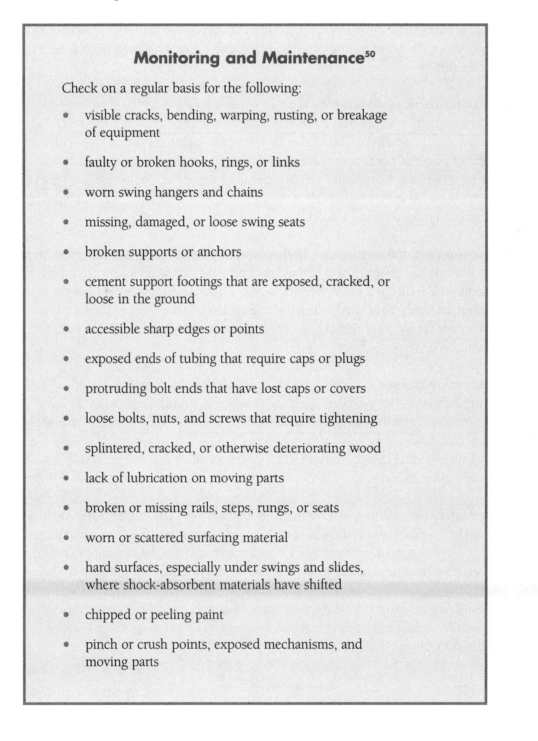

Monitoring and Maintenance[50]

Check on a regular basis for the following:

- visible cracks, bending, warping, rusting, or breakage of equipment

- faulty or broken hooks, rings, or links

- worn swing hangers and chains

- missing, damaged, or loose swing seats

- broken supports or anchors

- cement support footings that are exposed, cracked, or loose in the ground

- accessible sharp edges or points

- exposed ends of tubing that require caps or plugs

- protruding bolt ends that have lost caps or covers

- loose bolts, nuts, and screws that require tightening

- splintered, cracked, or otherwise deteriorating wood

- lack of lubrication on moving parts

- broken or missing rails, steps, rungs, or seats

- worn or scattered surfacing material

- hard surfaces, especially under swings and slides, where shock-absorbent materials have shifted

- chipped or peeling paint

- pinch or crush points, exposed mechanisms, and moving parts

Outdoor Structures

Some programs have areas with lots of grass, trees, plants, and playground equipment that is designed to match the needs and abilities of children under age 3. Others start with hard ground and very little equipment. Even if your program has few natural materials or structures, there are ways to make it appealing and comfortable for you and the children.

Natural materials—Find nearby places (a farm or gardening center) where you can obtain some bales of hay to put in the yard. If you keep them covered and protected from the rain, they will last a long time. Other natural materials you can bring are low tree stumps, driftwood logs (check for splinters), and large smooth stones. Be sure that the materials are nontoxic.

A garden—You do not need to have a plot of land to have a garden in your play yard. You can make a container garden by filling a wheelbarrow or large pots with rich soil.

Swings—Children can swing on swing sets and with you on a glider. Once infants can sit, you can place them in fully enclosed swings that are high enough off the ground for them to see what is going on nearby. Toddlers and twos can use bucket swings. Swings with a single-strap seat and no back support are not appropriate for children this young.

Slides—A number of companies make sturdy slide structures. Locate them on soft cushioning material. If your outdoor area has a hill, you can embed a slide in the ground, thereby making it safe for even very young children. Check a metal slide each time you take children outdoors on a sunny day, to be sure that it is not too hot.

Platforms and climbers—Climbers do not need to be higher than 18 inches from the ground, and cushioning material should be placed underneath and around them. Low, wide steps or a ramp can lead to a platform that is large enough for two or three children at a time. There should be handholds for children to grab when they need to steady themselves. Wooden or plastic structures with different levels provide challenges for mobile infants, toddler, and twos. You can even fasten a steering wheel on one level.

Sandboxes—Mobile infants, toddlers, and twos have a wonderful time playing with sand outdoors, where you do not have to worry about a mess. You can purchase or make a sandbox or use a large tractor tire. Make sure you have a way of covering the sand to protect it from animals.

Water tubs—A table, trough, or tubs to hold water will delight children on hot days. Make sure that whatever you use can be emptied easily after each use. A hose, by itself or with a sprinkler, is another way to provide water play outdoors.

Tires—Automobile tires, embedded in the ground, become structures for mobile infants, toddlers, and twos. Children can climb into and out of them and sit for a while. Drill holes in the tires so that water cannot collect and become a breeding site for mosquitoes.

Playhouses, boats, and tunnels—You can purchase playhouses or construct them with the help of families. An old rowboat, sanded and painted, would be a great addition to the playground. Tunnels made from expandable wire covered with cloth can be stored easily when not in use.

Cardboard cartons—While not permanent structures, the cartons from computers and household appliances can be transformed into tunnels, playhouses, cars, or places for children to be alone for a while. Cut large windows and doors so that adults can see children at all times.

Selecting Materials and Experiences for Different Ages

The way young children use outdoor equipment and materials differs according to their temperaments, developmental levels, and previous experiences.

Young Infants

You need to be very near young infants, so one of the first considerations is to arrange places where you will be comfortable sitting with babies and where you can observe everything that is happening. To put infants down, you need a protected area where they can be safe from children who walk and run. In providing materials and experiences for young infants, think about what they will be doing outdoors.

Watching—If young infants are carried or placed where they can see what is happening outdoors, you have a natural playground for them. Babies can safely observe their surroundings from an infant carrier, stroller, infant swing, or infant seat. When they are comfortable, infants are eager to watch such things as blowing leaves, other children, and you. You can enhance the environment by hanging colorful scarves and other fabrics from trees or structures where they will be blown by the wind. Hanging crystals or colored pieces of Plexiglas® from a fence or tree branch will create interesting light patterns.

Listening—Outdoors, the noise of traffic, the chirping of crickets and birds, and the shouts of children at play will interest young infants. You can also place wind chimes outdoors where infants can hear them when the wind blows or when you gently strike them.

Reaching and grasping—Place some toys on a blanket for infants to grasp and explore. For ideas, see chapter 11, *Playing With Toys*.

Moving and doing—Once infants can roll over and sit up, they need a flat, soft surface on which to move safely. They also need you to stay nearby.

Interacting—You are probably the most interesting part of the outdoor environment for young infants, just as you are interesting to them indoors. They will coo and respond as you talk about what is happening, sing to them, and draw their attention to interesting sights.

Mobile Infants

In addition to opportunities for sensory exploration, places for motor exploration are important for mobile infants. They crawl, pull up, cruise while holding onto structures or your hand, and soon walk. They still need a protected area where they will not be bumped by toddlers and twos who are moving quickly. Once mobile infants can walk on their own, run, and climb, they will want more freedom than an enclosed area allows, and your supervision will be critical to keeping them safe. To provide mobile infants with experiences they will enjoy, consider the kinds of activities that keep them busy and engaged.

Moving and exploring—Mobile infants need large enclosed spaces and places where they can climb, roll, slide, and swing safely. The structures described earlier will give them lots of appropriate challenges.

Pushing and pulling—Children who are just learning to walk enjoy sturdy toys that they can push and that help them keep their balance. Toy shopping carts and baby carriages are popular choices. Once they gain greater stability, they enjoy push-and-pull toys like toy lawn mowers and wagons.

Rolling and throwing—As discussed in chapter 11, *Playing With Toys*, balls are probably the best toys for mobile infants. Outdoors, you can add the challenge of large balls like beach balls, soccer balls, and basketballs. Tightly sewn bean bags to throw into a basket are another option.

Collecting, dumping, and filling—This is a favorite activity of mobile infants, and it is easy to provide the materials they need. Small pails and buckets with handles are perfect for collecting small objects, including toys that you bring outdoors and natural materials like leaves, pinecones, and rocks. A lot of dumping and filling can take place in the sand area if you include small plastic shovels, rakes, scoops, small watering cans, plastic cups, and funnels. Remove any small items that could be choking hazards.

Playing with water—This is an especially nice way for mobile infants to cool off on a hot day. They can walk through a sprinkler, play with water from a hose, or play with water in a trough or dish pans. Add some plastic cups and a few scoops for an added challenge.

In addition to these common activities for mobile infants, you can set up special activities, such as blowing and chasing bubbles, painting with water and large brushes, or finger painting with shaving cream on a smooth surface.

Toddlers

In addition to the materials and experiences you plan for mobile infants, toddlers will enjoy the following additions.

More room for active play—Toddlers are on the move, and they want to use their large-muscle skills. They need plenty of open spaces to run, structures to climb on and jump from, opportunities to slide and build, and surfaces on which to ride wheeled toys.

Riding toys—A smooth surface with pathways is an ideal place for toddlers to use trucks and other riding toys that they can push with their feet.

More things to push and pull—Add wagons and wheelbarrows that toddlers can fill with objects and move. They may also like pushing dolls or stuffed animals in a doll carriage.

Construction materials—Another favorite activity of toddlers is building, knocking down, and building again. Large plastic blocks are a great addition for outdoor play, as are empty boxes and planks that they can walk along. If you have bales of hay, tires, and driftwood, toddlers will use these materials as part of their building projects.

Twos

Twos can really take advantage of their time outdoors when offered a number of choices. In addition to the experiences described for infants and toddlers, twos are ready for more complex and structured outdoor experiences.

Gardening—Twos can help you plant and care for a variety of flowers, herbs, and vegetables. It is best to start with plants rather than seeds, which take too long to sprout for even the most patient 2-year-old. They can help water the garden, check the plants each day for changes, help with the harvest, and enjoy the results.

Recommended Plants[51]

- Plants that attract butterflies: butterfly bushes, asters, dill, parsley, hollyhocks

- Plants that provide color, texture, scent and taste: lamb's ears, sage, mint, marigold, basil

- Fruits and vegetables that are easy to grow: cherry tomatoes, yellow pear tomatoes, peas, string beans, melons, carrots, broccoli

---

Observing animal life—Twos are fascinated by living things. Notice their excitement when they see birds, ants, squirrels, caterpillars, and worms. You can attract birds by putting feeders in the yard. Bug boxes enable twos to collect and study caterpillars or worms that they may be reluctant to hold. You can provide a magnifying glass for closer examinations. Be sure to set all creatures free before returning to the room.

Art materials—On occasion, bring out large colored chalk, brushes and paint, and playdough. The colors look even brighter outdoors, so the art experience is different.

Neighborhood walks—Think of areas in your community where children can visit. For example, the children would enjoy playing in a neighborhood park, taking a trip to the corner market, or walking down the street to a large tree to collect and run through the falling leaves.

Riding toys—In addition to the riding toys that toddlers use, older twos may be ready for small tricycles and vehicles that they can pedal. Be sure to provide helmets.

Ball games—Twos can run to a ball and kick it with increasing control. Always include some balls for them in the outdoor area. You can enhance their ball play by providing baskets to throw balls into and by playing catch and kickball with them.

Including All Children

The outdoor play space should ensure that children with disabilities can have the same or equivalent experiences as other children. You need to be aware of what interests each child and bring each child into the activities.

Many adaptations are simply a matter of common sense and are easy to accomplish. For example, a ramp can make it easier to get strollers and wheelchairs in and out of the building. Remove equipment that overturns easily if a child pulls herself up on it or leans heavily against it. Position a child with disabilities near other children so they can interact with each other.

Caring and Teaching

A particular challenge in taking infants, toddlers, and twos outdoors is the time it takes to get them ready, especially when the weather requires snowsuits, mittens, and boots. Try to keep in mind that dressing is a valuable activity, by itself, and not just something you have to do to take children outdoors. For ideas, see chapter 10, *Getting Dressed*.

Meeting diapering and toileting needs when children are outdoors is another challenge. You must have a secluded area for diapering and toileting to protect children's privacy but, at the same time, you must maintain appropriate child-staff ratios. Some programs are fortunate enough to have a separate bathroom right off the play yard where a teacher can change a diaper or watch a child use the toilet while keeping an eye on what the other children are doing. If you have to go inside with a child, find out whether other children need to go as well. You can usually find a few toddlers and twos willing to go, so you will be able to take a small group with you, leaving other teachers to supervise the play yard. In many programs, several groups are outside at the same time, so more adults are supervising. You can also check and change diapers before going outdoors and make sure that children who use the toilet have had a chance to do so.

For walks, pack a shoulder bag or backpack with tissues, any special supplies for individual children, and a first-aid kit that contains emergency phone numbers and a cell phone or money for a pay phone. If you add a container of bubble-blowing solution, you will always have an engaging activity at hand.

It can be tempting for adults to think of going outdoors as taking a break from interacting with the children. While a change of scene is usually refreshing, children need you to remain on duty, observing, interacting, and sometimes playing with them. Children depend on you outdoors—just as they do indoors—to keep them safe and to respond in ways that make their experiences fun and meaningful.

Young Infants

Being outdoors offers young infants interesting sensory experiences.

Julio (4 months) often falls asleep after a brief period of looking around.

Jasmine (8 months) usually spends more time watching other children, sitting and playing on a blanket, swinging on a swing, and sitting on Janet's lap, reaching for objects that interest her.

To enhance children's pleasure and exploration, talk with them about what they are experiencing outdoors. Here are some examples of what you might say.

- Describe the experience: *It's a little cold outside today, isn't it? You are warm in your snowsuit and mittens, though.*

- Help them feel safe: *Here's a nice soft blanket for you to sit on. I'll sit right next to you.*

- Point out interesting sights: *Look how the wind is blowing the pretty fabric up and down, and up and down.*

- Enjoy interesting sounds together: *Do you hear the wind chimes?*

Mobile Infants

Mobile infants only need a little encouragement to take off outdoors, crawling, cruising, and climbing. Many like to join simple movement games. Almost all enjoy digging in the sand, playing with water, pushing wheeled toys, and dumping and filling containers.

__Willard__ (11 months) and __Abby__ (14 months) love going outdoors. Each morning, Willard looks up eagerly when Grace asks if he is ready to go outside. Abby sometimes asks Brooks, "Uh?" and goes over to the stroller.

As you interact with mobile infants, you can enhance their enjoyment and learning by talking with them.

- Encourage appreciation and respect for nature: *Let's sit here. We can watch the squirrel climb the tree.*

- Promote feelings of competence: *You climbed up, all by yourself!*

- Describe and identify familiar sounds: *Crunch, crunch, crunch. The leaves crunch under your feet when you walk on them.*

- Verbalize feelings: *Uh, oh. That siren surprised you, didn't it?*

- Promote cooperative play: *Let's roll the ball to Lianna now.*

Toddlers and Twos

Leo, Matthew, Gena, Valisha, and Jonisha know what to expect when they go outdoors. They jump right into exploring and using the equipment and materials their teachers provide. Through their experiences, they are learning new vocabulary and concepts. Their developing gross and fine motor skills give them more control as they explore, and their developing cognitive and language skills support more complex play.

Close supervision is a major challenge when you take toddlers and twos outdoors. They can move quickly and climb, slide, and jump in a flash. Stay alert and try to anticipate what children will do so you can be prepared to step in when needed. Here are some ideas for providing special activities and challenges for children this age.

Play simple movement games. Invite children to flutter like butterflies, wiggle like worms, or pretend to be baby birds who fly away and come back to the nest. Show children how to make their shadows move. Play "Follow the Leader" and "Can You Do What I Do?"

Call attention to different sensations. Point out the rough bark on a tree, the soft leaf of a lamb's ear plant, the prickly pinecone, and the smooth rock. Call children's attention to how the air smells after a rain and to the smells of freshly cut grass and various flowers.

Invent games that promote the development of gross motor skills. You can create a balancing path by laying boards or a piece of rope on the ground for children to walk along. Set up a bowling game where children try to knock down empty food boxes or plastic soda bottles by using a beach ball. Challenge twos to throw a beach ball into a laundry basket or large box. Invite children to chase bubbles that you blow.

Bring "indoor" materials outside. Encourage pretend play by placing props such as plastic vehicles, people, and animals in the sandbox. On warm days, bring books, musical instruments, and art materials outside for children to explore.

Enjoy the weather. You can still go outdoors when it is raining or snowing lightly. If the children are appropriately dressed, they will enjoy walking through puddles, catching snowflakes on their mittens, and making footprints in light snow. When the weather is too severe to go outdoors, bring some of the outdoors inside. Children can poke and dig in bins of snow or create a collage by sticking nontoxic leaves, twigs, and seeds on clear contact paper.

As always, interact with toddlers and twos outdoors in ways that support their development and learning.

- Introduce new words: *These silver maple seeds remind me of little helicopters. They spin around and around as they fall to the ground.*

- Follow children's interests: *Those ants are marching across the ground and going down those little holes. What do you think they are doing down there?*

- Encourage children to move and explore: *Let's see you jump like a grasshopper.*

- Ask open-ended questions: *What do you see? Where do you think that squirrel is going?*

- Stimulate imaginations: *What do you think the bird is saying when it chirps?*

Responding to and Planning for Each Child

As you observe children outdoors, think about the goals, objectives, and steps of the *Developmental Continuum*. Consider what each child is learning and how you might respond. Here is how three teachers use what they learn from their observations to respond to each child and to plan.

Observe	Reflect	Respond
Jasmine (8 months) sits on a blanket on the playground, holding a flower. She looks at it closely, turning it in her hands. She brings the flower to her face and rubs it on her nose and cheek. She looks at Janet, babbles, and smiles.	Jasmine is noticing particular characteristics of objects (*Objective 13, Shows a beginning understanding that things can be grouped*). She is using facial expressions and vocalizations to communicate (*Objective 17, Develops expressive language*).	Janet promotes Jasmine's language by responding, "Yes, I see that you have a yellow flower." She encourages Jasmine's examination of the flower by asking, "What does that flower smell like?" Janet leans over to smell the flower, inhaling deeply through her nose, to show Jasmine the meaning of her words.
Leo (18 months) walks around the park with Barbara and Donovan (16 months). Leo points to some fallen leaves and asks, "Dat?" He bends down, picks one up, and hands it to Barbara. She shows it to Donovan, who reaches out and touches it with his finger. Leo picks up another and hands it to Donovan. Donovan twirls the leaf in his hands. Leo picks up another and does the same.	Leo is having a brief play encounter with another child (*Objective 5, Plays with other children*). He is imitating the actions of others (*Objective 15, Engages in pretend play*). He is using word-like sounds to communicate (*Objective 17, Develops expressive language*).	Barbara says, "Leo, you found some leaves," to model expressive language for him. She kneels down so that she is on the same level as the children. To support their play, she points to their leaves and describes what they are doing. "Donovan, Leo gave you a leaf. Now you each have one."
Jonisha and Valisha (both 33 months) are bouncing a ball back and forth to each other on the playground. Valisha says, "I'm bouncing higher." "Me, too," Jonisha responds. "Ball goes higher and higher!" exclaims Valisha. Jonisha calls to LaToya, "Teacher, come see! Ball go so high!" Anton (32 months) stands near the girls, watching them. As LaToya approaches, Anton tugs at her sleeve, points at the girls, and says, "Me, too."	They are participating in coordinated play with each other (*Objective 5, Plays with other children*). Jonisha and Valisha are participating in a conversation for two or more turns (*Objective 18, Participates in conversations*).	LaToya acknowledges Jonisha's and Valisha's play. "Wow! You are bouncing that ball so high! You are also passing it back and forth to each other." LaToya wants to encourage the sisters to include others in their play. They frequently play together but not with other children. She says, "Anton is watching you pass that bouncy ball. I think he would like to bounce the ball with you."

Responsive Planning

In developing weekly plans, these teachers use their observations and refer to the *Developmental Continuum.* Here is what they record on their weekly planning forms.

> On the *Child Planning Form,* under "Current Information," Janet writes about Jasmine's exploration of the flower. She decides to take her group on a walk the following week to the park where many flowers are blooming. She records this on her *Group Planning Form* as a special outdoor experience for Wednesday. Under "Family Involvement," she makes a note to ask for a volunteer to come with the group.
>
> As Barbara reads her observation notes about Leo, she realizes that he recently played briefly with other children. Three of those encounters involved dramatic play props. She records this on the *Child Planning Form* and makes a note under "Plans" to encourage such play encounters by adding a prop that a few children can use at the same time. On the *Group Planning Form,* under "Changes to the Environment," she writes that she will add a three-seat steering bench to the pretend play props.
>
> LaToya has noticed that many of the children are engaging with each other for longer periods. She decides that she will add group mural painting, so she notes that on the *Group Planning Form* for Tuesday. She also writes a reminder to herself to get a roll of butcher paper from the supply room.

Make outdoor time a part of everyday life as you care for infants, toddlers and twos. You will enjoy the time you spend with them outside, and the benefits for the children will last a lifetime. The letter to families is one way to offer ideas about going outdoors with children.

SHARING THOUGHTS ABOUT GOING OUTDOORS

Dear Families:

Going outdoors gives children an entirely different environment to explore. Outdoors, they can stretch their large muscles, breathe fresh air, take in the sunshine (or the rain or snow), and enjoy the freedom of open space. They can marvel at the creatures they find on the playground, watch the wind blow the trees, and collect seeds and stones. We try to take the children outdoors every day, because we know how important it is for their overall development and learning.

When your child does this...	Your child is learning...
• crawls through the grass	• to explore with all senses
• climbs over a tree stump	• to use gross motor skills
• picks up pinecones to put in a bucket	• to group objects
• rolls a ball to another child	• social skills

What You Can Do at Home

Here are some activities to try next time you go outdoors with your child. You probably do some of them already. Perhaps others are new ideas.

- **Enjoy nature.** Talk about the breeze touching your cheeks. Roll down a grassy hill together. Plant a garden in your yard, a window box, or in a wheelbarrow that you can move as the sun moves. Take a bucket so your child can collect things such as stones and leaves. Be sure that the items do not present a choking hazard.

- **Take a texture walk.** Call your child's attention to natural materials and describe them. For example, you might point out *soft sand*, *rough pinecones*, and a *smooth rock*.

- **Invent games.** When your child walks well, create a balancing path by laying a piece of rope on the ground to walk along. Play a gentle game of catch. Set up a bowling game in which your child tries to knock down empty food boxes by rolling a beach ball.

- **Visit public playgrounds designed for children under age 3.** Playgrounds with equipment for very young children offer wonderful opportunities for children to practice their developing skills and to begin engaging with other children.

- **Take some "inside" activities outdoors.** For example, you might sit together under a tree and read a book. Give your child a paintbrush and water to paint the side of your house.

By working together, we can introduce your child to the joys and the wonders of the outdoors.

Sincerely,

Appendix

THE CREATIVE CURRICULUM®
FOR INFANTS, TODDLERS & TWOS

Goals and Objectives
At a Glance

SOCIAL/EMOTIONAL DEVELOPMENT

To learn about self and others

1. Trusts known, caring adults
2. Regulates own behavior
3. Manages own feelings
4. Responds to others' feelings with growing empathy
5. Plays with other children
6. Learns to be a member of a group
7. Uses personal care skills

PHYSICAL DEVELOPMENT

To learn about moving

8. Demonstrates basic gross motor skills
9. Demonstrates basic fine motor skills

COGNITIVE DEVELOPMENT

To learn about the world

10. Sustains attention
11. Understands how objects can be used
12. Shows a beginning understanding of cause and effect
13. Shows a beginning understanding that things can be grouped
14. Uses problem-solving strategies
15. Engages in pretend play

LANGUAGE DEVELOPMENT

To learn about communicating

16. Develops receptive language
17. Develops expressive language
18. Participates in conversations
19. Enjoys books and being read to
20. Shows an awareness of pictures and print
21. Experiments with drawing and writing

Teaching Strategies. ©2006 Teaching Strategies, Inc., PO Box 42243, Washington, DC 20015; www.TeachingStrategies.com

Individual Care Plan
Family Information Form

Child:	
Child's Date of Birth:	
Teacher:	
Family Member(s):	
Date:	

Arrival

What time will you usually arrive at the center? _____

What will help you and your child say good-bye to each other in the morning?

Diapering and Toileting

What type of diapers do you use? _____

How often do you change your child's diaper? When does your child usually need a diaper change?

Are there any special instructions for diaper changes?

Is your child beginning to use the toilet? If so, are there any special instructions for toileting?

Sleeping

How will we know that your child is tired and needs to sleep?

When does your child usually sleep? For how long does he or she usually sleep?

What helps your child to fall asleep?

We put babies to sleep on their backs. Is your baby used to sleeping on his or her back? (**Y / N**)

How does your child wake up? Does he or she wake up quickly or slowly? Does your child like to be taken out of the crib immediately or to lie alone in the crib for a few minutes before being held?

Eating

Babies:

Are you breast-feeding or bottle-feeding your baby? _____

If breast-feeding, will you come to the center to breast-feed? (**Y / N**)

    If so, at what time? _____

    If not, will you send expressed breast milk? _____

Bottle-feeding,

    What kind of formula do you use? _____

    How do you prepare the bottles? _____

    How much do you prepare at one time? _____

    How much does your baby drink at one time? _____

Does your baby drink bottles of water during the day? (**Y / N**)

    If so, when and how much? _____

Is your baby eating solid foods? (**Y / N**)

    If so, which ones? _____

    When? _____

    How do you prepare your baby's solid foods? _____

    How much does your baby eat at one time? _____

How is your baby used to being fed (in what position)? _____

Does your baby eat any finger foods? If so, which ones? _____

All Children:

What are some of your child's favorite foods? _____

What foods does your child dislike? _____

Is your child sensitive or allergic to any foods? If so, please list them.

Are there any foods that you don't want your child to eat?

Family Information Form, continued

Dressing

Is there anything special that we should know about dressing and undressing your child?

Awake time

How does your baby like to be held? What position does your baby prefer when awake?

What does your child like to do when awake?

How do you play with your child?

Departure

What time will you usually come to pick up your child? _____

What will help you and your child say hello to each other at the end of the day?

Individual Care Plan

THE CREATIVE CURRICULUM®
FOR INFANTS, TODDLERS & TWOS

Child:	
Child's Date of Birth:	
Teacher:	
Family Member(s):	
Date:	

Arrival	Eating

Diapering	Dressing

Sleeping	Departure

References

[1] National Association for the Education of Young Children. (1997). *Developmentally appropriate practice in early childhood programs serving children from birth through age 8: A position statement of the National Association for the Education of Young Children.* Retrieved June 28, 2006, from http://www.naeyc.org/about/positions/pdf/PSDAP98.PDF

[2] Maslow, A. H. (1999). *Toward a psychology of being* (3rd ed.). New York, NY: J. Wiley & Sons.

[3] Brazelton, T. B., & Greenspan, S. (2000). *The irreducible needs of children: What every child must have to grow, learn, and flourish.* Cambridge, MA: Da Capo Press.

[4] Erikson, E. (1993). *Childhood and society.* New York, NY: W. W. Norton & Company, Inc.

[5] Greenspan, S. (1999). *Building healthy minds: The six experiences that create intelligence and emotional growth in babies and young children.* New York, NY: Perseus Publishing.

[6] Bowlby, J. (1969). *Attachment and loss: Vol. 1. Attachment.* New York: Basic Books.

[7] Ainsworth, M., Blehar, M., Waters, E., & Wall, S. (1978). *Patterns of attachment.* Hillsdale, NJ: Erlbaum.

[8] Masten, A. S. (2001). Ordinary magic: Resilience processes in development. *American Psychologist, 56,* 227–238.

Benard, B. (2004). *Resiliency: What we have learned.* San Francisco, CA: WestEd.

[9] Piaget, J., & Inhelder, B. (2000). *The psychology of the child* (H. Weaver, Trans.). New York, NY: Basic Books.

[10] Vygotsky, L. S. (1999). The collected works of L. S. Vygotsky: Scientific legacy (M. J. Hall, Trans.). In R. W. Rieber, Ed., *Cognition and language: A series in psycholinguistics* (Vol. 6). London: Kluwer Academic/Plenum Publishers.

[11] Shonkoff, J. P., & Phillips, D. A. (Eds.). (2000). *From neurons to neighborhoods: The science of early childhood development.* Washington, DC: National Academy Press.

[12] Ibid.

[13] Ibid.

[14] Cole, M., Cole, S. R., & Lightfoot, C. (2005). *The development of children* (5th ed.). New York, NY: Worth Publishers.

[15] From *Temperament: Theory and Practice*, by S. Chess & A. Thomas, 1996, New York, NY: Brunner/Mazel, Inc. Copyright 1996 by Brunner/Mazel, Inc. Adapted with permission of Routledge/Taylor & Francis Group, LLC.

[16] Genesee, F. *Bilingual acquisition*. Retrieved March 21, 2002, from http://www.earlychildhood.com/Articles/index.cfm?FuseAction=Article&A=38

Snow, C. E. (1997, November 1). The myths around being bilingual. *NABE News, 29,* 36.

[17] American Academy of Pediatrics & American Public Health Association. (2002). *Caring for our children: National health and safety performance standards: Guidelines for out-of-home care programs: A joint collaborative project of American Academy of Pediatrics, American Public Health Association, and National Resource Center for Health and Safety in Child Care* (2nd ed.). Elk Grove Village, IL: The Academy.

[18] From *Heart Start: The Emotional Foundations of School Readiness* (p. 7), by ZERO TO THREE, 1992, Washington, DC: Author. Copyright 1992 by the author.
Retrieved February 7, 2006, from http://www.zerotothree.org/sch_read.html
Adapted with permission.

[19] Hart, B., & Risley, T. R. (1995). *Meaningful differences in the everyday experience of young american children.* Baltimore, MD: Brookes Publishing.

[20] Hart, B., & Risley, T. R. (1995). *Meaningful differences in the everyday experience of young american children.* Baltimore, MD: Brookes Publishing.

Snow, C. E., Burns, M. S., & Griffin, P. (Eds.). (1998). *Preventing reading difficulties in young children.* Washington, DC: National Academy Press.

[21] Weitzman, E., & Greenberg, J. (2002). *Learning language and loving it* (2nd ed., pp. 37–49). Toronto: The Hanen Centre.

[22] Schickedanz, J. (1999). *Much more than the ABCs: The early stages of reading and writing.* Washington, DC: National Association for the Education of Young Children.

[23] Geist, E. (2004). Infants and toddlers exploring mathematics. In D. Koralek, Ed., *Spotlight on young children and math*, Washington, DC: National Association for the Education of Young Children.

[24] National Council of Teachers of Mathematics. (2000). *Principles and standards for school mathematics.* Reston, VA: Author.

[25] National Association for the Education of Young Children. (2005). Teacher-child ratios within group size. *NAEYC early childhood program standards and accreditation performance criteria.* Retrieved June 14, 2006, from http://www.naeyc.org/accreditation/performance_criteria/teacher_child_ratios.html

[26] Greenman, J., & Stonehouse, A. W. (1994, September). Reality bites: Biting at the center—Part 1. *Exchange*. National Association for the Education of Young Children. (1996). Biters: Why they do it and what to do about it. *Early Years Are Learning Years*. Retrieved June 22, 2006, from http://www.naeyc.org/ece/1996/08.asp

[27] From *Parents as Partners in Education: Families and Schools Working Together* (6th ed.), by E. H. Berger, 2004, Upper Saddle River, NJ: Pearson Education. Copyright 2004 by Pearson Education. Adapted with permission.

[28] American Academy of Pediatrics & American Public Health Association. (2002). *Caring for our children: National health and safety performance standards: Guidelines for out-of-home care programs: A joint collaborative project of American Academy of Pediatrics, American Public Health Association, and National Resource Center for Health and Safety in Child Care* (2nd ed.). Elk Grove Village, IL: The Academy.

[29] Ibid.

[30] Ibid.

[31] National Institute of Child Health and Human Development. (2003, February). *Babies sleep safest on their backs* [NIH publication number 03-5355]. Bethesda, MD: National Institutes of Health.

[32] National Sleep Foundation. *Children's sleep habits*. Retrieved June 28, 2006, from http://www.Sleepfoundation.org/hottopics/index.php?secid=11&id=39

[33] Ibid.

[34] Ibid.

[35] American Academy of Pediatrics & American Public Health Association. (2002). *Caring for our children: National health and safety performance standards: Guidelines for out-of-home care programs: A joint collaborative project of American Academy of Pediatrics, American Public Health Association, and National Resource Center for Health and Safety in Child Care* (2nd ed.). Elk Grove Village, IL: The Academy.

[36] National Association for the Education of Young Children. (2005). Cleaning and sanitation frequency table. *NAEYC early childhood program standards and accreditation performance criteria*. Retrieved June 14, 2006, from http://www.naeyc.org/accreditation/criteria/sanitation.html

[37] Bronson, M. B. (1995). *The right stuff for children birth to 8: Selecting play materials to support development*. Washington, DC: National Association for the Education of Young Children.

[38] Assistive Technology Training Project. (1996). *Infusing assistive technology into early childhood classrooms*. Phoenix, AZ: Author.

[39] Nielsen, M., & Dissanayake, C. *Deferred imitation and the onset of pretend play in the second year*. Retrieved June 29, 2006, from http://www.warwick.ac.uk/fac/sci/Psychology/imitation/posters/m-nielsen.pdf

[40] Segal, M. (2004). The roots and fruits of pretending. In E. Zigler, D. G. Singer, & S. J. Bishop-Josef (Eds.), *Children's play: The roots of reading.* Washington, DC: ZERO TO THREE Press.

[41] Shonkoff, J. P., & Phillips, D. A. (Eds.). (2000). *From neurons to neighborhoods: The science of early childhood development.* Washington, DC: National Academy Press.

[42] Segal, M. (2004). The roots and fruits of pretending. In E. Zigler, D. G. Singer, & S. J. Bishop-Josef (Eds.), *Children's play: The roots of reading.* Washington, DC: ZERO TO THREE Press.

[43] Shonkoff, J. P., & Phillips, D. A. (Eds.). (2000). *From neurons to neighborhoods: The science of early childhood development.* Washington, DC: National Academy Press.

Ramsey, P. (1991). *Making friends in school: Promoting peer relationships in early childhood.* New York, NY: Teachers College Press.

[44] Segal, M. (2004). The roots and fruits of pretending. In E. Zigler, D. G. Singer, & S. J. Bishop-Josef (Eds.), *Children's play: The roots of reading.* Washington, DC: ZERO TO THREE Press.

[45] Hughes, F. (1999). *Children, play, and development* (3rd ed.). Boston, MA: Allyn and Bacon.

[46] Segal, M. (2004). The roots and fruits of pretending. In E. Zigler, D. G. Singer, & S. J. Bishop-Josef (Eds.), *Children's play: The roots of reading.* Washington, DC: ZERO TO THREE Press.

[47] Ibid.

[48] Cowley, J. (1999). *Mrs. Wishy-Washy.* New York, NY: Philomel Books.

[49] American Academy of Pediatrics & American Public Health Association. (2002). *Caring for our children: National health and safety performance standards: Guidelines for out-of-home care programs: A joint collaborative project of American Academy of Pediatrics, American Public Health Association, and National Resource Center for Health and Safety in Child Care* (2nd ed.). Elk Grove Village, IL: The Academy.

[50] From *Caring for our Children: National Health and Safety Performance Standards: Guidelines for Out-of-Home Child Care Programs: A Joint Collaborative Project of American Academy of Pediatrics, American Public Health Association, and National Resource Center for Health and Safety in Child Care* (2nd ed.) (p. 263), by American Academy of Pediatrics and American Public Health Association, 2002, Elk Grove Village, IL: The Academy. Copyright 2002 by AAP, APA, and NRCHSCC. Reprinted with permission.

[51] Torquati, J., & Barber, J. (2005). Dancing with trees: Infants and toddlers in the garden. Young Children, 60(3), 43.

General Resources

Baker, A., & Manfredi-Petitt, L. (2004). *Relationships, the heart of quality care: Creating community among adults in early care settings.* Washington, DC: National Association for the Education of Young Children.

Bardige, B. (2005). *At a loss for words: How America is failing our children and what we can do about it.* Philadelphia, PA: Temple University Press.

Bardige, B., & Segal, M. (2005). *Building literacy with love: A guide for teachers and caregivers of children birth through age 5,* Washington, DC: ZERO TO THREE Press.

Berk, L. (2004). *Infants and children: Prenatal through middle childhood.* Needham Heights, MA: Allyn & Bacon.

Brazelton, T. B. (1992). *Touchpoints birth to three: The essential reference for the early years.* Cambridge, MA: Da Capo Press.

Brilliant Beginnings, LLC. (1999). *Baby brain basics guidebook: Birth to 12 months.* Long Beach, CA: Author.

Carlson, V., Feng, X., & Harwood, R. (2004). The "ideal baby": A look at the intersection of temperament and culture. *Zero to Three, 24*(4), 22–28.

Day, M., & Parlakian, R. (2004). *How culture shapes social-emotional development: Implications for practice in infant-family programs.* Washington, DC: ZERO TO THREE Press.

Egeland, B., & Erickson, M. (1999). *Attachment theory and research.* Retrieved June 30, 2005, from http://www.zerotothree.org/vol20-2.html

Ezell, H. K., & Justice, L. M. (2005). *Shared storybook reading: Building young children's language and emergent literacy skills.* Baltimore, Maryland: Paul H. Brookes Publishing Co.

Gonzalez-Mena, J. (2005). *Diversity in early care and education: Honoring differences.* New York, NY: McGraw-Hill.

Greenman, J. (2005). *Caring spaces, learning places: Children's environments that work.* Redmond, WA: Exchange Press, Inc.

Greenman, J., & Stonehouse, A. (1996). *Prime times: A handbook for excellence in infant and toddler programs.* St. Paul, MN: Redleaf Press.

Grotberg, E. (1995). *A guide to promoting resilience in children: Strengthening the human spirit.* Retrieved June 30, 2005, from http://resilnet.uiuc.edu/library/grotb95b.html

Hart, B., & Risley, T. R. (1999). *The social world of children learning to talk*. Baltimore, MD: Paul H. Brookes Publishing Co., Inc.

Honig, A. (2002). *Secure relationships: Nurturing infant/toddler attachment in early care settings*. Washington, DC: National Association for the Education of Young Children.

Howes, C. & Ritchie, S. (2002). *A matter of trust: Connecting teachers and learners in the early childhood classroom*. New York, NY: Teachers College Press.

Jalongo, M. R. (2004). *Young children and picture books*. Washington, DC: National Association for the Education of Young Children.

Kohl, M. F. (2002). *First art: Art experiences for toddlers and twos*. Beltsville, MD: Gryphon House, Inc.

Lally, J. R., Griffin, A., Fenichel, E., Segal, M., Szanton, E., & Weissbourd, B. (2003). *Caring for infants and toddlers in groups: Developmentally appropriate practice*. Washington, DC: ZERO TO THREE Press.

Lally, J. R., & Mangione, P. (2006, July). The uniqueness of infancy demands a responsive approach to care. *Young Children, 61*(4), 14–20.

Lerner, C., & Dombro, A. (2000). *Learning and growing together: Understanding and supporting your child's development*. Washington, DC: ZERO TO THREE Press.

Miché, M. (2002). *Weaving music into young minds*. Albany, NY: Delmar.

Miller, K. (2000). *Things to do with toddlers and twos* (Revised ed.). Beltsville, MD: TelShare Publishing Co., Inc.

Neuman, S. B., & Dickinson, D. K. (Eds.). (2002). *Handbook of early literacy research*. New York, NY: The Guilford Press.

Olds, A. R. (2001). *Child care design guide*. New York, NY: McGraw-Hill.

Oser, C., & Cohen, J. (2003). *America's babies: The ZERO TO THREE Policy Center data book*. Washington, DC: ZERO TO THREE Press.

Pica, R. (2004). *Experiences in movement: Birth to age 8* (3rd ed.). Clifton Park, NY: Delmar Learning.

Raines, S., Miller, K., & Curry-Rood, L. (2002). *Story stretchers for infants, toddlers, and twos: Experiences, activities, and games for popular children's books*. Beltsville, MD: Gryphon House.

Sawyer, W. E. (2004). *Growing up with literature*. Clifton Park, NY: Delmar Learning.

Segal, M. (1998). *Your child at play: Birth to one year* (2nd ed.). New York, NY: Newmarket Press.

Shore, R. (1997). *Rethinking the brain: New insights into early development.* New York, NY: Families and Work Institute.

Torelli, L., & Durrett, C. (1998). *Landscapes for learning: Designing group care environments for infants, toddlers and two-year-olds.* Berkeley, CA: Torelli/Durrett Infant & Toddler Child Care Furniture.

U. S. Department of Health and Human Services, Administration for Children and Families, Administration on Children, Youth and Families, Head Start Bureau, Head Start Facilities. (2000). *Head Start center design guide.* Washington, DC: Author.

Index

curriculum goal and objectives
for, 48
parent's conflicting feelings toward
child care programs, 183
of parents of children with
disabilities, 215–216
temper tantrums, 154–155
Empathy, development of
curriculum goal and objectives for,
48
Enrollment forms, 190
Environment. *See* Outdoor experiences;
Physical environment
Equipment. *See* Materials and equipment
Erikson, Erik, 5, 7, 179
Esteem, 2
Evacuation cribs, 266
Experiences
with art. *See* Art
with food. *See* Food experiences
with imitating and pretending. *See*
Pretend play
with music and movement. *See*
Music and movement
with outdoors. *See* Outdoor
experiences
with sand and water. *See* Sand and
water experiences
with stories and books. *See* Stories
and books
with toys. *See* Toys
Expressive language, curriculum goal and
objectives for, 55

F

Facts to assess learning and development
analysis of, 175–176
collecting during observation,
171–174
Families
biting behavior and, 158
building partnerships with, 181–217
challenging situations with, 206–216
of children with disabilities, 167,
215–216
collecting materials from, 74
communicating with, 189–201,
204–205
concerns of, 182–184
conferences with, 198–200
conflicting feelings toward child care
programs, 183
cultural differences of, 186–187

diapering and toileting and, 244
differences among, 185–186
dressing and, 286
of dual language learners, 166, 191
getting to know, 185–188
involvement of, 184, 202–205
letters to. *See* Letters to families
mealtimes and, 253, 260
orientation for new families, 189–
191
outreach to, 192
planning to involve, 99, 184
resolving differences with, 206–208
stress of having an infant, 183
support for families experiencing
stress, 213–214
welcoming of, 188–192
working through conflicts with,
209–213
Family Conference Form, 199
Fathers, involvement of, 192. *See also*
Families
Fear and parents of children with
disabilities, 215
Feelings. *See* Emotions; Social/emotional
development
Fine motor skills. *See also* Motor skills
demonstration of, curriculum goal
and objectives for, 51
explanation of, 27
music and movement to promote,
350
toys and materials to promote, 75
Finger painting, 359, 361–363
Food experiences, 375–387. *See also* Eating
and mealtimes
caring and teaching during, 380–386
creating environment for, 377–379
letter to families about, 387
of mobile infants, 377, 381
responding to child's needs and,
385–386
of toddlers, 377–378, 382–384
of two-year-olds, 377–378, 382–384
of young infants, 377, 380
Friendship, stories and books about, 142
Frustrations, minimizing, 155, 282

G

Games. *See also* Play
during dressing, 282
to master separating and reuniting,
227

Gardens, 409, 413
Geometry and spatial relationships, 125–
126, 128
Goals and objectives for child
development, 44, 47–57. *See also*
specific routines and experiences
cognitive development, 52–54
language development, 55–57
physical development, 51
social/emotional development, 47–50
Good-byes. *See* Hellos and good-byes
Grandparents, involvement of, 192. *See*
also Families
Greenspan, Stanley
basic needs and, 2–4
emotional growth milestones and,
6–7
Greeting areas, 65, 188
Grief and parents of children with
disabilities, 215
Gross motor skills. *See also* Motor skills
demonstration of, curriculum goal
and objectives for, 51
explanation of, 27
music and movement to promote,
350
outdoor experiences to promote,
411–414, 417–418
toys and materials to promote, 75,
297, 298
Grouping items. *See* Classifying and sorting
Group Planning Form. See also Planning
forms
assessment of child, use of, 178
components of, 98–99
example of, 100, 103
purpose of, 98
use of, 96
Groups
learning to be member of, 140–142
curriculum goal and objectives
for, 49
sizes and teacher-child ratios, 143
Guilt and parents of children with
disabilities, 215

H

Handwashing, 79, 236, 237
Health considerations
colic, infants with, 255
diaper changing and, 237
eating and, 253–255
food experiences and, 379

for food experiences, 377–378
lists of appropriate, 75
for music and movement, 345–346
for outdoor experiences, 406–408
    outdoor structures, 409–410
    selection of, 410–413
for pretend play, 311–313
for sand and water experiences,
    392–393
selection and display of, 74, 76, 142,
    189, 294–298
for stories and books, 325–330
Mathematical relationships
    discovering, 122–128
    geometry and spatial relationships,
        125–126, 128
    mobile infants and, 123, 124, 125,
        126
    number concepts, 122–123, 127
    patterns and relationships, 124, 128
    promoting discovery of, 127–128
    sorting and classifying, 126–127,
        128
    toddlers and, 123, 124, 126, 127
    two-year-olds and, 123, 124, 126,
        127
    young infants and, 123, 124, 125,
        126
Meals. *See* Eating and mealtimes
Mirrors, 294
Mixed-age groups
    continuity of care and, 144
    meal times and, 251
    physical environment for, 80–81
Mobile infants. *See also* Infants
    age span of, xvii
    art and, 359–360, 367
    books for, 326
    cognitive development of, 29
    diapering of, 240
    dressing of, 284
    eating and, 257
    food experiences of, 377, 381
    geometry and spatial relationships
        and, 125
    language development of, 32–33,
        112, 114
    music and movement for, 346, 349
    number concepts and, 122, 123
    outdoor experiences for, 411–412,
        416
    patterns and relationships and, 124
    physical development of, 27–28
    physical environment for, 68, 70
    pretend play of, 311, 315
    sand and water experiences for, 392,
        395

scientific exploration and, 130, 131,
    133
self-regulation of, 147
separation from family member and,
    229
sleeping and nap time for, 272
social/emotional development of, 24
sorting and classifying and, 126
stories and books and, 333
stories and books for, 116, 326
toys for, 295–296, 303
writing and, 118
Mobiles, 294
Modeling behavior, 141, 148, 151–152,
    154
Molding skills, 360, 361
Motor disabilities. *See* Children with
    disabilities
Motor skills. *See also* Fine motor skills;
    Gross motor skills
    art and, 358
    diapering and toileting and, 234
    dressing and, 278
    eating and mealtimes and, 248
    food experiences and, 376
    hellos and good-byes and, 222
    music and movement and, 344
    outdoor experiences and, 405
    pretend play and, 310
    sand and water experiences and, 390
    sleeping and, 264
    stories and books and, 324
    toys and, 292
Mouthing toys, 294
Music and movement, 343–355
    caring and teaching during, 347–355
    creating environment for, 345–346
    instruments for, 346
    letter to families about, 355
    for mobile infants, 346, 349
    responding to child's needs and,
        352–354
    selection of materials for, 345–346
    supporting development and
        learning through, 344
    for toddlers, 346, 350
    for two-year-olds, 346, 351
    for young infants, 346, 348

NAEYC. *See* National Association for the
    Education of Young Children

Nap time. *See* Sleeping and nap time
National Association for the Education of
    Young Children (NAEYC)
    on dressing skills, 279
    on group size, 143
    on quality of care, 1
National Institute of Child Health and
    Human Development on SIDS, 266
National Sleep Foundation on infant sleep
    patterns, 268
Natural world. *See also* Outdoor
    experiences
    scientific exploration and, 131–132,
        134
Needs, basic, 2–4
Neighborhood walks, 413
Newsletters, use of, 197
Number concepts, 122–123, 127
Nursing reflexes, 255

O

Object permanence, 13
Objects, understanding and using
    curriculum goal and objectives for,
        52
Observations
    assessment based on, 168, 178
    documenting, 171–173
    planning based on, 95
    responses based on, 139
    setting up system for, 169–170
    Tracking Form, 170
Orientation for new families, 189–191
Outdoor experiences, 403–421
    caring and teaching for, 415–420
    for children with disabilities, 414
    creating environment for, 406–414
    letter to families about, 421
    mobile infants and, 411–412, 416
    responding to child's needs and,
        419–420
    selecting materials for, 410–413
    supporting development and
        learning through, 404–405
    toddlers and, 412, 417–418
    two-year-olds and, 412–413, 417–
        418
    young infants and, 410–411, 415–
        416
Overstimulation of children, 139, 146, 158

P

Painting. *See* Art
Parentese, 113
Parents. *See* Families
Patterns and relationships, 124, 128
Personal care skills, development of curriculum goal and objectives for, 50
Personality traits
  bonding with child and, 139
  temperament and, 36
Phonemes, 113
Phonological awareness, 16, 113, 116
Photographs
  class photo album, 203
  display of, 189, 223
Physical aggression, 153–154
Physical development
  art and, 358
  curriculum goal and objectives for, 51
  diapering and toileting and, 234
  dressing and, 278
  eating and mealtimes and, 248
  explanation of, 26–27
  food experiences and, 376
  hellos and good-byes and, 222
  of mobile infants, 27–28
  music and movement and, 344
  outdoor experiences and, 405
  pretend play and, 310
  sand and water experiences and, 390
  sleeping and, 264
  stories and books and, 324
  of toddlers, 28
  toys and, 292
  of two-year-olds, 28
  of young infants, 27
Physical disabilities. *See also* Children with disabilities
  adapting environment for, 81, 414
  positioning children with, 82
Physical environment
  to accommodate developmental needs, 67–72
  for art, 359–365
  for breast-feeding. *See* Breast-feeding
  for children with disabilities, 81–83
  conveying positive messages in, 83–85
  for diaper changing, 65–66, 235–236, 238
  for dressing, 279, 311–313

for eating and mealtimes, 67, 249–250
to encourage independence, 147
family room, 203
for food experiences, 377–379
frustrations, minimizing in, 155
for infants, 68–70
materials in, 74–76, 142. *See also* Materials and equipment
for mixed-age groups, 80–81
for music and movement, 345–346
organization of, 70, 73
outdoors. *See* Outdoor experiences
places for routines and experiences in, 65–67
planning and recording change in, 98
for playing with toys, 293–301
positive guidance strategies and, 150
for pretend play, 311–313
quiet places in, 224
safety and health considerations for, 77–79
for sand and water experiences, 391–394
setting up, 63, 64, 142, 205
for sleeping and nap time, 66, 265–267
for small groups, 141
for stories and books, 325–330
to support relationships, 143–144
for toddlers, 71–73
for toileting area, 236
for two-year-olds, 71–73
as welcoming environment, 188–189
Physical punishment, 154
Physical strain, methods to minimize, 83
Physical world, learning about
  art and, 358
  diapering and toileting and, 234
  dressing and, 278
  eating and mealtimes and, 248
  food experiences and, 376
  hellos and good-byes and, 222
  music and movement and, 344
  outdoor experiences and, 405
  pretend play and, 310
  sand and water experiences and, 390
  scientific exploration and, 129–130, 134
  sleeping and exploration of, 264
  stories and books and, 324
  toys and, 292
Physiological needs, 2
Piaget, Jean, 12–14, 17, 289
Pictures. *See also* Art; Photographs

awareness of, curriculum goal and objectives for, 57
Planning forms
  for art, 372
  child, 96, 97, 102
  examples of, 97
  for food experiences, 386
  group, 100–103
  for music and movement, 353
  for outdoor experiences, 420
  for playing with toys, 306
  for pretend play, 320
  for sand and water experiences, 400
  for stories and books, 339
  weekly, 96–103
Plans. *See also* Schedules
  amendments to, 104
  assessment of progress applied to, 177–178
  elements of, 98–99
  responsive, 95
    for art, 372
    for food experiences, 386
    for music and movement, 353–354
    for outdoor experiences, 420
    for playing with toys, 306
    for pretend play, 320
    for sand and water experiences, 400
    for stories and books, 339
  for transitions, 94–95, 145
Play, 291–307. *See also* Toys; *specific routines and activities*
  children with disabilities and, 167, 414
  function of, 12
  as learning experience, 161–163
  participation in, curriculum goal and objectives for, 49
  pretend. *See* Pretend play
  quiet play, promotion of, 75
  symbolic, 14
Poison Control Center, 407
Portfolios. *See also* Records and logs
  setting up system of, 169–170, 173–174
Positive guidance strategies, 149–150
Preoperational stage, 13, 289
Preparing food. *See* Food experiences
Pretend play, 309–321
  caring and teaching during, 314–321
  importance of, 14
  creating environment for, 311–313
  letter to families about, 321
  materials for, 311–313

of mobile infants, 311, 315
responding to child's needs and, 318–320
supporting development and learning through, 310
of toddlers, 312–313, 316
of two-year-olds, 312–313, 317–318
use of, 224, 279
curriculum goal and objectives for, 54
of young infants, 311, 314
Primary caregivers, 143
Print material, awareness of. *See also* Stories and books
awareness of, curriculum goal and objectives for, 57
Problem-solving ability, 6
curriculum goal and objectives for developing strategies, 54
Public Law 108-446, 41

Q

Quality care, 1

R

Reading. *See* Stories and books
Reasonable accommodation, 42
Receptive language, curriculum goal and objectives for, 55
Records and logs. *See also* Planning forms; Portfolios
journals to share information with families, 197
of sleep and nap time, 269
Redirecting behavior, 150
Rejection and parents of children with disabilities, 216
Relationships. *See also* Groups
building, 138–145
continuity of care and, 144
helping children with transitions, 144–145
importance of, 108–109
structure to support, 143–144
Resilience
development of, 10, 11
explanation of, 9
Rhythm

and language development, 113–114, 120, 264
and music and movement, 349, 351
Routines and rituals. *See also specific routines*
daily routines, adapting based on needs, 139
diapering and toileting. *See* Diapering and toileting
dressing. *See* Dressing
eating. *See* Eating and mealtimes
hellos and good-byes and, 223–224, 226, 227
with mobile infants, 147
music used during, 347
sleeping and napping. *See* Sleeping and nap time
with toddlers and two-year-olds, 147–148
with young infants, 146
Rules, use of, 149

S

Safety
of cribs, 266
in diaper changing, 235, 237–238
in eating and mealtimes, 250, 253–255
exploring and, 163
in food experiences, 379
in mixed-age groups, 80, 81
need for, 2
in outdoor experiences, 406–408
rules for, 149
in sand and water experiences, 391
of toys, 291, 293
Sand and water experiences, 389–400
caring and teaching during, 394–400
creating environment for, 391–394
letter to families about, 401
materials for, 392–393
mobile infants and, 392, 395
responding to child's needs and, 399–400
supporting development and learning through, 390
toddlers and, 392, 396–398
two-year-olds and, 392, 396–398
young infants and, 392, 394
Sandboxes, 410
Scaffolding, 14–15
Schedules. *See also* Plans
characteristics of appropriate, 87

daily, 86–93
for infants, 88–91
for toddlers, 91–93
for two-year-olds, 94
School readiness, 108
Scientific exploration, 129–135
mobile infants and, 130, 131, 133
natural world and, 131–132, 134
physical world and, 129–130, 134
promoting, 134–135
social world and, 132–133, 135
toddlers and, 130, 132, 133
two-year-olds and, 130, 132, 133
young infants and, 129, 131, 132
Secure attachment, 8, 9, 11
Self-awareness, 6, 140
learning about self, curriculum goal and objectives, 47–50
Self-regulation, 109
art and, 358
curriculum goal and objectives for, 47
development of, 6
diapering and toileting and, 234
dressing and, 278
eating and mealtimes and, 248
food experiences and, 376
loss of control and, 153–155
in mobile infants, 147
music and movement and, 344
outdoor experiences and, 404
pretend play and, 310
promotion of, 146–152
sand and water experiences and, 390
sleeping and, 264, 271
stories and books and, 324
in toddlers, 147–148
toys and, 292
in two-year-olds, 147–148
in young infants, 146
Sensorimotor stage, 13, 289
Sensory impairments, adapting environment for children with, 82
Separation anxiety, 24, 221. *See also* Hellos and good-byes
Shapes. *See* Geometry and spatial relationships
Sharing, 142, 148
Sheets and bedding. *See* Sleeping and nap time
SIDS (Sudden Infant Death Syndrome), 266
Sinks, 236
Size differences, understanding of, 127
Sleeping and nap time, 263–275
caring and teaching about, 268–274

responding to child's needs and, 305–306

safety of, 291, 293

selection and display of, 74, 76, 224, 294–298, 301

supporting development and learning through, 292

for toddlers, 296–297, 304

for two-year-olds, 298, 304

washing and sanitizing, 79

for young infants, 294, 302

Transitions. *See also* Hellos and good-byes

helping children with, 144–145, 148, 225

meeting with new families, 190

planning for, 94–95, 145

Transportation toys, 296, 297, 298

Trust

curriculum goal and objectives linked to, 47

development of, 5, 108, 138–140

between family and child care workers, 193–194, 226

separation anxiety and, 222

Tumbleform chairs, 81

Tunnels, as playground equipment, 410

Turn-taking, 142

Two-year-olds

age span of, xvii

art and, 362–363, 368–369

characteristics of, 72

cognitive development of, 31

competence, encouraging in, 155

dressing of, 285

eating and, 258–259

food experiences of, 377–378, 382–384

geometry and spatial relationships and, 126

language development of, 33, 113, 114

music and movement for, 346, 351

number concepts and, 122, 123

outdoor experiences and, 412–413, 417–418

patterns and relationships and, 124

physical development of, 28

physical environment for, 71–73

planning for, 101

pretend play of, 312–313, 317–318

sand and water experiences and, 392, 396–398

schedules for, 94

scientific exploration and, 130, 132, 133

self-regulation of, 147–148

separation from family member and, 230

sleeping and nap time, 273

social/emotional development of, 25

sorting and classifying, 127

stories and books and, 117, 328, 334–335

toilet learning of, 242–243

toys for, 298, 304

writing and, 118

U

U.S. Department of Agriculture (USDA) Child and Adult Care Food Program (CACFP), 254

V

Visual impairments. *See also* Children with disabilities

adapting environment for children with, 82

reading strategies for, 336

Vocabulary skills, 110–114, 119. *See also* Language development; Stories and books

Vygotsky, Lev, 14–15, 17

W

Walkers, 81

Water activities. *See* Sand and water experiences

Water safety, 407

Water tubs, 410

Weekly planning forms, 96–103

Wheel chairs, 81

Whiteboards, 188

Withdrawal and parents of children with disabilities, 216

Writing

experimentation with, curriculum goal and objectives for, 57

exploration of, 117–118, 121

mobile infants and, 118

toddlers and, 118

two-year-olds and, 118

Y

Young infants. *See also* Infants

age span of, xvii

art and, 359, 366

cognitive development of, 29

diapering of, 239

dressing of, 283

feeding of, 252, 255–256

food experiences of, 377, 380

geometry and spatial relationships and, 125

language development of, 32, 111, 113, 114

music and movement for, 346, 348

number concepts and, 123

outdoor experiences and, 410–411, 415–416

patterns and relationships and, 124

physical development of, 27

physical environment for, 68, 70

pretend play of, 311, 314

sand and water experiences and, 392, 394

scientific exploration and, 129, 131, 132

self-regulation of, 146

separation from family member and, 228

sleeping and nap time for, 271

social/emotional development of, 23–24

sorting and classifying and, 126

stories and books for, 116, 326, 332

toys for, 294, 302

Z

ZERO TO THREE, 108

Zone of proximal development (ZPD), 14–15

About the Authors

Diane Trister Dodge, M.S., founder and president of Teaching Strategies, Inc., is a well-known speaker and author of numerous books for teachers, administrators, and parents. She has worked in Head Start, child care, and public school programs as a teacher and trainer, and she has directed national projects on early childhood education. She served on the governing boards of the National Association for the Education of Young Children (1990–1994) and the Center for the Child Care Workforce. She currently sits on the boards of several other local and national organizations that serve young children and families.

Sherrie Rudick is the director of special projects at Teaching Strategies, Inc. She has more than 30 years' experience with early childhood and Head Start programs. During that time, she has been a teacher, child development center director, licensing specialist, trainer, reviewer, materials developer, and consultant. As a trainer, she has developed and conducted both individual training sessions and training conferences on the local, regional, and national levels. Ms. Rudick has co-authored materials that have been distributed nationally by the Department of the Army and the Head Start Bureau.

Kai-leé Berke, M.A., is a product development associate at Teaching Strategies, Inc. She has taught and cared for infants, toddlers, preschoolers, and kindergarteners in public, private, and Department of Defense programs. Before joining Teaching Strategies, Inc., she was the program administrator for a multi-site preschool organization. In addition to her local and national work as an early childhood trainer and consultant, she has served as an adjunct faculty member at Honolulu Community College and is currently teaching at Pacific Oaks College.

Order Form
Please type or print clearly.

4 Ways to Order

Order online
www.TeachingStrategies.com
15% discount or more for online orders

Order by phone
800-637-3652
Washington, DC area:
202-362-7543
8 a.m.–7 p.m. Eastern Time, M–F

Order by fax
202-350-5940
24 hours a day

Order by mail
Teaching Strategies, Inc.
P.O. Box 42243
Washington, DC 20015

Ship to:

NAME	
ORGANIZATION	
ADDRESS	

CITY	STATE	ZIP

PHONE	FAX

E-MAIL	

Bill to:

Your Teaching Strategies Customer Number: (If known)

NAME	
ORGANIZATION	
ADDRESS	

CITY	STATE	ZIP

PHONE	FAX

Order:

ITEM #	QTY	DESCRIPTION	UNIT PRICE	TOTAL
			$	$
			$	$
			$	$
			$	$
			$	$
			$	$
			$	$
			$	$
			$	$
			$	$

Please call for information on quantity discounts.

SUBTOTAL	$
SALES TAX CA, DC, IL: Add appropriate sales tax.	$
TOTAL	$

Method of payment

All orders must be accompanied by payment, P.O. number, or credit card information. Customers with an established credit history are welcome to use P.O. numbers.
First-time customers must enclose pre-payment with order.

❏ Check (payable to Teaching Strategies) ❏ Money order

❏ Purchase order (must include copy of P.O.) ❏ Visa ❏ MasterCard

❏ American Express ❏ Discover

CREDIT CARD OR PURCHASE ORDER NUMBER   EXPIRATION DATE

SIGNATURE OF CARD HOLDER

❏ Yes, I would like to receive occasional e-mail notifications about new Teaching Strategies products and special offers. I understand that Teaching Strategies will not share or sell my e-mail address with any other individual, company, or organization.

SHIPPING
United States: Orders up to $60.00—$5.00;
Orders over $60.00—12% of total.
International/U.S. Territories: $20.00 (first book)
+ $7.00 for each additional book.
Rush Delivery: Call for shipping charges.
Method: ❏ Ground ❏ 2-day ❏ Next-day ❏ International

Guarantee: Teaching Strategies guarantees your complete satisfaction. If you are not thoroughly delighted with the printed materials you order, return the item(s) in salable condition within 30 days for a refund (excluding shipping costs). We will gladly accept unopened CC-PORT software or Toolkits. However, we are unable to accept opened software or Toolkits (or components) with opened shrink-wrap. All video/DVD sales are final. Prices subject to change without notice. CCIT2

Thank you for your order.